KU-501-401

Environmental Studies

From Crisis to Cure

SECOND EDITION

R. RAJAGOPALAN

Former Professor
Indian Institute of Technology Madras

OXFORD

UNIVERSITY PRESS

OXFORD
UNIVERSITY PRESS

Oxford University Press is a department of the University of Oxford.
It furthers the University's objective of excellence in research, scholarship,
and education by publishing worldwide. Oxford is a registered trademark of
Oxford University Press in the UK and in certain other countries

Published in India by
Oxford University Press
YMCA Library Building, 1 Jai Singh Road, New Delhi 110001, India

© Oxford University Press 2011

The moral rights of the author have been asserted

First published 2011
Fourth impression 2012

All rights reserved. No part of this publication may be reproduced, stored in
a retrieval system, or transmitted, in any form or by any means, without the
prior permission in writing of Oxford University Press, or as expressly permitted
by law, by licence, or under terms agreed with the appropriate reprographics
rights organization. Enquiries concerning reproduction outside the scope of the
above should be sent to the Rights Department, Oxford University Press, at the
address above

You must not circulate this book in any other form
and you must impose this same condition on any acquirer

ISBN-13: 978-0-19-807208-9
ISBN-10: 0-19-807208-2

Typeset in Times New Roman
by Recto Graphics, Delhi 110 096
Printed in India by Akash Press, New Delhi 110 020

To
Malathi
who supported me fully
in my journey of 12 books

To Hai

All the best

R. [signature]

Feb 2013

Preface to the Second Edition

To the student

I welcome you to a new and possibly life-changing experience!

This is the second edition of a textbook for the course on Environmental Studies. This is more than a textbook, however. As you read the book, you may realize that this subject is different from many others: It is about you, and the future of your family, community, humanity, and this fragile planet.

We are today facing a grave environmental crisis. The unceasing industrial growth and economic development of the last 300 years or so have resulted in huge ecological problems: overexploitation of natural resources, degraded land, disappearing forests, endangered species, dangerous toxins, global warming, etc.

By studying this textbook on environmental studies, you will realize how human activities affect the environment.

About the book

This book is meant for the undergraduate students of all disciplines and it assumes very little background in mathematics or science. It is based on the University Grants Commission (UGC) syllabus that came out in the wake of the landmark judgment of the Supreme Court of India in 2003.

What are the special features of this book?

This book has variety and something of interest to everyone. Even as you cover the entire UGC syllabus, learn the concepts, and answer the questions, you will also:

- learn about the major environmental problems of the world and the threats mankind faces due to them
- find out what is being done about these problems
- discover how YOU can make a difference to the state of the environment
- read a large number of true environment-related stories about crises, solutions, successes, failures, interconnections, and inspirational individuals
- reflect on quotations, poems, and deeper issues
  I have also included in the book:
- List of books, articles, films and websites at the end of each chapter
- Ideas and guidance for carrying out meaningful field work (case studies and projects)
  To make things easier for you, the book also includes a glossary of terms.

The main text is in a question-answer format (sometimes called the Socratic method). This format promotes effective learning by making you an active learner. I have tried to anticipate the questions likely to arise in your mind. The question-format also lends itself to the SQ3R Method of study.

What is new in this edition?

Since I wrote the first edition in 2004, the global environment has changed much, generally for the worse. To the extent possible, I have updated all the chapters—the main text, stories, and references. I have also trimmed the chapters, making them easier to read. There are more exercises, including multiple-choice questions, which are often the favourite of examiners.

The chapter format has been substantially improved to enable you to

- study and understand the subject with ease and
- prepare well for tests and examinations.

How you can use this book for effective study using the SQ3R method?

How do you normally study a chapter? Plunge straight into it and read passively and quickly from the first section to the last? According to psychologists, this is the worst possible method! You may spend hours reading in that fashion, but that will not help you much when you face the examination.

This book enables you to follow a very effective and well-known technique of study called the SQ3R method. This technique makes you an active reader, so that you will understand and remember the material.

There are five related activities in the method:

Survey Before reading a chapter, make a quick survey of what the chapter contains. It is like looking at a map to plan your route before you begin a journey.

Question While you are surveying the chapter, make up questions that you would like the chapter to answer. This approach keeps your mind alert and concentrated.

Read Read each section of the chapter, looking for answers to your questions. Be an active reader as you search for the answers. Separate the key ideas from the supporting details and examples.

Recite After reading each section of the chapter, recall your questions and try to answer them. Do not move to the next section until you can recite the key ideas and answer the questions.

Review Immediately after finishing the chapter, go back and answer all the questions. Review again the next day and later.

How you should study a chapter in this book following the SQ3R method?

Step 1: Survey Before you begin reading the chapter
- Read the following:
  o Chapter title
  o Quotation: Try to see the connection between the quotation and the main topic of the chapter
  o This chapter is about…
  o The keywords and phrases are…
  o Title of the lead story
- Read the section headings (questions) and the titles of Boxes.
- Read carefully all the Key Ideas given in small boxes.
- Look at the tables, figures, pictures, cartoons, and other visuals in the chapter.

- Go through the following sections at the end of the chapter:
  o Review: A summary of the key points
  o Think critically: Deeper questions for reflection and discussion
- Read the questions given under Exercises

Step 2: Question While you are surveying the chapter, formulate the questions you expect the chapter to answer:

- Write down the section headings
- Convert the Box titles into questions and write them down.
- Add some of the questions given under Exercises—the ones you find interesting.
- Add your own questions.

While you survey the chapter and write down the questions, try to recall what you already know about the topics. Check whether you can answer any of the questions even without reading the chapter.

Step 3: Read Now you are ready to read the text.

- Select the section of the chapter you want to read.
- Read the Key Ideas.
- Look for text material that supports each Key Idea.
- As you read, look for answers to the questions you have written down.

Step 4: Recite After reading each section

- Try to answer the questions from memory: recite orally or write down in your notebook.
- Check back if you cannot answer a question.
- Make up mnemonics, if you find anything difficult to remember. A mnemonic is a word, sentence, poem, etc., that helps you remember something.

  When you are able to answer all the questions, move to the next section. Follow the steps Read and Recite for that section.

Step 5: Review After finishing all the sections of the chapter

- Review immediately:
  o Recite the Key Ideas and important points.
  o Answer the questions and do the exercises from memory. Note that the questions have been graded according to the level of difficulty.
  o Look for connections between sections.
  o Go through the section 'Learn more' at the end of the chapter. Access the websites and go through the books and articles. Watch the films, if you can.
  o Look for connections to other chapters.
- Review again the next day and later by reciting the Key Ideas and answering the questions.

  You can use the SQ3R method for any of your subjects. If you have questions about the SQ3R method, ask your teacher or write to me.

  Here are some websites that explain this method:

1. Virginia Tech: www.ucc.vt.edu/stdysk/sq3r.html and
   www.ucc.vt.edu/lynch/TextbookReading.htm
2. Sweet Briar College: www.arc.sbc.edu/sq3r.html
3. Study Guides and Strategies: www.studygs.net/texred2.htm

   In addition, Bethel University's website lists many online resources for improving academic skills—studying, learning, and taking examinations: http://cas.bethel.edu/dept/aesc/resources

Use the book to suit your learning style:

- Do you prefer concrete experience, like a true story or case study? Then, the true stories would interest you. Read the stories actively and find out what concepts they illustrate. Many are ongoing stories. Keep them updated by looking for concerned news items or magazine articles.
- Do you like to reflect or think about what you read in a textbook? If so, refer to the sections:
  o What does the story mean? (immediately after the story)
  o Think critically: Deeper questions for reflection and discussion.
- Are you inclined to learn theory? Then, the main text and boxes are for you.
- Are you happy doing something hands-on? Concentrate on the sections:
- Act: What you can do to conserve
- Learn by doing: Case study / Project
- Organize together: Eco-club activities and projects

If you are tired of studying and you want to relax, read the books, enjoy the poems, or watch the films recommended at the end of each chapter under 'Something different for a change'.

A note on the references

The material in this book has come from a variety of sources: books, textbooks, journal papers, magazine articles, news reports, documentary films, etc. Most of the websites cited were accessed during October–November 2010.

Additional web resources for students and teachers

You can find additional resources on the website created for this book by the publishers. Access the site www.oupinheonline.com, click on the title of this book, and follow the instructions.

Is this just a textbook?

This is, in fact, more than a textbook. It is about your life and what is in store for you. It is about the present and future of the earth. The text and the stories are meant to evoke surprise and shock, despair and hope, resolve and action. You will surely return to it even after the course. It may, in fact, change your life!

Give me your feedback—any errors, suggestions for improvement, additional material to be included, etc. My email address is rrgopalan2005@gmail.com.

R. Rajagopalan

Preface to the First Edition

To the student

'Oh, no! Not one more subject and one more book to be mugged up!' As it is, the load is heavy enough with so many tough and boring things to study. How can I manage the new course? Why should I bother about the environment?'

This could well be your response when told about the new compulsory course on Environmental Studies. As you read this book, however, you will discover that this subject is different from many others: It is about you, and the future of your family, community, humanity, and this fragile planet.

About the book

This book is meant for undergraduates of any discipline and it assumes no background in mathematics or science beyond the tenth standard. It is based on the new University Grants Commission (UGC) syllabus that came in the wake of the landmark judgement of the Supreme Court of India in 2003, to prescribe a course on the environment for colleges and to consider the feasibility of making it a compulsory subject at every level in college education.

A short extract of the Supreme Court judgement is given below:

> … for more than a century there was a growing realisation that mankind had to live in tune with nature, if life was to be peaceful, happy, and satisfied. In the name of scientific development, man started distancing himself from nature and even developed an urge to conquer nature. Our ancestors had known that nature was not subduable and, therefore, had made it an obligation for man to surrender to nature and live in tune with it.

Even as you cover the entire UGC syllabus, learn the concepts, and try the short-answer and essay questions, you will:
- learn about the major environmental problems, such as runaway growth, imperilled ecosystems, disappearing forests, endangered species, dwindling natural resources, escalating pollution, growing population, dangerous toxins, green laws, etc.;
- find out what is being done about these problems;
- discover how YOU can make a difference to the state of the environment;
- savour reading over one hundred short environment-related stories about crises, solutions, successes, failures, interconnections, and inspirational individuals; and
- reflect on the prologues, quotations, poems, and deeper issues.

In addition, this book will aid you in:
- finding ideas and guidance for meaningful field work;
- surfing the Internet for more information on environmental issues which interest you;
- locating books and magazines on the subject;
- choosing a satisfying and rewarding career in environment-related areas; and
- joining an environmental organization or forming one.

To make things easier for you, there is a glossary of terms.

This is in fact more than a textbook. It is about your life and what is in store for you. It is about the present and future of the Earth. The text and the stories are meant to evoke surprise and shock, despair and hope, resolve and action. You will surely return to it even after the course. It may in fact change your life!

A note on the references

The material in this book has come from a variety of sources: books, textbooks, journal papers, magazine articles, news reports, documentary films, etc. You will find at the end of the book an extensive list of references. Most of the websites cited were accessed during August–December 2004.

Feedback is welcome!

Many a topic covered in this book could fit in more than one chapter. In this matter, I have followed the UGC syllabus except for a few minor adjustments. The publishers and I will be delighted to receive feedback and suggestions from you on any aspect of the book such as:

- an evaluation of the content, style of presentation, production, other features, etc.;
- any errors, inconsistencies, wrong figures, unclear illustrations, difficult terms, etc.;
- topics to be included in the next edition;
- an update on the stories and any additional information you may come across;
- new stories of environmental degradation, conservation efforts, individual and group attempts, successes and failures;
- other websites, stories, poems, quotations, etc.; and
- your experiences in environmental conservation.

Your feedback will help us improve the book. All feedback can be sent to *rrgopalan2005@ gmail.com.* Thank you.

On a personal note

The writing of this book absorbed me totally for about a year. I went through various moods— curious, interested, mildly hopeful, extremely depressed. The horror stories were many, the hopeful ones were few. At times I wanted to give up, weighed down by the thought of the coming apocalypse. But I pushed on thinking of the one student whom the book may influence and convert into an environmentalist. The book is really for that unknown student. I hope, of course, that there will be many more than one!

Acknowledgements

I do not know what I would have done without the help of Alan and Ramjee. Apart from providing detailed comments and corrections on every chapter, they kept my spirits up, whenever I was discouraged. They were also my sounding board on many issues concerning the book.

I would not have embarked on this project, had I not been involved for the last five years in conducting environmental workshops at Auroville. I must thank Tency Baetens for inviting me to join the organizing team. It has been a great experience working with Alan, Bhavana, Claude, Harini, Lata, Prashanth, Tency, Tineke, Silvano, and others at Auroville.

It was my entry ten years ago into the International Ocean Institute (IOI) that made me think deeper on environmental issues. The Late Professor Elisabeth Mann Borgese, founder of IOI, was a great source of inspiration. I thank all my colleagues in IOI for their appreciation of my work with coastal communities. In particular, I am grateful to Krishan Saigal and Masako Otsuka for their constant support.

My friends in Navadarshanam—Ananthu, Atma, Jyoti, Om, Pratapji, Pushpaji, and Sudeshji—encouraged me in the task of writing this book and I thank them.

I would like to thank Francois Gamache for making my stay in Vancouver so comfortable that I could spend almost all my time on reference work in the libraries of that great city.

I am grateful to my friends who have always been a source of strength—Ahana, Chitra, Dilip, Muraleedharan, Narendran, Sekhar, Subramanian, Vishwanath, and many others.

I am very grateful to the authors of several excellent American textbooks on Environmental Science. In particular, I have drawn heavily from Botkin and Keller (1995), Chiras (2001), Cunningham and Saigo (1995), Enger and Smith (2004), Miller (2004), Nebel and Wright (1998), and Raven and Berg (2004). Their canvas was much wider and the books were aimed at undergraduates who had chosen Environmental Science as a subject. However, I learnt a great deal from reading their books and I have used many of their ideas. If this book is welcomed in Indian academia, they will have a share in its success.

My thanks for reprint permissions:

- Excerpts from pages 85 and 87–88 are from Eknath Easwaran, *The Compassionate Universe*, Penguin India edition, copyright 1989, reprinted with the permission of Nilgiri Press, P.O. Box 256, Tomales, CA 94971, *www.nilgiri.org*.
- Excerpts from the essay by Lois M. Gibbs, 'We Have Been Asking the Wrong Questions', in G. Tyler Miller, *Living in the Environment* 13e, copyright 2004, pp. 530–31, are reprinted with the permission of Lois M.Gibbs.

I have requested for reprint permission in the following cases:

- Excerpts from the Rio Summit speech of Severn Suzuki from David Suzuki, *Time To Change* (1994, Stoddart, Toronto), pp. 227–30.
- Excerpts from, 'How Can One Sell the Air?', from the book of the same name published by The Book Publishing Company, Summertown, USA.

I have taken many poems from websites and I record my appreciation for the creative work of the authors.

If the environmental lawyer M.C. Mehta had not filed the case in the Supreme Court in 1991 and again in 2003, this book would never have been written. He does not know me, but I must thank him not only for taking initiative in the matter of environmental education, but also for all the legal battles he has been fighting in the cause of India's environment.

I thank Oxford University Press India for supporting the idea of writing this textbook and for extending invaluable editorial help to me.

Finally, I thank Malathi, Kumar, and Anand for being patient with me all through the months I spent sitting before the computer screen.

R. Rajagopalan

Contents

MODULE 3   BIODIVERSITY   65

MODULE 4   RENEWABLE AND NON-RENEWABLE NATURAL RESOURCES   101

MODULE 5   ENVIRONMENTAL POLLUTION   169

MODULE 6 HUMAN POPULATION AND THE ENVIRONMENT 237

MODULE 7   SOCIAL ISSUES AND THE ENVIRONMENT   283

MODULE 8   FIELD WORK   331

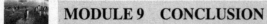

MODULE 9   CONCLUSION   337

Module 1

The Global Environmental Crisis

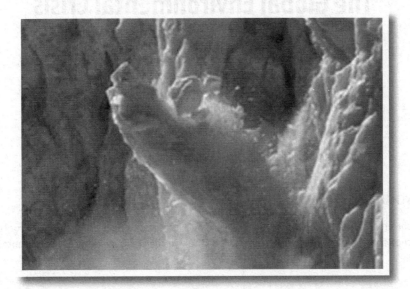

Chapter 1: The Global Environmental Crisis

The Global Environmental Crisis

Only after the last tree has been cut down,
only after the last river has been poisoned,
only after the last fish has been caught,
only then will you find that money cannot be eaten.

Native American Prophecy

THIS CHAPTER IS ABOUT...

Global environmental crisis and its causes, environmental indicators, ecological footprint, international agreements, public awareness, the interdisciplinary nature of environmental studies

THE KEYWORDS AND PHRASES ARE...

environment	ecology	environmental studies	ecological footprint
exponential growth	idea of progress	sustainable development	

THE STORY OF KALAHANDI: FROM FORESTS TO FAMINE

The monsoon has rarely failed this area. It gets an average annual rainfall of 1,250 mm, more than what Punjab receives. The water table in some places is very high. Yet, Kalahandi in western Orissa is frequently in the news for its extreme poverty and deprivation. Often it suffers from drought and sometimes it has floods. The people migrate to all parts of India looking for work and survival.

Kalahandi, however, was not always a place of hunger and deprivation. Nineteenth century travellers have talked about a mass of jungles and hills in the region. Just a few decades ago, it was all green here. The forests provided livelihood for six months and

agriculture provided for the next six months. With a large diversity of crops, it was one of the richest areas in eastern India. How did things change?

In the past, there was a network of about 30,000 traditional water-harvesting structures in the area. They included ponds, lakes, check-dams, and even tanks within paddy fields. The whole system was designed to suit the topography of the land so that no part of the rainwater went waste. What is more, the system was under the control of the community, which ensured proper maintenance and water-sharing through *jal-sabhas* (water councils).

Many tanks were built with the free labour provided by the people. There was also a social system to protect the forests in the catchment areas. About 50 per cent of the cultivated land was irrigated using the water bodies. Failure of rainfall did occur, but there was never any scarcity of water.

Came Independence and the troubles started. First, the government took over many of the structures, but did not maintain them properly. In other cases, fearing a takeover, the landowners converted the tanks into croplands. The focus shifted to large irrigation projects like the Hirakud Dam, though the canal system often did not suit the local topography.

Concurrently, the forests were being cut down for timber and the resulting erosion of the soil dumped a lot of silt on the catchment areas. Riverbeds also silted up, leading to floods downstream. A large amount of water was being lost as run-off. From then on, even a slight shortfall in rain brought water scarcity and a large-scale crop failure. Agriculture became a difficult proposition and people started migrating in large numbers, affecting community life and preventing any revival of the water harvesting system. Kalahandi thus slid into a vicious circle, from which it has never recovered.

What does the story of Kalahandi tell us?

Kalahandi is a classic case of environmental degradation leading to poverty and deprivation. Is Kalahandi a rare case or is it a typical one? Is there really a global environmental crisis? If there is a crisis, what is the cure? Such questions are addressed in this book.

Is there a global environmental crisis?

You can find many regular reports about the state of the world's environment (Box 1.1). In addition, there are many thematic and special reports (Box 1.2).

Here are some indicators of the current state of the planet, drawn from the various reports·

BOX 1.1

State of the planet: Regular reports

- The United Nations Environment Programme (UNEP) produces periodically a comprehensive global state of the environment report, called the Global Environment Outlook (GEO). GEO-4 was published in 2007.
- The Worldwatch Institute, an independent research organization in the US, publishes an annual State of the World report that lists the significant events of the previous year and covers current environmental topics.

- WWFN—World Wide Fund for Nature brings out every other year the Living Planet Report, a science-based analysis of the health of the planet.
- The Centre for Science and Environment (CSE), New Delhi, a public interest research and advocacy organization, issues periodical reports on the state of India's environment. They also cover current events in their magazine *Down To Earth*.

BOX 1.2

State of the planet: Examples of thematic and special reports

- UN World Water Development Report, published every three years
- Regular Assessment Reports from the UN Inter-governmental Panel for Climate Change (IPCC)
- UN Millennium Ecosystem Assessment Report (2005)
- Report of the World Commission on Dams (2000)

Population

- The world population is expected to reach 7 billion in 2011. It has taken just 12 years for the population to increase from 6 to 7 billion.
- India's population was about 1.2 billion in 2010. By 2030, we will overtake China in population.

More than 60,000 Indian villages lack sources of drinking water

Water and sanitation

- Two billion people live in countries that are water-stressed and, by 2025, two-thirds of the world population may suffer water stress. Some 80 countries suffer from serious water shortages now. Half the world population lacks sanitation facilities.
- In India, more than 60,000 villages are without a single source of drinking water. Diarrhoea, brought on by contaminated water, claims the lives of one million children every year. In addition 45 million people are affected annually by the poor quality of water.

Biodiversity

- Worldwide, 24 per cent of mammals, 12 per cent of birds, 25 per cent of reptiles and 30 per cent of fish species are threatened or endangered; this is 100 to 1,000 times the rate at which species naturally disappear.
- More than 10 per cent of India's recorded wild flora and fauna are threatened and many are on the verge of extinction.

Forests

- The net loss in global forest area during the 1990s was about 94 million hectares (ha). Tropical forests are being cleared at the rate of 70,000 to 170,000 sq km annually (equal to 21–50 soccer fields per minute)
- India's forest cover declined from 40 per cent a century ago to 22 per cent in 1951 and to 19 per cent in 1997. The quantitative decline is supposed to have been arrested since 1991, but the qualitative decline persists.

Land

- Each year, six million ha of agricultural land are lost due to desertification and soil degradation. This process affects about 250 million people in the world.
- India has nearly 130 million ha of wasteland compared to 305 million ha of biomass producing area.

Pollution

- At least one billion people in the world breathe unhealthy air and three million die annually due to air pollution.
- The World Health Organization consistently rates New Delhi and Kolkata as being among the most polluted megacities of the world.

Air pollution in a traffic jam in an Indian Metro

Coastal and marine areas

- Worldwide, 50 per cent of mangroves and wetlands that perform vital ecological functions have been destroyed.
- Over the past 40 years, India too has lost more than 50 per cent of its mangrove forests. The absence of mangroves on the Orissa coast accentuated the damage to life and habitation when the Supercyclone struck in 1999.

Disasters

- Across the world, the numbers of people affected by disasters have risen from an average of 147 million a year in the 1980s to 211 million a year in the 1990s. Floods, droughts, and wind storms accounted for more than 90 per cent of the people killed in natural disasters.
- India is the most disaster-prone country in the South Asian region. Drought, floods, earthquakes, and cyclones occur with grim regularity. 10,000 people died in the Orissa supercyclone of 1999, and 16,000 died in the Gujarat earthquake in 2001. In 2010, there were heavy floods in many parts of North India. Again in 2010, severe floods occurred in Pakistan, affecting more than 20 million people.

Energy

- More than two billion people in the world go without adequate energy supplies.
- India imports more than 50 per cent of its oil needs, primarily to feed the transportation sector.

Global warming

- There are clear signs of global warming: Global temperatures in 2010 were highest on record; permafrost and glaciers in the polar and other regions are melting; the very existence of many small islands is being threatened by the rise in the sea level.

The Melting Athabasca glacier in Canada (Image courtesy: http://commons. wikimedia.org/wiki/File:Melting_Toe_of_Athabasca_Glacier.jpg)

- In 2010, Delhi experienced the hottest April in 52 years. Hundreds of people died in India during the summer heat wave. There is evidence to show that some of the Himalayan glaciers are losing mass and becoming thinner.

Urbanisation

- More than half the world's population now lives in urban areas, compared to little more than one-third in 1972. About one-quarter of the urban population lives below the poverty line.
- About 23 per cent of the population in India's million-plus cities lives in slums. Dharavi in Mumbai, the largest slum in Asia, houses 500,000 people over a small area of 170 ha.

Overcrowding in an urban area, slums and apartments, crowded streets, traffic jams, etc.

We can go on with more statistics, but the picture must be clear to you. Severe environmental degradation is happening all over the world. What is the reason for this depressing state of affairs? Hundreds of scientists, environmentalists, politicians, social workers, and thinking citizens have come to two main conclusions:

KEY IDEA

We are using natural resources faster than they can generate and creating waste faster than it can be absorbed.

1. We are consuming natural resources at a rate much higher than that at which nature can regenerate them.
2. As we consume the resources, we are creating waste and pollution much faster than the rate at which nature can absorb them.

This is an unsustainable way of living and it can only lead to an environmental and social catastrophe.

Should we not worry more about problems such as poverty, armed conflicts, and terrorism than about the environment?

It is true that the world is facing many serious issues such as:

- Wars, local conflicts, and terrorism

- Exploding population
- Widespread hunger, poverty, and extreme inequalities
- Massive displacement of people due to environmental changes and development projects
- Emergence of new diseases
- Corruption in politics and the government
- Economic downturn and financial crisis

However, all such issues and the environmental crisis are inter-related. Here are some examples of such connections:

- Conflicts of any kind degrade the environment through the planting of landmines, destruction of irrigation systems and water resources, interference in planting and harvesting crops, etc. There is also the real danger of future wars being fought over scarce resources like oil and water.
- Rapid increase in population puts enormous pressure on natural resources such as water, land, and biodiversity.
- Environmental degradation leads to droughts, crop failures, and rural poverty. It also forces people to migrate to cities looking for livelihood. This in turn creates unsustainable urban demand for water, power, sanitation, and so on.
- Toxic waste from cities and industries give rise to new diseases.
- Corruption enables the violation of environmental laws and regulations, leading to greater degradation.

What is the crisis of environment?

The world is heading for an environmental disaster and, like the three monkeys, we do not want to see, hear, or talk about it. What is even worse, sometimes we do talk about it and then go about our business as if the environment and our lives were quite different.

Many environmental problems arise from the deliberate or inadvertent abuse, misuse, and overuse of natural resources by human beings. Land, water, energy sources, air, and space have all been adversely affected through human intervention.

Surely nature will take care of the problems over time?   The earth has existed for five billion years, humanity for three to five million years and civilization for 10,000 years. They have survived many crises and cataclysmic events. Looking back over the centuries, nature seems to have absorbed disturbances and stayed always in balance. Thousands of species have survived over a long period and, consequently, could be expected to continue to exist forever. Will we not survive the current environmental crisis too?

We may be correct in expecting the earth and many species to survive, but we may be wrong in assuming that humanity will also continue to exist along with nature in the same way. The reason is that there is something different happening now.

What is different about the current scene?

In the past, changes were always slow, but that is no longer true. Human activities have drastically increased the pace at which things change. What is happening now can be described by a simple mathematical curve or graph—the exponential growth of quantity with time. This curve is relatively flat in the beginning, but becomes steeper and steeper with time (Read Box 1.3 for an explanation of exponential growth.)

BOX 1.3

Concept: Exponential growth

Suppose you invest Rs 1,000 in a bank, which gives you an annual interest of 10 per cent. You ask the bank to reinvest the interest earned every year. (We call this compound interest.) At the end of one year, your account will have grown to Rs 1,100. At the end of the second year, the balance will be Rs 1,210 (Rs 1,100 + 110). Thus, every year, an increased amount of interest gets added to the principal. What will be the accumulated amount at the end of 50 years? Guess the amount before reading further!

In 50 years, the amount would have grown to more than Rs 117,000! If you did not know the power of compound interest, you would have surely underestimated the value. This kind of increase is called exponential growth.

Compare this growth with the case of simple interest. The initial deposit of Rs 1,000 will earn a constant amount of interest (Rs 100) every year. At the end of 50 years, the total amount will be only Rs 6,000 (original deposit of Rs 1,000 + interest of Rs 5,000). You can see for yourself how compound interest makes so much difference. This is the power of exponential growth.

Mathematically, any growth is exponential if the increase is at a constant rate per time period, rather than a constant amount. If you show exponential growth as a graph, the shape of the curve will be like the letter J. Figure 1.1 shows the growth of your investment of Rs 1,000 at a compound interest rate of 10 per cent. You can also compare the growth with a simple interest of same value.

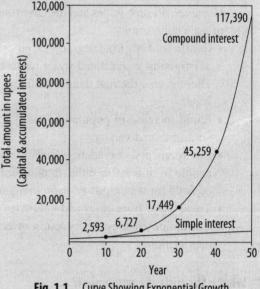

Fig. 1.1 Curve Showing Exponential Growth

Many natural phenomena exhibit exponential growth. For example, the population of the world has been increasing exponentially. With every case of exponential growth we associate 'a doubling time'. This is roughly the time it takes for the quantity to double in value. You can get the doubling time by dividing the number 70 by the growth rate of the quantity. This formula is derived from the basic mathematics of exponential growth. The world population doubles every 45 years or so.

Four such mega phenomena or spikes have been occurring, with profound implications for life on earth. These are the four quantities that are growing exponentially:

- Size of the human population (Figure 1.2)
- Production and consumption of goods and services (Figure 1.3)
- Concentration of carbon dioxide gas in the atmosphere (Figure 1.4)
- Number biological species becoming extinct every year (Figure 1.5)

A remarkable fact is that, in each case, the curve was flat over centuries until the spike began in recent times. What makes matters worse is that the four spikes are interconnected, each amplifying the others. Let us take a closer look at these phenomena.

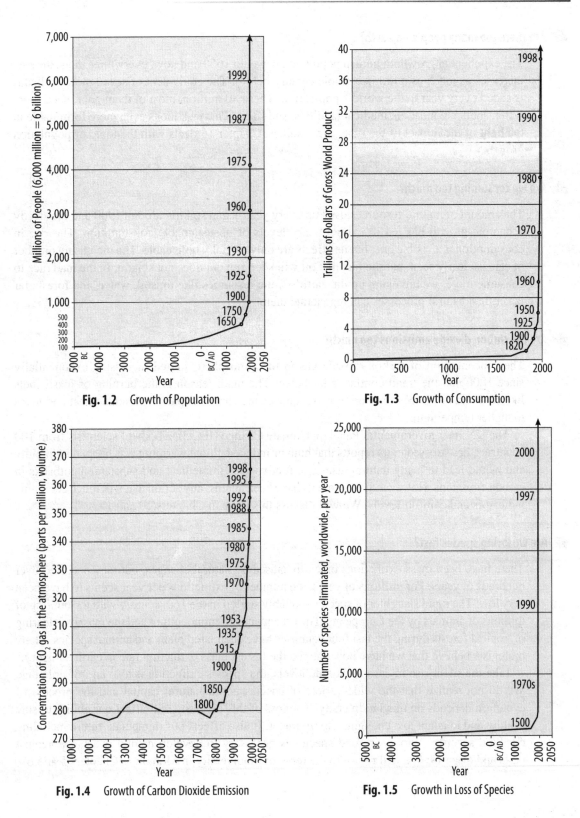

Fig. 1.2   Growth of Population

Fig. 1.3   Growth of Consumption

Fig. 1.4   Growth of Carbon Dioxide Emission

Fig. 1.5   Growth in Loss of Species

Are there too many people on earth?

The exponential growth in human population began in 1650 and now, every three days, the size increases as much as it did in a whole century before. The equivalent of seven more Kolkatas is added every year to the world's population. These 80 million, most of them poor, need food, water, shelter, education, medical facilities, and so on. This task looks even more formidable in the light of the impact of the other three spikes. Chapter 15 deals with the topic of population growth.

Are we consuming too much?

The amount of natural resources used up every year began spiking around 1900 and the steady economic growth has led to extraordinary levels of unsustainable consumption. The rise in consumption is a visible one, but its effects are only partially noticeable. The increasing number of cars is clearly seen, but the fact that oil will soon run out does not sink in. In the mad race to consume more, we are using up the earth's finite resources like topsoil, water, and forests far faster than natural processes can regenerate them.

Are the carbon dioxide emissions too much?

The concentration of carbon dioxide gas in the atmosphere started increasing exponentially since 1800 and the trend continues unabated. The main reason is the burning of fossil fuels like coal and oil. Excess carbon dioxide reduces the earth's capacity to radiate heat and leads to higher temperatures.

The UN Intergovernmental Panel on Climate Change (IPCC), a body of scientists from 100 countries, has stressed in its reports that human-induced global warming was happening rapidly and would lead to many natural disasters. It advocates immediate and substantial cutbacks in carbon emissions. However, governments have been against any action that will touch economic indicators and comfort levels. We will discuss this issue in Chapters 10 and 19.

Are we losing species fast?

There have been mass extinctions on earth caused by natural changes, but they occurred over hundreds of years. For millions of years, the number of extinctions per year seems to have been very low. The rapid slaughter of species probably started in the 16th century with the hunting of millions of animals by the Europeans. The ascendance of monoculture and the massive clearing of tropical forests during the last four centuries have decimated plant and animal species. Many biologists believe that we have now entered the fastest mass extinction rate in earth's history.

Like the silent rise in carbon dioxide levels, the species extinction is also an invisible one. We do not realize that the wide variety of species is our natural capital and the process of evolution depends on this biodiversity. The loss of this diversity will affect our ability to stay healthy and to adapt to a changing environment. It also affects our immediate future including our food security. Variety in food species is necessary to develop natural resistance against pests and diseases. We will return to the topic of biodiversity in Module 3 (Chapters 5 and 6).

Why should these quantities spike over the last two or three centuries?

The spikes are due to a fundamental change in our relationship with nature. This change began with the scientific and industrial revolutions that occurred in Europe in the 16th and 17th centuries. The new attitude towards nature came from the Idea of Progress that advocated the superior role of humans as masters of nature. We could indefinitely exploit nature and our progress towards a better life would be linear and continuous. Science and technology would help us in this quest for ceaseless progress and development.

Through colonialism and other ways, the Idea of Progress was conveyed to large parts of the world. Today, most countries swear by this notion of growth and development through science, technology, and industrial expansion.

Can we blame all our ills on the Scientific and Industrial Revolutions?

Clearly, these two revolutions marked the beginning of the exponential rate of consumption of natural resources by humans. However, there is also the view that the problems began much earlier, when humans shifted from being nomadic hunter-gatherers to settled agriculturists.

The current problem, however, is that we are living beyond our means. Our 'ecological footprint' is getting larger and larger.

What is meant by ecological footprint?

Assume that you live in a small house in a city. Let us say that the house is surrounded by a small garden and there is a compound wall that marks your plot of land. Can you isolate yourself in your home and continue to live indefinitely? You cannot, since you need many things from outside: food, water, material of different sorts and so on. Your garden may give you some vegetables, but it cannot provide you all the food items you need. There may be a well on your land, but the water may not be potable and you may have to depend on outside sources for drinking water.

Suppose we ask the question: How large a land will you need just to sustain you completely? That area is your ecological footprint.

KEY IDEA
Ecological footprint is the amount of biologically productive land and sea area required to sustain indefinitely an entity such as a person, a city's population, a country, etc. It accounts for the energy, food, water, and materials that the entity consumes and the wastes that it creates.

Let us do a mental experiment. Take the physical area of a city like Chennai and cover it with a huge glass hemisphere. We let in sunlight, but we do not allow any material to enter or leave the enclosure. How long will the city survive? Not many days!

The city cannot produce enough food for all the people. There will be severe water scarcity, because the tankers from the surrounding villages will stop entering the city. The enormous amount of solid waste generated every day cannot be sent away or dumped into the sea. The air trapped in the hemisphere will soon become so polluted that people will find it difficult to breathe. The 'carrying capacity' of the city area is not sufficient to sustain the lives of the population.

Suppose we are able to expand the size of the glass hemisphere to take in more and more of the surrounding area. Also assume that this area has diverse natural resources like a mini-earth. We can now ask another question: How large should be the area covered, if we want the city to survive indefinitely on the land, water and energy resources available within the hemisphere? That area is the ecological footprint of the city.

The millions of people living in Chennai have huge needs and they draw their requirements from a very large area surrounding the city. The ecological footprint of Chennai is many, many times larger than its actual area. Similarly, we can talk about the ecological footprint of a country. Or, we can compare the ecological footprint of a citizen of US with that of an Indian citizen.

We can express ecological footprint either in units of area or as the ratio of the area required to the actual area of the entity. For example, if Chennai requires for its survival an area three times its geographical spread, then its ecological footprint is three.

How is our environmental crisis connected to the idea of ecological footprint?   The larger the footprint, the more is the consumption of natural resources and the more is the environmental degradation. Most of the world's cities have footprints greater than one. Again, countries like the US have large footprints too.

What is humanity's ecological footprint?

KEY IDEA

Humanity's footprint is already more than 1.4. That is, we now require 40 per cent more than the earth's area to sustain our consumption of natural resources! Our footprint is also increasing steadily.

You will be surprised to find out the ecological footprint of humanity as a whole (Key Idea).

How is that possible? Common sense tells us that we could not be using resources from an area larger than that of the earth! We have only one earth. If our footprint is 1.4, how are we surviving at all?

We survive, because each year we are using up more than our annual share of the earth's resources. Currently, by September or earlier, we use up ecological resources that the earth regenerates in the whole year! The rest of the year, we survive by dipping into the quota of the future.

We draw more water from the ground than the amount of natural recharge. We catch fish faster than the rate at which they can re-populate. Our logging of trees is faster than the rate at which new trees grow.

Instead of living within the 'annual interest' that nature gives us, we have begun using up our 'natural capital'. In a sense, we are using resources that rightly belong to our children and grandchildren. We are living beyond our means.

In general, we are using resources faster than they can regenerate and creating waste faster than it can be absorbed. This is called 'ecological overshoot'. While this can be done for a short while, overshoot ultimately leads to the depletion of resources on which our economy depends.

What has the world done about the environmental crisis?

Even by the 1960s, the adverse environmental impact of unbridled economic growth was becoming clear. Books like Rachel Carson's *Silent Spring* set the tone for an environmental movement.

The UN Conference on Human Environment in 1972 held in Stockholm was the first international initiative to discuss environmental problems. In 1983, the UN set up the World

KEY IDEA
Sustainable Development: Development that meets the needs of the present without compromising the ability of future generations to meet their own needs.

Commission on Environment and Development (WCED) with Gro Harlem Brundtland of Norway as the Chairperson. The WCED Report, called *Our Common Future,* emphasised the need for an integration of economic and ecological systems. The Commission supported the concept of 'Sustainable Development' and defined it as given on the left (Key Idea).

This definition of sustainable development has been criticised for being interpretable in many ways. Yet, it has caught the attention of many people, since it seems to imply that development and environmental conservation can go together.

After Stockholm, the major effort was the UN Conference on Environment and Development (UNCED) held in 1992 in Rio de Janeiro. Attended by more than 100 Heads of State and 30,000 participants, UNCED came up with several documents including:

- The Rio Declaration on Environment and Development listing 27 principles of sustainable development
- *Agenda 21*, a detailed action plan for sustainable development in the 21st century
- The Convention on Biological Diversity

The next conference, popularly known as Rio+10, was held in Johannesburg, South Africa, in 2002. This Conference recognized that implementation of the Rio agreements had been poor. This Summit marked a shift from agreements in principle to more modest but concrete plans of action. Since Rio+10, however, most countries have ignored even these modest plans.

Why is there a general lack of public awareness about environmental issues?

There are many factors that limit our awareness of environmental issues. To the millions of poor people, the problems of daily existence are more important than environmental degradation. The more prosperous are afraid that, in the name of environment, their comforts may be taken away. In any case, most of us do not pay the real costs of exploiting nature.

There is also false anti-environment propaganda by vested interests like the large corporations, for whom constant growth is vital. At the political level, parties are more interested in short-term gains and would not take unpopular measures for conserving the environment. Further, in this age of extreme specialization very few can look at the larger picture of what is happening to the world. There is also paucity of reliable and clear information on the environment. To make matters worse, indicators like Gross Domestic Product (GDP) give us a misleading picture of what is desirable.

What is the role of environment-related studies?   If subjects like environmental studies, environmental science, or ecology are taught to everyone at the school and college levels, there will be an increase in the awareness level.

Could we define environmental studies and related terms?

Generally, there are two ways in which we use the term 'environment'. In one, the term refers to what surrounds an entity. Any entity, say a person, any living organism, a citizen, a company, etc., has its environment. We thus talk of the home environment, the business environment, the political environment, etc. An entity interacts with its environment, that is, it influences and is influenced by the environment, positively or negatively. For example, the natural environment affects human beings. We in turn have an impact (often a negative impact) on the environment.

In the second way, we use the word to mean just the natural environment: the air, water, soil, living beings, plants, trees, mountains, oceans, etc. The Oxford Advanced Learner's Dictionary defines *environment* as 'the natural world in which people, animals, and plants live'. This book takes up the uses related with this natural environment. Let us define some terms related to the environment.

Ecology is the science that studies the relationships between living things and the environment. It is often considered to be a discipline of biology.

Environmental Science is the systematic and scientific study of the environment and our role in it.

What then is *Environmental Studies,* which is the subject of this book? The two terms, *Environmental Studies and Environmental Science,* are often used interchangeably, but we could make a distinction.

Environmental Studies can be defined as the branch of study concerned with environmental issues. It has a broader canvas than environmental science and includes the social aspects of the environment. It does deal with science where necessary, but at a level understandable to the non-scientist.

Why do we say that these subjects are interdisciplinary?

The subject of environment is inherently interdisciplinary. We study the complex relationships that exist in our natural environment among people, animals, other organisms, water, soil, air, trees, ocean, and so on. The interconnections are numerous and involve many different disciplines. We need inputs from biology, botany, zoology, soil science, technology, oceanography, atmospheric science, economics, sociology, anthropology, ethics, and so on. A simple rule to remember is that everything in this world is connected. (Read the two stories in Box 1.4 and Box 1.5)

BOX 1.4

Connections: Drink coffee in US and make the songbird vanish in South America

How can drinking a cup of coffee in a chain shop in the US lead to the disappearance of songbirds in South America?

In recent years, chains of coffee shops have proliferated in the US and many other western countries. The coffee comes from Central and South America and the growers now face a heavy demand. Traditionally coffee is grown under the shade of the rainforest (without using chemicals) and the ripe berries are handpicked. In order to increase productivity and meet the new demand, the growers have been shifting to unshaded plantations treated with fertilizers and pesticides. Over the past 25 years, about 50 per cent of the shade trees have been replaced with unshaded plantations.

The shade plantations have always provided shelter for a large number of birds, vertebrates, and insects. Many migratory songbirds spend the winter

Contd

Box 1.4 Contd

in the rain forests. With a decrease in shade trees, there has been an alarming decline in the population of birds like warblers and orchard orioles.

Conservation groups like the Rainforest Alliance and the American Birding Association have initiated programmes to certify coffee as 'shade-grown' and encourage consumers to ask for such varieties. In fact, one brand already available is called Songbird Coffee!

There are thousands of such connections in nature. Even a simple act of ours could have wide ramifications over long distances.

BOX 1.5

Connections: Get rid of malaria, but invite the plague!

In mid-twentieth century, malaria was rampant in the Indonesian island of Sabah, earlier known as North Borneo. In 1955, the World Health Organization (WHO) began spraying the island with the dieldrin (a chemical related to DDT) on the mosquitoes. The attempt was successful and malaria was almost eradicated.

The dieldrin, however, did other things too. It killed many other insects including flies and cockroaches. The lizards ate these insects and they died too. So did the cats that ate the lizards. Once the cats declined, rats proliferated in huge numbers and there was a threat of plague. WHO then dropped by parachute healthy cats on the island.

The dieldrin had also killed wasps and other insects that consumed a particular caterpillar, which was somehow not affected by the chemical. The caterpillars flourished and ate away all the leaves in the thatched roofs of the houses and the roofs started caving in.

Ultimately the situation was brought under control. However, the unexpected chain of events showed the importance of asking at every stage the question: 'And then what?'

Is there hope for the future?

While this book describes the environmental crisis, it also contains many stories of hope, of successful efforts by individuals, voluntary groups, international organizations, and even governments.

Positive actions here and there are not enough, however. We must act individually and collectively to save the planet and the human species through sustainable development.

To begin with, each of us should see the environmental crisis as a real one needing urgent action from all of us. We have to move from a linear thinking to systemic or circular thinking that recognises complex interactions and natural cycles in the world.

We should examine beliefs, such as the following, that we have imbibed from our education and culture:

- 'The world works today, will work tomorrow.'
- 'Perpetual economic growth is necessary and good.'
- 'Happiness comes from consumption.'

Ultimately it is a question of changing one's mindset. If that happens to a sufficiently large number of people, we may yet begin managing our resources in a wise and sustainable way. We will return to this question in the final chapter of the book.

REVIEW: A SUMMARY OF THE KEY POINTS

- The world is facing a global environmental crisis.
- We are consuming natural resources at an ever-increasing rate, without giving nature time to regenerate them.
- We are also polluting the world so much that nature cannot absorb it all.
- Our unsustainable way of living can only lead to a catastrophe.
- The environmental crisis is rooted in our attitude of domination and exploitation of nature, based on the Idea of Progress.
- Many phenomena like population and consumption have been growing exponentially over the past 100–200 years.
- The concept of ecological footprint expresses the amount of land needed to sustain the lifestyle of an

entity—a person, a city, a country, etc.
- Humanity's ecological footprint is already more than 1.4. That is, we now require 40 per cent more than the earth's area to sustain our consumption of natural resources.
- There are several international agreements over the issues of environment and development, but the implementation has been poor.
- An accepted but questionable approach is that of 'sustainable development', that is, development that meets the needs of the present without compromising the ability of future generations to meet their own needs.
- Any study of the environment has to be an inter-disciplinary one.

EXERCISES

Objective-type questions

In each case below, choose the best answer out of the given set of choices:

1. What describes best the water and sanitation situation?
   (a) About 10,000 villages in India are without a single source of drinking water.
   (b) 50 per cent of the world population lacks sanitation facilities.
   (c) 65 per cent of the world population suffers from water stress.
   (d) 1.3 billion Indians do not get clean water.

2. Which of the following statements is true?
   (a) Nature can absorb the waste and pollution that we create.
   (b) Even if we continue with our current ways of living, nature will, in due course, take care of the problems that we create.
   (c) Our current consumption levels are unsustainable.
   (d) Natural resources have no limits.

3. Suppose there is a quantity that increases exponentially and we draw the graph of the quantity against

time. How would you best describe the resulting curve?
   (a) Its increase is directly proportional to the time. When the time doubles, the quantity also doubles.
   (b) It is a flat curve.
   (c) The curve goes up and down.
   (d) Its value doubles over a fixed time period and the curve becomes steeper all the time.

4. Humanity's ecological footprint
   (a) already exceeds the area of the earth.
   (b) cannot exceed the area of the earth.
   (c) now equals twice the area of the earth.
   (d) is less than the area of the earth.

5. Which of the following was **not** a conference on environment?
   (a) Stockholm UN Conference on Human Environment in 1972.
   (b) UN Conference on Environment and Development held in 1992 in Rio de Janeiro.
   (c) World Summit called Rio+10 held in Johannesburg in 2002.
   (d) Annual conference of the G8 countries

Short-answer questions

1. What are the two main causes of the environmental crisis?
2. Explain the concept of ecological footprint through an example.
3. List the major international conferences held on environment and development. What were the major outcomes in each case?

Long-answer questions

1. Explain the root cause of the current environmental crisis through the four spikes.
2. Give a non-mathematical explanation of exponential growth and compare it with linear growth. Give one or more examples.
3. Humanity's ecological footprint is 40 per cent more than the earth area. How then are we carrying on our 'business as usual'?

4. Why do we say that any study of the environment becomes an interdisciplinary one?
5. Give an update of the indicators of the state of the world and of India given in this chapter. Have any indicators changed for the better?

Think critically: Deeper questions for reflection and discussion

1. There is a view that all our problems and our domination over nature started when we started practising agriculture about 10000 years ago. Examine this view and give arguments in favour and against.
2. In your opinion, what should be the difference in the way the two subjects, environmental science and environmental studies, are taught to undergraduates?
3. Why are many environmental problems so difficult to solve? Is it because they have often many dimensions and many stakeholders with conflicting interests?

SOMETHING DIFFERENT FOR A CHANGE

1. Enjoy a poem: Here are the famous first lines of the poem *Auguries of Innocence* by the English poet, William Blake (1757–1827):

   > To see a World in a grain of sand
   > And a Heaven in a Wild Flower,

   > Hold Infinity in the Palm of your hand
   > And Eternity in an Hour.

2. Read *Ecotopia: The Notebooks and Reports of William Weston*, a novel by Ernest Callenbach, published in 1975. The book describes an ecological utopia. It was influential in the environmental movement.

ACTIVITIES

What you can do to conserve the environment

Practical ways of helping to save the environment are given in most of the succeeding chapters. To begin with, you could do the following:

1. Make a resolution that you would take one small action every day to conserve the environment. Act on the suggestions given in this book.
2. Join a local environmental group or voluntary organization and work with them at the local level.
3. Try to reduce your ecological footprint by examining the source of everything that you consume. Can you grow some vegetables and fruits in your backyard or terrace? Can you collect the rainwater that falls on your roof?

Organize together: Eco-club activities and projects

This is the start of a new semester or academic year. Make a good beginning by setting up an eco-club in your college. Write down its aims and possible activities. Elect a secretary and a small committee. In later lessons there are suggestions for eco-club activities.

You can also get ideas from the UN special programme for youth, called TUNZA. Access the website www.unep.org/tunza/youth.

Learn by doing: Idea for fieldwork

Study your neighbourhood, your town, or your ancestral village. What are the key environmental issues faced by the place? What are the conflicting interests in each case?

LEARN MORE

Books

Agarwal, Anil, Sunita Narain and Srabani Sen (eds) 1999, *State of India's Environment—5, Fifth Citizens' Report*, Centre for Science and Environment, New Delhi.

Ayres, Ed 1999, *God's Last Offer: Negotiating for a Sustainable Future*, Four Walls Eight Windows, New York. (on exponential growth)

Brown, Lester R., Janet Larsen and Bernie Fischlowitz-Roberts 2003, *The Earth Policy Reader*, Earth Policy Institute, Indian Edition, Orient Longman, Hyderabad.

Carson, Rachel 1962, *Silent Spring*, Indian Edition, Other India Press, Goa.

CSE 2000, *Our Ecological Footprint: Think of Your City as an Ecosystem*, Centre for Science and Environment, New Delhi.

Mason, Colin 2003, *The 2030 Spike: Countdown to Global Catastrophe*, Earthscan, London. (on exponential growth)

Sainath, P. 1996, *Everybody Loves a Good Drought: Stories from India's Poorest Districts*, Penguin Books India, New Delhi. (Stories on Kalahandi and other places)

UNEP 2007, *Global Environment Outlook 4*, Global Resource Information Division, UN Environment Programme, Division of Early Warning and Assessment, Geneva.

Wackernagel, Mathis and William E. Rees 1996, *Our Ecological Footprint: Reducing Human Impact on the Earth*, New Society Publishers, Gabriola Island, Canada.

WCED (World Commission on Environment and Development) 1987, *Our Common Future*, Oxford University Press, Oxford.

Articles

Lakshman, Nirmala 2001, 'Distress: A Way of Life in Kalahandi', *The Hindu*, May 13.

Mahapatra, Richard and Ranjan Panda 2001, 'The Myth of Kalahandi: A Resource-rich Region Reels under a Government-induced Drought', *Down To Earth*, Vol. 9, No. 21, March 31.

Websites

United Nations Environment Programme (UNEP): www.unep.org

Intergovernmental Panel on Climate Change (IPCC): www.ipcc.ch

UNEP Environmental Knowledge for Change: www.grida.no

Films

The 11th Hour: A film by Leonardo DiCaprio (A look at the state of the global environment including visionary and practical solutions for restoring the planet's ecosystems)

The Many Faces of Madness: A film by Amar Kanwar (on ecological degradation in India)

Module 2

Ecosystems

CHAPTER 2

Ecosystems: Basic Concepts

One cannot but be in awe,
when one contemplates the mysteries of eternity,
of life, of the marvellous structure of reality.
It is enough if one tries to merely comprehend
a little of this mystery each day.
Never lose a holy curiosity.

Albert Einstein
(1879–1955)
Father of Modern Physics and Nobel Laureate

THIS CHAPTER IS ABOUT...

Ecosystems (definitions, components, types, structure, energy flows, services, etc.), food chains, global cycles

THE KEYWORDS AND PHRASES ARE...

ecosystem	species	population	community
biosphere	biome	aquatic life zone	biota
abiotic conditions	ecotone	edge effect	food chain
food web	producer	photosynthesis	consumer
decomposers	trophic level	energy flow	ecological pyramid
pyramid of biomass	pyramid of energy	ecological succession	habitat
ecological niche	biogeochemical cycle	water cycle	carbon cycle
ecosystem service			

THE STORY OF THE HIMALAYAS: PARADISE IN DANGER

'If there is a paradise on earth, it is here, it is here, it is here'. So said the Moghul emperor Jehangir while visiting Kashmir in the early seventeenth century. The beauty of the great Himalayas is timeless.

The majestic Himalayas are not merely a range of mountains. They are considered to be the cradle of Indian civilization and have exerted great influence over Indian thought, culture, and of course, the environment. They are not just the 'abode of snow' (as the name implies), but the kingdom of the Gods.

If the Himalayas were not there, the rain clouds from the Indian Ocean would pass over the sub-continent, leaving India as a desert. Many rivers that nourish the land, including the great Indus, Ganga, and Brahmaputra, originate in the Himalayas. It is on the banks of the Indus that the Harappan Civilization flourished.

The Himalayas are spread over 600,000 sq km in a broad arc 2,500 km long between the Indus and the Brahmaputra. The current forest cover is about 31 per cent with an immense biodiversity, with flora and fauna varying extensively from one region to the other. One-tenth of the world's known species of higher altitude plants and animals occur in the Himalayas. It is not commonly known that the region also contains mineral and metal deposits. Over 50 million people inhabit the Himalayan belt.

Today, however, the paradise is in danger and has already suffered irreparable ecological damage. Human activities like forest clearing, road construction, and mountaineering have taken a heavy toll. These in turn have led to soil erosion, landslides, and floods. In addition, there are natural factors like avalanches and earthquakes. Global warming has increased the melting of glaciers.

With the growth of towns in the region, the commercial felling of trees has increased to unsustainable levels. Deforestation continues in spite of the resistance by the local people (for example, the Chipko movement and the efforts of activists like Sunderlal Bahuguna and Chandi Prasad Bhat),

creation of protected areas, and ban orders by the government.

Mountaineering and trekking teams leave behind enormous amount of garbage. They also consume large amounts of local vegetation as fuelwood and fodder. Their movements also disturb the wildlife in the mountains.

A dense network of roads has been built in the Himalayas. While they improve access for the local people, they also make it easy for outsiders to come in and exploit the forest resources. The very act of road construction using methods like blasting disturbs the ecosystem and leads to landslides and loss of vegetation. The debris also damages agricultural fields and human settlements.

The quarrying of stones for the construction of roads and building houses for the increasing population has been increasing in scale. This causes loss of vegetation and topsoil, lowers the water table, disturbs wildlife, and increases air pollution. The hydropower potential of the region has led to projects like the Tehri Dam, which do cause ecological damage.

In spite of their scale and grandeur, the Himalayas constitute a fragile ecosystem in delicate balance. That balance may have already been upset, with unpredictable consequences for the entire subcontinent.

Environmentalists, activists, international agencies, and the governments of the region are now working to save the Himalayan environment. Read Box 2.1 for the efforts of an inspiring individual.

BOX 2.1

The story of Sunderlal Bahuguna: A gentle warrior fights for the Himalayas

'Himalaya is a land of penance. Nothing in the world can be achieved without penance. I am doing this on behalf of all who are striving to save our dying planet. Why should a river, a mountain, a forest, or the ocean be killed, while we cling to life?'

This is what Sunderlal Bahuguna wrote to his friends when he undertook a second long fast in

1996 on the banks of the Bhagirathi River demanding a review of the Tehri Dam Project. He broke the fast on the seventy-fourth day on an assurance given by the then Prime Minister that the project would be reviewed.

A two-minute conversation (when he was thirteen) with Dev Suman, a Gandhian and a

Contd

Box 2.1 Contd

freedom fighter, completely changed the life of Sunderlal. He joined the non-violence movement, organised students, and was sent to jail even as a young boy. After independence he followed Gandhi's injunction that all the freedom fighters should go and work in the villages.

Bahuguna, and his equally committed wife Vimla, have been living in the Himalayas, working for the welfare of dalits, lobbying against deforestation, encouraging forest-based small-scale industry and campaigning for saving the Himalayan ecology. Bahuguna became well known, when he led the Chipko Movement against the commercial felling of trees in the Himalayas (See Chapter 7).

In 1981, Bahuguna walked 4,800 km across the Himalayas, from Kashmir to Kohima, carrying the message: 'Save the tree, save the future'. On the way, his group held meetings in countless villages on environment and development issues, talked to children, and learnt the problems faced by the people.

Later, his struggle was against the building of the huge Tehri Dam on the Bhagirathi River in Uttarakhand. He was convinced that the dam would destroy Garhwal-Kumaon Himalayas and create a perpetual flood threat. In the true Gandhian tradition, he went on fast several times on the Tehri issue.

In spite of all the efforts of Bahuguna and others, the Tehri Dam was completed in 2006, completely submerging the Old Tehri town and over 20 villages. Thousands of people were displaced.

Bahuguna, however, is undeterred. 'My fight is to save the Himalayas, and it will continue,' he says. 'My movement has not gone waste because it will give strength and direction to the fight ahead. Sooner or later my voice will be heard. Truth never dies; it ultimately prevails, no matter what. Our goal is to have a comprehensive Himalaya policy to save the hills. The Himalayas are a mountain of emotions, not rocks and boulders, and we must preserve and nurture it to save our culture, to save our souls'.

What do we learn from the story of the Himalayas?

The story shows that even large ecological systems like the Himalayas are being adversely affected by human activities. We can no longer assume that such natural systems would continue to function as before and provide us with the natural resources that we need.

Where do we start in our journey through environmental issues?

In this book, we will see how from the Himalayas to Kanyakumari, and in most other parts of the world, human activities are causing severe degradation of the environment. First, however, we should learn about nature itself—the ecological systems including forests, deserts, ocean, rivers, lakes, etc. That is the task of the next three chapters.

What is an ecosystem?

When you hear the term 'forest ecosystem', what comes to your mind? Surely you think immediately of trees, animals, birds, butterflies, and so on. The mention of the term 'ocean ecosystem' brings to mind a picture of waves, currents, fish, whales, and so on. An ecosystem (or ecological system) is a region in which living organisms interact with their environment.

Is there a more formal definition of an ecosystem?   Before we can define the term ecosystem in a formal way, we must get to know a few more basic terms. An organism is any living thing—

an animal, a plant, or a microbe. A mosquito, a fish, a plant, a rabbit, a tree, an elephant, a human being—all are organisms. A cell is the basic unit of life in organisms. An organism like bacterium consists of a single cell, while most organisms have many cells.

The organisms in this world can be classified into different species. You would know that human beings are a species and so are roses. A species is a set of organisms that resemble one another in appearance and behaviour. The organisms in a species are potentially capable of reproducing naturally among themselves. Generally, organisms from different species do not interbreed and, even if they do, they do not produce fertile offspring.

The members of a species living and interacting within a specific geographical region are together called a population. *Neem* trees in a forest, people in a country and golden fish in a pond are examples of populations. There is diversity in most natural populations. While there are broad similarities among the members, they do not all look exactly alike nor do they all behave in the same way.

The term population refers only to those members of a certain species that live within a given area. The term species includes all members of a certain kind, even if they exist in different populations in widely separated areas.

We need one more definition before we can come back to ecosystems. A community is the assemblage of all the interacting populations of different species existing in a geographical area. It is a complex interacting network of plants, animals and microorganisms. Each population plays a defined role in the community.

We are now ready for a more formal definition of an ecosystem:

An ecosystem is a community of living organisms (populations of species) interacting with one another and with its non-living physical and chemical environment. The interactions are such as to perpetuate the community and to retain a large degree of stability under varying conditions.

A puddle of water, a stream, a clump of bushes, a thick forest, or a large desert—all are ecosystems. The ecosystems of this planet are interconnected and interdependent and together they make up the vast biosphere.

What exactly is the biosphere?

To understand what the biosphere is, we should first know what the earth is like. It has several spherical layers. The atmosphere is a thin envelope of air around the earth extending about 50 km from the surface. That part of the atmosphere up a distance of 17 km from sea level is the troposphere that contains the planet's air. Above the troposphere is the stratosphere that contains ozone. It is this ozone that supports life by filtering out the harmful ultraviolet radiation from the sun.

The hydrosphere consists of the liquid water, ice, and water vapour, while the lithosphere is the earth's upper crust containing the fossil fuels and minerals. Then we have the biosphere, in which all the living organisms interact with each other and with their environment. The biosphere includes most of the hydrosphere, parts of the lower atmosphere and the upper lithosphere. That is, the biosphere is that portion of the planet and its environment, which can support life.

How are ecosystems classified?

The terrestrial portion of the biosphere is divided into biomes. We group similar or related ecosystems to form biomes. A biome usually has a distinct climate and life forms adapted to the climate. Deserts, grasslands, tropical rain forests, temperate forests, coniferous forests, and tundra are examples (Chapter 3). A biome is simply more extensive and complex than an ecosystem. It is the next level of ecological organization above a community and an ecosystem.

The non-terrestrial part of the biosphere is classified into aquatic life zones: Freshwater swamps, marshes, and bogs make up one type of aquatic zone. Lakes and rivers, estuaries, inter-tidal zone, coastal ocean, and open ocean are the other aquatic zones (Chapter 5).

There is no accepted system of classification of biomes and aquatic life zones. In fact, we often use the term ecosystem instead of biome and aquatic life zone.

What is the structure of an ecosystem?

> **KEY IDEA**
>
> An ecosystem has a living component, called the biotic community (or biota) and non-living components called abiotic conditions.

Let us now study ecosystems in greater detail (Key Idea).

The biotic community of species interact with each other and with the abiotic conditions in such a way as to perpetuate the species.

The biotic community includes the plants, animals and the microorganisms. Species in a community are mutually dependent in many ways. For example, in a forest ecosystem, the birds eat the fruits from the trees and build their nests in them. The birds, in turn, spread the plant seeds, helping the propagation of the tree species.

The abiotic conditions of terrestrial ecosystems include water, air, soil, nutrients, minerals, salinity and acidity levels, energy, sunlight, temperature, wind, rainfall, and climate. We could also include the latitude and altitude of the area and the frequency of fires. In short, we define all the conditions under which the organisms live. The abiotic conditions both support and the biotic community.

In aquatic ecosystems, the abiotic factors include the depth, turbidity, salinity and temperature of water, chemical nutrients, suspended solids, currents, and the texture of the bottom (rocky or silty).

What is the boundary of an ecosystem?   Where does the sea end and the land begin? What is the boundary line between a forest and the adjoining grassland? Natural ecosystems rarely have distinct boundaries. In fact, they are never truly self-contained and self-sustaining systems.

An ecosystem gradually merges with the adjoining one through a transitional zone called ecotone. You will find in the ecotone a mixture of species found in both the ecosystems. Often, the ecotone will have additional species not found in either ecosystem. Or, the ecotone may have greater population densities of certain species than in either of the adjoining communities. This phenomenon is called the edge effect. Ecotones could be studied as distinct ecosystems.

We can see the edge effect in the coastal zone, where the land and the ocean meet. Because of the flow of tides, the coastal zone does not have fixed boundaries on the seaward or landward directions. The area is rich in biological diversity and, in particular, it provides habitat for organisms that can survive in water as well as on land. It also contains unique plants like mangroves that thrive in salt water.

KEY IDEA

Ecotones, where two or more ecosystems meet, are very rich in biological diversity. This is called the Edge Effect.

An estuary, where a river meets the sea, is even more clearly an ecotone. Here, there is a constant exchange of seawater and freshwater and the biodiversity is very high. An example is the estuary in Chennai, where the river Adyar meets the sea. This area attracts a wide variety of organisms including many bird species.

What are food chains and food webs?

Food gives organisms the energy to do biological work like growing, moving, reproducing and maintaining themselves. The concept of a food chain should be intuitively clear to you. The insect is eaten by the frog, the frog becomes lunch for the snake, and the swooping hawk finishes off the snake and we thus have a food chain. It is just a sequence or organisms, in which each is the food for the next. All organisms, dead or alive, are potential sources of food for other organisms.

Food chains overlap, since most organisms have more than one item on their menu. Again, an organism could be found on the menus of many other organisms. Thus, we have a complex network of interconnected food chains called a food web.

If every organism must eat another organism for survival, where does the food chain start?   Obviously there must be at least one self-feeding organism that produces food and 'eats' it too! Such producers are in fact all around us—the green plants.

Producers take simple inorganic substances from their abiotic environment and make complex organic molecules using solar energy. These are the only organisms in an ecosystem

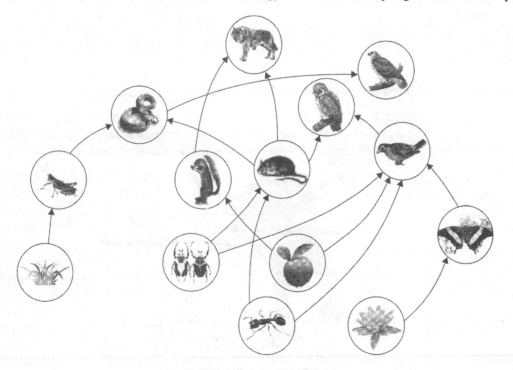

Fig. 2.1   Example of a Food Web

that can trap energy from the sun and make new organic material. All other organisms in this world are, directly or indirectly, dependent on the producers for their food.

The process used by producers to convert inorganic material into organic matter is called photosynthesis. The green plant takes in carbon dioxide from the atmosphere, water from the soil, and energy from the sun to make a kind of sugar molecule. In the process, it gives out oxygen.

The reaction that takes place can be represented as follows:

carbon dioxide + water + solar energy → sugar + oxygen

The green pigment chlorophyll in the plant traps the solar energy. Hence, we can say that photosynthesis takes place in the leaves.

The world depends on food made by the producers and, fortunately for us, producers come in all types and sizes, from microscopic single-cell algae, through small plants, to giant trees.

Other than producers, there are two other main categories of organisms: consumers and decomposers. Organisms that feed on producers or other organisms are called consumers. Decomposers get their nourishment from dead organic material (explained later).

Does photosynthesis take place in the ocean too? In aquatic ecosystems, a different process called chemosynthesis takes place. Here specialized bacteria convert simple compounds from their environment into more complex nutrient compounds without sunlight. They use instead, a different source of energy. Deep in the earth's core, heat is generated by the decay of radioactive elements. This heat is released at hot-water vents in the ocean depths. The bacteria use this geothermal energy for chemosynthesis. Later, these bacteria are consumed by many aquatic animals.

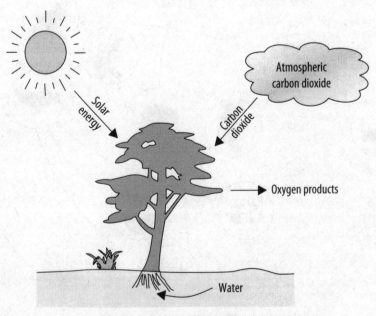

Fig. 2.2 Process of Photosynthesis

What are trophic levels?

Each organism in an ecosystem is at a specific feeding stage called the trophic level. The term comes from the Greek *trophos,* meaning nourishment. All producers are at the first trophic level and are also called autotrophs (self-feeding organisms). All other organisms that must consume organic matter for getting energy and for building their bodies are called heterotrophs or consumers.

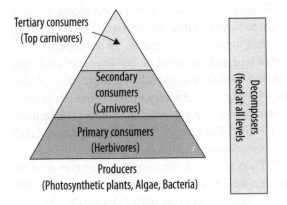

Tertiary consumers (Top carnivores)

Secondary consumers (Carnivores)

Primary consumers (Herbivores)

Decomposers (feed at all levels)

Producers (Photosynthetic plants, Algae, Bacteria)

Fig. 2.3   Trophic Levels

Consumers are classified as follows:

- Primary consumers or herbivores feed directly on producers and are at the second trophic level. When we eat fruits or vegetables, we act as primary consumers.
- Secondary consumers or carnivores (at the third trophic level) feed on other consumers. When we eat meat, we are secondary consumers.
- Tertiary consumers eat other carnivores and are at the fourth trophic level. Again, we are tertiary consumers when we eat the fish that eats the smaller fish that eats the algae. This chain may go on to one or two more levels.

Omnivores eat both plants and animals and hence they feed at more than one level. Human beings, bears, foxes, pigs, rats, and cockroaches are omnivores.

The trophic levels form a pyramid. At the base we have a large number of producers and high energy. As we go up the pyramid to higher trophic levels, there are fewer organisms and less energy. This is explained in a later section.

Detrivores are consumers that feed on detritus, which refers mainly to fallen leaves, parts of dead trees, and faecal wastes of animals. Ants, termites, earthworms, millipedes, crayfish, and crabs are examples of detrivores.

What is the role of decomposers?   Decomposers include fungi and bacteria that secrete digestive enzymes, which decompose organic matter into simple sugars. The decomposers then absorb the sugars for their own nourishment. They release the resulting simpler inorganic compounds into the soil and water. The producers take in these compounds as nutrients.

Detrivores and decomposers are essential for the long-term survival of a community. They play the vital role of completing the matter cycle. Without them, enormous wastes of plant litter, dead animal bodies, animal excreta, and garbage will collect on this earth. Also, important nutrients like nitrogen, phosphorus, and potassium would remain indefinitely in dead matter. Then the producers will not get their nutrients and this will make life impossible.

How does food become energy in organisms?   The organisms within an ecosystem are constantly growing, reproducing, dying, and decaying. They need energy for their activities.

When organisms eat food, they take in the chemical energy that is stored in carbohydrates. This energy is released within the cells of the organisms through a process called cell respiration, which is the reverse of photosynthesis. The sugar molecules are broken down in the presence of oxygen and water into carbon dioxide and water and energy is released in the process:

sugar + oxygen + water → carbon dioxide + water + energy

Cell respiration makes the stored chemical energy available for biological work. All organisms, including green plants, respire to get energy.

What is an ecological pyramid?

For most ecosystems, the main source of energy is the sun. Producers trap the solar energy and store it as sugar, starch, fats, and proteins. When primary consumers eat the producers, the energy also moves up the trophic level. During the transfer, however, about 90 per cent of the energy is lost to the environment as unusable heat.

> **KEY IDEA**
>
> It is a fundamental law of nature that energy can neither be created, nor destroyed. It can only be transformed from one form to another; during any such transformation, a part of the energy is lost as less useful heat.

As we move up the trophic levels, the amount of usable energy available at each stage declines. Thus, we have a pyramid of energy flow. If the producer has 10,000 units of energy, the primary consumer receives only 1,000 units and the secondary consumer gets only 100 units. The tertiary consumer is left with just 10 units. The energy flow is one-directional and the loss at each stage is simply released into the environment.

What about the matter? Each trophic level contains a certain amount of biomass, which is the dry weight of all the matter contained in the organisms. As we move up the trophic levels, the biomass also decreases drastically. At each level, we lose 90–99 per cent of the biomass. We call it a biomass pyramid.

There are two ways by which the biomass decreases with each level. First, much of the food taken in by a consumer is not converted into body tissues. It is stored as energy to be used by the consumer when needed. Second, much of the biomass, especially at the producer level, is never eaten and goes directly to decomposers.

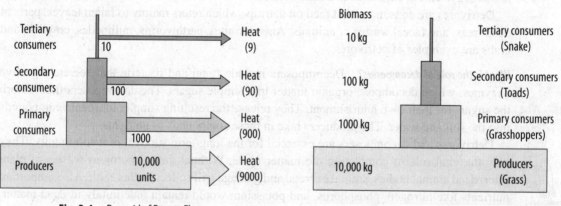

Fig. 2.4   Pyramid of Energy Flow   Fig. 2.5   Pyramid of Biomass

How does an ecosystem get established?

Consider the rocky surface of a barren hill that is left undisturbed. If there is some rain or moisture, moss starts growing in the minute cracks in the rocks. Slowly, the moss becomes a mat that holds any soil that comes its way. The seeds of small plants start growing on this soil and in turn the plants trap more soil. Shrubs and trees follow and the litter from the trees eliminates the original moss and even the small plants. Over time, more trees grow and ultimately there is a forest. As the big trees grow, many of the small plants under them disappear. This orderly process of transition from one biotic community to another is called primary ecological succession.

What is interesting about ecological succession?   A biotic community grows successfully and its very success makes the area more favourable to another community. When the second community moves in and prospers, the conditions become unfavourable to the first and hence it disappears.

Also note that, for succession to take place, there must be a diversity of species present in the area. It is not a matter of new species developing or even old species adapting to new conditions. The population of an existing species takes advantage of favourable conditions and prospers.

Ecological succession does not go on indefinitely. A stage is reached when all the species are in dynamic equilibrium among themselves and with the environment. This state is called climax ecosystem. During ecological succession, one biotic community gradually makes way to another, the second gives way to a third, and so on, until the climax stage is reached. Major biomes are examples of climax ecosytems.

Climax ecosystems could also change. If the drastic climate changes occur or if alien species are introduced into the ecosystem, a process of adaptation and succession follows. Left undisturbed, an ecosystem always moves towards a state of dynamic balance.

Why then so many hillsides remain barren?   Ecological succession can happen only when an area is left undisturbed. Any interference by human beings disturbs the process. For example, if shepherds take their goats to the hillside every day for grazing, no growth is possible.

What happens if a forest area is cleared by fire or by human beings and then left undisturbed? In this case, secondary succession takes place. The old soil is still present, but the microclimate in the clearing is different. The appropriate species from the surrounding ecosystem will first reinvade the area. Slowly, each biotic community will give way to another until the clearing becomes indistinguishable from the larger ecosystem.

What is a habitat?

Habitat is the area where a species is biologically adapted to live. The habitat of a given species or population is marked by the physical and biological features of its environment such as the vegetation, climatic conditions, presence of water and moisture, soil type, etc.

How do so many species live together in an ecosystem without fierce competition taking place? There are, of course, predator–prey relationships, but they do not lead generally to extermination of species. The reason is that each species in an ecosystem has found its habitat and, what is more, its own ecological niche within the habitat.

Monkey to Bird: Don't worry I am not going to eat you. You have your own ecological niche and I have mine.

The niche is characterized by the particular food habits, shelter-seeking methods, ways of nesting and reproduction, etc., of the species. It includes all aspects of the organism's existence—all the physical, chemical, and biological factors that it needs in order to live and reproduce.

KEY IDEA
Species in an ecosystem coexist because each has its ecological niche.

Where the organism lives, what it eats, which organisms eat it, how it competes with others, how it interacts with its abiotic environment—all these aspects together make up its ecological niche. When different species live in the same habitat, competition may be slight or even non-existent, because each has its own niche.

What are cycles in ecosystems?

We saw that energy flows through an ecosystem in one direction. Matter, on the other hand, moves through ecosystems in numerous cycles. The nutrients that organisms need to grow, live, and reproduce are continuously taken from the abiotic environment, consumed and then cycled back to the environment.

There are several such biogeochemical cycles (with biological, geological and chemical interactions), powered directly or indirectly by solar energy. They include the carbon, oxygen, nitrogen, phosphorus, and water cycles. With respect to matter, the earth is essentially a closed system. Matter cannot escape from its boundaries.

How does water circulate on earth?   The hydrologic or water cycle is powered by the sun and gravity. Solar energy evaporates water from the ocean, rivers, lakes, and other water bodies. Plants extract water from the soil through the roots and transport it to the leaves, from where it evaporates. This process is called transpiration.

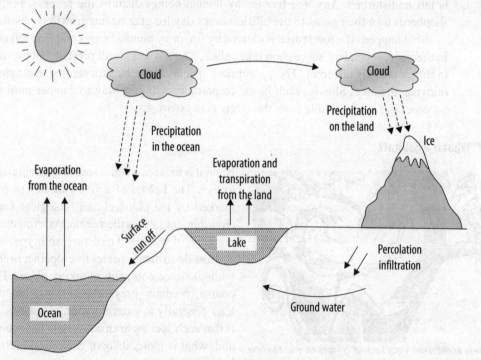

Fig. 2.6   The Water Cycle

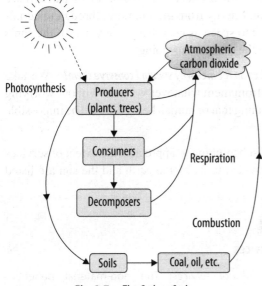

Fig. 2.7 The Carbon Cycle

KEY IDEA

Matter cycles through the earth and the atmosphere. These natural cycles provide what is needed by ecosystems.

Wind and air move the water vapour through the atmosphere. When the temperature falls, the vapour condenses into tiny droplets that form clouds. The next stage is precipitation as rain or snow, mostly over the ocean and partly over land. The water that falls on land may percolate through the soil and collect in aquifers. Or the water may flow back to the ocean as run-off though the rivers and streams.

We will return to the water cycle in Chapter 7.

What is the carbon cycle? Carbon dioxide constitutes just 0.035 per cent by volume of the atmosphere and yet it is vital to life. Plants take carbon from carbon dioxide in the air and they use chlorophyll to gather energy from the sun. From these inputs and water, plants make glucose as a basic building block. In this process of photosynthesis plants release oxygen. Animals breathe in this oxygen, digest their food (that comes from plants) and recombine the carbon and the oxygen to make carbon dioxide, which goes back to the plants. This is called the carbon cycle.

When we burn fossil fuels like oil, the carbon in the fuel combines with atmospheric oxygen to form carbon dioxide. Since we burn a lot of oil, there is a huge emission of carbon dioxide. This increase in carbon dioxide concentration upsets the carbon balance in the atmosphere. There are not enough growing plants to absorb all the excess carbon dioxide. Things become worse when we cut down forests and burn more trees.

Normally, carbon dioxide and other gases surround the planet like a blanket and capture the heat. This greenhouse effect is necessary up to a limit. The current excessive level of carbon dioxide, however, leads to a higher temperature and global warming. This results in climate change, which could lead to natural disasters like droughts and floods as well as a rise in sea level.

Like the water and carbon cycles, there are nitrogen, phosphorus, and sulphur cycles in nature.

How do I recognize an ecosystem when I have found one?

Ecosystems vary widely in size, complexity, biotic and abiotic components, the sharpness of the boundary, and so on. The key point, however, is that the ecosystem sustains life. Individual organisms or populations cannot sustain life indefinitely. No single species can produce all the food it needs, decompose all its wastes, and reuse the matter to produce more food.

An ecosystem is the minimal grouping of diverse organisms that interact and function together in order to sustain life. That is why we need to focus on ecosystems when we want to conserve a species or to use natural resources in a sustainable manner.

What ultimately sustains life in an ecosystem?   The sun is the primary sustainer of life on earth. It is a huge nuclear fusion reactor running on hydrogen. Energy from the sun flows through materials and living organisms and eventually goes back into space as heat. Only a tiny part of the sun's energy falls on earth, but that is enough to keep the ecosystems going.

Ecosystems are surely wonders of nature, but what do they do for me? Why should I conserve them?   We take nature and ecosystems for granted and we take from them whatever we want without worrying about the costs or repayment. Life on earth, including that of human beings, would be impossible without the help of ecosystems.

What services do ecosystems provide for us?   We are just beginning to appreciate the extent of services provided by ecosystems. The main services provided to us by the earth and the sun are listed in Box 2.2.

BOX 2.2

Ecosystem services

Ecosystem services are the benefits people obtain from ecosystems. Nature provides these services to us free of cost. They are of four types:

1. *Provisioning services:* The products obtained from ecosystems, including genetic resources (like seeds), wood, food, and fresh water.

2. *Regulating services:* The benefits obtained from the regulation of ecosystem processes, including the regulation of climate, water purification, flood control, and control of human diseases.

3. *Cultural services:* The non-material benefits people obtain from ecosystems including education, recreation and experiencing the beauty of nature.

4. *Supporting services:* Ecosystem services that are necessary for the production of all other ecosystem services. Some examples are biomass production, production of atmospheric oxygen, and soil formation.

What is the value of these ecosystem services that nature provides for free?   A team of ecologists, economists, and geographers tried to answer this question. Led by Robert Costanza, the team first divided the earth's surface into 16 major biomes and aquatic life zones. They then listed 17 goods and services provided by nature in each of these areas and examined over 100 studies that have tried to put a money value on such services. Finally, they came up with an estimate of the monetary value of ecosystem services.

Their conclusion was that the ecosystem services were worth more than US$ 36 trillion per year. This is comparable to the annual Gross World Product that is estimated to be US$ 39 trillion. Some experts believe that this is a conservative figure and that the real worth of nature could be much more, even a million times more.

We can ask ourselves the question: What should be the value of the natural capital of the world for it to give us an annual return of US$ 36 trillion? The answer is a mind-boggling US$ 500 trillion! Costanza's estimate involves many assumptions and omissions. Yet, it draws our attention to the enormous value of ecosystem services. Any estimate is better than not attaching any value at all for what we take from nature. Sometimes we can get an idea of the value of ecosystem services by working out the cost of replacing nature by a man-made system (See Box 2.3 for an example).

KEY IDEA

The ecosystem services provided free by nature are of enormous value.

BOX 2.3

Economics: Value of an ecosystem service

The citizens of New York used to be proud of their drinking water that was supposed to be tasty, pure, clean, and healthy. Sometime ago, however, the quality of the water, obtained from the Catskill watershed, fell below the standards set by the Environment Protection Agency.

A study found the cause of the problem: the increasing levels of activity in agriculture, industry, and urban development were together

- diminishing the actual forested area of the watershed and
- altering the biogeochemical cycles and the species composition

Two options were considered to solve the problem:

1. Buy and restore the watershed so that the forest will continue to provide natural purification and filtration: The estimated cost was US$ 1 billion.
2. Build and maintain a new purification and filtration plant: The capital cost would be US$ 6–8 billion and the annual operating cost US$ 300 million.

The first option was the obvious choice. This case gives you some idea of the value of ecosystem services.

Can we at all put a money value on life and nature? Some critics feel that placing a money value on ecosystem services is misleading and dangerous. They are infinitely valuable, since they are irreplaceable.

Beyond all these services, consider the rainbow in the sky, the sun rising from the ocean, the dance of whales, the grace of the deer, the shimmering oasis in the desert, or the snows on the mountain. What price can you put on these?

REVIEW: A SUMMARY OF THE KEY POINTS

- Ecosystems represent complex interactions among organisms and between them and the environment.
- Energy can neither be created, nor destroyed. It can only be transformed from one form to another; during any such transformation, a part of the energy is lost as less useful heat.
- Organisms have roles like producers, consumers, and decomposers in the food chain; they maintain the flows of matter and energy.

- An ecosystem always moves towards a state of dynamic balance.
- Every species has its ecological niche in an ecosystem.
- Water and carbon are continuously cycled in the biosphere.
- The sun is the primary sustainer of all life on earth.
- Ecosystems provide invaluable services to the biosphere, which includes the human beings.

EXERCISES

Objective-type questions

In each case below, choose the best answer out of the given set of choices:

1. Which of the following statements is true with regard to species?
   (a) The organisms in a species are capable of reproducing naturally among themselves.
   (b) Organisms from different species always interbreed and produce fertile offspring.
   (c) The members of a species living and interacting across the biosphere are together called a population.
   (d) Human beings form a species, but *neem* trees do not.

2. Which of the following statements is true with regard to ecosystems?
   (a) Ecosystem is different from ecological system.
   (b) There are no interactions between an ecosystem and its environment.
   (c) An ecosystem is a region in which living organisms interact with their environment.
   (d) Ecosystems are the same as populations.
3. Which of the following statements is true with regard to biomes?
   (a) The terrestrial portion of the biosphere is divided into biomes.
   (b) A biome is just a community of populations.
   (c) A biome is just a population of a species.
   (d) Biome stands for biological home.
4. Which of the following is **not** an abiotic condition?
   (a) Water
   (b) Soil
   (c) Temperature
   (d) Bacteria
5. Which of the following statements is true with regard to ecotones?
   (a) We can see the edge effect in an ecotone.
   (b) Ecotone stands for ecological tone.
   (c) Ecotone is the sharp line separating two ecosystems.
   (d) Ecotone will not contain the species found in the adjoining ecosystems.
6. What is the basis of all food chains?
   (a) Consumer
   (b) Producer
   (c) Decomposer
   (d) Detrivore
7. Which of the following statements is true with regard to energy?
   (a) There is no loss when mechanical energy is converted into electrical energy.
   (b) Energy can be created or destroyed.
   (c) Whenever energy changes its form, some part is lost.
   (d) As we move up the trophic levels, the amount of usable energy available at each stage remains the same.
8. Which of the following aspects is **not** associated with the ecological niche of a given species?
   (a) Ways in which the given species reproduces itself.

(b) Other species that consume the given species.
(c) Food consumed by the predator that consumes the given species.
(d) Food consumed by the given species.

Short-answer questions

1. Explain the differences between species, population, and community.
2. What is a biome? Give examples.
3. What are the main components of an ecosystem?
4. What are the abiotic factors in terrestrial biomes and aquatic life zones?
5. What is the edge effect and what is its importance?
6. Every organism is potential food for other organisms. Then who makes food first to get the chain going?
7. What is the main difference between a producer, a consumer, and a decomposer in an ecosystem? Explain through examples.
8. Explain a food chain and a food web.
9. What happens to the energy flow as we move up the trophic levels?
10. How can we describe the ecological niche of a species?
11. What are biogeochemical cycles? Describe the water and carbon cycles.
12. List the important ecological and economic services provided by ecosystems. What is the estimated value of these services?

Long-answer questions

1. Write an essay describing the Himalayas as a mountain ecosystem and explain the ecological problems the region is facing today. Try to add to the information given in this chapter.
2. Describe the processes of primary and secondary ecological succession.

Think critically: Deeper question for reflection and discussion

We, as human beings, are also part of ecosystems. We have, however, overcome the usual barriers and limiting factors faced by other species. We have interfered with the working of most ecosystems and are plundering the resources of ecosystems without any care. What would be the consequences of continuing this trend?

SOMETHING DIFFERENT FOR A CHANGE

1. Reflect on this hymn from the Atharva Veda:

   Mother of all plants,
   Firm earth upheld by Eternal Law,

   May she be ever beneficent and gracious to us
   As we tread on her.

2. Read the delightful book *The Cartoon Guide to the Environment* by Larry Gonick and Alice Outwater.

ACTIVITIES

Learn by doing: Case study / Project

1. Choose a small ecosystem like a pond or a garden that is relatively undisturbed. Observe the ecosystem over three months or more and keep a log of your observations. Try to identify the producers, consumers, and decomposers.

2. Choose a small animal or bird that you can watch in your back garden or a nearby park. Observe the behaviour of the organism regularly and keep a journal of your observations. Watch what the organism eats, what it rejects, where does it live, over which area does it move, how does it reproduce, which organisms are its predators, etc.

Organize together: Eco-club activities and projects

Observe Earth Day on April 22 to create awareness in your neighbourhood or institution about environmental issues. Earth Day has been an annual event for people around the world to celebrate the earth and our responsibility toward it. Earth Day is observed on April 22. More than a half billion people participate in the campaigns every year.

The first Earth Day was observed in the US in 1970. It was founded by Gaylord Nelson and organized by Denis Hayes. 20 million people participated in the event. It marked the beginning of the environmental movement. Since then Earth Day is observed every year in many parts of the world.

Your club can do a variety of things to observe Earth Day. Here are some examples:

• Volunteer for environmental action such as tree planting.

• Begin making your institution a green campus.

• Help launch a community garden.

• Urge your corporation councillors, MLAs and MPs to take environmental issues seriously.

Do something nice for the earth, have fun, meet new people, and make a difference. (For more information, access the website www.earthday.net)

LEARN MORE

Books

Burne, David 1999, *Get a Grip on Ecology,* Weidenfeld and Nicholson, London.

Callenbach, Ernest 1999, *Ecology: A Pocket Guide,* Indian Reprint, Universities Press, Hyderabad.

Savan, Beth 1991, *Earthcycles and Ecosystems,* Kids Can Press, Toronto, Canada.

Articles

Costanza, R. et al. 1997, 'The Value of the World's Ecosystem Services and Natural Capital', *Nature,* 387, 253–260, 15 May.

Lubchenco, J. 2001, 'Understanding Human Impact on Earth's Ecosystems', in Raven, Peter H. and Linda R. Berg, *Environment,* Harcourt College Publishers, Fort Worth, USA, p.65. (on ecosystem services including the case of New York City water supply).

Goldsmith, Katherine 1997, 'A Gentle Warrior', *Resurgence,* No.181, March/April, p.31. (on Sunderlal Bahuguna)

Tripathi, Purnima S. 2004, 'Tragedy at Tehri', *Frontline,* August 27, pp. 33–39. (on Sunderlal Bahuguna)

Film

Planet Earth: A BBC nature documentary.

CHAPTER 3

Forest, Grassland, and Desert Ecosystems

Forests precede civilizations,
deserts follow them.

Attributed to **François-René de Chateaubriand**
(1768–1848)
French author and politician

THIS CHAPTER IS ABOUT...

Ecosystems such as forests, grassland, deserts, and mountains

THE KEYWORDS AND PHRASES ARE...

biosphere reserve	coniferous forest	grassland	precipitation
rainforest	savanna	temperate forest	tundra

THE STORY OF THE NILGIRIS: BLUE MOUNTAINS IN PERIL

In 1818, the East India Company asked John Sullivan, the Collector of Coimbatore in South India, to investigate the origin of the fabulous tales that were being circulated concerning the 'Blue Mountains' to verify their authenticity and to send a report to the authorities. Sullivan set off towards the Nilgiris with a contingent of prisoners, elephants, dogs, ponies, and English huntsmen.

Above 1000 feet, the expedition had to abandon its animals and climb with cords and pulleys. After a week of hard ascent and several casualties on the way, the group reached a plateau of unparalleled beauty. This plateau became the hill resort of Ootacamund or Ooty.

The Nilgiris (Image courtesy: http://commons.wikimedia.org/wiki/File:Nilgiri-Hills.jpg)

The Nilgiris or the Blue Mountains are a mountain range at the junction of the Western and Eastern Ghats. With a maximum elevation of 2,600 m above mean sea level, the climate ranges from humid to semi-arid and from warm to cold conditions. The most striking feature of the Nilgiris is their massive appearance.

The Nilgiri Biosphere Reserve (NBR), with an area of 5,520 sq km, was established in 1986 and was included in the UNESCO Man and the Biosphere Programme in 2000. The NBR contains several dry scrub, dry and moist deciduous, semi evergreen and wet evergreen forests, evergreen sholas, grasslands and swamps. It is the home of the largest known population of two endangered animal species, the Nilgiri Tahr and the Lion-tailed macaque and the largest South Indian population of elephant, tiger, gaur, sambar, and chital as well as a number of endemic (unique to this area) and endangered plants

The biodiversity of NBR includes 3,300 flowering plants, 175 orchids, over 100 species of mammals, 350 species of birds, 80 species of reptiles and amphibians, 300 species of butterflies and innumerable invertebrates. Many of these species are endemic to the region.

The British began replacing the pristine vegetation by tea and coffee plantations and this process has picked up greater momentum in recent decades. Half of all the cultivated area, about 30,000 ha, is covered with tea, which now governs the economy of the district. Initially it brought in economic boom, but it has been an ecological disaster by promoting monoculture, excessive use of chemical pesticides and fertilizers, and an extremely dependent population. The eco-cultural degradation has been compounded further by the more recent crisis in the tea industry and stagnation in tourism.

The total population of NBR is more than one million, of which about one-third is tribal. The five Nilgiri peoples—Toda, Kota, Badaga, Kurumba and Irula—were linked in a ritual, economic and social symbiosis and they were known for their harmonious use of the environment. Over the past 40 years, however, the environmental degradation has had adverse consequences on the social, economic, and cultural life of these communities. They have been deprived of their traditional economy, culture, and lifestyle, which had a symbiotic relationship with the ecology of the Nilgiris. There were also conflicts with the immigrant repatriates from Sri Lanka.

Landslides have become more frequent in recent years. Often poor villagers have seen their homes destroyed in these incidents. Deforestation along with the conversion of land for agriculture, tea plantations, and residential houses, even on steep slopes, are the reasons for the landslides.

More than ten years ago, concerned citizens of the region came together under the 'Save the Nilgiris' Campaign. They have been able to get the government to pass laws and take other measures to protect the ecosystem. Thanks to their efforts, the government set up the Hill Areas Conservation Authority for Tamil Nadu. They have also campaigned against the excessive promotion of tea and eucalyptus plantations. More than anything else, they have created awareness among the people on environmental issues.

The Nilgiris are still a vast reserve of biological and cultural heritage with many unique characteristics. The local people continue to depend on the forests for their livelihood and well-being. It is possible even now to prevent further destruction of this unique ecosystem.

🐦 What does the Nilgiris story tell us?

KEY IDEA
Human beings have interfered and made an impact on 73 per cent of the land area.

In the previous chapter, we learnt how ecosystems function and how they try to reach a state of dynamic balance. However, human beings are now everywhere, interfering with the ecosystems. The Nilgiris case is an example of the damage that human impact can cause.

How far have human beings explored and disturbed this land?   If we exclude uninhabitable areas of ice, rock, desert, and steep mountains, we have made an impact on 73 per cent the land area.

Before we learn more about human impact on the environment, however, we should find out more about forests and other natural systems. That is the task of this chapter and the next.

What are the different types of biomes?

Recall from Chapter 2 that we group similar or related ecosystems to form biomes. A biome usually has a distinct climate and life forms adapted to the climate. Tropical rain forests, temperate forests, coniferous forests, tundra, grasslands, deserts, and mountains are examples. In this chapter, we will learn about these biomes.

Why do different regions have different biomes?   Temperature and precipitation are the two major factors that account for the differences in biomes from region to region. The term precipitation covers all the forms in which water comes down on earth, including rain, snow, hailstorm, etc. The mean values of temperature and precipitation as well as the way they vary over the year (and even over the day) will determine the kind of biomes we find in an area.

Different climates promote different communities of plants and animals. Again, the types and numbers of organisms may vary from location to location within a biome because of variations in the local climate and soil, and because of the natural and human-caused disturbances that occur in the area. Yet, the regions of a biome have broadly comparable biological communities.

Climate, plants, and animal species of regions vary with latitude and altitude. You can observe these changes as you move from the equator to the poles or from the base to the summit of a tall mountain. Again, in a thick forest, different communities are found at different levels.

What is wonderful is that every species has adapted to the climate and has found its ecological niche in the community. Left undisturbed, the biome reaches a stable state. It continues to be dynamic and undergoes changes that occur over long periods. The trouble comes, however, when humans enter the ecosystem and bring in rapid, often devastating, changes.

Let us now learn more about the different biomes, beginning with forests. Forests still cover about 20 per cent of land. Forests can be classified in different ways and one way is to divide them into tropical rain forests, temperate forests, coniferous forests, and tundra.

What are tropical rain forests?

As the name implies, tropical rain forests are found in the hot and humid regions near the Equator. These regions have abundant rainfall (2000–4500 mm per year) that occurs almost daily and the temperature varies little over the year. They are found in South and Central America, Western and Central Africa, Southeast Asia, and in some islands of the Indian and Pacific Oceans.

The enormous plant biodiversity is supplemented by an abundance of amphibians, reptiles, birds, monkeys, and small mammals, as well as predators like tigers and jaguars.

These rain forests are marked by a variety of tall trees and a dense canopy. There are at least three distinct stories or layers of vegetation. The soils are thin, acidic, and nutrient-poor. Little organic matter accumulates

KEY IDEA
Though they occupy just 2 per cent of the earth, tropical rain forests contain 50–80 per cent of all the terrestrial species.

since the litter that falls on the floor decomposes very quickly and the minerals are quickly absorbed by the roots.

Why are tropical forests considered so important?   Apart from preserving immense biodiversity, the tropical forests play a major role in recycling water. In a landmark research study conducted in the early 1980s in the Amazon, scientists found that a forest could return as much as 75 per cent of the moisture it received back to the atmosphere.

We have always been told that more trees meant more rain, but a Brazilian study (Hindu 1983) has given a scientific basis for this connection. The research showed that the forests could return enough amounts of water to cause the formation of rain clouds. Land that is covered by trees collects and returns to the atmosphere at least 10 times more moisture than deforested land does.

What are temperate forests?

Temperate forests have seasonal variations in climate, freezing in winter and warm and humid in summer. The annual rainfall is about 750–2,000 mm and the soil is rich.

Temperate forests are found in western and central Europe, eastern Asia, and eastern North America. They have deciduous (leaf-shedding) trees like oaks, maples, ash, and beech, and some coniferous trees like pines. Shrubby undergrowth, ferns, lichens, and mosses are also found.

These forests contain abundant microorganisms, and mammals like squirrels, porcupines, chipmunks, raccoons, hares, deer, foxes, coyotes, and black bear. Birds like warblers, woodpeckers, owls, and hawks, besides snakes, frogs, and salamanders are common.

What are coniferous forests?

These forests derive their name from the abundance of coniferous trees like spruce, fir, pine, and hemlock. A coniferous tree produces hard dry fruit called cones. Coniferous forests also contain smaller amounts of deciduous trees like birch and maple. They occur in the northern part of North America, Europe, and Asia.

In these forests, winters are usually long and cold. The precipitation is often light in winter and heavier in summer. The soils are acidic and humus-rich and there is much litter.

The main animals are large herbivores like mule deer, moose, elk, caribou; smaller herbivores like mice, hare, and red squirrels; predators like lynx, foxes, and bears. They are often important nesting areas for many migratory birds like warblers and thrushes.

What kind of forests do we have in the Arctic?

The forests in the Arctic are called tundra. They occur in the extreme northern latitudes, where the snow melts seasonally. There is no equivalent in the southern hemisphere, since there is no land in the corresponding latitude.

The region has long and harsh winters and very short summers. Precipitation occurs mostly in summer and the annual average is just 10–25 cm.

The species diversity is low, but those few species exist in large numbers. Mosses, lichens, grasses, and some dwarf trees are the main plants. The animal species include lemmings, weasels,

KEY IDEA

The Arctic tundra has been adversely affected by oil exploration and military use.

arctic foxes, hares, snowy owls, and musk oxen. Many bird species migrate here in summer and feast on the abundance of insects—mosquitoes, black flies, deerflies, etc.

The tundra is a fragile ecosystem. Even a casual hiking on the land causes enormous damage and regeneration is very slow. Large parts of the arctic tundra have been affected by oil exploration and military use. (Read Box 3.1 on the Arctic National Wildlife Refuge)

BOX 3.1

The story of the Arctic National Wildlife Refuge: Choosing between pristine nature and petroleum

It is one of the last remaining areas of unspoiled nature and it is now in trouble. The story of the Arctic National Wildlife Refuge (ANWR) in Alaska is a classic case of the environment vs development dilemma.

In 1980, the US Congress created the ANWR—7.3 million ha of undisturbed tundra, wetlands, and glaciers. It is home for an extremely diverse community of organisms, including polar bears, arctic foxes, peregrine falcons, musk oxen, snow geese, and many other animal species. It is also the calving area for large migrating herds of caribou. More than 150,000 caribou return here after wintering in Canada. All the tundra plant species like mosses, lichens, and dwarf trees are found here. Under a thin layer of soil there is permafrost, ice that does not melt even in summer.

The ecosystem is fragile and finely balanced. Any additional stress can do irreversible damage. Environmentalists have always argued for leaving the area undisturbed. Unfortunately for the region, however, it has deposits of oil!

The US Geological Survey estimates the reserves to be about 7.7 billion barrels, 2 billion of which could be extracted economically under current oil prices. There was always pressure to begin drilling

in ANWR, but the US Congress had allowed only exploration, with the condition that its approval was needed for any drilling activity. Faced with insatiable demand, rising prices of crude oil and uncertainties of imports, the US government and the oil companies are dead set on drilling in ANWR.

The pro-drilling groups point out that, in neighbouring Prudhoe Bay, oil is already being extracted and the infrastructure for drilling exists. No environmental impact has been reported. What is more, only 1.5 per cent of the total area will be encroached upon. There are sound economic reasons to extract oil from ANWR and reduce dependence on imports.

The environmentalists say that any drilling poses a permanent threat to the delicate balance of nature. Prudhoe Bay in fact has suffered damage—wolves and bears have been decreasing in numbers, resulting in an abnormal increase in caribou population. What is more, the oil will not last long, but we would have already sacrificed nature. In fact, the production in Prudhoe Bay has peaked and is now declining.

As the arguments go back and forth, the tundra is waiting to know its fate.

What is the state of the forests in India?

The Forest Survey of India (FSI) publishes every two years an assessment of India's forest cover. The India State of Forest Report 2009 (SFR 2009) presents an assessment based on satellite data of 2006–2007. The main findings of SFR 2009 are:

KEY IDEA

According to the Forest Survey of India, our forest and tree cover is 24 per cent of the land area and this cover is increasing over time. However, environmental groups do not fully accept this claim.

- Forest and tree cover of the country was about 78 million ha in 2007, which is 24 per cent of the geographical area. This includes 21 per cent forest cover and 3 per cent tree cover.
- There was a net increase of 0.18 million ha (0.23 per cent) in the forest and tree cover between 2005 and 2007.
- The increase in the forest cover between 1997 and 2007 was 3.13 million ha (4.75 per cent).
- The seven north-eastern states of India have nearly one-fourth of the country's forest cover. The region gained 59,800 ha of forest cover as compared to the previous assessment of 2005.

Environmentalists and voluntary organizations have been witness to unending deforestation in many parts of the country. They question the figures given in the official reports.

What are the important types of forests in India?

About 80 per cent of India's forests is spread over four types. Table 3.1 gives the distribution and the locations.

Table 3.1   Distribution of Indian Forests by Type

Type	Percentage	Locations
Tropical moist deciduous	37	Andamans, Uttar Pradesh, Madhya Pradesh, Gujarat, Maharashtra, Karnataka, Kerala
Tropical dry deciduous	28	North-south strip from Himalayas to Kanyakumari
Tropical dry evergreen	8	Western Ghats, Assam, Andamans
Subtropical pine	7	Himalayas
Others	20	
	100	

What is the impact of human activities and natural forces on the forests of the world?

In Chapter 9, we will be examining in detail the impact of humankind as well as the forces of nature on forest resources. The major impact on the forest ecosystem is the following:

- The clearing and burning of the forests for agriculture, cattle rearing, and lumber, result in loss of biodiversity, extinction of species, soil erosion resulting in the loss of vital topsoil, and disturbance of the carbon cycle leading to global warming.
- The clear cutting and conversion of forest land on hilly areas for agriculture, plantations, and housing leads to landslides and floods that affect people in the forests and on the plains. It also increases siltation of rivers.

Felling the last tree on earth

> **KEY IDEA**
> Human activities have a very adverse impact on forests.

- Many forests have been affected by acid deposition originating from industries.
- The harvesting of old growth forests destroys crucial habitat for endangered species.
- Pesticide spraying to control insects in forest plantations leads to poisoning all the way up the food chain and unintended loss of predatory hawks, owls, eagles; this could in turn lead to the increase of the pest population.
- Dams built in forest areas for hydropower and water drown huge areas, destroying species and depriving people of their lands; they could also induce earth tremors.
- In wilderness areas like the Arctic, oil exploration and military activities disrupt the ecosystem, contaminate areas, and lead to the decline of species.

What are grasslands?

Grasslands are regions where the average annual precipitation is high enough (250–1,500 mm) for grass and perhaps a few trees to grow. The rainfall is, however, erratic and uncertain and hence large groups of trees do not grow. It is hot and dry in summer with incidence of fires.

Grasslands are the vast expanses of plains and rolling hills in the interiors of continents. They are found in central North America, central Russia and Siberia, subequatorial Africa and South America, Southern India, and Northern Australia.

The soil is rich and deep supporting many grass species, sparse bushes, and occasional woodlands. The animals include large grazing mammals like bison, antelopes, wild horses, kangaroos, giraffes, zebras, and rhinos as well as predators like wolves, coyotes, leopards, cheetahs, hyenas, and lions. Birds, rabbits, and mongoose also flourish in grasslands.

There has been a large-scale conversion of grassland into croplands, since they are well suited for agriculture. They are also used as rangelands for animals.

Savannas are tropical grasslands with widely scattered clumps of low trees. They are marked by low rainfall and prolonged dry periods. The African savannas are known for their enormous herds of hoofed animals like gazelles, zebras, giraffes, and antelopes. There are predators like cheetahs, lions, hyenas, eagles, and hawks. During the hot periods, the larger animals migrate in search of water and grass. The smaller ones stay dormant or eat seeds.

How do we define a desert?

Desert is an area where the evaporation often exceeds the precipitation. The typical annual precipitation is between 25 and 50 mm spread unevenly over the year.

Deserts are found mostly in a band 30 degrees north and south of the Equator and occupy about 30 per cent of the land surface. This area is increasing with continuous desertification going on in many parts of the world. There is more on desertification in Chapter 10.

The largest deserts are in the interiors of continents, where moist sea air or moisture-bearing winds do not reach. There are also local deserts, which are rain-shadow areas on the downward side of mountain ranges.

How do plants and animals adapt to deserts? The soil has very little organic matter, but is rich in minerals. The plants have adapted to the dry conditions and conserve water by having few or no leaves. The giant saguaro cactus, for example, has a stem that can expand to store water. Many have thorns or toxins to protect themselves from being grazed.

Some plants have wax-coated leaves that minimize loss of moisture. Others have deep roots that reach the groundwater. Alternatively, some have widely spread, shallow roots that collect water after any rain and store it in spongy tissues.

Desert animals are usually small in size and they remain under cover during the day and come out to feed at night. Many have a thick external shell that minimizes evaporation loss. They can stay dormant during the driest periods. Frogs, reptiles, rodents, jack rabbits, foxes, and owls are some of the desert animals.

During the daytime, the sun heats up the ground and the temperature is high. The night can be quite cold, since the lack of vegetation allows the heat from the ground to radiate away quickly.

Is there any human impact on deserts? You may think that a dry and hot desert cannot be damaged much by human activity. In fact, the desert ecosystem is quite sensitive and delicate. A heavy vehicle driven on the desert can do enormous damage to the thin topsoil and the sparse vegetation. The disturbed area will take a long time to recover, because of the extremely slow rate of growth of vegetation and low species diversity.

> **KEY IDEA**
> Even deserts are affected by human activities.

Apart from soil destruction, there are other human disturbances to desert ecosystems. The creation of desert cities, depletion of groundwater supplies, land disturbance and pollution from mining, and storage of toxic and nuclear wastes are some of the human activities that cause damage.

How can we describe the Thar desert?

The Thar or the Great Indian Desert is spread over four states in India—namely, Punjab, Haryana, Rajasthan, and Gujarat—and two states in Pakistan and covers an area of about 446,000 sq km. Though smaller than the Sahara in Africa and the Gobi in Russia, it is the most populated desert in the world, with about 13 million people.

The average annual rainfall is between 100 to 500 mm and most of it occurs in a few showers during the monsoon. The only river in the region is Ghaggar, which enters Rajasthan from Punjab and dries up in the desert.

The Thar has no oasis, native cactus or palm trees. Yet, a variety of flora and fauna thrives in this area. Flowering plants like shrubs and wild grasses, trees like the Khejra, Babul, and Rohida, and fruit trees like Ber and Pilu are found here.

Sheep, goats, and camels are the common animals used by the people. The Asiatic wild ass, deer species like the black buck and the Indian gazelle, common Indian hare red lynx, jackal and wild dog. About 23 species of lizard and 25 species of snakes are found here and several of them are endemic to the region.

The Thar desert
(Image courtesy: http://commons.wikimedia.org/wiki/File:Sand_dunes_of_thar_desert.jpg)

Local communities like the Bishnois have traditionally protected the trees and the animals (Read Box 3.2).

BOX 3.2

The story of the Bishnois: Giving one's life for a tree

The Bishnois of Rajasthan have been known for their concern for trees, birds, and animals. In 1731, Abhay Singh, the King of Jodhpur, wanted large quantities of wood for burning bricks to build his new palace. He sent his Minister, Giridhardas, with woodcutters to cut the trees in the forests near the Bishnoi villages.

Amritadevi, a mother of three, wanted to save the trees. She hugged a tree and begged Giridhardas and the cutters to stop the operation. Her daughters too followed her example. Giridhardas ordered the men to proceed and they cut down the trees and

the women. The news spread and more villagers came to the rescue of the trees. But the cutting continued and by nightfall, 363 people had given their lives in the cause of the forest.

When the King heard the news, he was overcome with remorse. He then banned felling of trees in the Bishnoi forests forever.

Recently, the Government of India has instituted the *Amritadevi Wildlife Protection Award*, to be given to village communities that show valour and courage for the protection of forests and wildlife.

The increase of human and livestock population in the desert has led to deterioration in the ecosystem resulting in degradation of soil fertility and vegetation. The desert is on the increase due to overgrazing and deforestation of marginal land

Are mountains distinct biomes?

Mountains have unique characteristics and can be studied as distinct biomes. Of all the continents, Antarctica is the most mountainous. Elsewhere, thanks to its relative inaccessibility, a mountain often stands out as an island of rich biodiversity in the midst of a devastated landscape.

A mountain
(Image courtesy: http://commons.wikimedia.org/wiki/File:Rajgad_after_monsoon.jpg)

As you go up a mountain, you will see dramatic changes in climate, soil, and vegetation even over short distances. In a way, moving up a mountain is similar to moving from the Equator to the North Pole, since you can experience similar changes in the biomes. Beginning with low deciduous forest, you could move through coniferous forests to alpine tundra and snow.

Mountains perform many ecological services for us. The majority of the world's forests are in the mountains. Apart from being home to endemic species of plants and animals not found elsewhere, they are

KEY IDEA

Mountain ecosystems provide vital ecosystem services, but they are facing severe degradation.

also sanctuaries for animals driven away from the lowland by human activities.

Mountains play a vital role in the water cycle. They absorb precipitation in their soils and vegetation and slowly release the water through small streams. These streams often join together and become rivers. Thus the mountains act as a reservoir, storing water in the monsoon and releasing it during the dry season.

What is happening to the mountain ecosystems now? Man is out to plunder the mountains too: roads have been laid, forests have been cleared, rivers have been dammed, hill stations have been built, and minerals have been mined. The resulting degradation has many effects.

The barren slopes get further eroded when rains wash away the valuable topsoil that ends up as sediment on rivers, reservoirs, and the ocean. The mountains can no longer hold the water and hence there are floods during the monsoon and no water in summer. The biodiversity, of course, disappears.

Alarmed by such degradation, the United Nations declared the year 2002 as the International Year of the Mountain to focus attention on their condition. There is also the International Centre for Integrated Mountain Development (ICIMOD) in Nepal, which works for the sustainable development of mountains.

Ending on a hopeful note: Positive story

In the lead story of this chapter, we saw how the citizens' initiative, Save the Nilgiris Campaign, did produce positive results. Now read Box 3.3 for a famous success story in the annals of the Indian environmental movement.

BOX 3.3

The story of Silent Valley: A pristine valley saved?

Situated in the Kundali Hills of the Western Ghats, in Kerala, the Silent Valley Forests are considered to be one of the last remaining virgin tropical evergreen forests in India, a climax ecosystem. Covering an area of 90 sq km, it has many rare plants and animals. The tree diversity here is very high and is comparable to some rain forests.

In the late 1970s, the Kerala Government decided to build a hydropower project in the area to generate 240 MW of power and irrigate 100,000 ha of land. The project would have, however, submerged 500 ha of the forest.

Several organizations like the Bombay Natural History Society (BNHS) and the Kerala Sastra Sahitya Parishad (KSSP) formed a 'Save Silent Valley' Movement to urge the state government to abandon the project. International organizations like the World Wide Fund for Nature and the World Conservation Union (IUCN) supported the struggle.

The issue became highly politicised and the pro-dam groups came up with the slogan: 'Man or Monkey'. The reference was to the lion-tailed macaque that the conservationists were concerned about.

Finally, the continued agitation and the intervention of the then Prime Minister, Indira Gandhi, forced the government to shelve the project. In 1984, the area was declared a National Park. It is now part of the core area of the Nilgiris Biosphere Reserve.

REVIEW: A SUMMARY OF THE KEY POINTS

- Terrestrial biomes are determined by temperature and precipitation.
- Forest ecosystems still cover a large area on land.
- Human beings have interfered in about 73 per cent of land; even the Arctic has not escaped our attention.
- Tropical forests are the treasure chest of the world's biodiversity and they are being destroyed at a rapid pace.

- Forest ecosystems are experiencing serious ecological and social problems in India and the rest of the world.
- Deserts can be damaged easily and take very long to recover from any disturbance.
- Mountains are unique ecosystems providing valuable services.

EXERCISES

Objective-type questions

In each case below, choose the best answer out of the given set of choices:

1. Which of the following is **not** a biome?
    (a) Tundra
    (b) Tropical rainforest
    (c) earth
    (d) Desert

2. Which of the following is **not** found in a tropical rainforest?
    (a) Desert area
    (b) Rich diversity of plants and animals
    (c) Acidic soil
    (d) Abundant rainfall

3. Which of the following statements is **not** true with regard to global forests?
    (a) Forests are adversely affected by acid rain.
    (b) Forests are submerged by reservoirs created when big dams are built.
    (c) Cutting down forests leads to landslides and floods.
    (d) Forests lead to water scarcity.

4. Which of the following statements is true with regard to deserts?
    (a) Deserts are affected by human activities.

    (b) Plants do not adapt to deserts.
    (c) Animals do not survive in deserts.
    (d) Days and nights are always hot in deserts.

Short-answer questions

1. How do desert organisms survive the heat and lack of water?
2. Why are tropical rain forests important to us?
3. What are the ecosystem services provided by mountains?

Long-answer questions

1. How do biomes vary based on the temperature and precipitation of the region?
2. Describe the human impact on the world's forests.
3. What lessons can we learn from the two cases described in this chapter: The Nilgiris and the Silent Valley?

Think critically: Deeper question for reflection and discussion

How does one use the forest without harming it? What can we learn from tribal communities or the Native Americans in this regard?

SOMETHING DIFFERENT FOR A CHANGE

Here is a poem by the Chilean poet Gabriela Mistral (1889–1957). Besides being a poet, she was also a teacher and a diplomat.

Pine Forest
Let us go now into the forest.
Trees will pass by your face,

and I will stop and offer you to them,
but they cannot bend down.
The night watches over its creatures,
except for the pine trees that never change:
the old wounded springs that spring
blessed gum, eternal afternoons.

If they could, the trees would lift you
and carry you from valley to valley,
and you would pass from arm to arm,
a child running
from father to father.

ACTIVITIES

Act: What you can do to conserve forests

Join any group action (such as the 'Save Western Ghats Campaign') that may be going on in your area.

Learn by doing: Case study / Project

If possible, spend your vacation in a forest area, observing the biotic species and abiotic conditions, the lives of the local people, and efforts of environmental groups. Write a report on the environmental and social problems in the area and suggest solutions.

Organize together: Eco-club activities and projects

1. Observe July 1–7 as Vanamahotsava Week: The idea of observing a Vanamahotsava Week was started in India several decades ago. As the name implies, it was to be a forest festival with the participation of the people. Over the years, however, the practice lost its original appeal and has now become a mere ritual. Take the lead in putting some fresh life into this festival and promote planting and protecting trees in your college or in your neighbourhood.

2. Observe December 11 as International Mountain Day: The UN General Assembly designated December 11 as the International Mountain Day from 2003. Each year the observance focuses on a theme. For more information, access the website: www.fao.org/mnts/intl_mountain_day_en.asp.

LEARN MORE

Books

Publications Division 2010, *India 2010: A Reference Annual*, Ministry of Information and Broadcasting, New Delhi. (gives some statistics on India's forests)

Sagreiya, K.P. 1994, *Forests and Forestry*, National Book Trust, New Delhi. (provides a more detailed account of forests in India, but the statistics are not current.)

Article

Hindu 1983, 'Forests' Impact on Weather Patterns', *The Hindu*, Chennai, July 18, 1983. (on the study on the role of forests in water recycling conducted by a Brazilian team led by Eneas Salati of the University of Sao Paulo)

Websites

State of India's Forests: www.wildlifeinindia.com/forests-of-india.html

India State of Forest report 2009: www.fsi.nic.in/sfr_2009.htm

Film

The Children of the Amazon: A film by Denise Zmekhol, which documents changes to the people and the land in the Amazon as development takes over more of the rainforest.

CHAPTER **4**

Aquatic Ecosystems

For all at last return to the Sea—
to Oceanus, the ocean river,
like the ever-flowing stream of time,
the beginning and the end.

Rachel Carson
(1907–1964)
American marine biologist and nature writer

THIS CHAPTER IS ABOUT...

Ocean and coastal zone, ocean governance, coral reefs, mangroves, inland seas, estuaries, freshwater ecosystems (rivers, lakes, etc.)

THE KEYWORDS AND PHRASES ARE...

Aquatic life zone	plankton	nekton	benthos	mangroves
phytoplankton	zooplankton	coastal zone	open ocean	euphotic zone
bathyal zone	abyssal zone	coral reefs	zooxanthellae	estuary
wetland	UNCLOS	EEZ	Common heritage of mankind	

THE STORY OF THE GULF OF MANNAR: UNIQUE AQUATIC ECOSYSTEM IN PERIL

The island of Kurusadai, near Rameswaram, is a biologist's paradise. Even today you can see its dense foliage, shallow coral reefs, plants, and aquatic life with an extraordinary diversity of form and colour. This is just one example of the marine life in the Gulf of Mannar, one of the world's richest marine biodiversity regions.

The Gulf of Mannar Biosphere Reserve (GOMBR) is located in the southeastern tip of Tamil Nadu extending from Rameswaram to Kanyakumari. It covers an area of 10,500 sq km, includes 21 islands, and contains over 3,600 species of fauna and flora. They include mangroves, seagrass beds, algae, coral reefs, many fish species, marine turtles, dolphins, dugongs, and many migratory birds.

This biological paradise is now in trouble. The habitat is getting degraded, the marine species are threatened, and the people's livelihood seriously affected. The three main threats to the ecosystem are the destruction of the marine resources by bottom

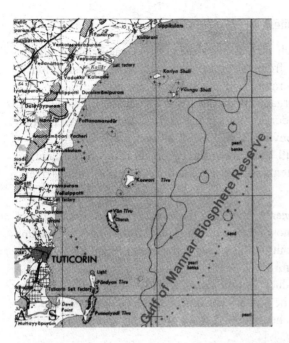

trawling, the mining of corals, and the pollution from industries.

The trawlers scrape the seabed using huge nets weighed down by chains. In the process, they destroy the breeding grounds of a large number of marine species. Since the nets are of fine mesh, they also bring up large amounts of smaller fish (bycatch), thus decimating the marine life. The traditional fisherfolk, on the other hand, use small boats and baiting methods that do not harm the non-target species.

There is a perpetual conflict between the two groups. The trawlers are expected to operate beyond three nautical miles from the shoreline and the fisherfolk within this distance. Each group accuses the other of violating the distance restriction. Mutual arrangements regarding times and days of operation do not work.

Illegal coral mining goes on unchecked in the area. Several hundred boats mine huge quantities of coral every day using levers and dynamite to break up the reefs. The catch is sent to cement companies as raw material. About 65 per cent of the coral reefs in the area are already dead, mostly due to human interference. The dugongs have disappeared and many marine species are threatened.

Over 100,000 people in 90 villages and hamlets in the area depend on fishing for their livelihood. Over the years, the variety and catch of fish have been steadily going down. As a result, there is more indebtedness among the fishermen.

The Gulf of Mannar was declared as a biosphere reserve in 1989 and was brought within the ambit of Man and the Biosphere Programme of UNESCO in 2001. This implies that fishing or any other activity is prohibited in the area. Such a restriction is unfair and unenforceable, as it goes against the traditional rights of the local fisherfolk. The only way to save the biosphere is by involving the local people as partners.

The Global Environmental Facility (GEF) has now provided support to the biosphere reserve through the GOMBR Trust. This body is responsible for the coordination of a management plan for the biosphere reserve in cooperation with government agencies, private entrepreneurs, and local people's representatives. Priority is being given to encouraging community-based management.

The Director of GOMBR Trust said in 2010 that the formation of the Trust and constant interaction with the locals had prevented mining of coral reef but the coastal communities were still smuggling sea horses, sea cucumber, and seaweeds. The biosphere reserve is still in a critical condition.

What do we learn from the Gulf of Mannar case?

It is once again a case of a unique natural environment, population pressure, people's livelihood issues, and local and international conservation efforts. The story tells us how valuable the ocean is and how human impact is adversely affecting the ocean ecosystems. Our task in this chapter is to learn more about different types of aquatic ecosystems: the ocean, rivers, lakes, wetlands, and so on.

How do aquatic ecosystems differ from terrestrial ones?

KEY IDEA

In aquatic life zones, the characteristics of water—salinity, light penetration, nutrient levels, waves, and currents—are the crucial factors.

Aquatic life zones, which include the ocean, rivers, lakes and wetlands, differ in many respects from terrestrial biomes. Unlike the situation in terrestrial biomes, temperature and precipitation are not the factors that determine the types of organisms that thrive in an aquatic life zone. First, water itself tends to moderate temperature and second, any precipitation falling on water cannot obviously be a major influence.

In this chapter, we will learn about the two main categories of aquatic life zones: saltwater systems (ocean, etc.) and freshwater systems (rivers, lakes, etc.).

What kinds of organisms do we find in aquatic life zones?   There are three main types of organisms in aquatic life zones: plankton, nekton, and benthos. The free-floating plankton are microorganisms that cannot swim easily and are buffeted about by the waves and currents. Plankton again are of two types: phytoplankton and zooplankton.

Phytoplankton are the photosynthetic producers of the ocean and they form the basis of the ocean's food web. The tiny zooplankton are the primary consumers that feed on phytoplankton. They in turn become the food for newly-hatched fish and small organisms and the food chain continues up the trophic levels.

The nekton, which are strong swimmers, include all the larger organisms like fishes, turtles and whales. The benthos are bottom-dwellers adapted to living on the floor of the water body. Some fix themselves to one spot like sponges, oysters, and barnacles. Others burrow themselves into the sand like worms and clams. Some others move about on the floor, like crawfish and brittle stars.

How large is the ocean and how important is it?

This planet should really be called ocean and not earth, because the ocean covers 71 per cent of the earth's surface. The ocean has an area of about 361 million sq km, an average depth of 3.7 km, and a total volume of 1,347,000 million cubic km. Seawater contains about 35 g of salt per kg.

Although we talk of different oceans in the world, there is just a single global ocean. For convenience, we have divided the ocean into the Pacific, the Atlantic, the Indian, and the Arctic. The largest geographical division is the Pacific Ocean that covers one-third of the earth's surface and contains more than 50 per cent of its water. The Pacific also has the deepest part of the ocean, the Mariana Trench, with a maximum depth of 11,000 m, which is 2,200 m more than the height of Mt. Everest!

KEY IDEA

We have explored just a small part of the ocean. Yet we know that it provides us with a variety of vital ecosystem services.

The global ocean is important to us in many ways. The biodiversity and resource-base of the ocean far exceeds that of the land. The ocean contains more than 250,000 species of plants and animals. This could well be an underestimate, since hardly 5 per cent of the ocean has been explored and mapped in detail. Every day, we are discovering new wonders about the ocean—its behaviour, services, and products.

The ocean provides many ecosystem services like regulation of climate and rainfall, cycling of nutrients, absorption of carbon dioxide, waste treatment, being a nursery for many species, storage of biodiversity and genetic resources, and protection from storms. The economic benefits include food items (fish, sea weed, and other items), fishmeal, oil and gas, minerals, medicines, building materials, transportation, recreation, and employment.

How do we divide the ocean into meaningful zones?

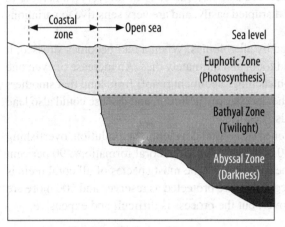

Fig. 4.1   The Zones of the Ocean

The large marine ecosystem is divided into two major zones: the coastal zone and the open ocean. The coastal zone extends from the high tide mark on land to the edge of the continental shelf, which is the submerged part of the continent. At this point, there is a sharp increase in the depth of water and from here onwards it is the open ocean. The coastal zone is discussed in a later section.

The open ocean is divided into three zones by depth. The euphotic zone is the upper part where there is enough light for the phytoplankton to carry out photosynthesis. Large fish like sharks and swordfish are found here. The bathyal zone lacks sunlight and hence contains no producers. Zooplankton and smaller fish that populate this zone have to move to the upper levels at night for feed.

The abyssal zone is the cold and dark zone at the bottom, reaching in places to a depth of 4,000 to 6,000 m. It is too dark for photosynthesis and yet there are producer organisms at this depth near hydrothermal vents. They are bacteria that can withstand temperatures of 200°C and they produce food through a chemical reaction.

What are coral reefs?

Coral reefs are one of the natural wonders of the ocean. On many beaches, these beautiful and colourful creations are on sale. Where do they come from and who makes them? Coral reefs are found in the shallow coastal zones of tropical and sub-tropical oceans, where light can penetrate. Apart being aesthetically appealing, they are also among the world's oldest, most diverse, and most productive ecosystems.

Corals are formed by huge colonies of tiny organisms called polyps. They secrete calcium carbonate (limestone) to form a protective crust around their soft bodies. When they die, their outer skeletons remain as a platform for others to continue building the coral. The intricate crevices and holes in the coral catacombs become the home for 25 per cent of all marine species.

The colour of the corals comes from zooxanthellae, the tiny single-celled algae that live inside the tissues of the polyps. In return for the home provided by the polyps, zooxanthellae produce food and oxygen through photosynthesis.

Why are coral reefs important?   Coral reefs are complex ecosystems that perform many ecological services. When polyps form their shells, they absorb some carbon dioxide as part of the carbon cycle. Reefs help protect the coastal zone from the impact of waves and storms. They are the nurseries for hundreds of marine organisms. In their biodiversity and intricacy of relationships, they can be called the rain forests of the ocean.

On the economic side, they provide fish, shellfish, building materials, medicines, and employment to people. Through tourism, they bring in valuable foreign exchange and give us the pleasure of enjoying the world under the sea.

Like many other parts of nature, coral reefs are also in trouble. They are very vulnerable to damage because they grow very slowly, get disrupted easily, and are very sensitive to variations in temperature and salinity.

Coral bleaching is the biggest threat faced by all colonies. When a reef becomes stressed, it expels the zooxanthellae, loses its colour and food, and ultimately dies. An increase of even one degree in the water temperature can trigger bleaching. Sediment runoff from land that smothers the reef and prevents photosynthesis is another stress. Any pollution and disease could also lead to bleaching. Direct physical damage can also occur.

60 per cent of the world's reefs are threatened by coastal development, pollution, overfishing and warmer temperatures. Of more than 100 countries with large coral formations, 90 per cent are experiencing decline of the reefs. Southeast Asia with the most species of all coral reefs is the most threatened region. 300 reefs in 65 countries are protected as reserves and 600 more are under consideration. Protected reefs do recover, but the process is difficult and expensive.

What is the importance of mangroves?

Mangroves are unique salt-tolerant trees with interlacing roots that grow in shallow marine sediments. Often they are found just inland of coral reefs. Mangroves provide valuable ecosystem services. Their roots are the breeding grounds and nurseries for many fish species like shrimp and sea trout. The branches are nesting sites for birds like pelicans, spoonbills, and egrets. They stabilize the soil, prevent erosion, and provide protection to the coast during cyclones. They are more effective than concrete barriers in absorbing wave action.

Mangroves occur all along the Indian coast covering 6,700 sq km, which is about 7 per cent of the world's total mangrove area. Some of the important mangrove forests are found in Andaman and Nicobar Islands, Sunderbans (West Bengal), Bhitarkanika (Orissa), Pitchavaram (Tamil Nadu), and Goa.

KEY IDEA

Coral reefs and mangroves provide invaluable ecosystem services (protection against storms, breeding grounds for fishes, etc.), but they are in decline all over the world.

In India and elsewhere, mangroves are fast disappearing due to coastal development, logging, and shrimp aquaculture. Between 1985 and 2000, the world lost half of its mangroves.

Before we move to the coastal zone and the fresh water life zones, let us look at a unique part of the ocean.

What is special about Antarctica and the Southern Ocean?

Antarctica is an icy continent, surrounded by the Southern Ocean. It is a fragile ecosystem and is relatively unexploited. The Antarctic ice cap contains 70 per cent of the world's freshwater. A thin layer on the ocean supports krill (very small shellfish), which is consumed by other fish, seals, penguins, and whales.

KEY IDEA

Antarctica is a sensitive indicator of the environment. Its ice shelves are breaking up, probably due to global warming.

Antarctica is a sensitive indicator of environmental changes. Between 1947 and 2000, the mean temperature of the Antarctic Peninsula went up by 2.5°C in summer and 5.6°C in winter. The reason could be global warming from the burning of fossil fuels. With increasing temperature, huge pieces of the ice shelf have been breaking off. Over a period of time, this melting of ice could raise global sea levels.

Seals and whales were first hunted in Antarctica, leading to the near-extinction of the southern fur seal, elephant seal, and the blue whale. The pollution from the rest of the world has now reached Antarctica. Radioactive particles from atomic testing as well as DDT and other chemical residues have been found in these waters. Tourism that is being promoted now will also have ecological consequences.

No country owns Antarctica, though several countries have made claims on parts of it. In 1991, 41 countries (including India) signed the Antarctic Treaty. They agreed to ensure that Antarctica is used for peaceful purposes, for international cooperation in scientific research, and does not become the scene or object of international discord. The treaty seeks to establish Antarctica as a zone free of nuclear tests and radioactive waste and includes agreed measures for the conservation of Antarctic fauna and flora.

Several countries including India have been conducting scientific research and exploration for oil and minerals in Antarctica. The first Indian expedition to Antarctica was sent in 1981 and since then Indian scientists have established two research stations, *Dakshin Gangotri* and *Maitri*, on the continent. Joint teams representing a number of scientific organizations in the country have participated in more than 20 expeditions to the continent.

Are inland seas also special?

These are large saline lakes that have salinities in excess of 3 g per litre and occur on all continents. They include the Caspian Sea, Dead Sea, Black Sea, and Aral Sea. They are sensitive ecosystems and their environmental importance is only now becoming clear. Most of the large inland seas of the world are facing environmental degradation. They were once healthy waters used for fishing, transport, etc. Now, however, human activities like overfishing, pollution, and diversion of inflow are decimating many of these water bodies. (Read about the Aral Sea in Box 4.1.)

BOX 4.1

The story of the Aral Sea: Death of a sea

The Aral Sea, on the border between Uzbekistan and Kazakhstan, was once the world's fourth largest freshwater lake. It was spread over 68,000 sq km in 1960. Over the past forty years, however, it has lost over 75 per cent of its volume and over 50 per cent of its area. How did such degradation happen?

The lake has no outflow other than evaporation and the inflow is from the rivers, Amu Darya and Syr Darya. In the 1950s, the USSR, in its insatiable drive for development, decided to divert the water from these two rivers to irrigate the desert area around the lake for planting cotton. The Soviets

Contd

Box 4.1 Contd

also constructed the world's longest irrigation canal (over 1,300 km long) to take the water into Turkmenistan.

Millions of hectares of cotton were planted and soon USSR became a net exporter of cotton. This success came with a cost to the Aral Sea. By the early 1980s, 95 per cent of the inflow had been diverted and by then the Sea had shrunk to a considerable extent.

The fish catch used to be 44,000 tonnes per year, providing livelihood for 600,000 people. Today, most of the 24 fish species are gone and the fishing industry has collapsed. These are hard times for the 35 million people living in the watershed.

The shoreline has receded by an incredible 100 km! Maynak, which was a seaport 25 years ago, is today 30 km from the shoreline. Abandoned boats dot the landscape. Toxic dust-salt mixture arises like a storm from the exposed seabed and gets deposited on the farmland, damaging crops. The dust also causes many illnesses including throat cancer and tuberculosis. The weather has changed for the worse, with summers getting warmer and the winters colder.

In 1994, the five republics of the region established a joint fund to prevent the complete disappearance of the Aral Sea. The World Bank and UNEP have given funds to improve the environment. Reviving the lake is a hard task, however. Even if all the diversion of water for irrigation is stopped now, it will take 50 years for the lake to fill up! The dilemma is that, with the collapse of the fisheries, irrigation for agriculture has become even more important. Do we want water on the farm or water in the lake?

By 2007 the Aral Sea had declined to 10 per cent of its original size, splitting into three lakes—the North Aral Sea and the eastern and western basins. By 2009, the south-eastern lake had disappeared and the south-western lake retreated to a thin strip. There is some good news, however. The North Aral Sea is making a recovery, due to the efforts of the Kazakh government, the World Bank, and scientists. A dam completed in 2005 raised water levels and decreased salinity, and increased the North Aral's span by 20 per cent. Some native plants and migrating birds like pelicans, flamingos, ducks, and even freshwater fish are coming back. While the South Aral Sea remains in crisis, the tentative revival of the North Aral Sea gives some hope.

Is not the ocean too vast to be spoiled by us?

The traditional view of the ocean is that of an unbounded domain with inexhaustible wealth. The apparent vastness of the ocean also gives the impression that it can accommodate all users and all kinds of uses and that any amount of waste will be absorbed by the marine system. We now know, however, that the ocean is a finite resource and that human activities are already having an extremely adverse impact on the ocean. The world over, fish-catches have been steadily declining because of pollution and overfishing with large trawlers and factory ships. Many fish species have disappeared forever.

The deep seabed has mineral as well as biological resources and many countries are now developing techniques to tap this wealth. The insatiable demand for petroleum has led to large-scale extraction of oil from the ocean with many negative consequences. The main shipping lanes of the ocean now carry very heavy traffic with consequent problems like large oil spills from giant tankers.

The dumping of hazardous waste, including nuclear material, into the ocean is raising pollution levels to great heights. Near the shore, heavy discharges from industry and sewage systems are also adding to the pollution. In fact it is estimated that 77 per cent of marine pollution originates from land.

Who controls the ocean activities?   For a long time the ocean area beyond the territorial limit was governed by the concept of the Freedom of the High Seas. This meant that any country or anyone could exploit the wealth of the ocean without any control. Now, however, the concept has been replaced by that of the Common Heritage of Mankind.

In a landmark agreement, many countries came together to draft the UN Convention on the Law of the Sea (UNCLOS), which came into force in November 1994. Apart from setting the territorial limit as 12 nautical miles (from the shoreline, this Convention establishes for every country an Exclusive Economic Zone (EEZ) up to a distance of 200 nautical miles from the shoreline. (One nautical mile is equal to 1.85 km.) Every country has the exclusive right to exploit the resources of its Exclusive Economic Zone (EEZ). What is beyond the EEZ is the International Area of the Seabed.

According to the Convention the ocean has to be used only for peaceful purposes and should be managed in the interests of all, including future generations. To control the ocean resources and to resolve disputes, two bodies have been established: the International Tribunal for the Law of the Sea, Hamburg, and the International Seabed Authority, Jamaica. The Seabed Authority controls the exploitation of resources in the International Area.

> **KEY IDEA**
> The UN Convention on the Law of the Sea now governs the use of marine resources. The ocean is seen as the Common Heritage of Mankind.

India has a coastline of over 7,000 km and an EEZ of two million sq km, which is two-thirds of our land area. The Seabed Authority has granted exclusive rights to India to explore 150,000 sq km in the Central Indian Ocean.

What is the coastal zone?

The coastal zone is the area of interaction between land and ocean, but there is no clear definition of the zone. On the seaward side, it is commonly taken to extend up to the gently sloping, shallow edge of the continental shelf. On the landward side, we could define the limit of the zone as the high tide line or even up to the watershed. Thanks to the edge effect, this zone shows very high levels of biodiversity. 90 per cent of all marine species are found in this zone.

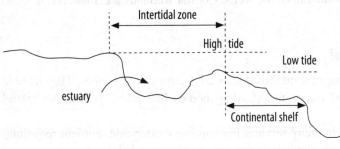

Fig. 4.2   The Coastal Zone

The coastal zone is easily affected by human activities. A general trend in the world is for the population to move towards the coastal zone. One estimate is that 60 per cent of the world population now lives within 60 km of the coast. This proportion is expected to increase to 75 per cent by 2025. Even conservative estimates suggest that at least 40 per cent of the population lives within 100 km of the coast. One incontrovertible fact is that the rate of increase of coastal population is higher than that of the general population.

Dumped garbage on Mumbai coast
(Image courtesy: http://commons.wikimedia.org/
wiki/File:Mumbai_environmentalproblems.JPG)

KEY IDEA

The coastal zone with its diversity is ecologically important, but it is being degraded due to population pressure, urban expansion, infrastructure development, and pollution.

Most of the large cities of the world are to be found on the coast. Twelve of the twenty most highly populated urban areas in the world are within 150 km of the coast and these include Mumbai and Kolkata. Coastal megacities have very large ecological footprints. In most cases, they dump enormous amounts of untreated sewage and industrial pollutants into the ocean.

Why are estuaries and coastal wetlands important?

Estuaries and coastal wetlands include river mouths, bays, mangrove forests, and salt marshes. Here the seawater mixes with freshwater and nutrients from rivers, streams, and runoffs. These ecosystems experience wide daily and seasonal fluctuations in temperatures and salinity levels because of tidal rhythms, variations in freshwater inflow from land and river, and the impact of storms.

The organisms in these ecosystems have to adapt to changing conditions. Yet, these ecotones are among the most fertile ecosystems, often more productive than the adjacent ocean or river. The main reasons are flow of nutrients from land, removal of waste products by tidal action, and the availability of sunlight.

Coastal saltwater wetlands are the ocean's nurseries, where many fish species spend the first part of their lives. These wetlands also protect coastlines from erosion and reduce damage from storms and cyclones. The flow of groundwater through coastal marshes prevents saltwater intrusion that would otherwise contaminate the wells. Coastal wetlands are, however, in steep decline all over the world.

How do we define freshwater life zones?

Aquatic zones with less than 1 per cent dissolved salts are freshwater life zones. They include flowing bodies like streams and rivers and standing bodies like lakes, ponds, and inland wetlands.

Freshwater ecosystems perform many services like climate moderation, nutrient recycling, flood control, waste treatment, groundwater recharge, providing a habitat for species, and preserving a pool of genetic resources and biodiversity. On the economic side, they provide food, drinking water, irrigation, hydropower, transportation, recreation, and employment.

Freshwater ecosystems are influenced by the local climate, soil, and resident communities as well as by the surrounding biomes. Anything that happens upstream will have an impact on them.

What are the general characteristics of rivers and streams?

The nature of any flowing-water ecosystem like a stream or a river varies greatly between its source and its mouth (where it meets the ocean or flows into another water body like a lake). A river often begins as a stream high in the mountains in a forest, which absorbs the precipitation and releases it slowly. In other cases, the river begins with the melting of snow or a glacier.

The source or headwater stream flows downstream rapidly over rocks or becomes a waterfall. Once it reaches the plains, it slows down. Other tributaries may flow into the river. Finally, it reaches the delta, the low-lying plains at the mouth, before flowing into the ocean. The delta is fertile thanks to the sediments carried along by the river.

Human activities are taking a heavy toll on the world's rivers. About 60 per cent of the 240 large rivers are strongly or moderately fragmented by dams, diversions, and canals.

What is the status of India's rivers?

More than 70 per cent of India's territory drains into the Bay of Bengal via the Ganga–Brahmaputra river system and a number of large and small peninsular rivers.

The Ganga and Brahmaputra rivers, together with their tributaries, drain about one-third of India. The Indus basin (in northwestern India) and a completely separate set of basins to the south (in Gujarat, Madhya Pradesh, Maharashtra) drain into the Arabian Sea.

The two most important west-flowing rivers of peninsular India are the Narmada and Tapti. The Narmada and its basin are undergoing large-scale, multipurpose development. The major rivers that drain into the Bay of Bengal are Mahanadi, Godavari, Krishna, and Kaveri.

India's rivers receive millions of litres of sewage as well as industrial and agricultural wastes. Most of the rivers have become sewage drains. Towns and villages using these rivers as water sources face severe contamination.

The pollution of the holy Ganga is often in the news (Read the lead story in Chapter 20). Repeated attempts to clean the Ganga have not produced results. Yamuna, which flows though Delhi, is just a massive sewer. Its 'holy' water, in which people wash themselves, has been declared unfit for human use.

Taking bath in the polluted Ganga

The question of interlinking Indian rivers is discussed in Chapter 7.

How can we study large lakes?

Lakes are natural bodies of standing freshwater, when precipitation, runoff, or groundwater seepage fills up depressions on land formed by geological changes. Lakes and their surrounding watersheds are unique and valuable ecosystems. Lakes store freshwater and give it to us in off-monsoon months. The water in lakes also recharges the groundwater. More than 90 per cent of all available surface freshwater is contained in lakes and reservoirs.

Lakes provide habitat for bacteria, fungi, algae, plants, plankton, molluscs, crustaceans, insects, fish, amphibians, reptiles, birds, and mammals. They support large numbers of threatened and endemic species.

Human communities that surround lakes depend heavily on lake biodiversity and natural lake processes for their water, food and way of life. Many of the world's poorest people depend on freshwater biodiversity for their protein needs.

> **KEY IDEA**
> Lakes provide fresh water, recharge the groundwater, and act as habitat for many aquatic species. But many lakes are shrinking in size and are becoming polluted too.

In many countries, lakes supply a large proportion of the drinking water. Lake Chapala (Mexico), which has been shrinking dramatically due to water diversion for inefficient irrigation, is the main water source for five million people in Guadalajara, Mexico. Although most lakes are relatively new to earth (in geological time) there are at least 14 lakes older than one million years. Many of the world's lakes, however, are in crisis. (Read about Lake Victoria in Box 4.2.)

BOX 4.2

The story of Lake Victoria: Reap what you sow

Lake Victoria is in East Africa, shared by Kenya, Tanzania, and Uganda. The second largest freshwater lake in the world and the source of the great Nile river, Lake Victoria is in serious ecological trouble leaving the local people in utter distress.

Until the 1980s, the lake had nearly 400 species of small colourful fishes called cichlids, not found anywhere else on earth. Each species had a slightly different ecological niche in the lake: some grazed on algae, others fed on dead organic matter at the bottom; some ate insects, shrimps, or even other cichlid species.

Cichlids provided a protein diet as well as livelihood to more than 30 million people around the lake. It was a happy story until an unsuspected villain came along in 1960. A new fish species, the Nile perch, was introduced in the lake to stimulate the local economy and the fishing industry.

The Nile perch was a large and voracious predator that fed on cichlids. Initially, there were enough cichlids for man and the predator. Over the next 20 years, however, the perch population steadily increased. As the harvest of Nile perch increased, the catch of other fishes started plummeting.

A strange combination of factors led to the decimation of the fishes. The perch of course was thriving at the cost of the cichlid. Further, the local people started cutting the forests nearby for fuelwood they needed for drying the large Nile perch. This cutting in turn led to soil erosion, which caused turbidity in the lake. Chemical fertilizers and untreated sewage from the land were also washed in.

Thanks to all the nutrients, there were frequent algal blooms and cultural eutrophication, leading to low oxygen levels in the lower depths. The cichlids were driven to the shallower waters, where the predators ate them up.

The local people could not afford the expensive perch and the small fishers were driven out by the mechanized boats. Poverty and malnutrition increased. Matters became worse when water

Contd

Box 4.2 Contd

hyacinth invaded large areas of the lake, blotted out sunlight, reduced oxygen levels further and hindered movement of small boats. The stagnant water promoted diseases spread by snails and mosquitoes.

How is the Nile perch doing? With the cichlids gone, it now feeds on tiny shrimp and its own young. It may also disappear after its 40-year domination. In effect, the fisheries have collapsed. The men from the area have been migrating in search of livelihood, leaving behind families in poverty, disease, and destitution. The World Bank is funding a Lake Victoria Environment Management Programme, but the progress is slow.

What about Indian lakes?   India had a very large number of lakes and ponds, constructed by the kings of old for storing water. Most of these lakes are polluted or have been drained and converted as cropland. Lakes in cities have become built-up areas.

What are freshwater wetlands and why are they important?

Wetlands are land surfaces covered or saturated with water for a part or whole of the year. They are shallow systems with black and rich sediments and abundant nutrients. They have vegetation adapted to thrive in saturated conditions.

There are three types of wetlands: swamps, marshes, and bogs. Marshes have no trees, but they contain grasslike plants (cattails, sedges, and reeds). Swamps have water-tolerant trees like red maple and cedar. Bogs are waterlogged areas saturated with groundwater or rainwater and may contain sphagnum moss and low shrubs.

Marshes and swamps are marked by full penetration of light and consequently high photosynthetic activity. Biomass production and species diversity are much higher than in the surrounding uplands. They provide habitat for migrating waterfowl, other birds, beavers, otters, muskrats, and game fishes.

Traditionally, wetlands were considered as wastelands that bred mosquitoes. They were drained and developed for agriculture, fish farming, or habitations. Their value as providers of ecosystem services is now being realized.

Wetlands control flooding by holding excess water and releasing it slowly. They help in recharging groundwater and in purifying water by trapping and holding pollutants in the soil. They are the major breeding, nesting, and migration staging areas for waterfowl and shorebirds.

They add moisture to the atmosphere, which could fall back as rain. They can even be used as sewage treatment plants that require little technology or maintenance. If they are managed well, they will not breed mosquitoes because of the presence of fish, insects, and birds.

Even as we realize their importance, however, they are shrinking rapidly all over the world. Almost half of them have disappeared over the past century and those that remain have been fragmented by 'development'. What is worse, some wetlands have been used as toxic waste dumps and landfills.

Ending on a hopeful note: Positive story

Box 4.3 gives an account of some success achieved in restoring the Chilika Lake in Orissa.

BOX 4.3

The story of Chilika Lake: New life for an old lake?

With an area of about 1,000 sq km, the Chilika Lake in coastal Orissa is the largest brackish water lagoon in Asia. Rich in fauna, it has been home to a variety of residential and migratory birds, many fish species and the Irrawady dolphin.

It is one of the largest wintering grounds for migratory waterfowl from all over the world. From October to December every year, birds migrate here from places as far away as Siberia and Australia.

Chilika was recognised as a biodiversity hotspot and was designated as a Ramsar site in 1982. This refers to the Convention on Wetlands, an intergovernmental treaty adopted in 1971 in the Iranian city of Ramsar. There are more than 1,200 Ramsar sites in the world.

During the later part of the 20th century, Chilika had been facing a number of ecological and social problems. Heavy siltation due to massive deforestation in the catchment area was reducing the lake area by two sq km every year. The blocking of its opening to the sea reduced the salinity level and many fish species were affected. The number of fish species dropped from 126 in 1930 to 69 in 1995. The poor drainage of water led to water logging in the agricultural lands around the lake.

200,000 fisherfolk and 800,000 people in the catchment area depend on the lake for their livelihood and the increasing population strained the resources further. The annual fish catch dropped from 8,800 tons to 1,600 tons during the decade of the 1990s.

Illegal prawn culture has been a problem, since this activity near the shore affects the fish. In 1999, the fishermen took direct action to destroy some shrimp farms and, in the police firing that followed, some of them were killed.

In 1993, Chilika had been placed on the Montreux Record, a list of Ramsar sites requiring priority conservation attention. By the end of 1990s, the lake appeared to be dying, with no hope of restoration. Positive developments were, however, in the offing.

The Government of Orissa created the Chilika Development Authority (CDA) for the restoration of the lagoon. The CDA commissioned the National Institute of Oceanography (NIO), Goa and the Central Water and Power Research Station (CWPRS), Pune to study the problems and suggest solutions.

The consultants pinpointed the decrease in the salinity level as the major cause of the problems. Acting on their recommendation, the CDA opened an artificial mouth connecting the lake and the sea in 2000. This intervention seemed to have a positive effect, since the fish catch started going up—4,900 tons in 2000–2001 and 11,800 tons in 2001–2002. The Irrawady dolphin was seen again and the seagrass meadows reappeared. The increase in salinity level also led to the shrinking of the undesirable invasive weed population.

The better exchange of water between the lagoon and the sea brought in more nutrients and flushed away the waste products. As a result, the productivity of the ecosystem increased. Thanks to the quicker drainage, the surrounding villages were not affected even in unprecedented floods of 2001.

The local people had been involved in the planning and implementation of the restoration work. Training programmes on appropriate land use practices and soil moisture conservation were conducted and women's self-help groups were formed. The Orissa Government also banned aquaculture in the lake area.

Impressed by the achievements, the Ramsar Bureau removed Chilika from the Montreux Record in 2002 and also conferred the Ramsar Wetland Conservation Award for 2002 on CDA for the successful restoration work involving the local community.

A success story? Not quite, say some environmentalists. The increased salinity appears to have affected the migratory birds and their numbers are declining. In addition, large scale poaching of the birds has also been reported. Illegal shrimp culture, overfishing, and the use of fine mesh nets are some of the other continuing problems. The Government of Orissa plans to regulate the fishing activities on Chilika.

REVIEW: A SUMMARY OF THE KEY POINTS

- Many large inland seas and fresh water lakes are facing severe environmental problems.
- The ocean is a treasure house of biodiversity and the provider of a whole range of ecological services.
- Coral reefs and mangroves are vital organisms that are under threat.
- The relatively unexploited Antarctica is now under pressure.
- The use of the ocean is now regulated by the UN Convention on the Law of the Sea.
- The coastal zone with its immense biodiversity is being degraded by development and population pressure.
- The importance of estuaries and wetlands are now being appreciated.

EXERCISES

Objective-type questions

In each case below, choose the best answer out of the given set of choices:

1. Which of the following factors **does not** determine the types of organisms that thrive in an aquatic life zone?
   (a) Salinity
   (b) Waves
   (c) Light penetration
   (d) Precipitation
2. Which of the following organisms is the 'producer' of the ocean?
   (a) Phytoplankton
   (b) Nekton
   (c) Benthos
   (d) Zooplankton
3. Which of the following statements is **not** true with regard to the ocean?
   (a) There is just a single ocean.
   (b) The ocean covers nearly three-fourths of the earth's surface.
   (c) The Indian Ocean has the deepest part of the ocean.
   (d) The biodiversity of the ocean far exceeds that of the land.
4. Which of the following statements is **not** true with regard to coral reefs?
   (a) Coral reefs are increasing in area everywhere.
   (b) Corals are formed by polyps.
   (c) Corals are the nurseries for hundreds of marine organisms.
   (d) Coral bleaching is the biggest threat faced by reefs.
5. Which of the following statements is **not** true with regard to mangroves?
   (a) Mangrove roots are the breeding grounds and nurseries for many fish species.
   (b) Mangrove branches are nesting sites for birds.
   (c) Mangroves stabilize the soil and prevent erosion.
   (d) Mangroves do not provide protection against cyclones.
6. Which international agreement governs the ocean?
   (a) UN Convention on the Law of the Sea
   (b) International Tribunal for the Law of the Sea
   (c) International Seabed Authority
   (d) Montreal Protocol

Short-answer questions

1. What are the factors that determine the types of organisms found in aquatic ecosystems?
2. List the main types of marine organisms. Who are the producers and consumers in the ocean?
3. Describe the main features of UNCLOS.
4. Explain why the following are important:
   (a) Coral reefs
   (b) Mangroves
   (c) Estuaries and coastal wetlands
   (d) Fresh water wetlands

Long-answer questions

1. Write essays on the importance of
   (a) the ocean and

(b) the coastal zone
with regard to economic and ecological services.

2. What are the general conclusions about the environmental problems of aquatic ecosystems you can draw from the cases described in this chapter?

SOMETHING DIFFERENT FOR A CHANGE

1. Enjoy the translation of an Eskimo song:

    The great sea has set me in motion
    Set me adrift
    And I move as a weed in river

    The arch of sky
    And mightiness of storms

ACTIVITIES

Act: What you can do to conserve aquatic ecosystems

If you are in a coastal town, join voluntary groups engaged in activities like beach clean up.

If there are ponds, lakes, or wetlands in or near your area, there could be groups trying to save them. If there is no group and if a water body is in peril, organise a group to make representations to the government and to create awareness in the community.

Learn by doing: Case study/Project

Locate a wetland and study it over a period of (at least) three months as an ecosystem. Trace the inflow and outflow of water. What are the plant and animal species found in the ecosystem? What kind of services does the wetland provide? What are the threats faced by the system and how best to face them? Write a report on your study.

Organize together: Eco-club activities and projects

1. Observe February 2 as World Wetlands Day, which marks the date of the signing of the Convention on Wetlands in 1971, in the Iranian city of Ramsar. On

Think critically: Deeper questions for reflection and discussion

There are still vast areas of ocean to be explored. How should we regulate exploration and exploitation of the ocean's resources?

Encompasses me
And I am left
Trembling with joy.

2. Read the classic novel *The Old Man and the Sea* by Ernest Hemingway or watch its film version with Spencer Tracy playing the main role.

this Day, government agencies, non-governmental organizations, and citizens undertake actions aimed at raising public awareness of wetland values and benefits in general and the Ramsar Convention in particular. For more information, access the Ramsar website www.ramsar.org

2. Observe April 5 as National Maritime Day. On this day in 1919, the *SS Loyalty*, the first ship of the Scindia Steam Navigation Company, sailed for the United Kingdom. Though the Day is celebrated more by seafarers and port authorities than others, you could use it as an opportunity to create awareness about the ocean. Use your creativity to bring life to an observance that has become a mere annual ritual!

3. Observe June 8 as World Oceans Day as adopted by the UN General Assembly. The Ocean Project and the World Ocean Network have helped to promote and coordinate World Oceans Day events worldwide with aquariums, zoos, museums, conservation organizations, universities, schools, and businesses. For more information, access the website www.theoceanproject.org.

LEARN MORE

Books

Carson, Rachel 2003, *The Sea Around Us*, Oxford University Press USA, New York. (Special commemorative edition of the 1951 classic with colour illustrations)

Richard, Bryan, Sarah Rickayzen, and Joan Barker 2007, *Ocean: Revealing the Secrets of the Deep*, Paragon Publishing, Bath, UK.

Articles

Menon, Parvathi 2003, 'A conflict on the waves', *Front-line*, Vol 20, No.6, March 28, pp. 65–73. (on the Gulf of Mannar)

Pattnaik, A.K. 2003, 'Chilika: Blue lagoon once more', *The Hindu Survey of Environment 2003*, The Hindu, Chennai, pp. 147–153.

Websites

UNESCO Man and the Biosphere programme: www. unesco.org

Gulf of Mannar Biosphere Reserve Project of Global Environment Facility: http://gefonline.org/project DetailsSQL.cfm?projID=634

Wetlands and the Ramsar Convention: www.ramsar.org

Chilika Lake:
- www.chilika.com (official website)
- www.angelfire.com/in/aquiline/chilika.htm (on the agitation against shrimp farms)

Films

The Blue Planet: A BBC documentary on the ocean.

Darwin's Nightmare: A documentary by Hubert Sauper on the effect of fishing the Nile perch in Lake Victoria.

End of the Line: A documentary by Rupert Murray about the devastating effects of overfishing.

Module 3
Biodiversity

CHAPTER 5

Introduction to Biodiversity

For each of the Big Five [extinctions],
there are theories of what caused them,
some of them compelling, but none proven.
For the sixth extinction, however,
we do know the culprit.
We are.

Richard Leakey
(1944–)
Kenyan paleoanthropologist, conservationist, and politician

THIS CHAPTER IS ABOUT...

Biodiversity—meaning, value, and loss, threatened and endangered species, extinction of species

THE KEYWORDS AND PHRASES ARE...

biological diversity	species diversity	genetic diversity	ecosystem diversity
biological extinction	ecological extinction	background extinction	mass extinction
keystone species	indicator species	sentinel species	habitat fragmentation
endangered species	threatened species	bioinformatics	

THE STORY OF THE INDIAN SMALL FARMER: SEEDS OF PLENTY OR SEEDS OF SUICIDE?

Prathap, Mahendra Reddy, Adinarayana—The names of just a few of the many small farmers of Andhra Pradesh who committed suicide in recent times. In most cases, an intolerable debt burden drove them to take their lives. They had all borrowed money for the inputs in their farming—seeds, fertilizers, and pesticides.

Until about the middle of the 20th century, such small farmers in India needed very little input from outside. They grew a variety of crops and kept aside some part of the harvest as seeds for the next year. They used organic manure and natural pesticides. Even if one crop failed, there were others to save the farmer from ruin.

Life was not easy, but the farmers were not in deep crisis either. However, India's population was growing and food was being imported. This was also the problem with many poor countries of the world.

The solution came in the form of the Green Revolution with the promise of plenty. The key element was new seeds called High Yielding Varieties (HYVs). Developed first in Mexico and then taken to many countries, the new seeds increased the yield per hectare to very high levels.

It was certainly a revolution in agriculture, but it came as a whole package. The HYVs needed large inputs of fertilizers, pesticides, and water. Further, the small number of laboratory-developed HYVs replaced the very large number of traditional varieties cultivated by farmers.

With the active encouragement of the government and international agencies, the Green Revolution was enthusiastically adopted in India. Food production increased and the country became self-sufficient.

The Green Revolution, however, changed the traditional agricultural practices. The farmers had to buy every year new seeds, fertilizers, and pesticides. Soon, the traditional varieties disappeared, leaving just a few HYVs. In other words, diversity gave place to uniformity. The seeds, however, came from the National Seeds Corporation or other certified government agencies.

From about 1998, another major change occurred with the entry into India of the international seed companies. They needed mass markets and they aggressively promoted the use of a small number of varieties.

The small farmer is now in the clutches of a new breed of entrepreneurs. They provide all the inputs at high prices, give credit at very high interest rates, and buy the crops at low prices. A crop failure due to spurious or low quality seeds, pest attack, or drought is often the last straw. The farmer is perpetually in debt and often the only escape is through suicide.

What is the basic cause of the farmers' problems?

The Green Revolution increased the yields, but created problems like soil degradation, falling productivity over time, increasing use of fertilizers, greater proneness to diseases, and excessive withdrawal of groundwater. At the basis of all the problems, however, is the loss of biodiversity. That is the topic of this chapter and the next.

What is biodiversity?

> **KEY IDEA**
> Biodiversity is the earth's primary life support system and is a precondition for human survival.

Biodiversity or biological diversity refers to the numbers, variety, and variability of living organisms and ecosystems. The term includes all the terrestrial, marine, and other aquatic organisms. It also covers diversity within species, between species, as well as the variation among ecosystems. It is concerned also with their complex ecological interrelationships.

What is species diversity?   Species diversity refers to the number of plant and animal species present in a community or an ecosystem. It varies a great deal between ecosystems. For example, species diversity is very high in tropical rainforests and coral reefs and low in isolated islands. You will find a large number of different plants and animals in an ecosystem with high diversity.

Genetic diversity is the variety in the genetic makeup among individuals within a species. Ecosystem diversity is the variety of habitats found in an area. It is the variety of forests, deserts, grasslands, aquatic ecosystems, etc., that occur in the area.

The following factors determine the degree of diversity in an ecosystem or community:

- *Habitat stress:* Diversity is low in habitats under any stress like harsh climate or pollution.
- *Geographical isolation:* Diversity is less in isolated regions like an island. If a species in an island disappears due to random events, it cannot be easily replaced. Organisms from the mainland have difficulties in reaching and colonizing the island.
- *Dominance by one species:* The dominant species consumes a disproportionate share of the resources. This does not allow many species to evolve and flourish.
- *Availability of ecological niches:* A complex community offers a greater variety of niches than a simple community and promotes greater diversity.
- *Edge effect:* We saw in Chapter 2 how there is always greater diversity in ecotones or transition areas between ecosystems.
- *Geological history:* Old and stable ecosystems like rain forests that have not experienced many changes have high diversity. An ecosystem like the Arctic has undergone many changes and this does not allow many species to establish themselves.

What is the value of biodiversity?

First, let us look at biodiversity purely from the human angle. Clearly, many organisms have utilitarian or instrumental value for us. They provide us with the following:

- Food that is directly eaten by humans, including grains, vegetables, fruits, meat, and fish. This is the consumptive value of biodiversity.
- Goods of various kinds like fuel, timber, paper, and medicines: Most of our current food crops came from wild tropical plants. The majority of the world's poor depends even now on traditional medicines derived from plants. Many of the new drugs developed by the pharmaceutical industry are also from plants and animals. Many useful microbes have been identified: while some are capable of cleaning up oil spills and toxic wastes, others can extract metals from ores. These are examples of productive use of biodiversity.

Ecological services: We have discussed in Chapter 2 the diverse ecological services provided by nature.

Recreation: The biodiversity of the planet enables activities like wildlife tourism, nature photography, trekking, and bird-watching.

Genetic resources: Biotechnology and genetic engineering use the genes of organisms to make new types of crops, medicines, etc.

Option value: We have the option of paying now for the future use of nature. For example, we might contribute now for the establishment of a wildlife park so that we (or the succeeding generations) can use and enjoy the facility later.

What is the medicinal value of biodiversity?   Hundreds of plants are still used in the traditional medicine of the developing countries. More than 60 per cent of the world's population depends directly on plants for their medicines. As a result, people have a vast and unique knowledge of the local plants and their medicinal values.

Modern pharmaceutical companies in the industrialised countries depend heavily on the plants in the developing countries in their search for new drugs. Some examples of plants from which very effective drugs have been developed are:

- rosy periwinkle from Madagascar for leukaemia,

- cinchona for malaria,
- rauwolfia serpentina for hypertension, and
- coca for anaesthesia.

The commercial value of plant-derived medicines is estimated to be US$ 50 billion a year. Yet, all the plants are taken from the poor countries without any compensation to them.

What value can we attach to the sheer beauty of nature and its biodiversity?   This refers to the non-utilitarian or aesthetic value of biodiversity. Just being close to nature gives many of us enjoyment and even spiritual solace. Writers, poets, artists, and composers derive inspiration from nature for their creative work.

> **KEY IDEA**
>
> Biodiversity has utilitarian, aesthetic, and ethical values.

Finally, we can look at biodiversity from the ecosystem point of view. It has then an intrinsic or ethical value. In this view, every species has a value and role in nature. It has a right to exist, whether or not it is known to be useful to humans. In fact, since humans have so much power over nature, they should perhaps conserve all species. The final ethical argument is that all life is sacred and must be protected.

How many species are there in this world?

We do not know exactly how many species inhabit this earth. Estimates range from 4 million to 100 million. The best guess is 10–14 million. Most of the species in the world are insects and microorganisms not visible to the naked eye.

How many species have been identified and named?   So far about 1.8 million species (not including bacteria) have been identified, named and catalogued. These include 270,000 plant species, 45,000 vertebrates, and 950,000 insects. Roughly 10,000 new species are identified every year.

> **KEY IDEA**
>
> Our knowledge of biodiversity is extremely limited.

Overall, our knowledge of species, biomes, and ecosystems is poor. Even out of the identified (1.8 million) species, only a third have been studied to some level. Among these, we understand the exact roles and interactions of just a small number of species. The new field of bioinformatics attempts to bring together all the biodiversity data using computers and information technology (Box 5.1).

BOX 5.1

Career: Bioinformatics

Bioinformatics is an emerging field with new opportunities. It combines biology with computer science and thus uses the power of information technology to study and conserve biodiversity.

Our knowledge of the world's biodiversity is still very poor and what little we know is also scattered in museums and research institutions all over the world. There is an urgent need to collate all the available information on species names, descriptions, distributions, status of populations, habitat requirements, interactions with other species, etc. This is one of the tasks of bioinformatics.

The main objectives of bioinformatics are to:

- Build computer databases to organize and store biological information

Contd

Box 5.1 Contd

- Develop computer tools to find, analyze, and visualize the information
- Communicate the information using the Internet

Two major bioinformatics programmes are the Species 200 Project, which collects baseline data set for studies on global biodiversity and the Global Biological Information Facility, which puts together 300 years of information from museums.

Indigenous knowledge of biodiversity is increasingly recognized as being very important. What was dismissed as primitive knowledge and quackery is now seen as a valuable storehouse of biodiversity knowledge. In agriculture, farmers have experimented over hundreds of years to develop local crop varieties and animal breeds best suited to the local conditions.

In medicine, local communities and medicine men in the villages possess a tremendous amount of knowledge about the uses of herbs and other plants in curing illnesses. In many cases, indigenous knowledge is far ahead of what scientists know. There are initiatives now to use such knowledge and compensate the community (Box 6.1, Chapter 6).

Where is all the biodiversity?

The vast majority of all species are in the developing countries. 50–75 per cent of all species are to be found in the tropical moist forests that account for just 6 per cent of the land area. A handful of soil in a tropical forest contains hundreds of species and more than a million individual organisms.

In the tropics and the sub tropics, where we also find most of the developing countries, there was always evolutionary activity giving rise to a rich biodiversity. Biodiversity is less in the colder northern regions because the recurrent ice ages there slowed down the proliferation of life forms.

The 19 most biodiverse nations of the world are listed in Table 5.1.

Almost all the plants eaten today in Europe originated in the developing countries (Table 5.2). The genetic diversity needed to maintain the world agricultural system is mainly in these places. Most of the medicinal plants too are also found only in the developing countries.

Table 5.1 The Mega-diversity Countries of the World

Australia	Madagascar
Brazil	Malaysia
Cameroon	Mexico
China	Myanmar
Colombia	Peru
Costa Rica	Philippines
Ecuador	South Africa
Ethiopia	Venezuela
India	Zaire
Indonesia	

Table 5.2 Origins of Food Plants

Plant	Place of origin
Potato	Andes, South America
Wheat	Turkey and Afghanistan
Bean	Central America
Coffee	Ethiopia
Soya, Cucumber, Orange	China
Rice	India

What about aquatic biodiversity?

We know very little about aquatic biodiversity, since we have explored and mapped less than 5 per cent of the ocean. Corals reefs, estuaries, and the deep-ocean floor contain enormous amount of biodiversity. The deep ocean species are mostly microbes living under the sea floor in a dark world without oxygen. Biodiversity is high near the coasts too, thanks to a variety of producers, habitats, and nursery areas.

What is the level of biodiversity in India?

India is one of the 19 mega-biodiversity countries and, so far, about 70 per cent of the total area has been surveyed for biodiversity assessment. 45,000 wild species of plants and 81,000 wild species of animals have been identified here. Together they represent 6.5 per cent of the world's biodiversity.

The actual numbers must be much higher since many biologically-rich areas like the Northeast have not been fully explored. The rich biodiversity is attributed to the presence of a variety of ecosystems and climates.

> **KEY IDEA**
> India is one of the 19 mega-biodiversity countries.

18 per cent of all plants found in India (including many flowering plants) are endemic. At least 166 crop species and 320 species of wild relatives of crops originated in India. We also have a large variety of domesticated species. For example, the number of rice varieties alone ranges from 50,000 to 60,000.

What is the biogeographic classification of India?

India can be divided into ten biogeographic zones:
- *Trans-Himalayan:* Extension of the Tibetan Plateau including the high-altitude cold desert in Ladakh and Lahaul-Spiti
- *Himalayas:* The entire mountain chain, diverse biotic provinces and biomes
- *Gangetic Plain:* Ganga River system
- *North-eastern zone:* Plains and non-Himalayan hill ranges
- *Desert:* Arid area west of the Aravalli high range, salty desert of Gujarat and sand desert of Rajasthan
- *Semi-arid zone:* Area between the desert and the Deccan Plateau including the Aravalli range
- *Western Ghats:* Hill ranges and plains running along the western coastline
- *Deccan Peninsula:* South and south-central plateau, south of the Tapti River.
- *Islands:* Andaman and Nicobar Islands
- *Coasts and Lakshadweep Islands*
  Each zone contains distinct species of flora and fauna.

What is meant by the extinction of species?

By extinction, we mean the complete disappearance of a species, that is, not a single member of the extinct species is found on earth. It is an irreversible loss and is called biological extinction.

Before a species goes biologically extinct, it goes through stages of local and ecological extinction. Local extinction means that the species is no longer found in the area it once inhabited. It is, however, present elsewhere in the world. Ecological extinction means that so few members are left that the species can no longer play its normal ecological role in the community.

Extinction is the ultimate fate of all species. Since multi-cellular organisms evolved on earth

570 million years ago, about 30 billion species have lived on this planet. Today, there are only about 14 million of them. This means that 99.9 per cent of all species that ever lived are extinct!

Over the life of the earth, environmental conditions have been changing, gradually or rapidly. Large-scale movement of the continents and climate change are examples. When such changes occur, the affected species must adapt itself, move to a more favourable area, or become extinct.

There are mainly two ways in which species become biologically extinct. Background extinction refers to the gradual disappearance of species due to changes in local environmental conditions. Thus, a process of natural and low-level extinction goes on continuously.

The Père David's Deer are critically endangered in the wild

KEY IDEA

99.9 per cent of all species that ever lived are now extinct.

The rate of background extinction has been generally uniform over long geological periods. On occasions, however, a second type, called a mass extinction, has occurred on earth.

What is a mass extinction?   Mass extinction is characterized by a rate of disappearance significantly higher than the background extinction. It is often a global, catastrophic event, with more than

65 per cent of all species becoming extinct over some millions of years. This is a brief period in geological terms, compared to 4.6 billion years the earth has existed.

Scientists believe that there have been five mass extinctions over the past 500 million years. In each case, the character of ecological communities changed dramatically. After each such extinction, it took 20 to 100 million years for the global biodiversity to recover.

The most severe extinction occurred about 225 millions years ago, when 95 per cent of marine species vanished. The most famous (and the last) mass extinction, however, took place about 65 million years ago, when the giant dinosaurs, which had ruled the world for 140 million years, were wiped out.

The Giant Panda
(Image courtesy: http://commons.wikimedia.org/
wiki/File:Panda_ChiangMaiZoo_humarkus.jpg)

Why did the mass extinctions occur?   Both biological and environmental factors would have led to mass extinctions. The suggested causes include global cooling, falling sea levels, predation, and competition. A more recent theory with considerable supportive evidence is that a giant comet or asteroid hit the earth. This event created huge clouds of dust that blocked out sunlight for so long that the majority of species died.

What is happening now to the world's species?

Before humankind became very active, the world was losing annually one out every million species. In early 20th century, we were perhaps losing one species a year. Now, we are losing one to hundred species a day and soon the rate of extinction is likely to be one thousand each day. These are estimates, but it is definite that we are losing species rapidly.

Over the next 50 to 100 years, as population and resource use grow exponentially, the rate of biodiversity loss will also increase sharply. Biologists estimate that 20 per cent of the current species will be gone by 2030 and 50 per cent by the end of the century. Distinguished scientists like Edward O. Wilson, Richard Leakey, and Norman Myers are convinced that the sixth mass extinction is under way. The effects of human-induced extinction of species will persist for thousands of generations to come.

> **KEY IDEA**
> Human activities are leading to the rapid extinction of many species.

Reports on the state of the world's biodiversity are not encouraging (Boxes 5.2 and 5.3).

BOX 5.2

Global Biodiversity Outlook 3

The Secretariat of the UN Convention on Biological Diversity (Chapter 6) published the Global Biodiversity Outlook 3 in 2010. The Introduction to this Report says in part:

This Outlook presents some stark choices for human societies. On one hand it warns that the diversity of living things on the planet continues to be eroded as a result of human activities. The pressures driving the loss of biodiversity show few signs of easing, and in some cases are escalating. The consequences of current trends are much worse than previously thought, and place in doubt the continued provision of vital ecosystem services.

The poor stand to suffer disproportionately from potentially catastrophic changes to ecosystems in coming decades, but ultimately all societies stand to lose...

...The action taken over the next two decades will determine whether the relatively stable environmental conditions on which human civilization has depended for the past 10,000 years will continue beyond this century. If we fail to use this opportunity, many ecosystems on the planet will move into new, unprecedented states in which the capacity to provide for the needs of present and future generations is highly uncertain.

BOX 5.3

2010 Global Study of Plants

In 2010, the Kew Gardens, UK, together with the Natural History Museum, London and the International Union for Conservation of Nature (IUCN) issued a report on the state of the world's plants. It was a global analysis of extinction risk for the world's plants. The main conclusions were:

- Of almost 4,000 species that were carefully assessed, over one fifth (22 per cent) were rated as threatened ones.

Contd

Box 5.3 Contd

- Plants are more threatened than birds, as threatened as mammals and less threatened than amphibians or corals.
- The most threatened habitat is the tropical rainforest.

- Most threatened species are found in the tropics.
- The most threatening process is man-induced habitat loss, mostly the conversion of natural habitats for agriculture or livestock use.

Many species we never knew about may have become extinct. Again, we can never be sure that a given species has finally become extinct. Members of a species may not be sighted for years and all of a sudden, one member may be found somewhere.

What are keystone species? Keystone species play roles affecting many other organisms in an ecosystem. They determine the ability of a large number of other species to survive. When a keystone species becomes extinct, it could result in a cascade of extinctions of other species.

An example of keystone species is a top predator like the grey wolf. If wolves go locally extinct (say, due to hunting) in an ecosystem, the populations of deer and other herbivores increase exponentially. The grazing pressure then drives many plants to extinction. Next, the small animals and insects that depend on the plants disappear.

What are indicator or sentinel species? They are very sensitive indicators of environmental problems. They give us early warning of problems that could potentially affect other species. Frogs and other amphibians are examples (Read Box 5.4).

BOX 5.4

The story of disappearing frogs: Early warning from a sentinel species

Scientists are puzzled and concerned at two events concerning frogs occurring in recent times: first, the sharp worldwide decline in frog populations and second, the large-scale occurrence of deformities among frogs in some places.

Why should we worry about mere frogs? Frogs and other amphibians are sentinel species, that is, they are very sensitive indicators of environmental problems. They give us early warning of problems that could potentially affect other species.

Amphibians are organisms that can live both on land and in water and include frogs, toads, and salamanders. These cold-blooded organisms first appeared 350 million years ago. There are 5100 known species of amphibians from small frogs to salamanders 1.5 m long. Since frog species live in small, specialized habitats, they are indicators of the environmental conditions in a variety of places.

Frogs are declining in numbers globally
(Image courtesy: http://commons.wikimedia.org/wiki/File:Frog_on_bough.jpg)

Frogs breathe through moist, absorptive, and permeable skins that are sensitive to pollutants

Contd

Box 5.4 Contd

in the environment. They lay gelatinous and unprotected eggs in ponds and these are very vulnerable to radiation and pollution.

Hundreds of amphibian species are vanishing or declining everywhere. According to the World Conservation Union (IUCN), 25 per cent of all known species are extinct, endangered, or vulnerable. In the US, 92 of the 242 native amphibian species are in decline. Worldwide, 32 species have become extinct in the last few decades and more than 200 species are in decline.

What worries scientists is the fact that the decline is not restricted to areas where there is a clear degradation of the environment or high levels of pollution. It is happening even in remote areas in pristine environments and also in protected parks and reserves. For example, all the seven native species in the Yosemite National Park are in trouble.

In 1995, a group of school children in Minnesota, US, discovered a large number of deformed frogs in a pond. In fact, 50 per cent of the leopard frogs in the pond were deformed, while the normal deformity rate is just 1 per cent. Soon, there were similar reports from most other parts of the US. Deformed frogs die early, before they can reproduce, thus leading to a decline in numbers.

Scientists believe that a number of reasons together are causing the problems with frog species. Agricultural pesticides in the water, increase in ultraviolet radiation in the atmosphere, infectious diseases, parasites, habitat loss, alien predators, and other such factors could be acting together on the amphibian populations.

The rapid disappearance of the tough, but sensitive, amphibians indicates a general deterioration of the global environmental health conditions. Further, the adult amphibians play an important role in ecosystems. For example, they eat more insects than birds do. If they die of pesticide poisoning, the many organisms like reptiles and birds that eat them will also be affected. Amphibians are also providers of pharmaceutical products.

What are the causes of biodiversity loss?

The major causes for the decline in biodiversity are the following:
- Habitat loss and degradation:
- Destruction of biodiversity-rich areas like tropical forests
- Destruction of coral reefs and wetlands
- Ploughing of grasslands
- Freshwater fish species threatened because dams and water withdrawals have radically altered river systems
- Pollution of freshwater streams, lakes, and marine habitats

Habitat fragmentation

For a species to survive it requires (among other things) a minimum extent of area in the ecosystem. For example, large animals like elephants and lions require large areas to move about. Due to human impact, many large, continuous areas of habitat are being reduced in extent or divided into patchwork of isolated fragments. This has many effects:
- Species become divided into smaller populations that cannot sustain themselves.
- Smaller fragments mean more edge area and this makes the species more vulnerable to predators and competitors as well as to wind and fire.
- Fragmentation creates barriers that limit the ability of the species to disperse and colonize new areas.
- Migratory birds face the loss of their seasonal habitats.

Commercial hunting and poaching

The illegal world trade in rare and endangered species of plants, birds, and animals is estimated to be US$ 8 billion per year, second only to arms smuggling. In this market, a live mountain gorilla fetches US$ 150,000 and a panda pelt US$ 100,000.

More than 37,000 plant and animal species are affected and these include rhinoceros, tiger, leopard, gorilla, butterfly, frog, tortoise, orchid, cactus, mahogany, etc. In addition, exotic pets and decorative plants are sold to collectors.

The poachers, mostly poor people in developing countries, depend on this trade for their livelihood. They collect specimens indiscriminately, killing young and old, male and female, often using very cruel methods. On an average, for each animal captured alive, 50 others are killed. What is worse, most of the live animals that are captured die in transit.

The tragedy is that the poacher finally gets very little, most of the money going to the middlemen. The country of origin also does not get any benefit, since no taxes or duties are paid. The country only loses its biodiversity for nothing.

Mass killing of birds and animals for sport or for commercial purposes has driven some species like the passenger pigeon to extinction (Read Box 5.5) and endangered others like the whale (Read Box 5.6).

BOX 5.5

The story of the passenger pigeon: Billions today, extinct tomorrow

On March 24, 1900, a young boy in Ohio, US, shot a bird. What was special about it? Well, it was the last wild passenger pigeon on earth. The bird was never seen again in the wild, though there were still some pigeons in zoos. In 1914, Martha, the last passenger pigeon in the world, died in Cincinnati Zoo and you can see the stuffed body in the National Museum of Natural History.

You might still wonder why we should worry about the extinction of a single bird. The passenger pigeon was not just another bird. It was the most abundant bird ever to have inhabited the planet. In the first half of the 19th century, there were 10 billion of them, in huge flocks, some containing more than 2 billion birds! In those days one could see a migrating flock of passenger pigeons that darkened the sky for three full days as they flew past!

How did they disappear? Their meat was good to eat, their feathers made good pillows, and their bones became fertilizer. What is more, it was easy to shoot them, since they moved in such large flocks

Male passenger pigeon

Contd

Box 5.5 Contd

and nested in long and narrow colonies. Their habitat and breeding grounds were also affected as forests were cleared.

From the middle of the 19th century, the hunting of passenger pigeons became big business. Traps, shot guns, dynamite, and even artillery were used to kill them in huge numbers. There was the case of one trapper alone killing three million birds.

In a few decades, billions of birds perished and the species became extinct. There cannot be a more tragic story of humankind's impact on the living organisms of this world.

BOX 5.6

The story of the blue whale: Hunted to extinction?

It is the world's largest animal. When fully grown, it could be 30 m long and weigh the equivalent of 25 elephants. Its heart is the size of a small car and a child can swim through its artery. Today, it is an endangered species.

The blue whale is a remarkable animal. For eight months, it is in the Antarctic, eating millions of krill (very small fish) by filtering them from seawater. Then it moves to warmer waters, where its young are born.

There were 200,000 blue whales before commercial whaling began. Today, the numbers are down to 3000–4000. It has been hunted to near extinction for its oil, meat, and bone. A blue whale matures sexually only when it is 25 and even then, it produces an offspring only every two to five years. Conservationists think that the number left is too few for the population to recover and avoid extinction.

Blue whales were caught in large numbers when they were in groups feeding in the Antarctic. Even otherwise, just due to their size, they are easy to spot and kill. An additional threat is the declining krill population in the Antarctic due to the melting of polar ice.

Whales in general have been under threat. Between 1925 and 1975, 1.5 million whales were killed, placing the many species on the road to extinction. The International Whaling Commission (IWC) was set up in 1946 to fix annual hunting quotas to countries. The IWC, however, had no powers to enforce the quotas.

In 1986, the IWC finally declared a moratorium on whale hunting. There was a sharp decline in the numbers killed. Japan and Norway have continued to hunt and Iceland resumed its practice in 2002. These countries want the IWC ban on hunting and the CITES ban on trading to be lifted citing large figures for current populations.

Conservationists question the IWC figures and argue that any relaxation will lead to overharvesting of all the species. They feel that these peaceful, intelligent, and social animals should be protected for ecological and ethical reasons.

The future of whales remains a question mark.

Introduction of non-native species

When a non-native species is introduced in an ecosystem and it has no predators, competitors, parasites, or pathogens to control its numbers, it can reduce or wipe out many local species. Hundreds of non-native species have been accidentally or intentionally introduced in coastal waters, lakes, and wetlands. Unintentional introduction occurs as stowaways in aircraft, through the ballast water of oil tankers and cargo ships, or as 'hitchhikers' on imported products like wooden packing crates.

In some cases, non-native species are deliberately introduced for getting some benefits. Initially, they may even be useful, but cause problems later by proliferating at the expense of local species.

In 1859, rabbits were introduced in Australia for sport shooting. Since the environment was favourable to them and there were no predators, their population exploded. They destroyed vast areas of rangeland, native wildlife, and sheep ranching. Finally, a disease virus was deliberately introduced to check their growth. We do not know what else the virus did!

Other causes of biodiversity decline

- Growing population and migration of farmers from overpopulated areas to fragile eco-systems
- Pollution or conversion of wetlands
- Over-exploitation of resources like overfishing in the ocean and excessive harvesting of medicinal plants
- Construction of large dams that flood large biodiversity-rich areas

Many species are affected by a combination of these reasons. An example is the decline of birds (Read Box 5.7)

BOX 5.7

The story of disappearing birds: Bleak future for winged wonders

If you like to watch the beauty of an eagle's flight, to listen to the song of a nightingale, or to enjoy the chatter of a parrot, savour the nice feelings. Soon you may not have this pleasure.

1200 bird species, out of 9800 known ones, are likely to become extinct within this century. Over 900 species are already either endangered or critically endangered. About 128 species have vanished over the last 500 years and 103 of them since 1800.

Birds perform valuable ecosystem services like seed dispersal, insect and rodent control, scavenging, and pollination. Many birds are sentinel species that warn us of impending or current problems. They could indicate high acidity levels in water, chemical contamination, arrival of new diseases, and effects of global warming.

Colombia, which has more than 1800 species, is the most bird-diverse country. India, with about 1250 species, ranks among the top ten bird-diverse countries of the world.

- The major threats to birds are:
- Habitat loss and fragmentation
- Introduction of non-native species: bird-eating snakes, rats, cats, mongooses, etc.; insects and pathogens
- Hunting and capture
- Collection for pet trade
- Longline fishing: Thousands of sea birds are caught in hooks and drown.
- Oil spills
- Pesticides and herbicides
- Skyscrapers, towers, and power lines kill millions of migratory birds.

Bird-lovers and bird-watchers all over the world are trying to save the winged wonders. The future, however, looks bleak for birds everywhere.

How do we declare species as being threatened or endangered?

For a species to survive and flourish, enough numbers must be present in the habitat to make reproduction possible. If density and population size fall below threshold values, the numbers start going down.

A threatened or vulnerable species is still found in reasonable size in its natural habitat, but the numbers are declining. Unless conservation measures are taken, it is likely to move into the next category, that is, the endangered list.

A species is declared as endangered when the number of survivors is so small that it could soon become extinct over all or most of its habitat. Unless it is protected, it will move into the critically endangered category, before it goes extinct.

What is a biodiversity hotspot?

If an area is unusually rich in biodiversity (mostly endemic) and this flora and fauna are under a constant threat of overexploitation, it is called a biodiversity hotspot. There are about 25 such hotspots in the world, mostly in the tropical forests.

The biodiversity hotspots together cover just 1.4 per cent of land and yet hold about 60 per cent of the world's biodiversity. One third of known species of the world are endemic to these hotspots.

A major reason why the hotspots are under great threat is that more than a billion people live near these areas in poverty. What is more, the rate of population growth in many of these areas is greater than the world average.

Is the biodiversity of India under threat?

At least 10 per cent of India's plant species and a larger percentage of its animal species are threatened. The cheetah and the pink-headed duck are amongst the well-known species that have become extinct. More than 150 medicinal plants have disappeared in recent decades. 10 per cent of flowering plants, 20 per cent of mammals, and 5 per cent of birds are threatened. Hundreds of crop varieties have disappeared and even their genes have not been preserved.

The biodiversity hotspots in India are the Eastern Himalayas and the Western Ghats. Both contain a large number of endemic species, which are now under threat.

What is the status of plant biodiversity in India? India had tremendous diversity of wild plants and to this farmers had added a large variety of crop species. There were thousands of rice and wheat varieties. As we saw in the beginning of the chapter, the Green Revolution encouraged farmers to plant the new high-yielding varieties (HYVs) replacing the indigenous ones. Over the years, the traditional species have disappeared. In place of 30,000 varieties of rice, Indian farmers now plant just 12 HYVs.

KEY IDEA
India's biodiversity is now under serious threat.

What will be the impact of biodiversity loss?

The poor people in the developing countries, who are dependent on biodiversity for their daily survival, will feel the impact first. Soon, however, the industrialised countries will also start experiencing the effects. Most of their food crops, medicines, textiles, spices, dyes, and paper originate from plants in the developing countries. The destruction of the rainforests means that less carbon will be absorbed and natural climate-control mechanisms are lost. This will have a major impact on the world's climate.

Why should we care? Many scientists and environmentalists believe that the mass extinction that is now underway could be the biggest of our environmental problems. Almost all the other problems are potentially reversible. The loss of biodiversity is not.

The conservationist Norman Myers said, 'We could push back the deserts, restore the topsoil, and allow the ozone layer to be repaired in a century or so. We could restore climate stability in the wake of global warming within a thousand years. But once a species is gone, it is gone for good.'

We will see in the next chapter what the world is doing to conserve biodiversity.

REVIEW: A SUMMARY OF THE KEY POINTS

- The earth's biodiversity is its primary life support system and vital to our survival.
- Biodiversity has instrumental, aesthetic, and ethical values.
- Our knowledge of the world's biodiversity is limited.
- Most of the biodiversity exists in the tropical developing countries and India is one of the mega-diversity countries of the world.

- Biological extinction goes on all the time and most of the species that ever lived are now extinct.
- Five mass extinctions have occurred so far and the sixth one is under way due to several human-induced reasons.
- A large number of species are in the threatened or endangered categories and need urgent conservation.

EXERCISES

Objective-type questions

In each case below, choose the best answer out of the given set of choices:

1. Which of the following statements is **not** true with regard to biodiversity?
   (a) Biodiversity refers to the numbers, variety, and variability of living organisms and ecosystems.
   (b) Biodiversity covers diversity within species and between species.
   (c) Biodiversity is not necessary for human survival.
   (d) Biodiversity covers variation among ecosystems.

2. When we enjoy the diversity in a forest, which kind of value are we placing on biodiversity?
   (a) Aesthetic value
   (b) Instrumental value
   (c) Option value
   (d) Utilitarian value

3. Which of the following statements is **not** true with regard to the species of the world?
   (a) Most of the species in the world are insects and microorganisms not visible to the naked eye.
   (b) We do not know exactly how many species inhabit this earth.
   (c) We have identified most of the species on earth.
   (d) Every year, we identify about 10,000 new species.

4. Where do we find the vast majority of species?
   (a) in the poorer countries.
   (b) in the richer countries.
   (c) in Europe.
   (d) in the US.

5. Which is the first stage in the process of a species becoming irreversibly extinct?
   (a) Ecological extinction
   (b) Mass extinction
   (c) Local extinction
   (d) Biological extinction

6. What is the estimated number of species that we are now losing every year?
   (a) One out of every million
   (b) 350 to 35,000
   (c) 350,000
   (d) One million

Short-answer questions

1. A witty person said that, 'To a first approximation, all species are extinct today'. Is this statement correct? If not, what is the correct situation about the extinction of species?

2. What are the suggested reasons for the five mass extinctions that have occurred so far?

3. How did the Green Revolution affect the diversity of food plants?
4. What are the factors that determine the level of biodiversity in an ecosystem?
5. What are the uses of biodiversity?
6. Distinguish between background extinction and mass extinction.
7. What are the human-induced causes of biodiversity loss?
8. What is the difference between threatened species and endangered ones?

Long-answer questions
1. Describe the different types of extinctions and explain how the coming sixth extinction is different.
2. Extinction is the ultimate fate of all species. Why then are we concerned about the decline of biodiversity?

Think critically: Deeper questions for reflection and discussion
1. Can you think of a situation in which human-induced extinction of a species would be morally justified?
2. Should we allow the patenting of life forms?

SOMETHING DIFFERENT FOR A CHANGE

1. Here are the words of Lao Tzu, the Chinese philosopher of the 6th century B.C., from his book *Tao Te Ching*:

In harmony with Tao
The sky is clear and spacious
The earth is solid and full
All creatures flourish together
Content with the way they are

Endlessly repeating themselves
Endlessly renewed

When humanity interferes with Tao
The sky becomes filthy
The earth becomes depleted
The equilibrium crumbles
Creatures become extinct.

ACTIVITIES

Act: What you can do to conserve biodiversity
1. When you go to the market buy local varieties of food items, fruits and vegetables in preference to those that have come from abroad or from a place very far from your town. Buying local species ensures that the diversity is conserved.
2. Change your food habits and start eating indigenous varieties of rice and wheat. You will be conserving biodiversity and at the same time eating more healthy food.

Learn by doing: Case study/Project
Select a small park or garden in your area. Prepare a biodiversity register: List all the species found in the place, find their scientific names with the help of a botanist and a zoologist. Interview long-term users of the place and find out if any loss of biodiversity has been observed or whether they have noticed new species. Write a report describing your observations and your recommendations for conserving the biodiversity of the place.

LEARN MORE

Books
Leakey, Richard and Roger Lewin 1996, *The Sixth Extinction: Patterns of Life and the Future of Humankind*, Anchor Books, Random House, New York.

Middleton, Nick 1999, *The Global Casino: An Introduction to Environmental Issues*, Second Edition, Arnold, London.

Wilson, Edward O. 2002, *The Future of Life*, Little, Brown, London.

Wilson, Edward O. 2006, *The Creation: An Appeal to Save Life on Earth*, W.W.Norton, New York

Youth, Howard 2003, *Winged Messengers: The Decline of Birds*, World Watch Paper 165, World Watch Institute, Washington, D.C.

Articles

Joshi, Sopan 2004, 'Inevitable Tragedy', *Down To Earth*, Vol.13, No.4, July 15, pp. 13–22. (on farmer suicides in Andhra Pradesh)

Rodgers, W. A. and H.S.Panwar 1988, *Biogeographical Classification of India*, Wildlife Institute of India, Dehradun.

Secretariat of the Convention on Biological Diversity 2010, *Global Biodiversity Outlook 3*, Montreal. (downloadable from www.cbd.int)

Websites

Articles by P.Sainath on farmer suicides: www.indiatogether.org/2004/jul/psa-seeds1.htm

www.indiatogether.org/2004/jul/psa-seeds2.htm

Article by Peter Rosset entitled 'Lessons of Green Revolution': www.foodfirst.org/media/opeds/2000/4–greenrev.html

2010 Report on the state of global plant species: www.kew.org/news/one-fifth-of-plants-under-threat-of-extinction.htm

Film

The State of the Planet: A BBC documentary on biodiversity and other ecological issues presented by David Attenborough.

CHAPTER 6

Biodiversity Conservation

If all mankind were to disappear,
the world would regenerate back to the rich state of equilibrium
that existed ten thousand years ago.
If insects were to vanish,
the environment would collapse into chaos.

Edward O. Wilson
(1929–)
American biologist, conservationist, and author

THIS CHAPTER IS ABOUT...

conservation of biodiversity

THE KEYWORDS AND PHRASES ARE...

in situ conservation   ex situ conservation   biotechnology   intellectual property rights

THE STORY OF OLIVE RIDLEY TURTLES: AN ANNUAL DANCE OF DEATH?

Every year, they visit us in thousands. After travelling thousands of kilometres in the sea to reach the Indian coast, they lay millions of eggs. Thousands of them, however, die gory deaths and are washed ashore. This is the tragic story of the Olive Ridley turtles and their annual migration to the Gahirmatha coast of Orissa.

The Olive Ridley is a small, hard-shelled marine turtle. The most dramatic aspect of its life history is the habit of forming great nesting aggregations, called 'arribadas'. These nesting concentrations occur in Mexico, Costa Rica, Nicaragua, Panama, and India.

It is a threatened or endangered species throughout its range and there is a ban on all Olive Ridley products under the Convention on International Trade in Endangered Animal and Plant Species (Box 6.2 below). In India, the killing or capture of the turtle is punishable under the Wildlife Protection Act, 1972.

The turtles face many threats as they move long distances to their nesting sites:

- In areas where recreational boating and ship traffic is intense, propeller and collision injuries are common.

- Turtles develop problems with their respiration, skin, blood chemistry, salt gland, and other functions due to a variety of reasons:
- Consuming marine debris such as plastic bags, plastic and styrofoam pieces, tar balls, balloons and raw plastic pellets. (Often, such items also contain toxic chemicals.)
- Moving through oil spills
- Ingestion of pesticides, heavy metals, and other toxic chemicals from various sources on land and sea

Orissa is one of the Olive Ridley mass nesting sites hosting as much as 50 per cent of the world's population. Gahirmatha supports perhaps the largest nesting population with an average of 400,000 females nesting in a given year.

The turtles start congregating off the coast by October–November every year. The couples mate in the sea and the females climb on to the sandy beaches to lay their eggs between January and March. A turtle nests up to three times per season, typically producing 100–110 eggs on each occasion.

After the females depart, it takes about 40 days for the eggs to hatch. During this period, the eggs are in danger. Some are washed away, others dry up in the sun, and yet others are eaten by birds and animals. The hatchlings again have a high mortality rate and it is a miracle that many of them make their way to the sea without their mothers to guide them.

The biggest threat to the turtles in Orissa is the mechanized fishing trawler. The turtles are either cut open by the rotary blades of the trawlers or suffocate in the fishing nets. More than 100,000 Olive Ridleys have been killed this way along the Orissa coast during the past ten years. Most of the trawlers operate illegally and they do not also care to use in their nets the turtle exclusion device (TED), which would allow the animals to escape.

There are attempts to save the turtles by the Forest Department as well as environmental organizations. They lack, however, the manpower and infrastructure facilities to monitor 280 km of the coastline. Gahirmatha itself is a marine sanctuary. But that does not seem to help the turtles.

The case of the Olive Ridley shows how difficult it is to conserve biodiversity.

What is the status of world biodiversity?

Let us review what we learnt about biodiversity in the previous chapter:

The biosphere is an extremely complex system with millions of known and unknown species—plants, animals, birds, bacteria, and viruses. Thousands of interactions take place every moment among these organisms and every link in this web is important for keeping the whole system stable.

Humankind has been interfering with the system far too much. They have cut many of the links in the web by destroying species with unknown consequences. Even if we are overestimating biodiversity loss, it is clear that the rate of extinction has gone up sharply due to human activities. We are losing more species than ever before. Instead of arguing over numbers or waiting to get reliable data, we must take precautionary steps to prevent further loss.

What is meant by biodiversity conservation?

KEY IDEA

While in situ conservation protects species where they are, ex situ conservation protects species in a place away from their natural habitat.

In biodiversity conservation, we study how human activities affect the diversity of plants and animals and develop ways of protecting that diversity. Conservation ranges from protecting the populations of a specific species to preserving entire ecosystems.

There are two main types of conservation. In situ (on-site) conservation tries to protect species where they are, that is, in their natural habitat. Ex-situ (off-site) conservation attempts to preserve and protect the species in a place away from their natural habitat. In general, in situ conservation is more cost-effective. In many cases, however, the ex-situ approach may be the only feasible one.

How is conservation done in situ?

In situ conservation requires the identification and protection of natural areas that have high biodiversity. This includes the establishment of national parks and reserves. Over the past few decades, there has been an increase in the number of reserves and the area covered.

The main objective is to preserve large areas of undeveloped land so that the ecosystems and the biodiversity can continue to flourish and evolve. Large animals like elephants need big reserves. Large reserves are also less vulnerable to disturbances, since their edge length is short relative to the area covered. If a reserve is split into patches, then corridors are provided to enable movement of the animals.

In situ conservation through reserves has its limitations. Many reserves do not receive the level of protection and management they need. Widespread encroachment by poachers, settlers, and others continues in many parks. Flora, fauna, as well as resources like wood and minerals continue to be exploited.

The local people living near the reserve are often seen as adversaries and are not involved in the conservation process. The chances of success are higher if the local people are consulted in the planning and design of the reserve. Ideally, the locals must be made partners in conservation. They should be allowed to use part of the reserve or a buffer zone for grazing, timber cutting, agriculture, fishing, etc. They could also be trained as guides and wildlife experts to restore degraded areas.

> **KEY IDEA**
> We do in situ conservation primarily by setting up national parks and reserves.

What is on-farm conservation?   A special case of in situ approach is on-farm conservation, which is a method farmers had been following all along. Faced with the problems of gene banks as well as in situ methods, we have rediscovered the important role of the farmer in biodiversity conservation. In this approach, there is a farmer-scientist partnership to collect, maintain, and improve the traditional plant varieties.

It is impossible to preserve all biodiversity in situ. Given the population and other pressures, we cannot set aside the required huge land area. Ex situ conservation is equally important. In some cases, where the population of a species has dwindled to extremely low levels, ex situ conservation may be the only way out.

How is ex situ conservation practised?

In this approach, we conserve biodiversity in an artificial setting. This includes the storage of seeds in banks, breeding of captive animal species in zoos, and setting up botanical gardens, aquariums, and research institutes.

How do seed banks work?   There are more than 100 seed banks in the world and they hold more than four million seeds maintained at low temperatures and low humidity levels. The majority of the banks are in the industrialised countries or indirectly controlled by them.

The banks store a very large amount of plant genetic material in a small space. The seeds are supposed to be safe from habitat destruction, climate changes, and general destruction. They can even help reintroduce extinct species.

There are, however, many problems with seed banks. Seeds are dried out before storage and some seeds cannot tolerate it. No seed remains alive indefinitely and every seed must be periodically germinated and new seeds collected for storage. This is an expensive and difficult process. It is said that a very large number of seeds in banks have not been germinated or tested for long and many be dead.

Fire accidents or power failures can permanently damage the seeds. One safeguard against such events is to subdivide the sample and store them in different banks. A more intractable problem is that the seeds in a bank have not been evolving in relationship to outer circumstances. When they are later reintroduced into the field, they may be less fit for survival.

Most of the seed banks concentrate on about 100 plants that give 90 per cent of our food. There is a need for many more banks to store many more species, particularly in the developing countries. In spite of the problems and limitations, however, seed banks remain an important method of preserving biodiversity for the future. If they are not managed properly, however, they may be giving us a false reassurance that we are conserving biodiversity.

The Great Banyan Tree at the Kolkata Botanical Gardens
(Image courtesy: http://commons.wikimedia.org/wiki/
File:Great_banyan_tree_kol.jpg)

KEY IDEA
Ex situ conservation is attempted by establishing seed banks, zoos, botanical gardens, aquariums, and research institutes.

What is the role of zoos in biodiversity conservation? Along with many other animals, zoos often preserve a few individuals of critically endangered species. If an animal breeds in captivity, the zoo may ultimately reintroduce the species into protected reserves.

Zoos need large spaces and huge funds. Only a small percentage of endangered species can be protected in zoos. The public tends to support the saving of large or popular species like the tiger, elephant, and panda. There is not much interest in protecting smaller or less attractive species, even if they are known to be very important for the ecosystem.

What about botanical gardens? There are over 1600 botanical gardens in the world, holding four million plants. They cover about 80,000 species or 30 per cent of all known species. The largest one is Kew Gardens in England, which has 25,000 species. When Britain was an imperial power, large numbers of plant species were taken from the colonies to the Kew Gardens.

Botanical gardens have a significant educational value for scientists and students. Like zoos, botanical gardens too face the problems of funds and space. They increasingly focus on rare and endangered species.

How can we use indigenous knowledge to conserve biodiversity? As discussed in Chapter 5, the best approach is to:
- involve local communities in the conservation process as partners,
- make use of their traditional knowledge (especially in medicine) for documenting the value of diverse organisms and for developing new products, and
- compensate the communities for the knowledge they have shared (Read about the Kani-TBGRI case in Box 6.1.).

BOX 6.1

The story of the Kanis: Compensating indigenous knowledge

In December 1987, a team of scientists were on a botanical expedition in the Western Ghats in Kerala. They had taken with them a few members of the Kani tribe as their guides. The scientists noticed that the guides were eating a fruit that seemed to keep them energetic even during tough treks. When the scientists tried it, they too felt a 'sudden flush of energy and strength'.

Initially, the Kanis were reluctant to reveal any information about the plant, saying that it was a sacred tribal secret not to be revealed to outsiders. After considerable persuasion, the tribals showed the team the plant Aarogyappacha as the source of the fruit.

The scientists, who were from the Tropical Botanic Garden and Research Institute (TBGRI), secured specimens of the plant and conducted investigations. They found anti-stress and other beneficial properties in the plant's active ingredients. Using Aarogyappacha and three other medicinal plants, they formulated a drug and gave it the name Jeevani.

TBGRI gave the right to manufacture the drug to a private company, Arya Vaidya Pharmacy (AVP) for a licence fee of Rs 10 lakh and a royalty of 2 per cent. The Institute, however, wanted the Kanis to get a part of the benefits as compensation for sharing their knowledge of the plant and its properties. The Kanis were to receive half the fee and half the royalty. This was the first case of an indigenous community receiving compensation in exchange for their traditional knowledge of plants and their uses.

The Kanis formed a trust, which would use the money for promoting the welfare of the community, preparing a biodiversity register to document their knowledge, and promoting conservation of biodiversity.

The arrangement has faced many problems, but it is a landmark attempt to ensure that indigenous communities get benefits from sharing their knowledge of biodiversity.

There is an international movement to conserve biodiversity through measures like documenting indigenous knowledge, assisting local communities to grow medicinal plants, make medicines and market them, saving and propagating traditional seeds, reintroducing traditional food items through restaurants. 'Seeds for Change' in the US and the Kokopelli Association in France are examples.

What is being done to protect wildlife?

Many countries have declared certain areas as reserves and restricted human activities in those areas. There are several thousands of national parks, sanctuaries, wildlife refuges, and wilderness areas in the world. They are partially or fully protected and they cover about one billion ha.

Many of the reserves are too small to sustain large species or they are too poorly protected. The developing countries have the maximum biodiversity, but they do not have enough funds and, in many cases, the expertise needed to manage protected areas well. Most reserves in the poorer countries suffer encroachment by land grabbers, loggers, miners, and poachers.

Why is it difficult to protect marine biodiversity?

We continue to view the sea as a huge natural resource that can absorb unlimited amounts of waste and pollution. Unfortunately, the damage to marine biodiversity is not visible to most people. At the same time, there is a tremendous pressure to expand human activities on the coast (Chapter 4).

What are the international efforts in biodiversity conservation?

In 1980, three organizations—United Nations Environment Programme (UNEP), World Conservation Union (IUCN), and World Wide Fund for Nature (WWF)—together prepared a World Conservation Strategy. It was a plan to conserve biodiversity, preserve vital ecosystem processes on which all life depends for survival, and develop sustainable uses of organisms and ecosystems. In 1991, they published a new version of this document entitled 'Caring for the Earth'.

Following the publication of the World Conservation Strategy and the holding of conferences like the 1992 Earth Summit, several international agreements and global initiatives have focussed on biodiversity conservation. The major ones are discussed below.

Convention on International Trade in Endangered Species of Wild Fauna and Flora (CITES)

This Convention has been in force since 1975 and 175 countries have signed it. Even though enforcement is difficult, CITES has helped reduce trade in many threatened species including elephants, crocodiles and chimpanzees (Box 6.2).

BOX 6.2

The story of CITES: Stop the trade, save the species

In 1989, the African elephant was declared as an endangered species. The elephants were disappearing primarily due to the ivory trade. By 2000, however, the elephant population had recovered in Namibia, Botswana, and Zimbabwe. This is one of the success stories of CITES, the Convention on International Trade in Endangered Species of Wild Fauna and Flora.

Beginning with 21 countries in 1975, CITES had 175 signatories in 2010. The Convention bans the hunting, capturing, and selling of endangered or threatened species. It lists over 900 species that cannot be traded as live specimens or wildlife products. It restricts the international trade of 29,000 other species that are potentially threatened.

The African elephant
(Image courtesy: http://commons.wikimedia.org/wiki/File:Elephant_near_ndutu.jpg)

Under the Convention, each country is bound to pass laws according to the CITES guidelines and many countries have done so. Enforcement of the laws is, however, lax in many countries, and even when a violator is caught, the penalties are mild. Further, a member country can exempt itself from protecting any of the listed species. Trade in endangered species still goes on, especially in countries that have not joined CITES.

Returning to the African elephant case, the recovery of the population is also causing a problem. In some places, the area is not enough for the large herds. They uproot many small trees, which in turn affect many other species. The local people want to hunt some of the elephants to keep the numbers down and to get economic benefits. In 1997, CITES moved the African elephant to a less restrictive, but a potentially threatened list, allowing the sale of stockpiled ivory to Japan.

Any ban on hunting and trading can only be a short-term measure. The better way is to educate consumers to stop buying the illegal products. If the prices and the market decline, the illegal trade will also stop.

UN Convention on the Law of the Sea (UNCLOS)

Thanks to UNCLOS (discussed in Chapter 4), countries now have jurisdiction over their territorial seas as well as their Exclusive Economic Zones. In effect, 36 per cent of the ocean surface area and 90 per cent of the fish stocks come under the control of individual countries. This provides a great opportunity for each country to protect its marine biodiversity (or to overexploit it!).

International Convention for the Control and Management of Ships' Ballast Water and Sediments

When a ship unloads at a port, its hull must be filled with water to maintain the ship's stability. As the ship then moves to another port, thousands of organisms travel with the water. When the ship takes in a new load at its destination, the ballast water and the organisms are released into the local waters. We saw in Chapter 5 how non-native species can destroy many local species.

The objective of the Convention on Ballast Water, adopted by 74 countries in February 2004, is to prevent, minimize, and ultimately eliminate the transfer of harmful aquatic organisms and pathogens through the control and management of ships' ballast water and sediments. Under the Convention, ships must have facilities to treat the ballast water before releasing it in foreign waters.

Convention concerning the Protection of the World Cultural and Natural Heritage

Adopted by UNESCO in 1972, this Convention seeks to encourage the identification, protection, and preservation of cultural and natural heritage around the world considered to be of outstanding value to humanity.

A number of the sites in the Heritage list are nature parks and reserves that conserve biodiversity. UNESCO's Man and the Biosphere Programme is a major effort in biodiversity conservation (Box 6.3).

BOX 6.3

The story of Man and the Biosphere Programme: Protect biospheres, save species

Alarmed at the rapid degradation of many ecosystems of the world, the United Nations Educational Scientific and Cultural Organization (UNESCO) began the Man and the Biosphere Programme in 1971. The plan was to establish at least one (ideally, five or more) biosphere reserves in each of the Earth's 193 bio-geographical zones. Each protected biosphere should be large enough to prevent gradual species loss and should combine conservation and sustainable use.

Each reserve must be nominated by the national government and should meet the basic requirements. It will contain three zones:

- *Core area:* The most important and fragile part of the ecosystem, which should be legally protected from all human activities, except research and monitoring

- *Buffer Zone 1:* The area in which non-destructive research, education, recreation, sustainable logging, agriculture, livestock grazing, hunting and fishing could be permitted as long as the activity does not harm the core area.

- *Buffer Zone 2:* The transition zone, in which conservation could be combined with more intensive and yet sustainable forestry, agriculture, grazing, hunting, fishing, and recreation

As of October 2010, there were 562 biosphere reserves in 109 countries. The seven Indian biospheres are Nilgiris, Nanda Devi, Sundarbans, Gulf of Mannar, Pachmarhi, Nokrek, and Simlipal. The major problem has been raising funds from local and outside sources to keep each biosphere going.

Other treaties that promote biodiversity conservation are the Convention on Wetlands (Chapter 4) and the Convention on the Conservation of Migratory Species of Wild Animals (1983).

The United Nations Environment Programme (UNEP) has initiated many regional agreements to protect large marine areas shared by countries. Under the UNESCO Man and the Biosphere Programme, many of the designated reserves are coastal or marine habitats. In addition, the World Conservation Union supports 1300 Marine Protected Areas covering about 0.2 per cent of the ocean area.

All these steps led finally to the Convention on Biological Diversity.

What is the Convention on Biological Diversity?

After five years of international negotiations, the Convention on Biological Diversity (CBD) was approved in 1992 at the Earth Summit in Rio de Janeiro and came into force in 1993. As of October 2010, 193 countries are parties to the Convention. India ratified it in 1994. The US signed the Convention in 1993, but has not ratified it.

The Convention has three main goals:

- Conservation of biodiversity
- Sustainable use of the components of biodiversity
- Sharing the benefits arising from the commercial and other utilization of genetic resources in a fair and equitable way.

Under the Convention, governments undertake to conserve and sustainably use biodiversity. They are required to develop national biodiversity strategies and action plans, and to integrate these into broader national plans for environment and development.

Other treaty commitments include:

- Identifying and monitoring the important components of biological diversity that need to be conserved and used sustainably.
- Establishing protected areas to conserve biological diversity while promoting environmentally sound development around these areas.
- Rehabilitating and restoring degraded ecosystems and promoting the recovery of threatened species in collaboration with local residents.
- Respecting, preserving and maintaining traditional knowledge of the sustainable use of biological diversity with the involvement of indigenous peoples and local communities.
- Preventing the introduction of, controlling, and eradicating alien species that could threaten ecosystems, habitats or species.
- Controlling the risks posed by organisms modified by biotechnology.
- Promoting public participation, particularly when it comes to assessing the environmental impacts of development projects that threaten biological diversity.
- Educating people and raising awareness about the importance of biological diversity and the need to conserve it.
- Reporting on how each country is meeting its biodiversity goals.

While CBD is a step forward, it has some drawbacks and implementation problems:

- It excludes the existing gene bank collections. Thus, four million seeds, which are also of high commercial value, are outside the control of CBD.

KEY IDEA

The Convention on Biological Diversity is the main international agreement for conserving global biodiversity.

- It encourages bilateral agreements, even though many biodiversity issues are regional or global. This has led to some poor countries signing agreements with rich countries or big corporations giving away the rights over their biodiversity.
- As with many international agreements, the implementation of CBD has also been slow and poor. The Convention does not provide for severe penalties for violations, nor does it have an enforcement mechanism.

What actions have we taken to conserve India's biodiversity?

The first protected area in the country was the Corbett National Park, established in 1936. Currently, there are more than 90 national parks, 350 wildlife sanctuaries, and 15 biospheres covering about 5 per cent of the land. In addition, there are several reserve forests.

In the national parks, habitations and private ownership of land are not permitted. Traditional activities like grazing and fuelwood collection are also prohibited. On the other hand, in sanctuaries some activities are permitted.

A biosphere belongs to the third category of protected areas. Here the wild flora and fauna are protected, but the people are allowed to live in the area and carry on their traditional activities. Table 6.1 lists the biosphere reserves of India.

Table 6.1   Biosphere Reserves of India

S.No.	Name of the site	Area in sq. km	Location (State or States)
1	Achanakamar—Amarkantak	3,800	Madhya Pradesh, Chattisgarh
2	Agasthyamalai	1,800	Kerala
3	Dehang Debang	5,100	Arunachal Pradesh
4	Dibru-Saikhowa	770	Assam
5	Great Nicobar	900	Andaman and Nicobar Islands
6	Gulf of Mannar	10,500	Tamil Nadu
7	Kanchanjanga	2,600	Sikkim
8	Manas	2,800	Assam
9	Nanda Devi	5,900	Uttaranchal
10	Nilgiri	5,500	Tamil Nadu, Kerala, and Karnataka
11	Nokrerk	800	Meghalaya
12	Pachmarhi	4,900	Madhya Pradesh
13	Rann of Kuchch	12,500	Gujarat
14	Similpal	4,400	Orissa
15	Sunderbans	9,600	West Bengal

In addition, there are special projects to protect certain animal species like the tiger and the elephant. For example, Project Tiger attempts to save the Indian tiger from extinction (Box 6.4).

BOX 6.4

The story of Project Tiger: More reserves, less tigers

The Sariska Tiger Reserve in Rajasthan is one of the 40 tiger reserves under Project Tiger. This Project was established in 1973 by the Government of India to conserve this endangered species.

According to official figures, India's tiger population has declined from roughly 40,000 a century ago, to about 3,700 now. Conservationists, in fact, believe that less than 2,000 are left.

In 2003, there were about 25 tigers in Sariska. In September 2004, the Wildlife Institute of India, Dehra Dun, sent a group of its students to the Sariska Reserve for training. The students trekked though 860 sq km of the reserve, but could not see a single tiger.

When the news of the missing tigers came out, the park authorities made frantic searches. The Rajasthan government continued to insist that there was evidence of tigers inside the Sariska Tiger Reserve. Yet, a survey carried out by the World Wild Fund for Nature (WWF) said that there was no evidence of any tigers in Sariska.

Prime Minister Manmohan Singh wanted immediate action by both the central government and state authorities. He called it the 'biggest crisis in the management of our wildlife' since the launch of Project Tiger and suggested immediate measures.

Meanwhile, tigers were reported missing in other reserves like Ranthambore, Simlipal, and Panna. The Central Bureau of Investigation began an inquiry. A gang of poachers were arrested in Jabalpur. The Prime Minister set up a Tiger Task Force.

The Task Force Report said that Sariska was just one example of the total collapse of the tiger conservation system. The report emphasized the close connection between the animals and the forest people. It wanted the forest-dwellers to be relocated wherever possible to relieve the pressure on the forests and tigers. However, this cannot be done everywhere due to the scarcity of land and the lack of funds. In most places, the forest must be shared between the people and the tigers, so that both can coexist.

Conservationists feel, however, that such coexistence will only harm both. Coexistence was possible in the past when forest-dwellers were few in number and did not exploit the resources. Now, the population is high, forests are shrinking, and there are also poachers. Exclusive tiger reserves are needed.

Keep the tigers in separate reserves or coexist with them? The debate goes on. Meanwhile, the number of tigers is shrinking.

KEY IDEA

We have established a large number of national parks, sanctuaries, and biospheres in India for protecting biodiversity.

What about ex situ conservation in India? There are 35 botanical gardens and 275 zoos, deer parks, safari parks, and aquaria. Two institutions engaged in conservation are the National Bureau of Plant Genetic Resources, New Delhi and the National Bureau of Animal Genetic Resources, Karnal.

How is indigenous knowledge being used to conserve biodiversity? Many local communities and voluntary organizations are now promoting conservation and sustainable use of biodiversity.

In 1996, the village of Pattuvam in Kerala created history by declaring its absolute ownership over all the genetic materials currently growing within its jurisdiction. The villagers had earlier prepared a detailed register of all the species found within the village. The village also set up a Forum for the Protection of People's Biodiversity, which would henceforth have to be consulted by any person or company who seeks access to the register and the genetic material it lists.

There are efforts all over India to document local biodiversity and indigenous knowledge. Some of the organizations involved in such work are the Foundation for the Revitalisation of Local Health Traditions and Green Foundation in Bangalore, Centre for Indian Knowledge Systems in Chennai, Beej Bachao Andolan in Tehri Garhwal, and Navadanya in Dehra Dun. Annadana (in Auroville near Puducherry) is the base of the South Asian Network of Soil and Seed Savers, established with the help of Kokopelli Association of France.

What has India done under the Convention on Biological Diversity?

In May 1994, India became a party to the Convention. In January 2000, the government released the National Policy and Action Strategy on Biodiversity. This document seeks to consolidate the on-going efforts of conservation and sustainable use of biodiversity and to establish a policy and programme regime for the purpose.

The Indian Parliament passed the Biodiversity Bill in December 2002. The main intent of this legislation is to protect India's rich biodiversity and associated knowledge. It seeks to check biopiracy and to prevent the use of our biodiversity by foreign individuals and organizations without sharing the benefits with us. One thrust area is the conservation of medicinal plants.

Foreigners running away with medicinal plants   *Exploitation by pharma companies*

The Government prepared a National Biodiversity Strategy and Action Plan in 2004, but has not implemented it (Box 6.5).

BOX 6.5

National Biodiversity Strategy and Action Plan

As required by the Convention on Biological Diversity, a National Biodiversity Strategy and Action Plan (NBSAP) for India was finalized in 2004. The NBSAP process was carried out by the Ministry of Environment and Forests (MoEF), Government of India, under sponsorship of the Global Environment Facility (GEF) through the United Nations Development Programme (UNDP). In a unique arrangement, Kalpavriksh, a non-governmental organization, undertook its technical coordination.

Based in Delhi and Pune, Kalpavriksh is an action group working on environmental education,

research, campaigns, and direct action since 1979. Kalpavriksh has been working on a number of local, national, and global issues.

The NBSAP process involved consultations and planning with thousands of people across the country, including tribal (adivasi) and other local communities, NGOs, government agencies, academics and scientists, corporate houses, students, armed forces, and other sections of society.

In order to reverse the erosion of biodiversity in India, the Action Plan focuses on three basic goals: conservation of biodiversity, sustainable use of

Contd

Box 6.5 Contd

biological resources, and equity in conservation and use.

Some important measures suggested in the Plan are:

• Restoration and regeneration of degraded ecosystems
• Recognition of community rights
• Development of alternative intellectual rights systems appropriate for indigenous knowledge

• Balancing of local, national, and international interests related to biodiversity
• Respect for cultural diversity
• Preventing deprivation of indigenous people from natural resources

Unfortunately, the NBSAP has not been implemented. It is time to revive it and take action to save India's biodiversity.

What is biotechnology?

Genes are the basic units through which an organism passes on its characteristics to its offspring. The pattern of genes in a plant or animal determines its potential physical shape, growth, and behaviour.

Biotechnology or genetic engineering manipulates the genes in an organism to change its characteristics. It can move a favourable gene from one organism to another. For example, biotechnology can make a plant resistant to specific pests or diseases. It can also produce new varieties of plants with some desired characteristics.

What are the benefits expected from biotechnology? Biotechnology claims to bring benefits in food, agriculture, and health. In agriculture, some possible products are the following:

• New crop varieties to double or triple yields per ha with less inputs
• Super plants that would produce their own fertilizer and pesticide.
• Plants adapted to grow in poor soils

What is the role of biotechnology with reference to biodiversity conservation?

Traditionally, farmers were always improving plant characteristics through methods like crossbreeding. This process, however, took many generations. Biotechnology enables a quicker and more focused way of modifying the genetic structure of plants and animals. It also provides techniques for moving genes between organisms that do not exchange genes naturally.

Biotechnology could lead to new and improved methods for preserving plant and animal diversity. By increasing the value of biodiversity, it could lead to better conservation.

What are the problems with biotechnology? Biotechnology is largely under the control or private industry in the richer countries. Their objective is to make products for the global market. Hence, their research favours uniformity over diversity.

Biotechnology companies prefer mass production of genetically identical seeds. Such seeds may not be appropriate to the small farmer in a developing country, whose needs are location-specific.

A more serious problem, however, is the patenting of seeds. Traditionally, the farmer had full control over the seeds. He retained apart of the harvest as seeds for the next year. Now, seeds are increasingly becoming commodities that the farmer has to buy every year.

Can seeds be patented?   Many countries like the US allow the patenting of seeds. There have been major controversies when American firms tried to patent Indian varieties like Basmati rice and turmeric. The patenting of plants or any life form is a complex issue.

Biotechnology can have serious impact on the developing countries in other ways too. For example, sweeteners developed from corn and other crops grown in the US have replaced sugar imports from the Caribbean and the Philippines. This has been a disaster for those economies. New substances, thousands of times sweeter than sugar, are now being developed using genes taken from tropical plants. They may mean an end to the sugar industry itself.

What are the basic issues in protecting wild flora and fauna?

There is often a conflict between conservation efforts and the livelihood issues of local communities. People capture or kill endangered animals often because of two related reasons: The poverty of the people combined with the willingness of rich to pay huge money for the products. What choice does the poor person have?

Should we try to protect all the endangered and threatened species?

From an ethical point of view, all life is sacred and must be protected. From a practical point of view, we are forced to decide which species we want to save. Money, scientific information, and trained personnel to do the job—all are in short supply. Clearly, we will be able to save only a limited number of species.

How do we choose the species we would try to save?   We need some criteria on which to base our choice. From a human point of view, we could choose those species that give us benefits now or likely to be useful in the future. The problem is that we do not have enough knowledge about the possible uses of thousands of species.

From a nature point of view, we could select those that are of most value to the ecosystem that is, the keystone species (Chapter 5). This may turn out to be good for the humans too. Another way is to simply choose species that have the best chance of survival. Given our constraints, it may be better to concentrate on a few strong species instead of many weak ones.

Ending on a hopeful note: Positive stories

1. Bhutan has taken very positive steps to conserve its rich biodiversity (Box 6.6).
2. One dedicated individual, Romulus Whitaker, has taken extraordinary efforts to protect snakes and crocodiles from becoming extinct (Box 6.7).

BOX 6.6

The story of Bhutan: Immense biodiversity, effective conservation

Bhutan or the Thunder Dragon, with its thick forest cover and immense biodiversity, is called the 'oxygen tank' or the carbon sink (Carbon cycle, Chapter 2) of the world. Out of an area of 40,000 sq km, 72 per cent is under forest cover. This ecosystem supports 7,000 species of plants, 165 species of mammals, and 700 species of birds. No wonder it is one of the 18 biodiversity hotspots of the world.

The diversity can be explained by Bhutan's wide range in altitude, topography, and climate. There are three climatic zones: sub-tropical, mid-mountain, and alpine. While the southern foothills get as much as 5,000 mm of annual rainfall, the northern regions receive as little as 500 mm. Numerous streams originate in the mountains, becoming six rivers that flow into India.

The Royal Government of Bhutan is fully committed to the conservation of the country's rich biodiversity. As early as 1964, Bhutan established two protected areas. In a major revamp In 1993, the country set up four national parks, four wildlife sanctuaries, and one protected area covering 10,513 sq km. Again, in November 2000, the government extended protection to a network of biological corridors, connecting key tiger habitats (with a population of 115–150 tigers). Now 35 per cent of the country's area is protected.

The government is determined to maintain a forest cover of at least 60 per cent with the cooperation of local communities. They face, however, many challenges like the fuelwood and timber needs of a growing population, smuggling of timber into India, and the entry of Tibetans who collect the valuable medicinal plants. Yet, Bhutan is a rare biologically diverse country that has an active programme of conservation. It may show the way to the rest of the world.

BOX 6.7

The story of Romulus Whitaker: Conserving snakes and crocodiles

The Irulas in Tamil Nadu are expert snake catchers. For long they were catching hundreds of snakes and selling them to the flourishing skin trade. When the trade in snakeskin was banned, they lost their livelihood.

At that point, Romulus Whitaker entered their lives. He helped them set up the Irula Cooperative Society for extracting snake venom and selling it to the institutes that make life-saving anti-venom. It was a win-win formula, since the killing of snakes stopped and the Irulas had a profitable occupation.

Romulus Whitaker came to India when he was seven. From his childhood, he had a natural affinity for snakes and in fact for all wildlife. When he was a school student in Kodaikanal, he used to wander in the Palani Hills and picked up the observation skills needed for dealing with wildlife. Later, he learnt snake-catching from Irulas and crocodile-catching from the natives of Papua New Guinea.

In 1972, Whitaker and some friends set up the Madras Snake Park in Chennai. Most of the snake-keepers in the Park are Irula tribals. The Park has 31 species of Indian snakes, all the three species of Indian crocodiles, four species of exotic crocodiles, and three species of Indian turtles.

Many species of reptiles including endangered species like the Indian python have been bred in captivity in the Snake Park. The offspring have been either released into the wild or made available for exchange with other Zoos.

Whitaker next established the Crocodile Bank, also in Chennai. In the early 1970s the crocodile was facing extinction in the country. The Crocodile Bank supplied breeding populace for restarting the species in Tamil Nadu as well as in the other parts of the country. Later, it became an international Crocodile Bank, gathering species, which were endangered in other countries as well.

Contd

Box 6.7 Contd

The Bank now has crocodiles from all over the world and has become a gene pool for all species. At the same time it is also a vibrant educational institution, because over 500,000 visitors come here every year. For the first time they encounter crocodiles as a non-menacing, interesting, and potentially viable animal, in terms of their ecological diversity.

Whitaker's life and work show that a single individual can make enormous contribution to biodiversity conservation through passion and dedication.

REVIEW: A SUMMARY OF THE KEY POINTS

- We can protect species in their habitat or away from their habitat and each method has its place.
- While there has been an increase in the number and area covered by the world's reserves, the management of many of the reserves is not satisfactory.
- Seed banks, zoos, and botanical gardens are important for biodiversity conservation, but they are beset with many difficulties.
- There are a range of international conventions and agreements to promote biodiversity conservation, the most important being the Convention on Biological Diversity (CBD).
- Under CBD, India has prepared a National Biodiversity Strategy and Action Plan.
- India has taken measures like the creation of biosphere reserves, protected areas, zoos, and botanical gardens for conserving biodiversity.
- Biotechnology promises immense benefits for agriculture, food production, and health, but brings with it many problems too.

EXERCISES

Objective-type questions

In each case below, choose the best answer out of the given set of choices:

1. Which of the following methods is **not** in situ conservation?
   (a) Setting up a national park
   (b) Establishing a reserve forest
   (c) Setting up a biosphere reserve
   (d) Building a seed bank

2. Which of the following methods is **not** ex situ conservation?
   (a) Breeding animals in a zoo
   (b) Setting up a botanical garden
   (c) Establishing a national park
   (d) Setting up an aquarium

3. Which is the most important international agreement for conserving all biodiversity?
   (a) Convention on Biological Diversity
   (b) CITES
   (c) UNCLOS
   (d) Convention on Ballast Water

4. Which of the following measures is **not** a part of India's National Biodiversity Strategy and Action Plan?
   (a) Restoration and regeneration of degraded ecosystems
   (b) Recognition of community rights
   (c) Preventing deprivation of indigenous people from natural resources
   (d) Allowing free export of medicinal plant species.

Short-answer questions

1. Distinguish between in situ and ex situ conservation. Explain the advantages and disadvantages of each approach.

2. What are the threats faced by the Olive Ridley turtles on the Orissa coast? What are the difficulties in saving them from being killed?

3. What are the main provisions of the Convention on Biological Diversity?

4. What are the benefits and problems of biotechnology?

Long-answer questions

1. Describe the major international efforts to save biodiversity. What has been the role of India in these efforts?
2. Describe the measures taken by India to save our biodiversity.

Think critically: Deeper questions for reflection and discussion

1. Diversity is not just about plants and animals. There is also human cultural diversity. The communities of this world differ in their agricultural practices, food habits, religion, spirituality, beliefs, medical systems, languages, literature, art, music, etc. This cultural diversity is also being threatened. Languages are becoming extinct, traditional knowledge of plants and their medicinal uses are being forgotten, and indigenous seeds are disappearing. Should this cultural diversity be conserved and if so, how can we do it?
2. Can we at all conserve all species? If that is not possible, how do we choose the species we should protect?

SOMETHING DIFFERENT FOR A CHANGE

1. Read, reflect, and puzzle over the following poem by the British poet Gerard Manley Hopkins (1844–1889):

Inversnaid

This darksome burn, horseback brown,
His rollrock highroad roaring down,
In coop and in comb the fleece of his foam
Flutes and low to the lake falls home.

A windpuff-bonnet of fawn-froth
Turns and twindles over the broth
Of a pool so pitchblack, fell-frowning
It rounds and rounds Despair to drowning.

Degged with dew, dappled with dew
Are the groins of the braes that the brook treads through,
Wiry heathpacks, flitches of fern,
And the beadbonny ash that sits over the burn.

What would the world be, once bereft
Of wet and of wildness? Let them be left,
O let them be left, wildness and wet;
Long live the weeds and the wilderness yet.

2. Read the classic books on tigers and wildlife by Jim Corbett and Kenneth Anderson and the recent *The Illustrated Tigers of India* by Valmik Thapar.

ACTIVITIES

Act: What you can do to conserve biodiversity

1. Do not buy any product made from killing endangered animal species. This includes products made from ivory,
2. Find out more about citizens' movements aimed at conserving biodiversity and join one of them as a volunteer. For example:
   (a) If you are in South India, join the movement to save the Silent Valley.
   (b) If you are in Orissa, join the groups trying to save the Olive Ridley turtles
   (c) If you are in Chennai, find out if you can help the Snake Park or the Crocodile Bank; you can also join the Turtle Watch on the Chennai beach

3. Volunteer for the 'Kids for Tigers' Programme, promoted by Sanctuary Asia magazine. The programme aims to bring out the vital connection between the survival of the tiger and the ecological security of the Indian subcontinent. (www.kidsfortigers.org)

Learn by doing: Case study / Project

Choose a small village and prepare a detailed biodiversity register listing the species found within the boundaries of the village. Take the help of a biologist to identify the plants. Before starting the project, discuss the issues of biodiversity and biopiracy with the villagers and explain the advantages of preparing a register. Involve the villagers, especially the youth, in the project.

Organize together: Eco-club activities and projects

Observe the International Day of Biological Diversity on May 22. This observance is supported by the Secretariat for the Convention on Biological Diversity. It is an opportunity to strengthen people's commitment and actions for the conservation of the world's biological diversity. Each year the Secretariat chooses a theme and provides posters and promotional material.

You could celebrate the day by organizing:

• meetings and lectures on the theme of biodiversity

• an excursion to a biodiversity-rich area with experts as guides

• activities for children;

• environmental clean-up activities.

You could also plan the Day as a people's event with colourful activities such as street rallies, bicycle parades, green concerts, essays, and poster competitions in schools, media events, tree planting, and public events in parks, nature conservancies and botanic gardens.

LEARN MORE

Book

UNEP, IUCN and WWF 1991, *Caring for the Earth: A Strategy for Sustainable Living,* United Nations Environment Programme, Nairobi, Kenya.

Articles

Anuradha, R.V. 2000, Sharing the Benefits of Biodiversity: The Kani—TBGRI Deal in Kerala, India, *Kalpavriksh*, Pune.

Das, Prafulla 2001, 'Orissa turtles: Dance of death', The Hindu Survey of the Environment 2001, *The Hindu*, Chennai, pp. 149–154.

Johnsingh, A.J.T. and Deki Yonten 2004, 'Beautiful Bhutan', *Frontline*, Vol. 21, No. 18, September 10, pp. 65–72.

Websites

CITES: www.cites.org

Convention on Biological Diversity: www.biodiv.org

Foundation for the Revitalisation of Local Health Traditions: www.frlht-india.org

International Convention for the Control and Management of Ships' Ballast Water and Sediments: http://globallast.imo.org/index.asp

Kalpavriksh: www.kalpavriksh.org

Project Tiger and the Task Force Report: http://projecttiger.nic.in/

Films

Rhino Rescue, a film by Dereck and Beverly Joubert for National Geographic Channel. This is a story of hope in Africa, the up and down tale of rhinos in Botswana. The rhinos are now back in Botswana having dodged extinction for the third time.

The Truth About Tigers, a film by the conservationist and film maker Shekar Dattatri. (www.thetruthabouttigers.org)

Module 4

Renewable and Non-renewable Natural Resources

CHAPTER 7

Water Resources

If there is magic in this planet,
it is in water.

Loren Eiseley
(1907–1977)
American anthropologist, philosopher, and naturalist

THIS CHAPTER IS ABOUT...

Water—needs, availability, and scarcity, water conflicts, water situation in India, solutions to the water crisis

THE KEYWORDS AND PHRASES ARE...

water cycle   virtual water   water footprint   rainwater harvesting   check dam

---

THE STORY OF CHERRAPUNJI: WETTEST PLACE ON EARTH, YET NO WATER TO DRINK

When the monsoon comes to this place, it does not rain, it pours. It could pour continuously for over two months and you may not see the sun for 20 to 25 days at a stretch. With an average annual rainfall of 11.5 metres, Cherrapunji is listed in every geography book as the wettest place on earth.

Some years it rains much more than the average. In 1974 the place received 24.5 metres of rain and the record for one day is 1563 mm. Yet, Cherrapunji, in the state of Meghalaya in North-east India, faces severe drought the rest of the year!

How is it that not a drop of the 11.5 metres of the rain remains to quench the thirst of the people? The answer lies in the destruction of forests. Once upon a time, the hills around Cherrapunji were full of dense

Villagers in Cherrapunji carting water from other areas

forests. These forests soaked up the heavy rain and released it slowly the rest of the year. Over the years, however, the forests were cut down. The heavy rains washed away the topsoil, turning the slopes into deserts. It is now a mining town with whole families and immigrants making a living out of extraction of coal and chalk. The dusty air chokes the life out of people.

There is no reservoir to store the water. For over twenty years, the residents have depended on a piped water supply that comes from afar. That supply is always erratic and undependable.

By tradition, the people of Cherrapunji celebrate the arrival of the rains every year with an elaborate festival. The rain gods do respond generously for four months. Yet the people do not have enough water for the next eight months!

What does the story of Cherrapunji tell us?

The story shows how important it is to have forests that would slow down the flow of rainwater and protect the topsoil, especially in the hills. Water is a unique resource and water scarcity is increasing in the world.

The UN World Water Development Report 2009 paints a grim picture of the water situation (Box 7.1).

BOX 7.1

World Water Development Report 2009

The UN publishes a World Water Development Report (WWDR) every three years, covering water and sanitation. The main conclusions of WWDR-3, issued in 2009, were:

- Demand for water has never been greater. Freshwater withdrawals have tripled over the last 50 years, while the area under irrigation doubled during the same period.
- Water demand for agriculture worldwide would increase 70–90 per cent by 2050, even though a number of countries are already reaching the limits of their water resources.
- The 10 largest water users (in volume) are India, China, the US, Pakistan, Japan, Thailand, Indonesia, Bangladesh, Mexico, and the Russian Federation. Total water use is highest in India (646 cu. km a year).
- By 2030, 47 per cent of world population will be

living in areas of high water stress. In Africa alone, by 2020, between 75 and 250 million people may experience increased water stress due to climate change. Globally, 700 million people could be displaced in the coming decades because of a scarcity of water.
- An estimated 5 billion people (67 per cent of the world population) may still be without improved sanitation in 2030. Half a billion people now lack access to adequate sanitation in Africa alone.
- Almost 80 per cent of diseases in developing countries are associated with water, causing some three million early deaths. For example, 5,000 children die every day from diarrhoea, or one every 17 seconds. In all, about one tenth of all illnesses worldwide could be avoided by improving water supply, sanitation, hygiene, and management of water resources.

Why is water a unique resource?

Water is a prerequisite for the existence of life. Human beings, animals and plants cannot survive without water and the human body itself is mostly water. We can go without food for even 30 days or more, but we cannot go without water even for a few days. When the water content in the body drops just by 1 per cent, there is thirst. If it drops by 10 per cent, there is a danger of death.

Water is the most critical limiting factor for many aspects of life like economic growth, environmental stability, biodiversity conservation, food security, and health care. In most cases of water use, there is no other substitute. In the case of energy, one source can often replace another, but water as a resource is mostly irreplaceable.

The good news about water is that we can reuse it many times. It may change its form, but we can always get it back. In fact, the molecules in the water we use have been around for millions of years. The earth holds the same quantity of water as it did when it was formed.

> **KEY IDEA**
> There is plenty of water on earth, but many millions face water scarcity.

The paradox of the water situation is that there is scarcity amidst plenty. As we shall see, there is in this world a lot of water and yet there are millions of people facing acute water scarcity.

How much water do we need?

We need water for personal use, agriculture and industries. At home, water is necessary for drinking, cooking food, washing, cleaning, toilet use, and gardening (Box 7.2).

BOX 7.2

Domestic water needs

In India, the urban water supply systems are designed for a daily consumption of 135 litres per capita (See Table).

Many urban residents consume much more than this norm. (Note how much water the flush toilet consumes!) People in our villages manage with much less water.

Use	Litres / Person / Day
Drinking	3
Cooking	4
Bathing	20
Flushing	40
Washing clothes	25
Washing utensils	20
Gardening	23
Total	135

In agriculture, we need water for growing food items like rice, wheat, vegetables, fruits, coffee, tea, and sugarcane. Non-food items like cotton also use water. Factories, thermal and nuclear power plants, etc., require large amounts of water. Industries use water for cleaning, as a coolant, and as part of the manufacturing process.

Nature and the rest of the earth need water too! We often forget that animals need water to drink and to clean themselves. A cow, for example, must drink four litres of water to produce one litre of milk. Natural systems like wetlands, lakes, and deltas also need water.

The absolute minimum for domestic use is 50 litres per person per day, though 100 to 200 litres is often recommended. Adding the needs of agriculture, industry, and energy sectors, the recommended minimum annual per capita requirement is about 1700 cu. m.

In addition to using water directly, we also consume water indirectly (Box 7.3).

BOX 7.3

Virtual water and water footprints

In addition to the direct use of water for our needs, there is also an indirect use of water in making many items that we eat, drink, or use (See Table below). This 'virtual' water is often hidden from us.

Item and quantity	Water used (litres)
Paper (1 A4 sheet)	10
Potato (100 g)	25
Cup of coffee (125 ml)	140
Milk (1 litre)	1000
Sugar (1 kg)	1500
Rice (1 kg)	3400
Cotton T-shirt (500 g)	4100
Pair of shoes (bovine leather)	8000
Beef (1 kg)	16000

140 litres of water   *1 cup coffee*

Image courtesy (coffee tree): http://commons.wikimedia.org/wiki/File:Coffee_tree_in_Buon_Me_Thuot_city.jpg.jpg; coffee (http://commons.wikimedia.org/wiki/File:Caf percentC3 percentA9_au_lait.jpg)

'Water footprint' is an indicator that measures both direct and indirect water use of a consumer or producer. The water footprint of an individual, community or business is defined as the total volume of freshwater that is used to produce the goods and services consumed by the individual or community or produced by the business. The concept is similar to that of ecological footprint (Chapter 1).

The water footprint of a country = (Yearly amount of domestic water used to produce all goods and services consumed within the country) + (Yearly amount of virtual water in the goods and services imported into the country). We get the per capita water footprint by dividing the total amount by the population (See Table below).

Country	Water footprint cu.m per capita / per year
US	2480
Thailand	2220
Germany	1545
Pakistan	1220
India	980
China	700
Global Average	1240

In absolute terms, India has the largest water footprint in the world.

How is the available water used in the world?

Human beings use about 54 per cent of all accessible freshwater supplies in the world. By 2025, this share will increase to 70 per cent. This will have serious implications for all other forms of life including plants. Table 7.1 shows the current pattern of water use in the world by humankind.

Table 7.1   Pattern of Water Use
(Percentage of total water consumed by each sector)

Sector	Global use percentage	Percentage use in industrialised countries	Percentage use in developing countries	Percentage use in India
Agriculture	70	30	82	80
Industry	22	59	10	15
Domestic	8	11	8	5

KEY IDEA

Since the total water available is finite, greater consumption by one sector can only result in less supply for other sectors.

It is significant that domestic consumption accounts for only 8 per cent and yet there is worldwide scarcity of drinking water. Agriculture continues to consume the major portion of the available fresh water. However, there is a clear difference in the water use between the developing countries and the industrialized countries. While agriculture takes the bulk of the supply in the former, industry consumes more than agriculture in the latter. This shows that there will be a severe problem in the developing countries once they industrialize to the level of the rich countries.

Now that we know how much water we need and how we use what we have, let us find out how much water is there in the world.

How much water is there in this world?

We know that 97 per cent of the world's water is in the ocean, too salty to drink. Of the remaining 3 per cent, two-thirds is locked up in relatively inaccessible icecaps and glaciers. That leaves a mere 1 per cent or 14 million cu. km. Again, half of this amount is groundwater and most of it lies too far underground.

How do we get fresh water every year?   A key element of the water cycle (Chapter 2) helps us get a regular supply of fresh water. Annually, about 430,000 cu. km of water evaporates from ocean and only about 390,000 cu. km falls back over the ocean as precipitation. The remaining 40,000 cu. km moves from the ocean and falls on land as rain and snow. The first advantage is that we get this supply every year. Second, as the water evaporates from the ocean and falls on land it loses its salt content and thus becomes potable.

KEY IDEA

The global water cycle provides us with fresh water every year.

Is the annual supply of fresh water enough for our needs?   There is indeed an annual fresh supply of 40,000 cu. km and this amounts to about 5,700 cu. m per person per year (for a population of 7 billion). This appears to be plentiful, since the minimum annual needs of a person is only about 1,700 cu. m. By this token, we should be comfortable with regard to the water situation. Yet, there is worldwide water scarcity.

How do we measure water scarcity?

If a country has about 1700 cu.m per person per year, it will experience only occasional or local water problems. If the availability falls below this threshold value, the country will begin to experience periodic or regular *water stress*. At the next stage, when the figure falls below 1,000 cu.m, the country will suffer from chronic *water scarcity*. The lack of water will then begin to adversely affect human health and well-being as well as economic development. If the annual per capita supply falls below 500 cu.m, the country will reach the stage of *absolute scarcity*.

As of 1995, 31 countries, with a combined population of 460 million, faced either water stress or water scarcity. By 2025, 48 countries with more than 2.8 billion people will be in this category. By 2050 the number of countries facing water stress or scarcity will rise to 54, and their combined population to 4 billion people—40 per cent of the projected global population of 9.4 billion.

Why is water becoming scarce?

A number of reasons have led to increasing water scarcity since the middle of the 20th century. While the demand for water has been going up sharply, the available amount has been going down. Exploding population, rapid industrialization, and increasing irrigation needs (due to methods like the Green Revolution) have pushed up the demand.

At the same time, the supply has also been adversely affected. The rapidly increasing pollution of rivers, lakes, as well as the groundwater is reducing the usable supply. Pollution has made many water sources unfit for use. Incredibly small amounts of substances like oil can pollute huge amounts of water.

In many places the rates of extraction of groundwater for irrigation are so high that ancient aquifers are getting depleted. As a result, water tables are falling, notably in India, China, and US (which together produce half the world's food). The major rivers of the world are drained dry before they reach the sea. The Yellow River in China, the Ganga in India, the Amu Darya in Central Asia, the Nile in Egypt, and the Colorado in US are examples.

People waiting for water

Distribution of the available water is also uneven over space and time. Some areas of the world get too much water while other places get too little. The transport of water over long distances is impractical.

Further, in some regions rainfall occurs over a short period in the year leading to floods in monsoon and drought in summer. The runoff, aided by deforestation, reaches the ocean quickly before it can be used. Much of the rain also falls in remote places that are inaccessible. Some of the rain is also needed to maintain special ecosystems like wetlands, lakes, and deltas. Global warming, which is now occurring, is changing the rainfall patterns.

> **KEY IDEA**
> Even as the demand for water goes up sharply, the availability is going down.

In addition, there is a gross inequity in the allocation of water resources. In general, the richer groups corner more of the water supply. The urban areas again draw a great deal of water from the surrounding areas depriving the poorer rural people of their needs.

Why do many cities face severe water scarcity?

The megacities of the world, many of them in the poorer countries, need a lot of water and this water is often drawn from the neighbouring villages and far off rivers and lakes. Even if a city gets good rain, the water is not retained in the area. Buildings, paving, and roads cover most of the land and the rainwater does not percolate into the ground.

Megacities also pollute the water and release large amounts of wastewater into the rivers and the ocean. Currently, less than 20 per cent of urban wastewater worldwide is treated. The increasing use of flush toilets also results in enormous wastage of potable water. Further, in many cities, more than half the available supply is lost through leaks and rotting pipelines.

Will there be enough water for irrigation?

Today irrigation takes away 70 per cent of the usable water in the world. There has been a five-fold increase in use of water for irrigation over the 20th century. The situation became worse since the adoption of the Green Revolution package. In many countries 50 per cent or more of the food production comes from irrigated land. These include countries like India, China, Egypt, Indonesia, Israel, Japan, Korea, Pakistan, and Peru. By 2025, up to four billion people will live in countries that will lack water to produce their own food.

Even now, inefficient and outdated practices of irrigation continue, leading to wastage of water. Many fields are flooded and though some water gets to the root zone helping the growth of the plant, 50 per cent is wasted as it percolates, evaporates, or runs off.

Most new land brought into agriculture uses groundwater that is depleting fast. Meanwhile, available agricultural land is also lost due to salinization, reservoir siltation, shift of water use, etc. Salinization is often the result of raising water tables, which happens due to the flooding of the fields. As the water evaporates it leaves behind salt on the topsoil. The siltation of reservoirs in big dams has often cut their lives to a mere 20 or 25 years. As mentioned earlier, cultivation is stopped in some places in favour of selling water to a nearby city. As a result of all this loss of cropland, the total irrigated area may in fact be decreasing.

The farmers take 85 per cent of the water and the fields are often over-irrigated. This is primarily because the farmers get free electricity and subsidized pumps and thus do not pay the real economic price of water.

The world over, large dams and canal systems are going out of fashion due to spiralling costs, environmental concerns, and displacement of people. Protest movements in many places have stalled the construction of dams.

> **KEY IDEA**
> We cannot continue to meet the heavy and ever-increasing demand for irrigation water and this could affect our food security.

Globalisation and industrialization increases demands for water from industry and urban areas in different parts of the world. The rapid increase in population also means that more water is needed for food and drinking purposes. All these facts seem to indicate that there is not much scope for increasing irrigation at the same rapid rate of the last century. It is also a sobering thought that all irrigation-based societies have failed in the past!

Why are there so many conflicts over water?

Around the world, more than 200 water bodies are shared by two or more countries. Conflicts are brewing over the water available in many rivers and river basins.

Strife over water is erupting throughout the Middle East, from the watersheds of the Nile to the Tigris and Euphrates Rivers. Likewise, there is a problem in the Ganga-Brahmaputra

Basin, where Bangladesh, India, and Nepal dispute the use of water. India and Nepal want to exploit the basin's huge hydroelectric power-generating potential, whereas Bangladesh wants the water managed in such a way as to minimize flooding during monsoon months and water shortages during dry months.

Of equal concern are the water conflicts between states in India that share river basins, such as Karnataka and Tamil Nadu, which share the Cauvery River. Inequitable distribution and use of water resources, sometimes arising from development projects, leads to disputes.

The third category of conflicts is between industries and local communities on several issues: excessive water consumption by industry resulting in reduced availability for irrigation; preferential treatment for industry in pricing; and pollution of groundwater, rivers, and other local water bodies from the discharge of wastewater.

> **KEY IDEA**
> Water conflicts are increasing at the local, national, and regional levels.

Agitations and public interest litigation on water issues are increasing and more conflicts at all levels are expected in the future (Box 7.4).

BOX 7.4

The story of Plachimada: Who owns the water?

If a soft drink industry owns a piece of land, can it exploit the groundwater without any limit? This is the core issue in what has come to be known as the Plachimada case in Kerala.

In January 2000, Hindustan Coca-Cola Beverages began drawing groundwater and producing cola in Plachimada. The Panchayat received an annual income of about Rs 600,000 in the deal. In addition, the plant provided employment for about 400 people.

By early 2002, the villagers started noticing changes in the water quality in the area. They felt that the plant was drawing too much water from the ground and this was affecting the harvest of rice and coconuts. In April 2002, the villagers started an agitation against the plant.

The Panchayat cancelled the company's licence. The matter went to court, which ordered the plant not to draw water from the ground and to find alternate sources of water. The Judge said that the company had no right to extract excessive natural wealth and the Panchayat and the government were bound to prevent it. The groundwater was a national resource, which belonged to the entire society and not to the company even though it owned the land.

In 2010, a Government Committee indicted the company for causing incalculable harm to the ecology and the people of Plachimada. The panel assessed the overall cost of the damage at Rs 216.26 crores and recommended setting up of a tribunal with judicial powers to make Coca Cola pay individual claims.

The Plachimada struggle is still going on and we do not know how the story will ultimately end. The case, however, has become the focal point for the debate on the people's right to water and a company's right to exploit the water under its land.

What is the water situation in India?

India and China are counted as water hotspots in the world primarily because of the large population that has to be provided with food and drinking water. Table 7.2 shows how the per capita availability has been going down in India.

Table 7.2 Water Availability in India

Year	Per capita availability of water (cu. m)
1951	5000
1990	2400
2007	1800
2030	1300 (estimate)

In India, more than 60,000 villages are without a single source of drinking water. Diarrhoea, brought on by contaminated water, claims the lives of one million children every year. In addition 45 million people are affected annually by the poor quality of water.

While the increasing population is one cause of India's water crisis, the problem has been compounded by the steady deterioration, disuse, and disappearance of the traditional tanks and ponds. These water bodies were very effective in retaining the rainwater and recharging the groundwater. The local communities took care of these resources.

Over the last 100 years or more, these tanks were neglected and many of them disappeared. Deforestation of the hills coupled with the absence of tanks has increased the runoff into the sea.

In recent years the extraction of groundwater using bore wells operated by electric or diesel pumps has reached gigantic proportions. Free electricity and the Green Revolution package have sharply increased the water usage. One estimate is that the extraction is already twice the recharge rate. In many states water tables have been dropping at alarming rates.

As India develops, industries need water more and more. The total available water is limited and hence any increase of supply to industries means taking water away from irrigation and domestic use.

What about urban water supply in India?

Our municipalities have to bring drinking water from outside the cities. For example, during summer water for Chennai comes from many surrounding agricultural villages. The farmers find it more profitable to sell the water than cultivate the fields. Water for Chennai is also brought from the Krishna River, Mettur, and other places far away. This clearly constitutes an unwelcome shift in water use that will ultimately threaten our food security.

Chennai, in fact, gets an average rainfall of 1290 mm per year, which is more than the national average. Yet, 90 per cent of this rain is lost in runoff, evaporation, and flow into the sewage system.

Bangalore gets its water from 90 km away and 500 m below its altitude. Apart from increasing the cost of supply of water, this practice also deprives the rural areas of much-needed water.

How much water do Indian industries consume?

We have no reliable figures on water consumption by Indian industry, with the estimates ranging from 40 to 67 billion cu.m. We are sure, however, that the amount is increasing rapidly. It is estimated that the water demand of Indian industry will triple over the next 20 years.

KEY IDEA

In India, the per capita availability of water is steadily going down, even as the needs of industry and agriculture are going up.

In India, thermal power plants use about 87 per cent of total industrial consumption. The efficiency of water use in Indian industry is way behind international standards. Another important aspect of industrial use is the pollution of water bodies caused by wastewater discharge.

There is no incentive for Indian industry to reduce consumption, since it gets water at ridiculously low prices. In order to attract industrial units to an area, State governments often offer assured water supply at low rates. The pricing in most cases ignores the opportunity cost of water (that is, benefit from possible alternative use) as well as the damage caused by the pollution of supplies by the discharge of wastewater.

In several parts of India, there are conflicts between industries and local communities over the use of water (Box 7.4).

What do the optimists say?

Even in this grim situation, there are optimists who believe that there will be dramatic solutions that would once and for all solve the water problem. Such dreams include:

- Transport of water in huge bags by sea.
- Towing of icebergs to needy places.
- Discovery of new deep aquifers full of water.
- Finding a new cheap energy source that will make desalination affordable.
- Interlinking rivers (Box 7.5)

BOX 7.5

Interlinking Indian rivers

The idea of linking rivers has been around for a long time. However, in 2002, the Supreme Court of India, acting on a public interest petition, directed the Government to interlink rivers within ten years. In response, the Government set up a Task Force to build national consensus, work out the detailed plans and complete the entire work by 2016.

Three major advantages were cited in favour of the scheme: droughts will never occur, floods in rivers like the Ganga and Brahmaputra will cease to be problems and an additional 30,000 MW of hydropower will be generated.

The budget for the project ranges from Rs 5,600 to 10,000 billion. Even the lower estimate equals 25 per cent of our GDP, 2.5 times our tax collection and double our present foreign exchange reserves. Obviously, funds of this magnitude will have to be raised from international sources. Even if we succeed in raising the funds, the annual interest

alone would amount to Rs 200 to 300 billion. The water will have to be priced high to meet such a burden. Will the farmers and other users be ready to pay the charges?

It is doubtful if a political consensus can ever be achieved on the project. Would the states be willing to share freely all the river waters? Even the current inter-state water problems have defied amicable solutions. It is not even clear that the rivers like the Ganga, the Brahmaputra, the Mahanadi and the Godavari are water-surplus. The sources of such rivers are drying up and the rivers themselves are choked with silt.

The likely ecological consequences of building over 200 reservoirs and a network of crisscrossing canals cannot even be assessed now. Judging from the experience of Narmada Dam and other large projects, the consequences could be disastrous. Environmentalists and social activists fear large-

Contd

Box 7.5 Contd

scale submergence of habitats, forests and fertile land, heavy destruction of wildlife habitats and biodiversity, displacement of large populations, and so on. In some places enormous amounts of energy will have to be spent pumping water uphill.

In the past, every single irrigation project in India has resulted in heavy cost and time overruns. The project to interlink rivers is likely to meet a similar fate.

Most experts, however, believe that there are real limits to the availability of water and that we are fast reaching them. A realistic solution is to find ways of using water more efficiently.

Is there a way out of the water crisis?

Here is a list of possible solutions to the water crisis in India and elsewhere:

- Reduce demand:
    - Educate people to use less water
    - Install water-saving devices like self-closing taps and dual-flush toilets.
    - Use decentralised wastewater-recycling systems in homes, apartment blocks, campuses, and industries, using natural methods like planted filters.
    - Adopt composting toilets to save water and also to minimise the sewage disposal problem.
    - Adopt agriculture practices that require less water:
        - Replace water-hungry crops by those requiring less water
        - Promote crops that can tolerate salty water
        - Return to indigenous species that can withstand drought
        - Switch to organic and natural farming
        - Get more crop per drop: Use drip irrigation, sprinkler method, etc.
        - Persuade people to change to a vegetarian diet that would require less water for production.
        - Reduce industrial consumption through recycling, reuse and new water-efficient technologies.
- Catch the rain where it falls
    - Retain water on land as long as possible through check dams and contour bunds allowing it to percolate into the ground.
    - Implement rainwater harvesting in urban and rural areas (Box 7.6)
    - Restore traditional system of ponds and lakes.
- Adopt decentralized systems of water supply and sanitation
    - Plan many small local catchments in place of large ones.
    - Implement a large number of small-scale schemes.
- Adopt fairer policies
    - Give control of water sources to the community
    - Price water properly
    - Remove inequities in access to water

KEY IDEA

We can meet the water crisis only by reducing demand, harvesting rain, implementing decentralized systems, and adopting fairer policies.

BOX 7.6

Rainwater harvesting

There are two ways in which rainwater can be harvested. One way is to slow down the flow of water on land through bunds and check dams. The longer the water remains on land, the more it percolates into the ground. This way it recharges the aquifers and wells. This method is best suited for rural areas.

The second way is to collect and store rainwater. This is a very effective method for our cities. The rainwater that falls on the roof can be collected, filtered, and stored. A surprisingly large amount of water can be collected in this way.

Suppose you live in the city of Delhi. Your house has a terrace area of 100 sq m. How much of rainwater can you collect in one year?

Average annual rainfall in = 910 mm
Delhi

Amount of rain falling on = Roof area × rainfall
100 sq m area

$$= 100 \text{ sq m} \times 0.91 \text{ m}$$
$$\doteq 91 \text{ cu. m}$$
$$= 91{,}000 \text{ litres}$$

For a family of five, consuming 750 litres a day, this rainwater will last for 120 days or one third of the year!

Rainwater harvesting in a house

Normally, rainwater is good enough to drink. As a precaution, however, you could avoid using water from the first rain of the monsoon. Rainwater harvesting systems usually incorporate first rain separators. As long as the storage is completely closed, the water remains good for a long period. Rooftop rainwater can also be used to recharge groundwater. We dig a few percolation pits around the house and fill it with gravel. Water from the roof is directly let into these pits. It percolates into the soil and recharges the groundwater, if the soil is porous. After a while, the water levels in the area will go up and the wells will have enough water. Water from stormwater drains can also be diverted into percolation pits.

Ending on a hopeful note: Positive stories

Read Boxes 7.7 and 7.8 for some positive stories.

BOX 7.7

Hopeful signs: Water conservation in India

In recent times a number of initiatives have been taken by individuals, communities, NGOs and even by government agencies to implement measures for water conservation and management. Some of the well-known cases are:

- Auroville: The spectacular efforts of this international community near Puducherry over the past 35 years in afforestation, water conservation, wastewater treatment, etc., are models to follow. Auroville is now working with local communities and the government to rejuvenate the traditional ponds and get the control back to the people.
- Tarun Bharat Sangh, Alwar, Rajasthan: This NGO, founded by Rajendra Singh, built thousands of

Contd

Box 7.7 Contd

earthen check dams in villages with community participation. As a result, water tables rose, dead rivers came back to life, and farming improved. (Box 7.8)

- Ralegaon Siddhi, Maharashtra: Through the efforts of Anna Hazare, the people have constructed sand percolation tanks and brought back the greenery.
- Gram Gaurav Pratishtan: In Maharashtra, the late Mr Vilas Salunke introduced the idea of a Pani Panchayat for a fair sharing of water.

- Tamil Nadu: Rainwater harvesting was made compulsory in the state in 2003.
- Efficient water use by industry: Faced with water scarcity, increasing costs, and protests by local communities, several industries like Arvind Mills, Chennai Petroleum Corporation, and J.K.Papers have implemented water conservation measures and have benefited by them.

BOX 7.8

The story of Rajendra Singh: The rivers that came back to life

In 1985, five young men led by Rajendra Singh came to Kishori Village in Alwar, Rajasthan. They belonged to the Tarun Bharat Sangh (TBS), founded by Singh. They had come to the village 'wanting to fight injustice against all people', but had no clue where to start. Advice came when they met Mangu Lal, an old man in Gopalpura: 'Build *johads* and you will get results', he told them. A *johad* is a small earthen check dam that captures and conserves rainwater. A typical *johad* would be about 1,400 feet long, 20 feet high and 50 feet wide.

Rajendra Singh beside a check dam in Rajasthan

Taking the advice seriously, TBS built the first *johad* in Gopalpura. The next year, the wells in the village had water even in summer. Following this success, another *johad* was built in Bhaonta in the Aravali Hills. In this case, the result was even more dramatic, since the Arvari River, which had gone dry, now came back to life. Mangu Lal had been proved right and the mission of TBS was clear.

In village after village in this drought-stricken part of Rajasthan, TBS built *johads* with the active participation of the villagers. To date, hundreds of *johads* have been built in a large number of villages, bringing back to life more rivers: Ruparel, Bhagwani, Sarsa and Jahajwali. As the rivers returned, so did the men who had gone away from the villages looking for work in the cities. Agricultural yields and

milk production increased and diesel consumption by pumps went down drastically.

TBS succeeded because they ensured the complete involvement of the villagers in the task. A TBS Team would visit a village only if invited. Meetings would be held and work would start only when the villagers were convinced of the feasibility of the project and were ready to contribute at least a third of the cost. Their contribution was in the form of their own labour and their knowledge of the traditional methods.

A detailed study of the work by Prof.G.D.Agarwal talks about the low cost of the structures and the

Contd

Box 7.8 Contd

perfection with which they were built, even though no engineering calculations had been made. Further, the structures withstood the heavy rainfall in 1995 and 1996. Agarwal calls it 'the largest-ever mobilisation of people in the cause of environmental regeneration'.

TBS had to face difficulties created by local mine owners and even the government. But they went ahead with their work. In 2001, Rajendra Singh received the Ramon Magsaysay Award for Community Leadership. Singh responded that the villagers really deserved the honour. They taught him the value of water. He only helped them revive their 'dying wisdom'. He has come to be known as the 'Water Man' of India.

REVIEW: A SUMMARY OF THE KEY POINTS

- Water is essential to life and is in most cases irreplaceable.
- The water cycle helps us get a regular annual supply of fresh water.
- There is only a finite amount of water in the world.
- The paradox of the water situation is that there is scarcity amidst plenty, primarily due to the impact of human activities.
- By the middle of the century, most countries in the world (and cities in particular) will be facing water scarcity. India will face severe problems.

- Even places with heavy rainfall can experience water scarcity in other seasons, if water management is poor.
- The world's food security may be threatened due to shortage of irrigation water.
- There could be future wars over water issues.
- There are effective ways of conserving and reusing water, which can be followed by anyone.
- There are many examples of successful water conservation efforts in India.
- The attempts to interlink Indian rivers will have financial, social, and ecological consequences.

EXERCISES

Objective-type questions

For each question below, choose the best answer out of the given choices:

1. What is the most important reason for water scarcity even in a high-rainfall place such as Cherrapunji?
   (a) Forests have been cut down.
   (b) Too much water is consumed.
   (c) Forests do not retain water.
   (d) There is no reservoir.

2. Why is water a unique resource?
   (a) There is a finite amount of water in the world.
   (b) Water is often polluted.
   (c) We cannot meet the demand.
   (d) Water has no substitute.

3. Which of the following statements is true with regard to water?
   (a) There is not enough water available per capita.
   (b) We cannot reuse water.
   (c) There is a lot of water and yet there is scarcity.
   (d) The total amount of water in the world is constantly decreasing in quantity.

4. Which of the following statements is true with regard to water use and sanitation in the world?
   (a) Human beings are using less water than before.
   (b) Water contamination is not the main cause of diseases.
   (c) 50 per cent or more of the population lacks sanitation facilities.
   (d) People are never displaced due to water scarcity.

5. Which country uses the maximum amount of water by volume?
   (a) US
   (b) China
   (c) Pakistan
   (d) India

6. Which of the following items uses the maximum amount of water per kg during its production?
   (a) Rice
   (b) Beef
   (c) Potato
   (d) Sugar

7. Which of the following statements is true with regard to roof-top rainwater harvesting?
   (a) The water cannot be used at home.
   (b) The water is very expensive.
   (c) Large amounts of water can be collected even with small roof area.
   (d) Only the first rain must be collected.

8. Which of the following statements is **not** true with regard to small earthen check dams?
   (a) They are easy to build and are not expensive.
   (b) They help recharge the local water table.
   (c) They can bring back dead rivers.
   (d) They have not been helpful in water conservation.

9. Globally, which sector uses the maximum percentage of water?
   (a) Agriculture
   (b) Industry
   (c) Homes
   (d) Hotels

10. Which of the following statements is **not** true with regard to the water situation in India?
    (a) Thousands of villages have no source of drinking water.
    (b) Per capita availability of water is going down.
    (c) Millions of children die due to contaminated water.
    (d) Our cities have enough water supplies.

Short-answer questions

1. What is the natural process that provides us with fresh water every year? How does it work?

2. The annual per capita requirement of water is 1700 cu.m, while the annual fresh water supply is at least 3 times more. Why then do we have water scarcity?

3. What are the levels of water availability that indicate water stress and water scarcity?

4. What are the special problems that big cities face on the water issue?

5. Describe the global pattern of water use across sectors. What are the main differences between the industrialized countries and the developing countries with regard to water use?

6. What is the implication of the statement, 'Any increase of water supply to one user means taking it away from another user'?

7. What is the link between water scarcity and food security?

8 What are the main reasons for water scarcity in India?

9. How can we reduce the total demand for water?

10. What is the importance of rainwater harvesting?

11. What are the pros and cons of the plan to interlink Indian rivers?

12. Give two examples of successful Indian attempts in water conservation.

13. What are the lessons we can learn from the efforts of the Tarun Bharat Sangh?

Long-answer questions

1. What are the reasons for the worsening water situation in so many countries? What is likely to happen in another 40 years or so?

2. What negative role do cities play in the water scene? How can this be corrected?

3. Why do conflicts occur over water?

Think critically: Deeper questions for reflection and discussion

1. There is very little control in India over the use of water by industry. Should the government impose stricter regulations on the use of water and the discharge of wastewater? Should the government also ensure that the industry pays a fair price for the water? Will such control increase the costs for industry and push up the prices?

2. If more water is taken by industry, less water will be available for agriculture. If industry does not enough water, economic growth will suffer; if agriculture is deprived of water, food security will be hit. What is the way out of this dilemma?

3. Should water be considered as a common resource or a private one? Do all citizens have a right to adequate access to water? Should water be privatised and fair prices charged for it?

4. Is it ethical to exploit the groundwater on your land without any restriction? Remember that the groundwater may have seeped in from the surrounding lands. A neighbour may take the trouble of recharging the groundwater and the geology may be such that all that water collects under your land.

SOMETHING DIFFERENT FOR A CHANGE

A poem by Lovemore Dhoba of the Youth Water Action Team:

Water Laments

Mother of all lives,
A root that gives life
Life serving creature
You used to dedicate all these names to me.

But look at what your sons,
Your daughters and grandchildren are doing to me

Tossing, my innocent soul,
As if I am of their age,
Sewage dumped in me
As if I am of no significance to their lives

Their industrial effluent,
Domestic garbage,
All left for me to swallow

Sanctions, very soon sanctions
I am going to lift up sanctions
Against you cowards

ACTIVITIES

Act: What you can do to conserve water

1. Start with yourself: Measure the daily water that you use and try to reduce the amount
2. Examine the usage pattern of water in your family or in any one family. Educate them to use water with more care and efficiency
3. On a regular basis, check all the public taps and pipelines in your area and arrange to plug the leaks
4. Take the initiative to implement rainwater harvesting in your house, apartment block or in your college campus

Access the website www.wateruseitwisely.com for more than 100 ways of saving water.

Learn by doing: Case study / Project

1. Choose a village, town or city as a unit for study. Examine the water situation in the place by finding answers to the following questions and write a report:
   - Where does the water the people use come from? What is its ecological footprint?
   - How much does it cost the users?
   - How much does it cost to supply the water?
   - What is the pattern of water use by the people?
   - Where does the wastewater go?

2. Examine the water usage of a small community (a village, a locality in a city, an apartment block) and write a report on actions that could be taken for conserving water:
   - How can the demand for water be reduced?
   - How can the ecological footprint of the water they get be reduced?
   - What other environment-friendly ways of getting water can one implement?
   - How can the quality of the water be protected?
   - How can the people reuse and recycle the water?
   - How can you educate the users about the proper use of water?

Organize together: Eco-club activities and projects

1. Observe World Water Day on March 22, as designated by the UN. The objectives of World Water Day is to focus attention on the need to:
   - address the problems relating to drinking water supply;
   - increase public awareness on the importance of conservation, preservation, and protection of water resources and drinking water supply

To observe the Day, you could:
   - promote mass media education programmes.

- focus on school children and youth.
- publish and diffuse documentaries.
- organise conferences, round tables, seminars and expositions related to the conservation and development of water resources
- promote community and self-help programmes
- increase public and private sector support for water conservation

For more information access the websites www.worldwaterday.org and www.unesco.org/water/

2. Join the World Youth Water Action Team. YWAT is a non-governmental, global organization of students and young professionals who aim to increase awareness, participation, and commitment among young people in water-related issues.

YWAT wants to establish a global movement of young people who are interested in water and who either participate in and/or initiate local community initiatives and/or form local YWAT units. Another objective is to influence decision-making processes in the field of water-related issues. To join YWAT you have to be between 18 and 30 years old and become active in awareness-raising activities. YWAT membership is voluntary.

For more information, access the website www.ywat.org.

LEARN MORE

Books

Agarwal, Anil and Sunita Narain (eds) 1997, *Dying Wisdom: Rise, Fall and Potential of India's Traditional Water Harvesting Systems,* Centre for Science and Environment, New Delhi.

Agarwal, Anil, Sunita Narain and Indira Khurana, (eds) 2001, *Making Water Everybody's Business: Practice and Policy of Water Harvesting,* Centre for Science and Environment, New Delhi.

Barlow, Maude 2007, *Blue Covenant: The Global Water Crisis and the Coming Battle for the Right to Water,* Books for Change, Bangalore.

Barlow, Maude and Tony Clarke 2003, *Blue Gold: The Fight to Stop the Corporate Theft of the World's Water,* Indian reprint, Leftword Books, Delhi.

de Villiers, Marq 1999, *Water,* Stoddard, Toronto.

Postel, Sandra 1992, *The Last Oasis: Facing Water Scarcity,* World Watch Environmental Alert Series, Earthscan, London.

Postel, Sandra 1999, *Pillar of Sand: Can the Irrigation Miracle Last?* W.W. Norton, New York.

UNESCO 2009, *Water in a Changing World: UN World Water Development Report 3,* UNESCO Publishing, Paris and Earthscan, London. (downloadable from www.unesco.org)

Articles

James, Barry 2003, 'Water: A flood of promises, a trickle of progress, *The New UNESCO Courier,* October, pp. 38–61.

Krishna Kumar, R. 2004, 'Resistance in Kerala', *Frontline,* Vol.21, No.3, February 13, pp. 38–40. (on Plachimada)

Vijayalakshmi, E. 2003, 'Calling the shots: Cola major gets a taste of panchayat power in Kerala', *Down To Earth,* December 15, pp. 15–19. (on Plachimada)

Websites

International Water Management Institute: www.iwmi.cgiar.org/

Pacific Institute Water Project: www.worldwater.org

Tarun Bharat Sangh: www.tarunbharatsangh.org

Films

Bringing home Rain, a documentary by Sushma Veerappa and Rainwater Club (on rainwater harvesting in a village)

Drinking the Sky, a BBC Earth Report documentary by Joost de Haas (on Cherrapunji)

Flow: For the Love of Water, a documentary by Irena Salina (2008)

Thirst, a documentary by Alan Snitow and Deborah Kaufman (2004)

CHAPTER 8

Energy Resources

Human beings and the natural world are on a collision course.
We must move away from fossil fuels to cut
greenhouse gas emissions.

World Scientists' Warning to Humanity (1992)

THIS CHAPTER IS ABOUT...

Energy—needs and sources, energy consumption, renewable and non-renewable energy sources

THE KEYWORDS AND PHRASES ARE...

fossil fuel	fuel cell	Hubbert curve	peak oil	photovoltaic cell

THE STORY OF WOMEN HEADLOADERS: NOMADS WITH HOMES?

Basumati Tirkey, a 35-year-old resident of Bangamunda village in Orissa, walks nine km every day, carrying a load of 35 kg of fuelwood, to earn Rs 15. And she has spent a lifetime doing so.

Basumathi is just one of the 11 million desperate women in India who eke out a living collecting and selling fuelwood. 70 per cent of women living in and around forest areas are engaged in this work. It is estimated that, in an average village in a semi-arid region, a woman walks more than 1,000 km a year to collect firewood alone. No wonder they are called 'nomads with homes'.

The UN Food and Agricultural Organization estimates that the fuelwood business in India has a turnover of US$ 60 billion. It must be the most valuable non-timber forest activity and yet it is the last resort of the poorest of the poor. It is generally

Forest guard to headloader: 'You are anti-environment. Pay me something'

regarded as being a threat to the forests and an illegal activity. In fact, a substantial part of the huge turnover ends up as payments to the forest guards or profit for the middlemen.

Fuelwood is still the most preferred (and often the only available) energy source in the rural areas and a major source for the urban poor too. It is estimated that 47 per cent of the total energy consumed by households in India is from firewood, 17 per cent from animal dung and 12 per cent from crop residues. This leaves just 24 per cent for commercial energy.

While many millions like Basumati make their living by collecting and selling fuelwood, millions more collect wood just for their daily energy needs. Because of low incomes these poor people are unable to shift to commercial fuels like kerosene. All this collection of wood puts a tremendous pressure on the environment and leads to deforestation and loss of green cover.

What does the story of Basumati and others mean?

With increasing population, the demand for fuelwood keeps going up, even as the availability is going down. The challenge is to provide sufficient energy for the poor without degrading the environment.

Is there a global energy crisis?

Different groups have different perceptions on the question of an energy crisis. This is because of the huge disparity in the needs, availability, and consumption of energy between the rich and the poor of the world. One third of the world's population, that is, more than two billion people, lack access to adequate energy supplies. At least three billion people depend on fuelwood, dung, coal, charcoal, and kerosene for cooking and heating. On the other hand, the industrialised countries, with only 25 per cent of the global population, account for 70 per cent of the commercial energy consumption.

In countries like the US, any hint of shortage of oil supplies or even a small increase in the price of oil is considered a crisis. In the poorer countries like India, the shortage or increasing price of fuelwood in a village could be a crisis. An urban resident in India faces frequent power cuts, especially in summer, and thus experiences an energy crisis.

> **KEY IDEA**
> There is a huge disparity in energy needs, availability, and consumption between the rich and the poor of the world.

There are also widely varying forecasts about energy reserves. Some believe that there will be enough energy for a long time to come; others are sure that a severe shortage is only a few years away.

What are our energy needs?

We need energy to carry out almost all of our activities:

Transportation   This is the world's fastest growing form of energy use. That is largely due to the rise of the private car. There are more than 600 million cars on the road now and 40–50 million more are added every year. Around the world, we are taking more trips and travelling greater distances.

Buildings   Energy use in buildings is rising rapidly. The International Energy Agency predicts that world electricity demand will double between 2000 and 2030, with most rapid growth in people's homes.

Manufacturing   We use a major part of global energy for manufacturing our vehicles, buildings, appliances, and even our food and clothes. We need energy to make an item (embodied energy), to use it during its life (operation and maintenance), and to dispose it off when it is no longer useful (waste management).

What is the global energy consumption pattern?

About 24 per cent of energy is used for transportation, 40 per cent for industry, 30 per cent for domestic and commercial purposes, and the remaining 6 per cent for other uses including agriculture. About 30 per cent of the energy goes into the production of electrical power, which in turn is used by different sectors.

Why do we often hear about energy consumption in the US?   With just 4.6 per cent of the world's population, the US consumes 24 per cent of the total commercial energy produced. This exceeds the total amount used by the next four countries, namely, Japan, Germany, Russia and China. India, with 16 per cent of the population, accounts for just 3 per cent of the total energy.

A comparison of per capita consumption of energy for transportation shows the stark differences among countries. For every 100 units of energy consumed by a US citizen for transportation, a Danish citizen uses 45 units, a Japanese 30 units, and an Indian just 2 units! 76 per cent of Americans get to work by driving alone in a car, while just 5 per cent use public transportation.

> **KEY IDEA**
> While the US and other industrialized countries consume disproportionately large amounts of energy, countries like India and China wish to catch up with them.

Why should we worry about what the US does?   First, we should note that 92 per cent of the energy used in the US comes from non-renewable fossil fuels that release huge volumes of emissions. The US has 3 per cent of the world's oil, but consumes 26 per cent of the crude oil extracted in the world. They also waste tremendous amounts of energy. Clearly, their ecological footprint is very large and that affects the whole world.

Now, many countries including India and China are striving to reach the level of prosperity of the US. If all of us start consuming energy at the same rate as US citizens, the world will run out of fossil fuels in a few years!

What are our sources of energy?

The sources of energy are of two types—non-renewable and renewable. Non-renewable sources are limited in supply and get depleted by use. Oil and coal are examples. Renewables are replenished by natural processes and hence can be used indefinitely. Solar energy is an example.

99 per cent of our energy comes from the sun. The commercial energy we pay for is just 1 per cent of the energy we use. Without the sun, life on earth would not exist, since the average temperature would go down to −240°C. It is this solar energy that gets stored in plants as biomass. The plants use the energy for photosynthesis that produces food.

The world's commercial energy comes mostly from fossil fuels like oil, coal and natural gas. It is difficult to get precise data on consumption by fuel, but Table 8.1 gives a rough idea.

Table 8.1   Global Consumption of Energy by Fuel

Energy source	Percentage of total energy	Sub-total percentage
Non-renewable sources		
Oil	32	
Coal	21	
Natural gas	23	
Nuclear	6	
Non-renewables Total		82
Renewable sources		
Biomass (mainly wood)	11	
Solar, wind, hydro and geothermal power		
	7	
Renewables Total		18
Total	100	100

What exactly are fossil fuels and why are they non-renewable?

Fossil fuels (coal, oil, and natural gas) are the remains of organisms that lived 200–500 million years ago. During that stage of the earth's evolution, large amounts of dead organic matter had collected. Over millions of years, this matter was buried under layers of sediment and was converted by heat and pressure into coal, oil, and natural gas.

Once we discovered them, we began consuming them faster and faster. From 1859 to 1969, the total production was 227 billion barrels. (In the oil industry, the barrel is the preferred unit and one barrel contains 159 litres.) 50 per cent of this total was produced during the first 100 years, while the next 50 per cent was extracted in just ten years!

Today, our consumption rate is extremely high. We consume in one day what the earth took one thousand years to form! Fossil fuels continue to be formed, but at an extremely slow pace. That is why fossil fuels are considered to be non-renewable.

> **KEY IDEA**
> Our rate of oil consumption very high and the reserves are finite. We are clearly on an unsustainable path.

Where does all the oil go?   The millions of cars, trucks, and buses whizzing along the world's highways consume enormous amounts of oil. Oil is easy to carry and hence it is the preferred fuel for transport. Petroleum is also needed for making fertilizers, pesticides, and thousands of other products.

> **KEY IDEA**
> The term Peak Oil refers to the maximum rate of the production of oil in any area under consideration, recognising that it is a finite natural resource, subject to depletion.

Why is there a worldwide concern about oil?

The extraction of crude oil from the earth is not a simple process. When a new oil field is tapped, oil gushes out, but not for long. We have to wait for the oil to seep slowly into the well from the surrounding rocks. For this and other reasons, the maximum annual production cannot exceed

10 per cent of the remaining reserves. Oil production is thus subject to the phenomenon of peaking (Box 8.1).

BOX 8.1

Peak oil

The production of oil is governed by the Hubbert curve (Figure 8.1), proposed by the geophysicist M. King Hubbert. In any oil field, the annual production increases until about 50 per cent of the reserve has been extracted. The production peaks at this point and thereafter declines because it becomes increasingly more difficult and expensive to extract the remaining oil. At some point, the energy expended in extraction exceeds the energy yield from the extracted oil. Then the field is abandoned.

The Hubbert curve is applicable also to countries and regions. The production in the US peaked as far back as 1970 and ever since it has been declining. The world peak may have been reached already, or it will do so very soon.

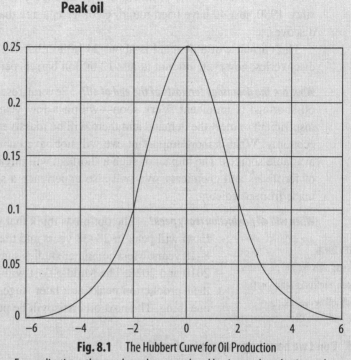

Fig. 8.1 The Hubbert Curve for Oil Production

For applications, the x and y scales are replaced by time and production scales.

'Oil peak' does not mean 'running out of oil', but it does signify the end of cheap oil. The countries of the Middle East now have most of the oil and, when · their production peaks, prices will soar. Any sharp increase in the price of oil will, of course, deeply affect many aspects of our lives.

The environmental costs of oil have been horrendous: air pollution, damage to ecosystems, carbon dioxide emissions, global warming, and so on. Major and minor oil spills have caused untold damage to the ocean, coastal zones, and marine life. In addition, the ballast water from the tankers has carried deadly organisms and toxic substances to far-off lands.

How much oil is still left and how long will it last?

The estimated recoverable reserves are 1.4 to 2.1 trillion barrels. About 70 per cent of the world's crude oil reserves are with the countries of OPEC (Organization of the Petroleum Exporting Countries). Currently, it has 12 members: Algeria, Angola, Ecuador, Iran, Iraq, Kuwait, Libya, Nigeria, Qatar, Saudi Arabia, the United Arab Emirates and Venezuela. Saudi Arabia alone accounts for 25 per cent of the total oil reserves.

The OPEC countries often give inflated figures, because the amount they are allowed to produce is a function of the declared reserves. Even large oil companies are known to falsify figures.

Currently, there are 1500 major oil fields in operation, of which the 400 large ones account for 60–70 per cent of the production. The discovery of new big fields peaked in 1962 and, since 1980, just 40 have been found. Geologists agree that there are no big ones left for us to discover.

The current world demand is about 24 billion barrels per year and is rising. Current new discoveries, however, amount to just 12 billion barrels per year and this is declining!

What are the doomsday forecasts of the end of oil?   Several research groups have suggested that an oil shortage is imminent. Very soon—within a few years, perhaps—oil from wells will be insufficient to meet the demand and there will be massive disruptions in transportation and the economy. What is more important, we will not have enough time to switch from oil to other available sources. The impact of such a shortage will threaten global food security, due to lack of fertilisers and chemicals. We will also experience a shortage of 500,000 goods currently made from petroleum.

When will oil production really peak?   The optimists think that world production (other than Middle East) will peak in 28–38 years and the pessimists swear that we have only 8–18 years. Most computer studies suggest that the peak will occur between 2010 and 2020. The Middle East will then have most of the oil and, when their production peaks at a later stage, prices will soar. We can be sure of one thing: The next oil crisis will be permanent!

> **KEY IDEA**
> World oil is likely to peak fairly soon. High prices and shortages will follow peak oil.

Don't we have huge amounts of coal?

At current rates of use, the world's coal reserves will probably last for another 200 years. There are, however, many problems with coal use. Coal has to be mined from underground or from the surface. Underground mines, besides being dangerous, also cause lung disease among the miners.

Among the fossil fuels, coal is most harmful to the environment. The mines create major land disturbances and the burning of coal causes severe air pollution. Coal is currently responsible for 36 per cent of carbon dioxide emissions in the world. In addition, it releases huge amounts of radioactive particles into the atmosphere, more than a properly operating nuclear power plant. Every year, air pollution from coal kills thousands of people and causes respiratory diseases in thousands more.

Is natural gas a good option?

Natural gas, a mixture of methane, butane, ethane and propane, is found above most oil reserves. While propane and butane are liquefied and removed as LPG, methane is cleaned and pumped into pipelines.

About 40 per cent of the total natural gas is in Russia and Kazakhstan. The available reserves are expected to last 200–300 years. Its abundance, low production cost, and low pollution make it the ideal fuel during the transition from fossil fuels to renewable sources. However, long pipelines are needed to carry natural gas.

What are the pros and cons of nuclear power?

In a nuclear reactor, neutrons split the nuclei of elements like Uranium and Plutonium and in the process release energy as heat. This high-temperature heat is used to produce steam, which runs the electric turbine.

In 1953, the US President Eisenhower announced that nuclear power will be 'too cheap to meter'. At that time it was predicted that, by the end of the century, nuclear power would be generating most of the world's electricity. This source seemed the ideal answer to the energy problem. The fuel supply seemed unlimited, the environmental impact was thought to be very low, and safety appeared to be assured. Things, however, turned out to be very different.

What went wrong with nuclear power?   The plants cost much more than the estimates, the operating costs were high, the technical problems were more intractable than expected, and the economic feasibility came to be doubted. But worse was to come.

The plants generate large amounts of deadly radioactive waste. The low-level waste must be stored safely for 100–500 years, while the high-level waste remains radioactive for a mind-boggling 240,000 years! Sixty years after the advent of nuclear power, we have no satisfactory way of storing the waste. Meanwhile more wastes are piling up in the plants. In addition, plutonium (a by-product of certain nuclear reactions) removed from old nuclear warheads have also to be stored somewhere.

Nuclear power plants as well as nuclear weapons testing have created thousands of contaminated sites, particularly in the US and the former USSR. The cost of cleaning them up will run into millions of dollars. Similarly, decommissioning an old plant costs more than the original construction!

The biggest problem, however, has been the loss of public confidence over the safety of the plants. Several minor accidents were followed by the major one in Chernobyl, which released radioactive dust over thousands of square kilometres and may ultimately cause between 100,000 and 475,000 cancer deaths (Read Box 14.3, Chapter 14).

What is the status of nuclear power?   Today, there are about 440 nuclear power reactors operating in 30 countries. Nuclear power accounts only for about 6 per cent of the total commercial energy.

> **KEY IDEA**
> Coal, natural gas, and nuclear power have associated problems and cannot easily replace oil.

Given the worldwide concerns about nuclear power, there was for some time little growth in nuclear energy. In fact, countries like Germany and Sweden even decided to phase out nuclear power within the next 20–30 years. However, nuclear power is back in contention now. 58 new reactors are currently being constructed in 14 countries including India. In the US, the lives of many reactors have been extended from the original 40 to 60 years.

Why can't we move to safer renewable sources?

An estimated US$ 200–250 billion in invested in energy-related infrastructure every year and another US$ 1.5 trillion is spent on energy consumption, with nearly all of this investment going to conventional energy. Thus, the world has been locked into indefinite dependence on unhealthy, unsustainable, and insecure energy structures. However, things are improving now, with rapidly increasing investments in renewables like solar and wind power.

What kind of energy do we get from the sun?

We receive from the sun a pure, non-polluting, and inexhaustible form of energy. Solar energy comes from the thermonuclear fusion reaction constantly taking place in the sun. All the radioactive and polluting by-products of the reaction are safely left behind in the sun, 150 million km away.

An enormous amount of solar energy falls on this tiny planet Earth. What we get from the sun in one month is more than the energy stored in all the fossil fuels we have. Also, using this vast amount of energy does not pollute the biosphere in any way.

Why then are we not using solar energy for all our needs? There are difficulties in using solar energy. It is a diffuse source falling evenly over a vast area and the first problem is to collect it efficiently. The second problem is to convert it into a usable form like electricity.

You can guess what the third problem is: What do we do when it is cloudy and the sun does not shine? We must have an efficient way of storing the energy. All research in solar energy is about finding cost-effective ways of collection, conversion, and storage.

How do we convert solar energy directly into electricity? This conversion is done by a photovoltaic cell (or PV cell), which consists of two layers of silicon. The lower layer has electrons that are easily lost and the upper one readily gains electrons. When light energy strikes the cell, it dislodges electrons from the lower layer. This sets up an electric current through the circuit carrying the electrons to the upper layer. Each cell generates only a small amount of power, but many cells, placed together on a panel, creates enough power to run an appliance.

The power from a solar panel is usually stored in a battery, to which we connect the appliance. Thus the energy is generated and stored when the sun shines on the panel and is used whenever needed. The direct current from the battery can be converted into alternating current through an inverter. You can then run normal appliances like a fan or television.

PV cells are used today in watches, pocket calculators, toys, etc. Larger solar panels can light up a house, run an irrigation pump, operate traffic lights, and so on. Solar power is a viable alternative in remote areas where power lines cannot be taken due to cost or difficulty of access. For example, Ladakh in the Himalayas is powered by solar panels and this has made a tremendous change to the people's lives.

How has the solar water heater become so popular in some Indian cities? The water heater is a simple and successful use of solar energy.

It absorbs solar radiation as heat and transfers the heat to the water. An efficient design of heater uses evacuated tube collectors. The collectors are made of parallel rows of transparent glass tubes, each of which has inner and outer tubes.

Solar water heater on a rooftop
(Image courtesy: Gilabrand, http://commons.
wikimedia.org/wiki/File:Solarboiler.jpg)

The vacuum in the space between the two tubes minimizes conductive and convective heat loss.

The collector is placed at a suitable angle to catch the sun's radiation. Cold water moves through a smaller pipe in the inner tube, gets heated, and collects in a tank. An electric heater element is also provided in the tank as backup for cloudy days.

Since electric water geysers are energy-guzzlers, solar heaters are a very good option. They pay back their capital cost in reasonable time. Soft bank loans are also available for buying such heaters. Some cities in India have made it mandatory for all new houses to install solar water heaters.

Why can't we directly focus the sun's rays on the material we want to heat? Make a parabolic reflector, something like a dish antenna and place a bowl with rice at the focal point. You will soon have your lunch ready. In fact, solar cookers of this type are available in India and some hotels and community kitchens use them.

In the international community of Auroville near Pudducherry, there is a large solar bowl, 15 m in diameter. It concentrates the sun's energy on to a tube that carries a special liquid. The hot liquid in turn heats water to produce steam, which is used for cooking. The solar kitchen serves 2,000 meals every day.

> **KEY IDEA**
> Solar energy is renewable and non-polluting, but the challenge is to find cost-effective ways of collection, conversion, and storage of energy.

For home needs there are small box-type solar cookers. Food cooked this way saves fuel, tastes better, and is good for the health. Put it out in the sun facing in the right direction and food will be ready in an hour or two depending on the food and the intensity of sunlight.

What about tapping wind energy?

If you travel from Nagercoil to Kanyakumari in South India, you will see hundreds of sleek-looking windmills slowly rotating and generating electricity. India is now a leading player in the wind energy scene. Globally, wind farms produce about 200 GW (Giga Watts) of energy. Europe produces 70 per cent of it with Denmark as the leader (Box 8.2). Europe plans to generate 10 per cent of its electricity from wind by 2025.

BOX 8.2

The story of Denmark: Life after oil

In 1998, the 4,400 residents of Brundby on a Danish island decided that they would give up fossil fuels in ten years. There are now more than twenty wind turbines generating as much energy as the island consumes from fossil fuels. Home heating, which is a necessity in Denmark, is through hot water made from burning straw.

Over six years, the island cut its energy consumption by 25 per cent, drastically reduced emissions of nitrous oxide, sulphuric acid, and carbon dioxide. The European Union plans to replicate in 100 other communities so that 12 per cent of the total energy in the Union would come from renewables by 2010.

Denmark has been making huge investments on developing green technologies. Twenty per cent of its electricity is now generated by renewable sources. It is also a world leader in wind power. Its windmills and generators are exported to many countries including India. The Danish wind power company, Vestas, has set up a manufacturing unit in Chennai.

A wind farm
(Image courtesy: James McCauley, http://commons.wikimedia.
org/wiki/File:Windmills.jpg)

Wind energy produces electricity at low cost, the capital costs are also moderate, and there are no emissions. Wind farms can be quickly set up and easily expanded.

Where is the catch?   Obviously, you need steady winds of a certain velocity and not every place is suitable. In any case, you will need some form of backup for windless days. It is a case of high land use, though attempts have been made to use the space below the windmills for agriculture or grazing. There is some noise pollution and the monotonous view of hundreds of windmills is visual pollution. In addition, there is a fear that windmills could interfere with the flight of migratory birds.

Is hydropower a good alternative?

20 per cent of the world's electricity comes from hydropower. In order to get sizable amount of power, we need a high dam on a river with a large reservoir. The potential energy of the water falling from a height runs the turbine.

Hydropower has several advantages. The cost of generation is low and there are no emissions. The reservoir can provide water for irrigation round the year and can also be used for fishing and recreation. It also gives drinking water to towns and cities.

What is the bad news?   Dams cost a lot of money and take years to build. Most of the suitable rivers of the world have already been dammed and it is now difficult to find new spots. The reservoir drowns large areas of farmland, wildlife habitats, and places of historical and cultural importance. An example is Tehri town, which disappeared under the waters of a dam.

> **KEY IDEA**
> Hydropower depends on dams, which cause ecological damage and displacement of people.

Large dams also cause large-scale displacement of local communities. The people lose their lands and become environmental refugees. Often, compensation for the lost land is meagre (and not even paid on time) and resettlement never satisfactory. Dams impede the migration of fish along the river and reduce the silt flowing downstream. In fact, the sediments pile up against the dam and reduce its useful life. There is a worldwide movement against the building of large dams.

There are other renewable sources like tidal energy, ocean thermal energy, geothermal energy, and energy from biomass (plant material and animal wastes). They are useful as small-scale alternatives, but cannot yet satisfy the world's enormous appetite for energy. In particular, they are not yet suitable for transportation.

What about the hydrogen economy?

Many experts believe that, as we run out of fossil fuels, we will move towards using the element hydrogen as the main fuel to run the world's economy. When hydrogen burns and gives us energy, it combines with oxygen to produce water vapour. In this process, there is no air pollution or emission of carbon dioxide.

This is good news again! What are we waiting for?   There is some bad news too. Hydrogen is not available in a free state: it is locked up in water and in compounds like petrol and methane. We need energy and an effective method to get the hydrogen out. We can split water by heat or by a process called electrolysis to get hydrogen. We can also get it from fuels like petrol, natural gas and methanol. Thus the first problem is one of collection.

As in the case of solar energy, we have the problem of storage too. Hydrogen is highly explosive and if it is stored as compressed gas, the tank will be large, heavy and costly. Only large buses and trucks could hold the tanks. If we store it as a liquid, we need very low temperatures and this will require energy. Another method being tried out is storage as solid metal hydride. Here again, energy is needed to release the hydrogen when we want it.

What about fuel cells that are often in the news?   A fuel cell is so called because it is an electrochemical unit like a battery. The fuel cell burns hydrogen to produce electricity. In the process, hydrogen combines with oxygen to produce water vapour. Thus there is no pollution and it runs continuously as long as there is input.

Unlike a battery, the fuel cell draws its input (hydrogen and oxygen) from outside. Again, a battery requires recharging, but the fuel cell does not. Finally, there is no toxic output when a fuel cell is discarded.

Fuel cells were developed as far back as 1960 for space applications. The progress since then has, however, been slow. There are now experimental buses and cars running on fuel cells, but they are very expensive. Automobile companies like Daimler-Chrysler, Honda, and General Motors have made prototype fuel-cell cars.

KEY IDEA

Hydrogen appears to be the dream fuel, but it takes energy to produce it first. Storage of hydrogen is also a problem.

What are the problems with using hydrogen?   First, it takes energy to produce hydrogen. Obviously, against this input, we should get much more energy from the hydrogen we produce.

Second, if this input energy comes from fossil fuels, there will be environmental effects. Third, the situation is even worse, if we produce the hydrogen from fossil fuels themselves. Finally, we have not fully solved the problem of storing hydrogen.

Where is the hydrogen economy then?   We must find first cost-effective ways of producing hydrogen from water using renewable energy like solar. We should solve all the storage problems too. In the best scenario, we would be using electrical and thermal energy produced by renewable sources like solar and incorporate hydrogen as the fuel for transport (Box 8.3).

BOX 8.3

The story of Iceland: World's first hydrogen economy?

Iceland promises to become the world's first hydrogen economy over the next 25–30 years. For this purpose, the Government of Iceland has teamed up with companies like Daimler-Chrysler, Royal Dutch Shell, and Norsk Hydro. The project is the brainchild of the chemist Bragi Arnason.

The project will produce hydrogen from seawater using the country's abundant renewable energy sources: wind, geothermal and hydropower. Hydrogen will run buses, cars, fishing vessels, and even factories. Royal Dutch Shell will operate hydrogen filling stations.

Iceland's experiment could become a model for other countries.

We must remember, however, that neither hydrogen nor any other wonder fuel, for that matter, is going to save us if we keep increasing our energy use or even maintain the current usage levels. The hydrogen economy will be viable only if we use energy much more efficiently and reduce our consumption levels. As of now, there is no sign of this happening.

> **KEY IDEA**
> Renewable sources such as solar energy, wind power, hydrogen, and hydropower all have limitations.

Once again we face the same hurdle: There is a natural limit to the amount of resources on this planet. When we overstep that limit, we will inevitably face an insurmountable hurdle.

Given all the limits and difficulties, are we using energy efficiently?

Increasing the efficiency of energy use will be equivalent to finding free sources of energy. There is tremendous scope for increasing energy efficiency in all our activities. For example, just replacing the incandescent bulb with a compact fluorescent lamp (CFL) reduces consumption by 75 per cent. The initial cost is more, but over time it pays back. At the same time, we are doing a service to society by consuming less energy. Incidentally, the cost of CFLs has been steadily coming down.

The internal combustion engine (I.C. Engine) that runs our automobiles is another device that wastes 90 per cent of the input energy. Driven by the first oil crisis, the fuel efficiency of American cars gradually increased between 1973 and 1985. Since then, however, it has levelled off primarily because of the consumer craze for the so-called Sport Utility Vehicle (SUV), minivan, etc. and because of the availability of cheap oil.

Makers like Toyota and Honda have introduced hybrid electric cars with much higher fuel efficiency. They run on petrol and a battery. The battery is kept charged by the petrol engine and an electric motor provides energy for acceleration and hill climbing. When the car is braked, part of the heat generated is used to charge the battery.

Whenever we use energy, some waste is inevitable. However, there is a large amount of avoidable waste in energy use. One estimate is that we waste more than 40 per cent of commercial energy we buy. Examples are vehicles and furnaces that waste fuel and poorly designed buildings that use up huge amounts of energy for heating and cooling. There is also the huge inefficiency of conventionally-fuelled power stations and big transmission losses.

Technology exists today for increasing the efficiency of most appliances by 50 per cent or more. As the demand for energy-efficient appliances increase, the prices will also come down. We must always consider the lifecycle cost of devices, that is, the total of the initial cost and the operating costs over the lifetime of the device. Such an approach will make us take better decisions that will save cost and energy.

> **KEY IDEA**
> Our first task is to use energy very efficiently.

How is the energy scene in India?

In India, about one-third of the energy comes from non-commercial sources. The rural population depends heavily on fuelwood, dung, and animal waste. In the urban areas, there are large numbers of non-motorized vehicles like bicycles, rickshaws, handcarts, and animal carts.

India ranks sixth in the world in total energy consumption. Our per capita energy consumption is 490 units (kg of oil equivalent), compared to 8,000 units in the US and 1,300 units in China.

Though we have abundant coal reserves, we have very little oil. More than 25 per cent of our primary energy needs is met by import of crude oil and natural gas.

In 2007, of the total energy used in India, 40.8 per cent came from coal, 27.2 per cent from biomass, 23.7 per cent from oil, 5.6 per cent from natural gas, 1.8 per cent from hydropower, and just 0.7 per cent from nuclear plants.

Table 8.2 gives approximate figures of India's production and consumption of fossil fuels. India is the sixth largest net importer of oil in the world, importing 70 per cent of its needs.

Table 8.2   Production and Consumption of Fossil Fuels in India
(2009 Data)

Fossil fuel	Production	Consumption
Crude oil	680,000 barrels/day	3 million barrels/day
Natural gas	1.4 trillion cu.ft	1.8 trillion cu.ft
Coal	610 million tons	680 million tons

India has 19 nuclear power reactors in operation. Four more are being added and 20 further units are planned.

We have major programmes for renewable energy. The government is promoting wind farms, solar energy, hydropower as well as waste-to-energy projects. Several wind farms have been set up in South India. Solar pumps, water-heaters, and lighting systems are widely available, though the initial costs are high.

Are we trying to conserve energy?

It is clear that we must conserve energy by improving efficiency at each of the stages: Production, transmission, and utilisation. According to estimates, we can save up to 40 per cent of energy in India through conservation. The Energy Conservation Act (2001) specifies energy standards and promotes energy audits.

The Bureau of Energy Efficiency (BEE) is the agency that implements the Act. Among other activities, BEE awards star ratings to brands of appliances such as fluorescent lamps, refrigerators, and air-conditioners. Each tested brand gets a rating of 1 star (least energy efficient) to 5 stars (most energy efficient). The voluntary scheme will be made compulsory later.

What does it all amount to?

No wonder fuel is going to save us if we keep increasing our energy use or even maintain the current usage levels. Once again we face the same hurdle: There is a natural limit to the amount of resources on this planet. When we overstep that limit, we will inevitably face an insurmountable hurdle. We can survive only if we use energy much more efficiently and reduce our consumption levels. As of now, there is no sign of this happening.

Meanwhile, our intensive energy use is leading to global warming and climate change. We will discuss these topics in Chapter 19 (Social Consequences of Development and Environmental Changes).

Ending on a hopeful note: Positive stories

Two initiatives, one international and the other in India, attempt to bring solar lighting to the poor people (Boxes 8.4 and 8.5). Boxes 8.6 and 8.7 list a few tips to save electricity and energy.

BOX 8.4

The story of One Million Lights

One Million Lights is a part of the World of Color public charity, a nonprofit organization based in Palo Alto, US. The mission of One Million Lights is to improve the daily lives of children and adults by providing clean and healthy lighting.

To accomplish this, they are distributing solar lights to families around the world. These solar lights replace environmentally toxic kerosene lamps and enable children to study at night. Their goal is to distribute one million (1,000,000) solar lights to replace kerosene lamps. One Million Lights also works with local schools to increase awareness of global issues.

BOX 8.5

The story of a solar campaign: Lighting a Billion Lives

The Energy and Resources Institute (TERI), New Delhi, has launched an initiative called 'Lighting a Billion Lives' (LaBL)—a campaign to promote the use of solar lighting devices by the poor.

Over 1.6 billion people in the world lack access to electricity and roughly 25 per cent of them are in India. These people are forced to light their homes with kerosene lamps, dung cakes, firewood, and crop residue. Lack of lighting or poor lighting affects their livelihood, health, environment, safety, and children's education.

The LaBL Campaign plans to bring solar light into the lives of one billion rural people. The distribution and servicing of solar lanterns is done by local entrepreneurs trained by TERI in association with its grass-roots level (government and NGO) partners. These local entrepreneurs are village youth, women, elders, or teachers. The lanterns are supplied by product partners.

The rural entrepreneurs are selected and trained to manage and run central solar lantern charging/distribution centres from where people rent the lanterns for a reasonable fee. The entrepreneurs are responsible for generating awareness, finding customers, maintaining the solar lanterns and operating the charging stations. Thus apart from providing reliable and ensured lighting to households at an affordable rate, the Campaign also facilitates entrepreneurial development among rural communities.

The campaign is being implemented according to a necessity index that has been developed for each state in India. Funds to the tune of Rs 230 billion need to be raised for providing lanterns to 65 million rural households in India. But this amount is less than half of total implied subsidy on kerosene consumption in the country. Further, each solar lantern saves 40–60 litres of kerosene/year, leading to a total saving of Rs 100 billion burned each year in kerosene and wick lamps.

Thousands of lanterns are already in use in a number of states in India and neighbouring countries.

BOX 8.6

Save electricity at home and in the office

- Turn off lights and fans when you leave a room.
- Shut off personal computers, television sets, set-top boxes, music systems, etc., when not in use: All appliances consume energy even on standby mode.
- Install automatic switch-off devices for areas like staircases.
- Replace all the bulbs in your home with Compact Fluorescent Lamps (CFL), or even better, with Light Emitting Diodes (LEDs). Thanks to lower power bills, you can recover the cost in a few months.
- If you can afford it, install a solar lighting system: Apart some saving electricity, it will give you light during power breakdowns.

- If you use hot water, install a solar water heater in place of an electric geyser.
- Use a solar cooker, say, for rice and dal: It saves gas and the food tastes better.
- Buy energy-efficient appliances when you replace old ones or you need new ones. Check always the specifications for energy consumption figures and look for the BEE star rating.
- Iron a pile of clothes at a time, instead of one or two at a time.
- Run a washing machine only when there is a full load.
- Avoid using kitchen machines every day. Grind spices once or twice a week.
- Build your house following the principles of ecological architecture.

BOX 8.7

Save energy in transportation

- Minimise the use of automobiles for your personal transport.
- Keep your vehicles tuned for low consumption of fuel.
- Avoid idling your vehicle at signals and traffic jams: Ten seconds of idling uses more fuel than in restarting the vehicle.
- Use bicycle for local work like shopping.

- Use public transport whenever possible: One busload of people takes 40 vehicles off the road during rush hour, saves 70,000 litres of petrol, and avoids over 175 tons of emissions every year.
- Join car pools.
- Live near your place of study or work, if possible.
- Check fuel consumption data while buying a new vehicle.
- Avoid air travel; if you can, go by train instead.

REVIEW: A SUMMARY OF THE KEY POINTS

- There is a serious fuelwood crisis in India and other developing countries.
- The end of cheap oil is not far away. Fairly soon, prices will soar, and there will be widespread repercussions.
- There will be serious depletion of energy resources, if countries like China and India seek to copy the

energy consumption levels of the richer countries.
- Energy efficiency can and must be increased.
- We must use the most sustainable, least polluting sources with high efficiency.
- Almost all sources of energy have their limits and problems.

EXERCISES

Objective-type questions

For each question below, choose the best answer out of the given choices:

1. Which source provides the maximum percentage of energy to the people of India?
   (a) Fuelwood or firewood
   (b) LPG
   (c) Animal dung
   (d) Electricity

2. Which of the following statements is true with regard to global energy?
   (a) We know clearly how much of reserve energy we have.
   (b) The industrialized countries consume a huge part of the total energy.
   (c) Energy supply is evenly distributed across all countries and within countries.
   (d) Fuelwood is easily available for the poor people in the developing countries.

3. Which is the world's fastest growing form of energy use?
   (a) Manufacturing
   (b) Buildings
   (c) Transport
   (d) Home consumption

4. Which of the following statements is **not true** with regard to fossil fuels?
   (a) We consume as much fossil fuel in one day as what the earth took one thousand years to form.
   (b) Fossil fuels are non-renewable sources of energy.
   (c) The burning of fossil fuels causes environmental damage.
   (d) Fossil fuels continue to be formed at a rapid pace.

5. Which of the following is a renewable energy source?
   (a) Natural gas
   (b) Coal
   (c) Wind
   (d) Nuclear reactor

6. Which of the following is **not** a problem with regard to solar energy?
   (a) Efficient collection of energy
   (b) Conversion of energy into electricity
   (c) Not being a renewable source
   (d) Storage of energy

7. Which of the following is **not** a problem with regard to hydropower?
   (a) It is a renewable source.
   (b) People have to move to other places.
   (c) Dams submerge large areas.
   (d) Dams get silted up.

8. What is the main problem in using hydrogen as fuel?
   (a) The burning of hydrogen produces no emissions.
   (b) The burning of hydrogen produces water.
   (c) Hydrogen can be produced from water.
   (d) It takes energy to produce hydrogen.

Short-answer questions

1. What is the main source of energy for this planet and how does it give us the energy?
2. List the various forms of commercial energy and give the proportion of each in the total.
3. Which country consumes the maximum amount of energy and why is this fact relevant?
4. Why are fossil fuels non-renewable?
5. Explain the Hubbert curve and the concept of peaking.
6. Compare the advantages and disadvantages of oil, coal, and natural gas as energy sources.
7. What are the special problems of nuclear power?
8. How is solar energy converted to electrical power and what are the problems in this regard?
9. What are the prospects of getting more hydropower?
10. What are the hurdles in moving to a hydrogen economy?
11. How can we improve energy efficiency?

Long-answer questions

1. Describe the fuelwood situation in the developing countries, emphasising the relationship between poverty and environment.
2. Describe the different scenarios with respect to the availability of oil. Which scenario appears reasonable to you and why?
3. Explain how almost every source of energy has its limits.

Think critically: Deeper question for reflection and discussion

Given that almost every source of energy has its limits and problems, what should be our attitude to using energy in this world?

SOMETHING DIFFERENT FOR A CHANGE

1. A short poem by the Sufi poet, Jalaluddin Rumi (1207–1273), for you to reflect on:

   Every moment
   the sunlight is totally empty
   and totally full.

2. Read the novel *Oil Dusk: A Peak Oil Story* by John M. Cape and Laura Buckner.

ACTIVITIES

Act: What you can do to conserve energy

Each one of us can take action to conserve energy in our personal life and work places. We can save energy at home, in the office, and in transportation (Boxes 8.6 and 8.7).

Learn by doing: Case study / Project

Do an energy audit of your college. Examine the consumption of all forms of energy over three months and find out how much energy each activity consumes.

Find out also the cost aspects. Come up with proposals for a) reducing the demand, b) increasing the energy efficiency and c) ways of using renewable energy.

Organize together: Eco-club activity

Observe December 14 as the National Energy Conservation Day. On that day, National Energy Conservation Awards are given to industrial units who have taken exception initiatives on energy conservation.

LEARN MORE

Book

Deffeyes, Kenneth S. 2008, *Hubbert's Peak: The Impending World Oil Shortage*, Princeton University Press, Princeton, NJ.

Articles

Das, Anjana and Vikram Dayal 1998, 'An Energy Shortage Closer to Home', *The Economic Times*, 15 January.

Field, Ted 1993, 'Wood-starved and footsore-global fuelwood shortage—World Forests', *American Forests*, July-August.

Mahapatra, Richard 2002, 'Phulmai's Walk', *Down To Earth*, Vol.11, No.14, December 15, pp. 25–34.

Mahapatra, Richard 2003, 'The Multi-billion-dollar Fuelwood Trade is the Last Resort for India's Poor', *InfoChange News & Features*, June (from the website www.infochangeindia.org)

Websites

1992 World Scientists' Warning to Humanity (Union of Concerned Scientists USA): www.ucsusa.org/about/1992–world-scientists.html

India Energy Portal set up by the Energy and Resources Institute: www.indiaenergyportal.org

Life After the Oil Crash: http://www.lifeaftertheoilcrash.net/

Lighting a Billion Lives: http://labl.teriin.org/

One Million Lights: www.onemillionlights.org

Post Carbon Institute's Energy Bulletin: http://energybulletin.net/

Films

A Crude Awakening: The Oil Crash, a documentary by Basil Gelpke and Ray McCormack (2006)

Blind Spot, a documentary by Adolfo Doring (2008)

Crude Impact, a documentary by James Jandak Wood (2006)

Who Killed the Electric Car?, a documentary by Chris Paine that explores the creation and destruction by the US auto maker General Motors of the battery electric car, called EV1, in the mid-1990s (2006)

CHAPTER 9

Forest Resources

The best time to plant a tree was twenty years ago.
The second best time is now.

Anonymous

THIS CHAPTER IS ABOUT...

Forests—global status, resources, services, logging, conservation, community involvement

THE KEYWORDS AND PHRASES ARE...

extractive reserve	Joint Forest Management	old-growth forest	sacred grove
second-growth forest	social forestry	sustainable forest management	

THE STORY OF THE ANDAMAN AND NICOBAR ISLANDS: LAST CHANCE OR LOST OPPORTUNITY?

It is a complex case involving a century of forest exploitation, the rights of indigenous people, inward migration, road development, and finally an intervention by the Supreme Court. Through it all, the plunder of the forests has continued unabated.

The Andaman and Nicobar Islands contain some of the finest tropical evergreen forests in the world. They are also rich in biodiversity with a variety of known and unknown species of flora and fauna.

The British established a Forest Department on the islands in 1883 and began the extraction of timber using convict labour. Even after Independence, however, logging has continued without a break. This has led to forest degradation. Further, the resulting soil erosion has resulted in heavy flow of sediments into the coastal waters that has smothered and killed a substantial amount of corals. Mangroves and corals have also been adversely affected by extraction. Species like the saltwater crocodile and the Andaman wild pig have become endangered.

The indigenous communities have been seriously affected with their traditional occupations threatened and rights violated. Communities like the Great Andamanese, the Onge, the Jarawa, and the Sentinelese have lived and flourished here for at least 20,000 years, but they could soon become extinct.

About 150 years ago the population of the tribal communities was estimated to be at least 5,000. Over the years, there has been a substantial government-supported migration of people from other parts of the country into the Islands. Today, in a total population of 500,000, the four indigenous communities put together account for a mere 500. The current total population, however, is much more than the size that the Islands can support. Already, there is a scarcity of drinking water.

A major factor affecting the forests and the communities is the 340-km-long Andaman Trunk Road (ATR). Originating in Port Blair in South Andaman, the ATR cuts across the islands to reach Diglipur in the North. In some places, it traverses through virgin tracts of forestland in the Jarawa Reserve. The ATR has increased the interaction between the Jarawas and the settlers as well as the tourists and eroded much of the natives' original way of life.

Responding to a public interest petition, the Supreme Court of India passed several orders in 2002: ban on the commercial exploitation of timber from the islands' forests, ban on the transport of timber to any other part of the country, removal of encroachments, restrictions on inward migration, phasing out of monoculture plantations, reducing sand mining on the beach, and closure of the Andaman Trunk Road in areas where it passes through the Jarawa Reserve.

One might think that it was a happy ending. The local administration, however, did not implement many of the orders. Several months after the passing of the court deadlines, they filed a petition asking for a review of the orders. Perhaps a great opportunity to implement a model conservation programme was lost.

Then came the tsunami of December 2004, which hit the Islands with devastating effect: over 3,500 people dead or missing; nearly 8,000 ha of fertile land rendered useless; nearly 1,000 boats completely damaged; and more than 150,000 head of cattle lost. The tsunami also destroyed coral reefs, mangroves, and the coastal ecology. There have also been several earthquake warnings since then.

The ecology of the Islands and the fate of the tribes continue to be in the balance. Meanwhile, the environmental degradation goes on and the tribes are withering away.

What does the case of Andaman and Nicobar Islands tell us?

The case of Andaman and Nicobar Islands is typical of what is happening to the world's forests. Massive deforestation through the extraction of timber, opening up of forests through road-building, population pressures, problems of indigenous people, and similar issues plague forests everywhere.

What is the state of the world's forests?

It is difficult to assess the extent of the world's forests. Data supplied by countries are often not reliable, though satellite imagery is being increasingly used to verify data from ground surveys. The definition of a forest also varies from one assessment to another.

The highlights of two global forest assessments are presented below, one from the World Commission on Forests and Sustainable Development (WCFSD) and the other from the UN Food and Agricultural Organization (UN FAO).

Following the Earth Summit in 1992, an independent World Commission on Forests and Sustainable Development (WCFSD) was established. The Commission had 22 members including M.S. Swaminathan and Kamla Chowdhary of India.

The Commission held public hearings in Asia, Africa, Europe, Latin America and the Caribbean, and North America. It met with forest communities, farmers, industry executives, etc. It took note of what scientists, economists, foresters, government officials, and other specialists involved in national and international forest policy had to say. It listened to

KEY IDEA
The rate of deforestation in the world shows signs of decreasing, but is still alarmingly high.

the views of environmental groups. The main conclusions of the 1999 WCFSD Report are given in Box 9.1.

BOX 9.1

World Commission on Forests and Sustainable Development (WCFSD)

The main conclusions of the 1999 WCFSD Report were:

- The world's remaining forested areas amount to about 3.6 billion hectares in 1999, down from about 6.0 billion ha 8000 years ago.
- 56 countries have lost 90–100 per cent of their forests.
- Over the last two decades of the 20th century, 15 million ha of forests were lost annually, largely in the tropics.
- About 14 million ha of tropical forests have been lost each year since 1980 due to conversion into cropland.
- Forest decline threatens the genetic diversity of

the world's plants and animals. About 12.5 per cent of the world's plant species, and about 75 per cent of the mammal species are threatened by forest decline.

- In developing countries alone, some US$ 45 billion per year is lost through poor forest management.
- In Europe, forests are declining due to drought, heat, pests, and air pollution. The number of completely healthy trees in European forests fell from 69 per cent in 1988 to 39 per cent in 1995.

The Commission concluded, 'The decline is relentless. We suspect it could change the very character of the planet and of the human enterprise within a few years unless we make some choices'.

The UN FAO carries out a Global Forest Resources Assessment every five years. The 2010 Assessment (FRA 2010) examined the current status and recent trends for all types of forests in 233 countries. Its key findings are given in Box 9.2.

BOX 9.2

Global Forest Resources Assessment 2010

The key findings of the UN FAO Global Forest Resources Assessment 2010 were:

- Forests cover 31 per cent of total land area. The world's total forest area is just over 4 billion hectares, which corresponds to an average of 0.6 ha per capita.
- The rate of deforestation shows signs of decreasing, but is still alarmingly high. Deforestation (mainly the conversion of tropical forest to agricultural land) shows signs of decreasing in several countries but continues at a high rate in others. Insect pests and diseases, natural disasters and invasive species are causing severe damage in some countries.
- South America and Africa continue to have the largest net loss of forest. In Asia, the forest area increased between 1990 and 2010 as a result of

large-scale afforestation efforts, particularly in China.

- Primary forests account for 36 per cent. The area of planted forest accounts for 7 per cent of total forest area. Large-scale planting of trees is significantly reducing the net loss of forest area globally.
- Legally established protected areas cover an estimated 13 per cent of the world's forests.
- Forests store a vast amount of carbon.
- 12 per cent of the world's forests are designated for the conservation of biological diversity. 8 per cent of the world's forests have protection of soil and water resources as their primary objective.
- 30 per cent of the world's forests are primarily used for production of wood and non-wood forest products. Wood removals increased

Contd

Box 9.2 Contd

between 2000 and 2005 and fuelwood accounted for about half of the removed wood.

- Around 10 million people are employed in forest management and conservation, but many more are directly dependent on forests for their livelihoods.
- Significant progress has been made in developing forest policies, laws and national forest programmes. 80 per cent of the world's forests are publicly owned, but ownership and management of forests by communities, individuals and private companies is on the rise
- The number of university students graduating in forestry is increasing.
- There are many good signs and positive trends towards sustainable forest management at the global level.

Estimates of forest cover in India were given in Chapter 3.

How are forests classified from the point of view of exploitation as a resource?

There are mainly three categories of forests: Old-growth, second-growth, and plantations. Old growth or frontier forests are uncut forests that have not been seriously disturbed by human activities or natural disasters for several hundred years or more.

Second-growth forests result from ecological succession (Chapter 2) that takes place when forests are cleared (by human activities or due to natural disasters) and then left undisturbed for long periods of time.

Plantations are managed forests of commercially valuable trees. They are created mostly by clearing old-growth or second-growth forests. Plantations promote monoculture, concentrating on one or a few species. Being less diverse than natural forests, they are more prone to diseases and other disturbances.

There is now an increasing reliance on plantations as the source of industrial wood. This is a new development and half of all the plantations of the world are less than 15 years old. More than 60 per cent of plantations are in Asia, many owned by foreign companies.

What are the products and services provided by forests?

Industrial wood and fuelwood: According to FRA 2010, reported wood removals amounted to 3.4 billion cu. m annually in the period 2003–2007. Considering that informally and illegally removed wood, especially fuelwood, is not usually recorded, the actual amount of wood removals is undoubtedly higher. As mentioned in Box 9.2, half the wood removed is fuelwood, mostly produced and consumed in the developing countries. The remaining half is industrial wood, 80 per cent of which comes from the industrialised countries.

Non-wood products: In many of the poorer countries, especially in Asia, non-wood forest products (NWFP) such as food, fibre, honey, and medicinal plants form an important source of income and a critical component of food security and well-being. Some forests are also sources of minerals.

Ecosystem services Forests provide a range of services like soil generation, soil and water conservation, purification of air and water, nutrient recycling, maintenance of biodiversity,

KEY IDEA

Forests provide a range of invaluable products, ecosystem services, and other contributions.

providing habitat for animals, mitigation of climate change, and absorption of carbon. Forests contain about half of the world's biodiversity. Natural forests have the highest species diversity and endemism among all ecosystems.

Other contributions Forests provide employment and income, recreation, education, scientific study, protection of natural and cultural heritage, aesthetic pleasure, and spiritual solace.

How much of the wood goes into making paper?

Paper is the world's fastest growing use of wood. Worldwide, 40 per cent of the wood is used for making paper and this figure is expected to reach 60 per cent by 2050. The US alone accounts for 30 per cent of the world's paper use, consuming one billion trees a year and releasing 100 million tons of toxins every year during processing.

India has about 600 paper mills with an annual capacity of 8.5 million tons. Of the raw material they use, 39 per cent comes from wood and bamboo, 31 per cent from agricultural residues, and 30 per cent from waste paper. Even though waste paper is abundant in India, the industry imports annually about 1.2 tons of it costing US$ 116 million.

Reforestation has not kept pace with the world demand for paper. The amount of paper recycled has also been too small to make any difference. Some countries like the Netherlands and Germany recover over 70 per cent of waste paper. India has a recovery rate of just 18 per cent, mainly because we have a poor collection and segregation system.

In the industrialized countries, about 50 per cent of the paper is used for packaging, 30 per cent for writing, 12 per cent for newsprint, and 8 per cent for paper tissue and towels. American retailers send out 17 billion catalogues to potential customers and 95 per cent of this paper is discarded unread! Such junk mail culture is now spreading to countries like India.

Contrary to general belief, computers have not brought in the paperless office. In fact, studies have shown that paper consumption has increased by about 40 per cent after the introduction of computers and email.

Logging leads to deforestation
(Image courtesy: Przykuta; http://commons.wikimedia.org/wiki/File:Zrywka_drewna_776.jpg)

In what ways are forests being destroyed?

Commercial logging methods directly and indirectly lead to deforestation. In many places, for obtaining one cubic metre of logs, two cubic metres of standing trees are destroyed. New extractive technologies can cut trees very quickly. When some species are selected for logging, non-target species are also damaged.

Logging companies create infrastructure, especially roads, in forests to make their tasks easier. However, roads provide easier access to interior parts and encourages the entry of invasive species, hunters, poachers, tourists, plant collectors, and people in general. This, in turn, leads to further exploitation of the resources.

Another area of concern is the depletion of forest-based wildlife due to the commercial harvesting and trade of bushmeat. This practice of killing wild animals for meat is prevalent in Africa, where many primates and antelopes are threatened.

The construction of dams in forests invariably causes enormous damage. Dam reservoirs inundate and destroy forests and their biodiversity.

What is the impact of deforestation?

Deforestation exposes soils and shade species to wind, sunlight, evaporation, and erosion. Soil fertility goes down due to the rapid leaching of essential mineral nutrients. Topsoil is eroded and this accelerates siltation in dams, rivers, and the coastal zone. The increased sedimentation harms downstream fisheries.

Forest making way for farms

KEY IDEA
Deforestation has a series of adverse effects on the planet and the people.

When the forest disappears, there is no regulation of the flow into rivers. As a result, floods and droughts alternate in the affected areas.

Deforestation, degradation, and fragmentation of forests affect many species and lead to the extinction of some. In particular, migratory birds and butterflies suffer due to the loss of their habitat.

Local and global climate changes can occur. Studies have shown that about 97 per cent of the water absorbed from the soil by the roots evaporates and falls back on land as precipitation. When a large forest is cut down, the regional rainfall pattern may be affected.

Deforestation may also lead to global warming by releasing carbon stored in the trees. If the trees burn, the carbon is released immediately. If the trees are cut and removed, half the carbon remains in the form of branches, twigs, etc. When they decompose, the carbon is slowly released.

Clearing of forests affects the local communities, who lose their sources of food, fuel, construction materials, medicines, and areas for livestock grazing. What is more, they lose their culture and way of living.

What is the role of forest fires?

Wildfires, usually started by lightning, have an ecological role. The combustion frees the minerals locked up in the dry organic matter. The mineral-rich ashes are necessary for the growth of plants. The vegetation usually flourishes after a fire.

Fires remove plant cover and expose the soil, which stimulates the germination of certain types of seeds. They also help control pathogens and harmful insects. Occasional fires burn away some of the dry organic mater and prevent more destructive fires from occurring later on. For all these reasons, prevention of fires is not necessarily good for a forest.

Intentional or accidental human-induced fires do cause damage. Such fires have become a major problem in large forests, especially in countries like Canada and the US. In a number of developing countries, fires continue to be used for land clearing with adverse consequences.

➤ What is the relationship between forests and climate change?

Forests both influence and are influenced by climate change. They play an important role in the carbon cycle and the way we manage forests could significantly affect global warming.

Forests hold more than 50 per cent of the carbon that is stored in terrestrial vegetation and soil organic matter. Hence, deforestation contributes significantly to net emissions of carbon dioxide into the atmosphere.

If the predicted global warming occurs, the impact on forests is likely to be regionally varied, dramatic, and long-lasting. Even now, we can see how any extreme weather has great impact on forests. For example, the 1999 storms in Europe caused heavy damage to forests and also to trees outside forest areas.

Climate change also causes more forest fires than usual. In many countries, there was an increase in wildfires during the 1990s compared to the previous decades, possibly due to climate change.

International agreements such as the Kyoto Protocol on Climate Change (Chapter 19) may have a great impact on forest management. Under this agreement, a country with forests earns emission credits, since its forests absorb carbon dioxide. These credits are tradable, that is, a developing country can sell its credits to an industrialised country that has exceeded its quota of emissions. The latter would invest in afforestation and reforestation projects in the developing country. The Kyoto Protocol, however, is set to expire in 2012.

➤ What are the international and national initiatives in forest conservation?

Sustainable forest management was first discussed at the international level at the Earth Summit in 1992. There were major differences between the industrialised countries and the developing countries and the summit could only come up with a set of non-binding principles.

The International Tropical Timber Organization (ITTO) was set up in 1983 under the UN Commission for Trade and Development (UNCTAD). ITTO brings together the producer and consumer countries and is a major platform for issues concerning sustainable forest management. In 1985, FAO, UNDP, World Bank, and World Resources Institute came up with the Tropical Forestry Action Plan, later revamped and renamed as the National Forest Action Programme.

The Kyoto Protocol (Chapter 19), Convention on Biological Diversity (Chapter 6), and the Convention to Combat Desertification (Chapter 10) are three of the international agreements that have a bearing on forests.

Declaring forests as protected areas or as biosphere reserves is a measure adopted by most countries. This is also supported by initiatives like the UNESCO Man and the Biosphere Programme. The protected area approach has been discussed in Chapter 6 under biodiversity conservation.

The UN Forum on Forests (UNFF), created in October 2000, is a permanent high-level intergovernmental body with universal membership. In 2007, the UN General Assembly adopted the Non-Legally Binding Instrument on all types of forests negotiated by the UNFF earlier that year. The purpose of this instrument is to:

- strengthen political commitment and action at all levels to implement effectively sustainable management of all types of forests and to achieve the shared global objectives on forests
- enhance the contribution of forests to the achievement of the internationally agreed development goals, including the Millennium Development Goals, in particular with respect to poverty eradication and environmental sustainability
- provide a framework for national action and international cooperation.

What is sustainable forest management?

The UN FAO defines sustainable forest management (SFM) as the stewardship and use of forests and forest lands in a way, and at a rate, that maintains their biodiversity, productivity, regeneration capacity, vitality and their potential to fulfill, now and in the future, relevant ecological, economic and social functions, at local, national, and global levels, and that does not cause damage to other ecosystems.

In simpler terms, SFM seeks to achieve a balance between society's increasing demands for forest products and benefits, and the preservation of forest health and diversity. This balance is critical to the survival of forests, and to the prosperity of forest-dependent communities.

SFM is the use of the world's forests in such a way that that they continue to provide resources now without depriving future generations of their needs. One of the principles of SFM is to involve the local communities fully in forest management. Implementing this principle is, however, difficult since forests departments are usually very reluctant to lose their control over forest resources.

SFM has also become an element in the climate change negotiations. As mentioned earlier, the Kyoto Protocol would compensate countries for the benefits their forests provide to the world. The industrialised countries are ready to support SFM in the developing countries so that they can buy the credits and continue to pollute the atmosphere.

According to FRA 2010, there was mixed progress towards sustainable forest management. While many trends remained alarming, there were also many positive developments over the last 20 years. However, all regions and subregions displayed a mixture of positive and negative trends, which made it difficult to say anything definite about the level of progress towards sustainable forest management.

At the same time, FRA 2010 noted the following:

- Significant progress has been made in further developing an enabling framework for sustainable forest management.
- A large number of forest policies and laws have been created or updated.
- National forest programmes now cover close to 75 per cent of the world's forests.
- An estimated 52 per cent of the total forest area had been designated as permanent forest estate or its equivalent.

Certification of timber as coming from sustainable forests is another approach to SFM (Box 9.3).

KEY IDEA
Many steps have been taken for forest conservation at national and international levels with mixed results.

BOX 9.3

Forest Certification

How can we halt deforestation and save the remaining forests? One way is to act as a responsible consumer and buy wood only from companies that follow sustainable practices. How do we locate such companies? Forest certification is meant to help us.

Certification is a voluntary market-based approach that that enables us to identify forest products backed by high environmental standards. It focuses on the quality of forest management rather than on that of forest products.

The two main certification bodies are:

1. Forest Stewardship Council (FSC): Producers have to meet certain principles and standards for good forest stewardship. They can then use the FSC trademark for product labelling. By 2010, FSC had certified as well as managed more than 135 million hectares in 81 countries. Certification is based on sustainability of timber resources, socio-economic benefits provided to local people, and forest ecosystem health including preservation of wildlife habitat and watershed stability.

2. Programme for the Endorsement of Forest Certification (PEFC): This international NGO promotes Sustainable Forest Management (SFM) through independent third-party certification. PEFC is an umbrella organization. It works by endorsing national forest certification systems developed through multi-stakeholder processes and tailored to local priorities and conditions. It seeks to ensure that timber and non-timber forest products are produced with respect for the highest ecological, social and ethical standards. Thanks to its eco-label, customers and consumers are able to identify products from sustainably managed forests. With about 30 endorsed national certification systems and more than 220 million hectares of certified forests, PEFC claims to be the world's largest forest certification system.

Certification is also possible through the Pan-European Forest Council (PEFC), Canadian Standards Association (CSA), Sustainable Forest Initiative (SFI), ISO 14001 Standards, etc. Most of the certified area is in Europe, Canada and the US. India has just begun the process.

There is a growing demand for certified wood. Environment-conscious consumers have welcomed certification, though some producers consider it a restrictive practice.

How can local communities be involved in forest conservation?

Many local communities have lived in or near forests and used them in a sustainable manner. In the 20th century, however, there were two developments in this regard. Due to increase in population and poverty, new groups migrated into the forest areas and began overexploiting the resources. When governments began protecting forests and declaring them as protected areas, they viewed the local people as enemies of the forests and tried to prevent them even from entering the area. The result was an increase in illegal use of the resources and conflicts.

It is now increasingly being realized that local people should be seen as partners in conservation. Most programmes now involve the local communities in planning, decision-making, and implementation. In return for controlled access to the forests, the locals can provide labour and help in conservation. They can become excellent guides in ecotourism.

What are extractive reserves? Extractive reserves are protected forests, in which local communities are allowed to harvest products like fruits, nuts, rubber, oil, fibres, and medicines in ways that do not harm the forest. The objective is to improve the lives of the people, while conserving the biodiversity.

The approach believes that the local people would have a greater stake in conservation if they get the benefits they were earlier enjoying. It recognizes the fact that, in many instances, we have to use land and forest in order to preserve them.

How are communities involved in forest conservation in India?

In India and some other countries, communities living in or near the forests are involved in conservation in three ways: Joint Forest Management, social forestry, and sacred groves.

What is Joint Forest Management?   Around the 1980s, the Government of India came to recognize the important role of local communities in forest conservation. They introduced the concept of Joint Forest Management (JFM) for working closely with the local user communities in the protection and management of forest resources.

In JFM, the local communities are involved in the planning of the conservation programme. They are allowed controlled access to the forest areas and permitted to harvest the resources in a sustainable manner. In return, they become the guardians of the forest.

Participation of locals in forest conservation

KEY IDEA

The importance of involving local communities in forest management is now well recognized.

What is social forestry?   Social forestry refers to the planting of trees, often with the involvement of local communities, in unused and fallow land, degraded government forest areas, in and around agricultural fields, along railway lines, roadsides, river and canal banks, in village common land, government wasteland and panchayat land.

The term 'social forestry' was first used in India in 1976 and the idea has been adopted in many Asian countries. A major controversy has been the planting of eucalyptus trees under social forestry. Eucalyptus was chosen for the majority of social forestry projects because it survives on difficult sites and out-performs indigenous species in growth, producing wood very rapidly. However, it has some adverse ecological impacts on soil nutrients, water hydrology, biodiversity, and wildlife.

What are sacred groves?   The traditional sacred groves of India play an important role in community participation and conservation of biodiversity (Box 9.4).

BOX 9.4

The story of sacred groves: Conservation by fear of God!

It could be just a few trees or a whole forest. No tree or plant is cut here, no animal or bird is killed, and no form of life is harmed. No one would dare, because it is protected by the local deity. Some even have a temple within.

The sacred groves of India are a unique traditional institution devoted to the conservation of forests and biodiversity. They are referred to in the ancient texts and thousands of them must have existed. They were protected by local communities through social traditions and taboos that incorporate spiritual and ecological values. (Recall also the story of the Bishnois of Rajasthan in Box 3.2, Chapter 3.)

Preserved over the course of many generations, sacred groves represent native vegetation in a natural or near-natural state. They are thus rich in

Contd

Box 9.4 Contd

biodiversity and are banks of species and genetic diversity. They often contain species that have disappeared in other places. Rare medicinal plants are also found in the groves.

Many groves have water sources that help the local communities. The groves absorb water during the monsoon and release it slowly during the dry period.

Over time, hundreds of these groves have disappeared under the pressure of population and development. However, according to one survey, over 13,000 groves still survive as patches across the country. Other estimates give the number as being between 100,000 and 150,000. Only groves in remote parts remain undisturbed, while others need protection.

In recent years, there has been an increasing interest in documenting and conserving the sacred groves.

How can wood be used more efficiently?

Currently, enormous quantities of wood are wasted, primarily in countries like the US in many ways: inefficient use as construction material, excessive packaging, excessive junk mail, inadequate paper recycling, not reusing wooden shipping containers, etc. There is great scope to reduce such wastage.

Tree-free paper can be made from natural fibres and agricultural residues from wheat, rice, and sugarcane. China plans to make 60 per cent of its paper from tree-free pulp. A number of publishers in the world now use paper from forest-friendly sources.

What should we do to save the world's forests?

The summary recommendations of the World Commission on Forests and Sustainable Development (WCFSD) were:

1. Stop the destruction of the earth's forests: their material products and ecological services are severely threatened.
2. Use the world's rich forest resources to improve life for poor people and for the benefit of forest-dependent communities.
3. Put the public interest first and involve people in decisions about forest use.
4. Get the price of forests right, to reflect their full ecological and social values, and to stop harmful subsidies to lumber companies.
5. Apply sustainable forest management approaches so we may use forests without abusing them.
6. Develop new ways of measuring forest capital so that we know whether the situation is improving or worsening.
7. Plan for the use and protection of whole landscapes, not the forest in isolation.
8. Make better use of knowledge about forests, and greatly expand this information base.
9. Accelerate research and training so sustainable forest management can become a reality quickly.
10. Take bold political decisions and develop new civil society institutions to improve governance and accountability regarding forest use.

There is no sign, however, of these recommendations being implemented.

Ending on a hopeful note: Positive stories

There are remarkable stories from all over the world of individuals and groups going to great lengths to save or plant trees. Some examples are:

- *Chipko*, the people's movement to save the forests of Tehri Garhwal (Box 9.5)
- The Green Belt Movement started by Wangari Maathai in Kenya (Box 9.6)
- The planting of roadside avenue trees in Karnataka by Thimmakka and Chikkanna (Box 9.7)
- The unbelievable two-year tree-sit by Julia Butterfly Hill to save the redwood trees of California (Box 9.8)

BOX 9.5

The Story of *Chipko*: The Women who Saved the Trees

On March 26, 1974, a group of men arrived stealthily in the forest next to Renni Village in the Garhwal District of Himalayas. They had been sent by a contractor to begin cutting down 2500 trees in the forest. Anticipating resistance from the villagers, the contractor had ensured that all the men were away on that day.

Word of the arrival of the axe-men spread in the village and the women came out of their houses. About 25 of them, led by Gaura Devi, confronted the contractor's men. They pleaded with the men not to start the felling operations, but the men responded with threats and abuses. As the confrontation continued, more women joined the protest. Ultimately, the men were forced to leave, since the women did not budge.

This small event was a milestone in the *Chipko* Movement, which became known all over the world as a symbol of people's action in preventing the destruction of the environment. '*Chipko*' means 'to cling' or 'to hug hard'. The vision of women hugging the trees and successfully confronting the loggers fired the spirit of environmentalists the world over.

The *Chipko* Movement spread rapidly across the Himalayan Region in the seventies led by dedicated activists like Sunderlal Bahuguna and Chandi Prasad Bhat. The contract system allowed rich contractors from the plains to make huge profits from cutting trees on the hills. The Movement was a response of the hill communities to the unfair and destructive nature of this system. The government had to abolish the contract system and stop the indiscriminate felling of trees, at least for some years.

The *Chipko* Movement brought unprecedented energy and direction to environmental preservation in India. It remains one of the celebrated environmental movements of the world.

BOX 9.6

The story of Wangari Maathai: Nobel Prize for noble work

She started a movement that planted 30 million trees in 20 countries. She campaigned for women's rights and greater democracy in her country. She defied a corrupt regime, was vilified and forced to leave her country for some time and even assaulted by the police once.

Contd

Box 9.6 Contd

Wangari Maathai, the first woman in East Africa to get a Ph.D., was a Professor at the Nairobi University in Kenya when she launched the Green Belt Movement (GBM) in 1977. Her objective was to empower the people and to show that they can choose to destroy or build the environment. GBM encouraged poor women to plant millions of trees to combat deforestation and to get in return enough fuelwood.

The movement has set up 5000 tree nurseries run by women and disabled persons. Seedlings are given free to groups and individuals. For every tree that survives for three months, the planter receives a small payment. By 1988, 40,000 people were planting trees and in due course the movement spread to many other African countries.

Wangari came into limelight when she led a protest against the building of a 62–storey building in the middle of Freedom Park, Nairobi's most popular public space. The then President, Daniel

Arap Moi, labelled her and the GBM as subversive. Faced with intense persecution, she had to leave the country for a while. Her marriage broke up too.

When Wangari returned to Kenya, she took up the cause of political prisoners. She criticised the President for allowing deforestation and displacing people. She stood solid and unbowed through all the persecution she suffered.

The political climate changed in Kenya in 2002, when Mwai Kibaki came to power. Wangari became a Member of Parliament and also the Assistant Minister for Environment. In October 2004, she was awarded the Nobel Peace Prize.

BOX 9.7

The story of Thimmakka: Trees as children

There is something special about the 300 towering avenue trees on a four km stretch of the road from Kudur and Hulikal in Karnataka. All of them were planted and cared for by an elderly couple, Thimmakka and Chikkanna.

Thimmakka was born about 80 years ago in the town of Gubbi and was married off at an early age to Chikkanna of Hulikal Village. They were landless labourers working on farmlands. Thimmakka could not have children and the couple were often lonely in the evenings.

About 60 years ago they decided to plant trees on the main road to Kudur. The couple thought that the trees would provide shade for the villagers, who had to walk often on the hot and dusty road.

They chose the peepul tree (*Ficus religiosa),* created a small nursery, and began planting the saplings. They built thorn guards around the saplings, watered them daily until they took root. They tended each tree until it was 10 years old.

Every year they planted 15 to 20 trees, until they had covered the entire stretch of four km. They took care of the trees as if they were their children. In fact, Chikkanna quit working so that he could devote himself full time to this task. The trees grew tall and have been providing shade for the road users, shelter for many birds and animals, and biomass for the fields.

Chikkanna died in 1990. Since 1995, many honours have come Thimmakka's way: National Citizen's Award, Priyadarshini Vrikshamitra Award, etc.

BOX 9.8

The story of Julia Butterfly Hill: The woman who wouldn't come down

In December 1997, Julia Butterfly Hill climbed a redwood tree in California and sat down on a platform high up in the tree. And she remained there for two years! Here is her remarkable story.

The coastal redwood trees, which grow in California, are some of the tallest and oldest trees on the planet. They are also unique: they grow nowhere else. Yet they continue to be cut by timber companies for making into furniture.

In the early 1990s, members of an environmental group erected a small platform and began living in one of the huge Pacific redwoods, which had been slated for cutting. They named the tree 'Luna'. The purpose of this 'tree-sit' was, firstly, to prevent the tree being cut and, secondly, to draw wider attention to what was happening. For the timber company in this area of North California was not only cutting redwoods, it was also engaged in clear-cutting entire forests of trees. The result of this was that the soil was destabilized, resulting in massive erosion of topsoil and frequent landslips on precipitous hillsides. Clear-cutting also threatened other forms of life, which depended for their existence upon the forests.

Most people could only stay up the tree for a few days at a time, and, as winter approached, there were fewer volunteers. Then a young woman named Julia Hill became involved. The first time she went up for five days. After she came down again, she heard that nobody else was available to continue the sit. So she went up again. She didn't come down again for two years!

Of course, she was supplied with provisions by a support team on the ground. But she was living on a tiny platform 180 feet up near the top of a tree, which was exposed on the top of a ridge. She survived two of the toughest Californian winters ever, protected by no more than a thin tarpaulin.

The timber company did everything they could to make her come down. They brought a helicopter generating huge updrafts close to the tree and they trained bright lights on the tree at night and played loud music. They cut other trees surrounding Luna, and they also threatened to cut the tree while she was living in it. Finally they stationed guards around the tree for a while in an attempt to starve her out.

A number of times she was close to giving up. She contracted frostbite, she broke a toe, and she was almost blown out of the tree by storms. Sometimes she didn't sleep for a week. Yet she survived. She stayed. How? She wanted to protect Luna for the thousands of people across the country for whom she had become a symbol of hope, 'a reminder that we can find peaceful, loving ways to solve our conflicts, and that we can take care of our needs without destroying nature to satisfy our greed.'

Above all, she built up a remarkable relationship with Luna itself. In the middle of one of the worst storms, when she was in danger of being blown down to her death, she found herself asking Luna what she should do. Luna told her to imitate the trees, to bend with the wind and not to try to fight it.

She became a celebrity, an inspiration for thousands of people, a symbol of what one individual was willing to do to stand for her beliefs. Finally, after protracted negotiations with the timber company who owned the tree, an agreement was signed by which Luna was protected from logging in perpetuity. After two years, on December 18, 1999, Julia came down to a huge reception.

Julia set up the Circle of Life Foundation to activate people through education, inspiration and connection to live in a way that honours the diversity and interdependence of all life.

REVIEW: A SUMMARY OF THE KEY POINTS

- Forests provide invaluable products and services.
- Forest cover is depleting rapidly, especially in the tropics, due to many reasons and this will have serious consequences for the environment.
- In order to conserve forests, we have to reconcile the diverse, and often conflicting, interests of the environmentalists, government officials, and local communities.
- A number of national and international measures have been introduced for sustainable forest management, but implementation has been poor.
- Local communities are increasingly being involved in forest conservation.

EXERCISES

Objective-type questions

For each question below, choose the best answer out of the given choices:

1. Which of the following statements describes best the status of global forests?
   (a) The definition of a forest varies from one assessment to another.
   (b) The rate of deforestation shows signs of decreasing, but is still alarmingly high.
   (c) The forest cover has stabilized since 1999.
   (d) Asia continues to have the largest net loss of forest.

2. What are plantation forests?
   (a) They are old-growth forests.
   (b) They are second-growth forests.
   (c) They are more diverse than natural forests.
   (d) They are managed forests.

3. Which of the following items is **not** provided by natural forests?
   (a) Fuelwood
   (b) Honey
   (c) Medicinal plants
   (d) Monoculture

4. Which of the following statements is true with regard to paper?
   (a) The consumption of paper has gone down with the advent of computers.
   (b) Paper is made only from bamboo.
   (c) Most of the used paper is recycled.
   (d) Most catalogues and junk mail are discarded unopened.

5. Which of the following statements is true with regard to deforestation?
   (a) It adversely affects local communities.
   (b) It does not lead to global warming, since trees absorb carbon dioxide.
   (c) It does not affect rainfall pattern.
   (d) It does not lead to the loss of topsoil.

6. Which of the following statements is true with regard to forest certification?
   (a) It is carried out only by the UN Forum on Forests.
   (b) It is now compulsory.
   (c) It enables the consumer to make responsible choices.
   (d) India's reserve forests are all covered by certification.

7. Which of the following statements is **not** true with regard to Joint Forest Management?
   (a) It recognizes the important role of local communities in forest conservation.
   (b) The local people are allowed controlled access to the forest areas.
   (c) The local people are not permitted to harvest the resources, since the forest belongs to the government.
   (d) The local people act as the guardians of the forest.

8. What did the word *Chipko* become famous for?
   (a) It is the name of the people's movement to save the forests in the Himalayas.
   (b) It means 'hugging trees'.
   (c) It is a song of the hill communities.
   (d) It happened only in Renni village.

Short-answer questions

1. Describe the efforts of any two individuals who have worked for the conservation of trees or forests.

2. Explain in your own words the problems facing the forests of Andaman and Nicobar Islands.
3. What is state of the world's forests according to global assessments?
4. What is the difference between old-growth and second-growth forests?
5. What are the ecosystem services provided by forests?
6. What is the impact of deforestation on the environment?
7. Are natural fires good or bad for the forests? Explain.
8. How can local communities be involved in forest conservation?
9. How can we save the remaining forests of the world?

Long-answer questions

1. Study the full report of the World Commission on Forests and Sustainable Development and write a critical review.
2. Write an essay on the international initiatives in forest conservation.

Think critically: Deeper questions for reflection and discussion

1. Should we ban international trade in tropical timber?
2. How would you react to the destruction of tropical forests, if you were:
   (a) a poor landless farmer in Brazil
   (b) owner of a biotechnology company
   (c) an environmentalist

SOMETHING DIFFERENT FOR A CHANGE

1. Here is a well-known piece by the American poet Robert Frost (1874–1963) for you to reflect on. Incidentally, this poem was found on Jawaharlal Nehru's desk after his death.

   ### Stopping by Woods on a Snowy Evening

   Whose woods these are I think I know.
   His house is in the village, though;
   He will not see me stopping here
   To watch his woods fill up with snow.

   My little horse must think it's queer
   To stop without a farmhouse near
   Between the woods and frozen lake
   The darkest evening of the year.

   He gives his harness bells a shake
   To ask if there's some mistake
   The only other sound's the sweep
   Of easy wind and downy flake.

   The woods are lovely, dark, and deep,
   But I have promises to keep,
   And miles to go before I sleep,
   And miles to go before I sleep.

2. Watch the film *They Killed Sister Dorothy*, a documentary by Daniel Junge about the nun who was promoting forest conservation and people's livelihood in the Amazon. She was murdered by the powerful ranchers of the area.

ACTIVITIES

Act: What you can do to conserve forests

1. Plant trees wherever you can—in your compound, neighbourhood, park, streets, under power lines, on the denuded slopes of a hill, etc., but take care to choose an appropriate tree: for example, banyans next to buildings is not a good idea, as their strong root systems may damage the foundation!
2. Contribute to organizations that promote tree planting and have 'adopt a tree' programmes.
3. Join voluntary groups in your area or city that work to save existing trees and plant new ones.
4. Save the forests by saving paper:
   • Buy recycled, handmade or tree-free paper
   • Use both sides of the paper, one-side paper for notes, etc.
   • Reuse paper envelopes
   • Write to companies to take your address off their mailing list

Learn by doing: Case study/Project

1. Many states have programmes to promote Joint Forest Management. With the permission of the concerned forest department, study any one programme. Spend a few days or weeks living with the forest communities. Interview local people as well as foresters. Write a report evaluating the JFM. Focus on the situation before and after the implementation of JFM.

2. Study any movement against a specific development or conservation project in a forest area like the construction of a dam or the establishment of a protected area. Write a report giving your assessment of the situation. Suggest alternatives that may be acceptable to the government and the people.

Organize together: Eco-club activities and projects

Observe March 21 as World Forestry Day. The Day is celebrated in forests around the world for people to consider the benefits of forests to the community such as catchment protection, providing habitat for animals and plants, areas for recreation, education and scientific study, and as a source of many products including timber and honey. World Forestry Day also aims to provide opportunities for people to learn how forests can be managed and used sustainably for these purposes.

LEARN MORE

Books

Hill, Julia Butterfly 2000, *The Legacy of Luna*, HarperCollins, San Francisco.

Maathai, Wangari 2006, *Unbowed: A Memoir,* Knopf, New York.

Articles

DTE 2003, 'Sacred Groves: for Fragments' Sake', *Down To Earth,* Extra Supplement, Vol.12, No.15, December 31.

Sekhsaria, Pankaj 2002, 'Logging Off, For Now', *Frontline,* Vol.19, No.1, January 18, pp. 65–67.

Sekhsaria, Pankaj 2003, 'Andaman's Last Chance: An Opportunity Lost', *The Hindu Survey of the Environment 2003,* The Hindu, Chennai, pp. 129–131.

Websites

Forest Stewardship Council: www.fsc.org

Independent World Commission on Forests and Sustainable Development: www.iisd.org/wcfsd/finalreport.htm

Julia Butterfly Hill: www.circleoflifefoundation.org

Programme for the Endorsement of Forest Certification: www.pefc.org

Sacred groves: www.sacredland.org/world_sites_pages/Sacred_Groves.html

UN FAO Global Forest Resources Assessment 2010: www.fao.org/forestry/fra/fra2010/en/

Wangari Mathaai: www.greenbeltmovement.org and www.nobelprize.org/peace/lauraetes/2004/index.html

CHAPTER 10

Land, Food, and Mineral Resources

We abuse land because we regard it as a commodity belonging to us.
When we see land as a community to which we belong,
we may begin to use it with love and respect.

Aldo Leopold
(1887–1948)
American wildlife ecologist and naturalist

THIS CHAPTER IS ABOUT...

Land, agriculture, fisheries, mining

THE KEYWORDS AND PHRASES ARE...

biodynamic farming	bio-intensive farming	desertification	green revolution
natural farming	organic farming	permaculture	

THE STORY OF PUNJAB: POVERTY OF PLENTY?

Punjab has been known as India's granary and a success story of the Green Revolution. Today, however, it is a story of degraded soil, depleted water tables, reduced productivity, and farmer suicides. How did things change so quickly?

Partap Aggarwal, a pioneer in natural and organic farming, interviewed Punjab farmers and this is what he found:

Approximately in the mid-sixties, a whole new package was developed by the agricultural university in Ludhiana and implemented throughout Punjab with unprecedented energy. It consisted of a high yielding dwarf wheat seed, a regimen of chemical fertilizer and pesticide use, and most importantly an

irresistible bait of a guaranteed lucrative support price. The subsistence farmers were initially suspicious of the chemicals but the package as a whole was offered on the basis of 'take it or leave it'.

The yields, however, were high and the farmers began to prosper. As the farmers' income rose, they began to stretch the land area under wheat and rice to the limits. As cultivation became more intensive and gap between crops narrowed, the farmers felt the need to buy tractors and other machinery. As their cash income grew, more machinery and chemicals followed.

Soon, with higher incomes, the farmers' lifestyle too began to change; large and small brick houses began to replace traditional mud structures; modern gadgets such as refrigerators and motorized two-wheelers as well as cars came into fashion. Clothes became fancier and people more sedentary. Now, almost all Punjab farmers use labour from Bihar, some entirely depend on them. Many more young men and women seek college education than 20 years ago.

Food habits have changed. The list is endless. Under these circumstances, even if the farmers want to stop producing the lucrative cereal crops, they cannot.

The soil has now lost its natural capacity to nourish the crops and the farmers have to keep on adding fertilizers. Naturally, the cost of production is going up. It was not a good idea to grow two heavy crops of cereals on the same land year after year. The water table is also going down. The farmers are now caught in the vice-like grip of high-input cultivation, many are in deep debt, and some have committed suicide.

The farmers are also concerned about the long-term effect of the poisons they spray on the crops and the soil. For example, they notice the effect on birds. One old farmer said, 'The birds are more or less gone. There are no vultures to eat the dead animals. In fact one does not see or hear any birds except an occasional crow, dove or egret. I think this is a bad omen, but most people do not seem to care.'

What does the future hold for this state?

What does the Punjab crisis tell us?

Indeed, things have changed in Punjab. But problems like soil degradation, falling water tables, and increasing use of chemicals are not unique to Punjab. Such environmental problems are now common in many parts of India and the world. In this chapter, we will examine the reasons for the crisis.

What is the importance of land as a natural resource?

The land area of the earth, about 140 million sq km, occupies less than a third of the surface. Yet, it is vital for our existence since it is land that:
- preserves terrestrial biodiversity and the genetic pool,
- regulates the water and carbon cycles,
- acts as the store of basic resources like groundwater, minerals, and fossil fuels,
- becomes a dump for solid and liquid waste, and
- forms the basis for human settlements and transport activities.

Even more important, the topsoil, just a few centimetres in thickness, supports all plant growth and is hence the life support system for all organisms, including humankind.

What is the condition of the world's land surface? UN studies estimate that 23 per cent of all usable land (excluding mountains and deserts, for example) has been degraded to such an extent that its productivity is affected. The main causes are deforestation, fuelwood consumption, overgrazing, agricultural mismanagement (planting unsuitable crops, poor crop rotation, poor soil and water management, excessive input of chemicals, frequent use of heavy machinery like tractors, etc.), establishment of industries and urbanization.

Soil erosion and degradation, which occur due to loss of green cover, strong winds, chemical pollution, etc., have severe effects on the environment. They affect the soil's ability to act as a buffer and filter for pollutants, regulator of water and nitrogen cycles, habitat for biodiversity, etc.

How serious are waterlogging and soil salinity?

When irrigation is not accompanied by proper drainage, waterlogging occurs. This in turn brings salt to the surface, where it collects at the roots of plants or as a thin crust on the land surface. Rapid evaporation of groundwater also adds salt to the soil.

Pakistan, Egypt, India, and the US are some of the countries worst affected by salinization and waterlogging. In Egypt, 90 per cent of all farmland suffers from waterlogging. In Pakistan, two-thirds of all irrigated land is salinized. In India, 12–25 per cent of land is waterlogged or salinized.

What is the scale of desertification and what is being done about it?

Desertification is land degradation in arid and semi-arid areas caused by human activities and climatic changes. It occurs slowly, as different areas of degraded land spread and merge together, rather than through advancing desert. It is a slowly but clearly progressing 'skin disease' over the planet. The desertification problem remains poorly understood, but estimates suggest that a third of the earth's land area is affected, that is, about 50 million sq km.

One fifth of the world's population is threatened by the impacts of global desertification. Its effects can be seen all over the world, in Asia, the African Sahel, Latin America, throughout North America and along the Mediterranean. Cultivable land per person is shrinking throughout the world, threatening food security, particularly in poor rural areas, and triggering humanitarian and economic crises.

Fertile topsoil takes centuries to form, but it can be washed or blown away in a few seasons. Human activities such as over-cultivation, deforestation and poor irrigation practices combined with climate change are turning once fertile soils into barren patches of land. When large barren patches merge together, a desert comes up.

The international community has long recognized that desertification is a major economic, social and environmental problem of concern to many countries in all regions of the world. The Earth Summit in 1992 supported a new, integrated approach to the problem, emphasizing action to promote sustainable development at the community level. The UN Convention to Combat Desertification was adopted in 1994 and entered into force in 1996. Over 180 countries are now parties to the Convention.

Among practical measures undertaken to prevent and restore degraded land are prevention of soil erosion; improved early warning system and water resource management; sustainable pasture, forest and livestock management; aero-seeding over shifting sand dunes; narrow strip planting, windbreaks and shelterbelts of live plants; agroforestry ecosystems; afforestation and reforestation; introduction of new species and varieties with a capacity to tolerate salinity and/or aridity; and environmentally sound human settlements.

KEY IDEA

Erosion, waterlogging, salinization, and desertification are some of the ways in which land has been degraded.

What is the impact of urbanization and industrialization on land?

More than 50 per cent of the world's population now lives in urban areas and this figure is expected to go up. Urban areas constantly need more land for settlements, infrastructure, industries, leisure activities and the like and hence increase pressures on land. More and more agricultural land gets converted into urban colonies. Larger cities affect even larger areas outside them, thanks to their widening ecological footprint (Chapter 1).

We see solid waste piled up on many urban streets. Outside the city, there are large dumps of waste brought from the city. It is estimated that about two million hectares of land have been degraded due to waste disposal and landfills.

Urban agriculture has been expanding globally over the past 25 years. In Sao Paulo in Brazil and Havana in Cuba, for example, urban home gardens have been very successful. While urban agriculture provides locally grown food and helps recycle organic matter, it can also cause pollution of water and soil if chemicals are used.

What is the future of land as a resource?   With increasing world population, there will be intense pressure on land, particularly in Africa and Asia. More intensive land use will be needed to feed the people. More land will also be brought into agriculture by converting forests and grasslands.

Where does the world's food come from?

Food comes from three sources:
- croplands that provide 76 per cent of the total, mostly grains
- rangelands that produce meat mostly from grazing livestock, accounting for about 17 per cent of the total food
- fisheries that supply the remaining 7 per cent.

What is the global food availability?   There is enough food in the world to provide at least 2 kg per person a day including grain, beans, nuts, fruits, vegetables, meat, milk and eggs—enough to make most people fat! The problem is that many people are too poor to buy readily available food. At least 700 million people do not have enough to eat. Every year hunger kills 12 million children worldwide.

India now produces annually 180–210 million tons of food grains, 5 million tons of meat products, and 6 million tons of fish. The increase in grain production since the 1960s is ascribed to the Green Revolution.

> **KEY IDEA**
> There is enough food for every person in the world, but millions do not have the money to buy food.

What is meant by the Green Revolution and what has been its impact?

The Green Revolution (See also Chapter 5) refers to the rapid increase in world food production, especially in the developing countries, during the second half of the 20th century, primarily through the use of lab-engineered high-yielding varieties of seeds. It was hailed as a success story of agricultural science and technology. It is now clear, however, that it has brought in its wake many problems too.

In the middle of the last century, there were severe food shortages in many developing countries. With growing populations, countries like India had to import food. The answer to this problem came from Mexico.

In the early 1940s, Mexico's wheat yields were low and the country was importing 50 per cent of its food. Under a research programme set up to increase the production of grains, the American agricultural scientist, Norman E. Borlaug developed a high-yielding variety of wheat through new concepts in plant breeding. It was a variety that could respond to high inputs of fertilizer and irrigation. Between 1950 and 1965, Mexican wheat yields increased 400 per cent and a Green Revolution had been born.

By mid-1960s, the Green Revolution was fully adopted in India too. The new high-yielding varieties (HYVs) increased the production and made multicropping possible. Ultimately India achieved self-sufficiency in food.

The Green Revolution, however, was a clear shift from traditional agriculture. It came as a package of HYVs along with high inputs of chemical fertilizer, pesticide, water, and agricultural machinery like tractors. It was an energy-intensive method: apart from the energy that went into the making of the inputs, energy was again needed to run the machinery and to pump water.

Governments had to subsidize many of the inputs to keep the farming going. The Green Revolution also made the developing countries dependent on foreign technology.

KEY IDEA

While the Green Revolution increased yields dramatically, it is a high-input system that has degraded the soil, lowered water tables, reduced biodiversity, and impoverished the small farmer.

The farmers found that they had to buy the seeds every year and that, year after year, the inputs had to be increased to maintain the productivity levels. On the whole, the Green Revolution has benefited large landowners and not the subsistence farmers. (Recall the story of Punjab)

A large number of traditional varieties have disappeared. Currently, just 12 HYVs provide most of the world's food and they are more prone to diseases and pest attacks compared to the traditional varieties. The soil has also been getting degraded and drained of its nutrients through the excessive use of chemicals.

What is the way out for agriculture?

One way out of the crisis is the gradual shift from chemical agriculture to organic farming. Organic farming does not use chemical fertilizers and chemical pesticides. It is in fact a return to the traditional methods like crop rotation, use of animal and green manures, and some forms of biological control of pests.

Organic farming is based on the following principles:

- Nature is the best role model for farming since it uses neither chemicals nor poisons and does not demand excessive water.
- Soil is a living system and not an inert bowl for dumping chemicals.
- Soil's living populations of microbes and other organisms are significant contributors to its fertility on a sustained basis and must be protected and nurtured at all costs.
- The total environment of the soil, from soil structure to soil cover, is more important than any nutrients we may wish to pump into it.

Organic farming can, over a period of time, reverse soil degradation and improve soil health. Conversion to organic farming will mean initial problems and economic losses as the soil recovers, but it will be a better option in the long term. Worldwide, there is an active movement towards organic farming and farmers can get advice and support from many groups.

Organic farming is used as a general label for the following systems of agriculture:

- Reliance on the soil's natural fertility enhanced through composting and vermiculture: While simple composting is the natural conversion of organic matter into manure, vermiculture uses earthworms to speed up the process.
- Natural farming or no-tillage farming, pioneered by Masanobu Fukuoka of Japan.
- Biodynamic farming: exploiting bio- and solar rhythms in farming, based on the ideas of Rudolf Steiner
- Bio-intensive farming: Intensive garden cultivation using deep-dug beds

> **KEY IDEA**
> Organic farming is a way out of the agricultural crisis.

- Permaculture: An approach that goes beyond organic farming is Permaculture, developed by Bill Mollison and David Holmgren (Box 10.1).
- LEISA: Low External Input Sustainable Agriculture developed by Dutch farmers and scientists committed to organic farming

BOX 10.1

The story of Permaculture: Designing sustainable human settlements

In the 1960s, environmental issues came into the public agenda, especially in the industrialised countries. People became concerned about problems like the loss of biodiversity, overconsumption of non-renewable resources, pollution of air, water, and soil by chemicals and waste products, etc. In response to these issues, two Australians, Bill Mollison and David Holmgren, developed the concept of Permaculture, short for Permanent Agriculture.

Permaculture is a philosophy and an approach to land use, which weaves together microclimate, annual and perennial plants, animals, soils, water management, and human needs into intricately connected, productive communities.

The main features of Permaculture can be summarised as follows:

- It is a system for creating sustainable human settlements by integrating design and ecology.
- It is a synthesis of traditional knowledge and modern science, applicable to both urban and rural situations.
- It takes natural systems as a model and works with nature to design sustainable environments, which will provide basic human needs as well as the social and economic infrastructures, which support them.
- It encourages us to become conscious part of the solutions to the many problems, which face us, both locally and globally.

Permaculture has spread to other parts of the world including India.

What are genetically modified crops?

Genetic modification of crops through biotechnology has been proposed as the ultimate answer to the world's food and agriculture. Recall from Chapter 6 that biotechnology is the manipulation of living organisms or cells to create a product or an effect. Biotechnology makes use of microorganisms, such as bacteria, or any biological substance, for specific purposes.

An important aspect of biotechnology is genetic engineering or genetic modification (GM). All life is composed of cells that contain genes, and genes are made of molecules called DNA. The DNA molecule of an organism contains information about its characteristics and behaviour. Genetic engineering manipulates the genes in an organism to change its characteristics. It can move a favourable gene from one organism to another.

GM can make a plant resistant to specific pests or diseases. Bt Cotton and Bt Brinjal are examples. Bt stands for the bacterium *Bacillus thuringiensis*, which acts as a microbial pesticide. Each strain of this bacterium specifically kills one or a few related species of insect larvae. Scientists introduce the Bt gene into the plant's own genetic material. Then the plant manufactures the substance that destroys the pest.

GM can also produce new varieties of plants with some desired characteristics, such as herbicide tolerance, virus tolerance, and resistance to drought and salinity. However, there are strong opinions in favour of and against the introduction of GM crops.

Those who support GM crops give arguments such as:
- GM is the only way to produce enough to feed the increasing world population.
- Plants will be resistant to pests, droughts, water salinity, and even climate change.
- There will be a reduction in the use of fertilizers and pesticides.

Those who oppose GM raise questions such as:
- How do we know the unintended consequences of GM foods, such as long-term effects on humans and other organisms?
- We know that a GM crop contaminates the non-GM varieties grown nearby. What would be the effects of such contamination on biodiversity?
- Can the farmer grow seeds for the next planting or is he perpetually dependent on the seed company? Would GM lead to domination of agriculture by a few large companies?
- Is it ethical and safe to introduce animal genes into plants and vice versa?

KEY IDEA

While GM crops are hailed as the ultimate solution to the agricultural crisis, questions remain about their safety and efficacy.

Bt Cotton is a GM crop currently cultivated in India in large areas. However, the results of using Bt Cotton have been mixed. Meanwhile Bt Brinjal created a major controversy (Box 10.2). Both these GM crops have been developed jointly by the giant US Corporation Monsanto and the Indian firm Mahyco.

BOX 10.2

The story of Bt Brinjal: Ban it or plant it?

Bt Brinjal is a genetically modified brinjal created by inserting a gene from the soil bacterium *Bacillus thuringiensis* into the plant. The objective is to give the Brinjal plant resistance against certain insects.

Bt Brinjal created a controversy in India. The proponents say that Bt Brinjal would be beneficial to small farmers because it is insect resistant and increases yields. The opponents have concerns about its possible adverse impact on human health and bio-safety, livelihoods and biodiversity.

The Genetic Engineering Approval Committee (GEAC) of the Ministry of Environment and Forests (MoEF) recommended the release of Bt Brinjal in India. However, faced with opposition from several citizens' groups, Jairam Ramesh, the Minister for Environment and Forests, arranged public consultations across the country before taking a final decision on this issue.

At the end of the consultations in February 2010, the Minister imposed 'a moratorium on the release of Bt Brinjal till such time studies establish the safety of the product from the point of view of its long-term impact on human health and environment, including the rich genetic wealth existing in Brinjal in our country, to the satisfaction of both the public and professionals'.

Contd

Box 10.2 Contd

Sharad Pawar, the Agriculture Minister, disagreed with the ban. He said that the ban would 'set the clock back', demoralise Indian scientists, and jeopardize R&D crucial to food security. Prime Minister Manmohan Singh then decided that MoEF should not take such decisions unilaterally. After Bt Brinjal, there are many more GM food crops awaiting GEAC approval—25 kinds of rice, 23 kinds of tomatoes, many types of groundnut, pigeon peas, potato, mustard, sugarcane, soy and okra.

As we await the final verdict, we could ask, 'If Bt Brinjal is approved, what will happen to the 2,500 indigenous varieties of the country?'

While agriculture is going through a crisis, fisheries, the other major source of food, has its share of problems too.

How important is fish as a food source and where does fish come from?

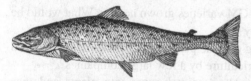

About two million people, mostly in the developing countries, depend on fish as their main source of food. 55 per cent of the fish comes from the ocean, 33 per cent from aquaculture, and 12 per cent from inland freshwater fishing in rivers, lakes, reservoirs, and ponds. Aquaculture is the artificial production of fish in ponds and underwater cages. A third of the world's fish harvest is used as animal feed, fishmeal, and oils.

It is a wrong notion that the vast open sea holds unlimited amount of fish. 80–90 per cent of global commercial fish catch comes from coastal waters within 300 km of the shoreline.

Is there a fisheries crisis?

The world's fisheries are in fact in deep crisis. An environmental and social catastrophe is in the making, but most consumers of fish do not perceive it.

A massive increase in global fishing began in the 1950s and 1960s with the rapid induction of new technology: factory trawlers, satellite positioning, acoustic fish finders, spotter planes, huge nets, etc. Industrial fishing technology employed in the modern trawlers operating in all the seas began locating and catching the last remnants of all varieties of fish stocks. Soon the rate of harvest exceeded the rate of fish population growth.

The first sign of problem was the collapse of the world's largest fishery, the Peruvian anchovy in 1972. The decline in the North Atlantic started in the mid-1970s and over the next two decades most of the cod stocks in New England and Eastern Canada collapsed. Centuries of fishing tradition came to an end.

80 per cent of the marine fish stocks are now fully exploited, overexploited, or in a state of depletion. Large-scale fisheries are very likely to collapse within a few decades in most areas.

We are now fishing down the food web. Once the larger fishes are exhausted, the fleets start catching the smaller fish. These being often the prey of the larger fish, there is further decline of the latter. Meanwhile, we are also removing the species living on the ocean floor through bottom trawling, which is like clear cutting a forest. This removes the species at the base of the food web.

The tragedy is that the massive harvesting of fish was not driven by nutritional needs, but by the demand for luxury foods or livestock feed. The rich countries actively encouraged the unsustainable exploitation through heavy subsidies to their fishers. Apart from overexploitation, fisheries are threatened by pollution of water bodies, climate change, destruction of mangroves and coral reefs,

> **KEY IDEA**
> The global fisheries have nearly collapsed.

What is the state of India's fisheries?

The current annual fish production is about 6 million tons, with a roughly equal share for marine and inland fisheries. About 460,000 tons of fish are exported. Ten million people depend directly or indirectly on fishing for their livelihood.

The catch per vessel has been going down in all the coastal states. This is because there are about 35,000 small mechanised boats and two million artisanal crafts competing for the fish.

To add to the problems, the government announced a new deep sea fishing policy in 1991, opening up Indian seas to foreign vessels in the name of joint ventures. When industrial fleets have depleted the huge fisheries of the Atlantic and the Pacific, how long will Indian stocks last?

India has about 1,000 freshwater fish species, but this diversity is under threat. Overharvesting, competition from newly-introduced exotics, and pollution are taking their toll.

What is the way out for global fisheries?

Some recommendations given by experts to save global fisheries are:

- Adopt an ecosystem-based approach by considering the food needs of the key fish species
- Eliminate any fishing gear that destroys the ocean floor or catches non-target species as bycatch
- Establish marine reserves as no-fishing zones to help populations recover
- Move away from the notion that the ocean will always give us all that we demand
- Employ traditional aquaculture integrated with agriculture (for example, raising fish in paddy fields at appropriate seasons)

Let us turn to mining, which is a major activity in human exploitation of natural resources.

What are minerals and mining?

A mineral is any substance that is naturally present in the earth's crust and is not formed from animal or vegetable matter. The earth's geological processes have formed these minerals over millions or billions of years and hence they are non-renewable.

Mining is the process of extracting and processing minerals. Over 100 minerals are mined and these include metals like gold, iron, copper, and aluminium and non-metals like stone, sand and salt. Apart from minerals, coal is the major material that is mined from the earth.

What are the environmental and social impacts of mining?

Underground mining has little direct effect on the environment, but it can cause long-term problems like subsidence and pollution of aquifers. In underground mines, the workers are at great risk. Accidents like flooding and collapse are common and the work itself causes severe health problems like respiratory illnesses.

Surface or open cast mining destroys all vegetation in the area and pollutes the landscape with the dust that is thrown up. Once the available material is mined out, large craters are left behind. When hills that act as watersheds are mined away, the water tables go down.

The processing of the mined material, often done on site, using in many cases mercury, cyanide, and large quantities of water, pollutes rivers and other water bodies. The waste material like slag is often far greater in quantity than the usable part and is left behind as unsightly, unstable, and dangerous heaps.

Mining has huge social impacts. Mining-induced displacement and resettlement leads to the following problems for the communities:

- Loss of land, livelihood, and even cultures.
- Increased health risks due to contamination of natural resources such as land and water: Resettled populations often do not have access to safe water and sanitation
- Changes in population dynamics: Since trained manpower is usually not available locally, the workers come from outside.

What is the status of mines and minerals in India?

Here are some facts about mining in India:

- India produces as many as 86 metals and minerals.
- 80 per cent of mining in India is for coal.
- India has over 3,500 legal mines.
- Illegal mining is a major problem in the country. In the past five years, 180,000 cases of illegal mining were registered across 17 states.
- Over 1 million people are employed in the industry.

> **KEY IDEA**
> Mining is necessary, since we need metals and minerals. But it has serious environmental and social impacts.

- Mining has adversely affected biodiversity, ecosystems, local cultures, and communities.
- About 10 million people have been displaced from mining areas and 75 per cent of them have not received proper compensation. The tribal communities are worst affected.

The case of the Aravalli Hills in Rajasthan is typical of the Indian mining scene (Box 10.3).

Ending on a hopeful note: Positive stories

The success of Cuba in shifting to organic farming is a classic case (Box 10.4). There are organic farmers in India who get as much (if not more) yield in comparison to chemical farming (Box 10.5).

BOX 10.3

The story of the Aravalli Hills: Mining vs *Jal, Jangal, Jameen*

The Rajasamand Lake in Rajasthan had not dried up for at least 300 years. It did so in 2001. The likely reason: a decade of marble mining in Rajnagar area.

The Aravalli Hills, spread across Haryana, Rajasthan, and Gujarat, are the lifeline of the three states as they control the climate and drainage system. The hills act as the watershed for the region. Unfortunately, however, the hills are also repositories of immense mineral wealth including talc, marble, and granite.

(Image courtesy: P.K.Niyogi, http://en.wikipedia.org/wiki/File:Aravalli_Hills.jpg).

The mining and related industries employ about 175,000 workers and 600,000 others are indirectly dependent on the mining operations. 9,700 industrial units in Rajasthan alone are connected with mining.

Forest cover has been depleted by 90 per cent over the past 20 years since large-scale mining began. When the mines reach below the underground water level, a cone of depression is formed that sucks water from the surrounding areas, drying up wells and affecting agriculture.

Several studies have pointed out that the natural drainage system and the water table of the entire region have been badly affected over the years. Pollution levels have also increased.

Studies have shown that the labourers are not provided with any health care. Lung diseases like tuberculosis and silicosis are common, making the labourers invalids or killing them by the time they are forty. Child labour constitutes 10–15 per cent of the workforce and women workers 30–40 per cent, and their condition is the worst.

Environmentalists have charged that owners generally mine in much larger areas than are legally allocated to them. They fear that all the minerals in Rajasthan will be exhausted within 50 years, if the mining goes on at the current rate. According to them, mining affected water, forest, and land. While mining led to the depletion of water in wells, mining waste destroyed fertile land.

In 2002, the Supreme Court of India imposed a blanket ban on mining activities in the Aravallis. The basic premise for the ban was the argument that the Aravallis came under the category of forestland. Later, the Court constituted a high-level monitoring committee to suggest ways and means for the overall ecological restoration of the hills and give environment clearance for all mines seeking renewal of their leases.

In February 2010, the Supreme Court directed the cancellation of 157 mining leases operating in the Aravalli Hills and asked the Forest Survey of India to carry out satellite imagery of the entire 50,000 sq km range spread across 15 districts of the State to assess the extent of ecological damage.

BOX 10.4

The story of Cuba: From crisis to a success story

Imagine a country that suddenly finds itself with no fertilizer or pesticide for its fields and all imports of meat, grains, and processed foods gone. Most countries would not be able to recover from such a crisis, but this is the story of one country that did.

The small island of Cuba has been for long under severe economic sanctions by its neighbour, the US. It had depended on the Soviet Union and the Eastern Bloc for exchanging its sugar for fertilizers, oil, and grains. When the Soviet Union collapsed in 1989,

Contd

Box 10.4 Contd

Cuba's economy and food security were seriously threatened. The people were facing starvation.

The Cuban government's answer was a major shift to organic farming. The strategy was to transform derelict city plots into well-funded vegetable gardens under the supervision of organic farming associations. Thousands of gardens across Cuba began producing organic vegetables and many other crops. Organic farming on small family plots currently provides employment to 326,000 people out of a population of 12 million.

The gardens use organic compost and mulch instead of chemical fertilizers, biological pest control methods instead of chemical pesticides, and other environment friendly techniques. Giant greenhouses produce vegetables in all seasons. Organic sugar and coffee are now being produced.

The organic gardening associations bring together farmers, farm managers, field experts, researchers, and government officials to develop and promote organic farming methods. Its aim is to convince Cuban farmers and policy-makers that

An organic farm

the country's previous high-input farming model was too import-dependent and environmentally damaging to be sustainable, and that the organic alternative has the potential to achieve equally good yields.

The Cuban success in shifting to organic farming points the way to the rest of the world.

BOX 10.5

The story of Ramesh Dagar: Small, organic, and profitable!

With agriculture in crisis and small farmers committing suicide, who would believe that one can make more than Rs 10 lakhs a year from one hectare of land? Well, Ramesh Chandar Dagar in Sonipat, Haryana can show you how.

Dagar used to wonder whether a small farm could be made viable and, four years ago, he started experimenting on one hectare within his farmland. His experiment with integrated organic farming has been a success. He now practises it in all the 44 hectares he owns and is busy spreading the message to others.

Integrated organic farming is about more than just avoiding chemicals. It includes many other practices like bee-keeping, dairy management, biogas production, water harvesting, and composting. The key element in Dagar's experimental plot is the cyclic, zero-waste approach. The paddy waste goes into vermicomposting as well as mushroom

production, the dung is fed into the gobar gas plant with the sludge going into the composting pit, and so on. The excess compost is sold.

A pond collects rainwater that is used to wash the buffaloes and other purposes. Fish is grown in the pond and regularly harvested. Bee-keeping increases crop output through effective pollination and the honey too has a good market. The farm uses solar power for pumping and lighting.

Dagar grows all seasonal vegetables, fruits, paddy, wheat, mushroom, and flowers. He has begun growing lettuce, baby corn, and strawberry for export. The sale of compost and honey brings in the maximum income. He keeps experimenting with new crops and new ideas.

Dagar has set up the Haryana Kisan Welfare Club and its members are now busy spreading the message of integrated organic farming.

REVIEW: A SUMMARY OF THE KEY POINTS

- The world's land surface is continuously degrading, soil is becoming unhealthy, and desertification is increasing.
- There is enough food available in the world to feed everyone, but poverty keeps millions of people hungry.
- While the Green Revolution increased crop production dramatically, it has led to many problems in the long term, leading to a crisis even in states like Punjab.
- The wise option for agriculture seems to be to shift gradually to organic farming minimizing or altogether avoiding chemical fertilizers and chemical pesticides.
- There are many examples of successful adoption of organic farming.
- There is a global fisheries crisis with most fish stocks in collapse or decline.
- Mining has become more intense and widespread and causes many environmental and social problems.

EXERCISES

Objective-type questions

In each question below, choose the best answer out of the given choices.

1. Which is the most important support for all plant growth and all life?
   (a) Topsoil
   (b) Fertilizer
   (c) Farming
   (d) Pesticide

2. Which of the following is **not** a problem associated with land?
   (a) Waterlogging
   (b) Salinization
   (c) Desertification
   (d) Climate change

3. Which of the following statements is true with regard to food on this planet?
   (a) There is unlimited amount of fish.
   (b) There is enough food to feed every person.
   (c) Every person is able to buy food.
   (d) Green Revolution has solved the problem of hunger.

4. Which of the following statements is **not** true with regard to the Green Revolution?
   (a) It increased crop yields.
   (b) It needs fertilizers and pesticides.
   (c) It requires decreasing inputs over time.
   (d) It uses high-yielding varieties of seeds.

5. Which of the following statements is true with regard to organic farming?
   (a) It uses chemical fertilizers.
   (b) Over time, it makes the soil healthier.
   (c) It uses chemical pesticides.
   (d) It does not use animal or green manure.

6. Which of the following statements is **not** true with regard to GM crops?
   (a) They could have greater resistance to pests.
   (b) They are proven to be completely safe.
   (c) They could resist drought or salinity.
   (d) They could reduce the amount of fertilizer needed.

7. Which of the following statements is **not** true with regard to global fisheries?
   (a) Most of the marine fish stocks are now fully exploited or overexploited.
   (b) We are now fishing down the food web.
   (c) The demand for luxury foods and livestock feed has led to overexploitation.
   (d) The rate of fish population growth exceeds the rate of harvest.

8. Which of the following statements is **not** true with regard to communities in mining areas?
   (a) They often lose their land and livelihoods.
   (b) All of them get employed in the mines.
   (c) They often do not have access to fresh water and sanitation.
   (d) They are displaced from their land.

Short-answer questions

1. In what ways is the world's land surface getting degraded?
2. What are the sources of our food and is there enough food in the world for all?
3. Explain in brief the basic principles of organic farming.
4. Why is there a global fisheries crisis?
5. What are the environmental and social impacts of mining?

Long-answer question

Write an essay on the Green Revolution answering questions such as: Under what conditions was it introduced? What benefits did it bring? What are the problems now being faced by the farmers who have adopted the Green Revolution package? What is the likely long-term impact of the Green Revolution on the environment?

Think critically: Deeper questions for reflection and discussion

If India has excess food stocks that are rotting, why are millions still going hungry? Why can't we implement a 'Food for Work' Programme and distribute the excess food?

SOMETHING DIFFERENT FOR A CHANGE

A poem by the American farmer, environmentalist, and poet, Wendell Berry:

> Sowing the seed,
> My hand is one with the earth.
> Wanting the seed to grow,
> My mind is one with the light.
> Hoeing the crop,
>
> My hands are one with the rain.
> Having cared for the plants,
> My mind is one with the air.
> Hungry and trusting,
> My mind is one with the earth.
> Eating the fruit,
> My body is one with the earth.

ACTIVITIES

Act: What you can do to conserve land and other resources

1. If you have some land or even just a terrace, grow vegetables using organic methods.
2. If you have more land and you cultivate any crops, vegetables, or fruits:
   (a) Plant only indigenous species
   (b) Prefer polyculture to monoculture
   (c) Do composting or vermicomposting and use mulch
   (d) Shift to organic farming
   (e) Use drip irrigation
   (f) Plant appropriate trees wherever possible
3. If you have no space at all, start a community garden for vegetables and herbs.
4. Buy your food from local markets, small traders and not from supermarkets

5. Buy only organically-grown food and if it is not available locally, form a consumer group to procure and distribute organic food.
6. If you are a non-vegetarian, find out more about vegetarianism and, if convinced, become a vegetarian.
7. To save minerals and metals:
   (a) Buy durable products that will last long
   (b) If you are buying a car, buy a small and efficient one
   (c) Do not buy soft drinks in metal containers
   (d) Repair and reuse old bicycles

Learn by doing: Case study/Project

Spend some time at an organic farm and a 'normal' farm following the Green Revolution approach. Study the methods used in the farms and compare them. Write a report detailing the environmental and economic aspects. Describe also how the 'normal' farm can convert itself into an organic one.

Organize together: Eco-club activities and projects

1. Observe October 16 as World Food Day (WFD). This is a worldwide event designed to increase awareness, understanding and informed, year-round, long-term action on the complex issues of food security for all. WFD is an effort by private voluntary organizations, governments, and the international system, carrying out many programs and projects, and working in different ways to build public will in the struggle for hunger alleviation and world food security. Each year WFD highlights a particular theme on which to focus activities.

   You can observe WFD by increasing awareness, understanding, information, services, support, advocacy, and networking with regard to food issues. You can get more information and help from the FAO website. www.fao.org/wfd/

2. Observe November 21 as World Fisheries Day. It was initiated by the World Forum of Fish Harvesters and Fish Workers (WFF). The Forum's main aim is to save the lives of all those who are dependent on the oceans by promoting sustainable fisheries and by preserving marine ecology. The World Fisheries Day is observed with the idea of highlighting preservation of marine ecology, creating and sustaining public awareness, initiating and strengthening action at various levels. The World Fisheries Day is not only for the fish-harvesters and fish-workers but also for all who care for and wish to nurture this planet.

3. Observe June 17 as the World Day to Combat Desertification and Drought (For information access the website www.unccd.int)

LEARN MORE

Books

Alvares, Claude (ed.) 1996, *The Organic Farming Sourcebook,* The Other India Press, Goa.

Fukuoka, Masanobu 1978, *The One-Straw Revolution: An Introduction to Natural Farming,* Indian Reprint 1985, Friends Rural Centre, Rasulia, M.P.

Morrow, Rosemary 1993, *Earth User's Guide to Permaculture,* Kangaroo Press, East Roseville, Australia.

Patel, Raj 2007, *Stuffed and Starved: Markets, Power and the Hidden Battle for the World's Food System,* Portobello Books, London.

Tompkins, Peter and Christopher Bird 1991, *Secrets of the Soil,* Viking Arkana, London. (on biodynamic farming)

Articles

Aggarwal, Partap 2004, 'Punjab Pilgrimage', Private communication.

Dasgupta, Kumkum 2001, 'Poverty Amidst Plenty: The Punjabi Tale', *UNESCO Courier,* January.

Jamwal, Nidhi 2004, 'Small Farms Can be Profitable', *Down To Earth,* Vol. 12, No. 23, April 30, pp. 50–52. (on Ramesh Chandar Dagar)

Sebastian, Sunny 2003, 'Rajasthan: Mine Over matter', *The Hindu Survey of the Environment 2003,* The Hindu, Chennai, pp. 117–121. (on Aravalli Hills)

Zytaruk, Melinda 2003, 'Life After Oil', *Alternatives Journal,* Vol. 29, No. 4, Fall, pp. 2–25. (on organic farming in Cuba)

Websites

Genetically Modified Food in India: www.indiagminfo.org/

Mines, minerals, and people (India): www.mmpindia.org/

Permaculture Society of India: http://permaculture.in/

Social, economic, and environmental impacts of mining: www.miningandcommunities.org

Film

Poison on a Platter, a documentary by film-maker Mahesh Bhatt on GM foods in India.

Module 5
Environmental Pollution

CHAPTER 11

Air and Noise Pollution

*There's so much pollution in the air now that
if it weren't for our lungs
there'd be no place to put it all.*

Robert Orben
(1927—)
American magician and professional comedy writer

THIS CHAPTER IS ABOUT...

air pollution, noise pollution

THE KEYWORDS AND PHRASES ARE...

decibel   photochemical smog   primary air pollutant
smog   secondary air pollutant

THE STORY OF JUVENILE ASTHMA: POLLUTED AIR, SUFFERING CHILDREN

Eight-year-old Moni caught pneumonia during winter rains three years ago and she is now an asthmatic, visiting the government hospital every week. Her father, who earns Rs 60 per day, spends Rs 80 per week on her treatment. The family of five cannot buy rations and the house rent is six months overdue.

Moni is not alone. Seven-year-old Umesh Kumar, one-year-old Mushtab, and many more children among the poor of Kanpur city are all asthmatics, condemned for a long period of medical treatment and unaffordable expenses. Anuj Rawal is perhaps among the few happy people of the city, since

his medical shop sells Rs 50,000 worth of asthma medicines every month!

Kanpur is one of the worst polluted cities in India. It is home to many textile mills and leather units. The most popular form of transport is the rickety three-wheeler tempo, which spews out volumes of smoke from old engines. Dust is thick in the air and the smog never goes away. And the hospitals are full of juvenile asthmatics. The story is the same in the shanties of Delhi, slums of Mumbai, or colonies of Chennai.

WHO estimates that 10–15 per cent of Indian children in the 5–11 age group suffer from asthma. It costs an average of Rs 300 per month to buy a child's asthma medicines. Since there is little awareness of asthma among the poor and even health officials, often the disease is not even diagnosed. Even if it is diagnosed, the child is given steroids because they are cheap. Steroids will have long-term adverse effects on their health.

Several studies have shown the link between pollution and asthma. According to a Delhi study, the city's polluted air is responsible for a 40 per cent increase in asthma cases. More people were admitted to the emergency ward on days when the air pollution was high.

What do we learn from the juvenile asthma case?

Indira Gandhi told the 1972 Stockholm Conference on the Human Environment that poverty was the worst form of pollution. The juvenile asthma case shows that when poverty and pollution come together the result is doubly tragic.

Air pollution can have serious effects and so can noise pollution. These are the topics for this chapter.

What is air pollution?

Air pollution is said to exist if the levels of gases, solids, or liquids present in the atmosphere are high enough to harm humans, other organisms, or materials. The pollution could have natural causes like a forest fire or the eruption of a volcano. Our primary concern, however, are human activities, which are today responsible for most of the air pollution. Further, much of the pollution caused by humans is concentrated in thickly populated urban centres (Box 11.1).

BOX 11.1

The story of Mexico City: Saving a choked city

Just living and breathing the air here is equivalent to smoking two packets of cigarettes a day. It is the second largest city in the world and it has also the second worst level of air pollution.

Mexico City is located in a bowl-shaped valley with mountains on three sides. It has a population of more than 20 million, which is constantly on the increase. There are more than three million vehicles that emit four million tons of pollutants annually. Many of the vehicles are old ones that emit more pollutants than normal.

Emissions from 36,000 industries and leakage of LPG (liquefied petroleum gas) from thousands of containers add to the air pollution. The air also contains particles of dried faecal matter from the

millions of tons of sewage dumped on the land near the city.

The Mexican government has taken several steps to reduce the air pollution:

Contd

Box 11.1 Contd

- The hillsides have been reforested to reduce the particulate matter produced by wind erosion; in all, 25 million trees have been planted.
- Some refineries have been closed, others upgraded
- Cleaner fuel has been imported from the US

and unleaded petrol has been introduced; old vehicles have been banned.
- Public transport is being improved and one day a week personal cars have been prohibited.

With these measures, there has been some improvement, but there is still a long way to go.

Primary air pollutants are harmful chemicals that are released directly from a source into the atmosphere. Secondary air pollutants are also harmful chemicals, but they are produced from chemical reactions involving the primary pollutants.

Primary air pollutants include the following:
- Particulate matter: This includes both solid particles and liquid suspensions. Soil particles, soot, lead, asbestos, and sulphuric acid droplets are examples.
- Oxides of carbon and nitrogen and sulphur dioxide
- Hydrocarbons like methane and benzene

Secondary air pollutants include the following:
- Ozone: It is a form of oxygen and is a pollutant in the troposphere or the layer of the atmosphere closest to the earth's surface. It is a beneficial component in the stratosphere from 10 to 45 km above the earth (Chapter 19).
- Sulphur trioxide: This is formed when sulphur dioxide reacts with oxygen. In turn, sulphur trioxide combines with water to form sulphuric acid.

What are the sources of outdoor air pollution?

The sources of outdoor air pollution are:
- Burning of fossil fuels in
  - automobiles, domestic cooking and heating
  - power stations and industries (primarily the chemical, metal, and paper industries)
- Mining activities leading to dust as well as fires (Box 11.2)
- Burning biofuels, tropical rainforests, wastes of all kinds, etc.
- Natural emissions from animals, decaying organic matter

BOX 11.2

The story of Jharia: City of fire

In 2000, the town's temple snapped in two and flames leapt out from underneath, spewing noxious gases. The underground fires that had been raging for several decades had reached the residents' doorsteps!

Jharia in the state of Jharkand is now a town surrounded by fires. Raging in the coalmines underground, the fires are now visible on the surface. At night, the smoky haze makes Jharia resemble a cremation ground. Every possible outlet

Contd

Box 11.2 Contd

from the mines spits fire. Danger lurks at every step.

Coal fires occur naturally like forest fires. Lightning, forest fires, or frictional heat inside the earth's crust can trigger the spontaneous combustion of coal. These fires burn away coal, raise the atmospheric temperature, and cause land subsidence. Smoke from these fires contains poisonous gases such as the oxides and dioxides of carbon, nitrogen, and sulphur. Jharia is today among the ten most polluted towns of India.

Jharia has a 100-year history of coal fires. Neglected for long and stoked by relentless mining, the fires have consumed 40 million tons of India's best coking coal and rendered 1,800 million tons out of bounds. The fires now cover about 17 sq km. There have been many gas eruptions, accidents and deaths of miners.

The estimate of the cost of extinguishing the fire ranges from Rs Four to Ten billion. It may be worthwhile, because there is coal worth Rs 30 billion still to be extracted in the area. Bharat Coking Coal Ltd, the public sector company that owns the mines, is said to have spent Rs 1 billion so far to put out the fires, without much success.

The state government wants to evacuate the 300,000 people of Jharia, abandoning 100,000 houses. For the residents of Jharia, mere existence now is hell on earth. They live in constant fear of a major subsidence that could cause the entire town to collapse. Yet, they do not want to leave the town.

Will the entire town be evacuated so that mining can go on? Or will the fire be put out incurring high costs? Or more likely, will the precarious existence of the people continue without any action being taken?

Temporary, but severe, air pollution can occur due to disasters like earthquakes, volcano eruptions, dust storms, leak of gases (like the Bhopal case), and armed conflicts, etc. Even festivals (Diwali with its crackers, for example) can create air pollution. Dust storms are typically formed in desert areas and from there they can spread to places thousands of kilometres away (Box 11.3).

Industries and automobiles are by far the main contributors to outdoor air pollution across the world.

BOX 11.3

The story of Chinese dust storms: The fifth season

Schools were closed, many flights had to be cancelled, and hospitals crowded with patients suffering from breathing difficulties. This was the scene in Seoul, South Korea on April 12, 2002.

The cause was a huge dust storm that had originated in China. It marked the arrival of the 'fifth season', one of severe dust storms that the Koreans and the Chinese have come to fear. Such dust storms have now become a regular feature between winter and spring.

The amount of particulate matter in the Seoul air is normally 70 micrograms of dust per cubic metre. If this figure reaches 1,000 micrograms, many would have breathing problems. On that day, the figure was 2070 micrograms per cu m.

Apart from affecting the health of many, such dust storms lead to worker absenteeism, lower retail sales, problems in dust-sensitive factories like the ones making computer chips, etc. Hence, they are

Contd

Box 11.3 Contd

a threat to the economy. On occasions, the storms from China have even reached the US.

The storms create havoc in China itself, including the capital, Beijing. The real burden of the storms, however, falls on the Chinese farmers who live at their source. The dust and sand destroy crops, damage trees and orchards, kill animals, fill up water wells, and blow away fodder. Perhaps the worst effect is that they take away the topsoil.

Why do these storms occur? In its efforts to feed 1.3 billion people, China is overgrazing its range-lands, overploughing the cropland, overpumping the aquifers, and overcutting the forests. The land is becoming barren in northern and western China and the strong winds of late winter and early spring generate these huge dust storms. They carry away the fine particles and deposit them in the lungs of bewildered Koreans or even Americans!

Efforts to halt the desertification through afforestation have had only a limited success. The key seems to be to relieve the pressure on the land created by the grazing of 290 million sheep and goats. How will the Chinese do it?

What is the role of automobiles in creating air pollution and other environmental problems?

The automobile is one of the most desired items of consumption today and the demand seems insatiable. From about 50 million in 1950, the numbers increased to 600 million in 2010. The US alone has 25 per cent of all the cars in the world. China is now the second-largest car market in the world.

The automobile contributes to a range of environmental problems by increasing air and noise pollution, adding to solid waste, accelerating global warming, taking a heavy toll of life through accidents, using up natural non-renewable resources like oil and metals, etc.

Lead pollution caused by automobiles has been a serious problem. Lead was added to petrol for preventing the 'knocking' of the engine. Lead, however, is extremely poisonous and tends to accumulate in most biological systems. Large accumulation of lead in the body can result in paralysis, blindness, and even death. It can also affect the mental development of unborn children. Lead addition in petrol is now banned in most countries.

Automobiles contribute to pollution

Automobiles need roads and highways, which have many adverse environmental effects. They use up land and consume resources like steel and cement, which require heavy energy inputs and pollute the environment. Congestion and traffic jams cause enormous loss of man-hours as well as fuel. In cities, automobile emissions are a major cause of smog.

What is smog?

KEY IDEA

A range of human activities, including the use of automobiles, cause increasing air pollution in the world.

Smog is a form of outdoor pollution and the term was originally used to describe a combination of smoke, fog, and chemical pollutants that poisoned the air in industrialised cities like London. Now the term refers to the effects of air pollution not necessarily associated with smoke particles. It is used to describe air pollution that is localized in urban areas, where it reduces visibility.

What is common now in cities is photochemical smog formed by the chemical reactions between sunlight, unburnt hydrocarbons, ozone, and other pollutants. Photochemical smog can be seen as a hazy shroud on warm days in congested cities. It is an irritant to humans and very toxic to plants. In developing countries, leaded fuel, old engines, industrial emissions, and fuelwood burning combine to create severe smog.

What are the levels of outdoor air pollution in India?

India is now the second fastest growing auto market after China. Sales of all vehicles from April 2009 to March 2010 reached a total of 12.3 million (1.95 m passenger vehicles, 0.53 m commercial vehicles, 9.37 m two-wheelers, and 450,000 three-wheelers).

The exponential growth of vehicles, outdated vehicle technology, bad fuel quality, poor maintenance of vehicles, poor traffic management and planning, all contribute to vehicular pollution. The problem is compounded by the unwillingness on the part of vehicle owners and the auto industry to accept emission norms and the lack of efficient public transport.

Trucks and buses run on diesel, which has high sulphur content. The old engines emit vast quantities of suspended particulate matter, leading to heavy air pollution over many cities.

Air pollution caused by automobiles

KEY IDEA

The air pollution in a large number of Indian cities much more than the prescribed limits.

The Central and State Pollution Control Boards have been measuring the Ambient Air Quality in Indian cities. They measure parameters such as suspended particulate matter (SPM), nitrogen oxide, and sulphur dioxide and compare the values with the National Standards.

In 2009, the levels of SPM (less than 10 micrometre) were worse than the standard in 91 cities. The 10 worst affected cities were Jharia, Ludhiana, Khanna, Delhi, Ghaziabad, Kanpur, Gobindgarh, Lucknow, Amritsar, and Gwalior. The Annual Average SPM for these cities ranged from 190 to 260 microgram per cu. m, against the National Standard of 60 units. The main cause of pollution is the emission from vehicles and industries. Box 11.4 describes how the air in Delhi improved in recent times and became polluted again.

Polluted air is affecting the health of the people, particularly children. In Delhi alone, one out of every 10 school children suffers from asthma (Recall the story of juvenile asthma).

BOX 11.4

The story of Delhi's air pollution: Supreme Court clears the air

Delhi had for long been an extremely polluted city. There was often a haze and many people had breathing problems. Responding to a public interest petition, the Supreme Court of India issued a series of orders beginning from 1985 to improve Delhi's environment. These orders included:

- mandatory use of the less-polluting CNG (Compressed Natural Gas) by all buses and commercial trucks
- shifting of all highly polluting industries out of Delhi.

Contd

Box 11.4 Contd

- phasing out of leaded petrol and of all commercial vehicles older than 15 years.

After many delays and court interventions, the orders were implemented by December 2002. Gradually, the air became cleaner and it seemed to be a success story.

Delhi, however, seems to have lost all the gains made. The SPM in residential areas went up from 150 microgram per cu. m in 2001 to 209 units in 2008. Some of the reasons for this worsening pollution are:

- Adding 1,000 new personal vehicles each day on its roads—double the number added in the pre-CNG days
- Growth in personal diesel vehicles, which pollute more than the petrol vehicles.

- Decreasing use of public transport

The Delhi story shows how difficult it is to tackle air pollution in the major cities.

A CNG bus in Delhi
(Image courtesy: http://delhitourism.nic.in/delhitourism/images/dtc_bus.*jpg*)

What are the effects of outdoor air pollution?

At low levels air pollutants irritate the eyes and cause inflammation of the respiratory tract. If the person already suffers from a respiratory illness, air pollution may lead to the condition becoming chronic at a later stage. It can also accentuate skin allergies.

Many pollutants also depress the immune system, making the body more prone to infections. Carbon monoxide from automobile emissions can cause headache at lower levels and mental impairment and even death at higher levels.

Particulate matter can reduce visibility, soil clothes, corrode metals, and erode buildings. On a larger scale, air pollution leads to acid rain, ozone layer depletion, and global warming. These effects are discussed in Chapter 19.

How can outdoor air pollution be reduced or controlled?

Outdoor air pollution can be reduced by adopting cleaner technologies, reducing pollution at the source, implementing laws and regulations to make people pollute less, introducing appropriate transportation policies, etc.

Automobile emissions can be reduced through various measures:

- Making cleaner and fuel-efficient cars (Read discussion in the next section)
- Using lead-free petrol in existing cars
- Introducing policies that encourage the building and use of mass transit systems and discourage the use of personal transport (Examples are efficient and low-cost public transport, congestion charges in city centres, separate lanes for car pools, heavy tax on personal cars, tax incentives on electric cars, etc.)
- Shifting from diesel to natural gas for trucks and buses (Read Box 11.4)

Particulate matter in the air can be reduced by:
- Fitting smokestacks with electrostatic precipitators, fabric filters, scrubbers, or similar devices
- Sprinkling water on dry soil that is being excavated during road construction

How can we make cleaner cars?

There are options for making cars that would pollute less than current models: electric cars, hybrid cars, and hydrogen cars. All three types have been under development and prototypes have been made and tested.

The electric car is run by a motor powered by electricity. It produces virtually no emissions and the design is simple. The power usually comes from a battery inside the car. You can charge the battery using normal electric power. The battery needs recharging after running a certain distance (current models give about 200 km) and hence long trips are not possible. One can move around within a city. Though there is no net reduction in pollution, the electric car certainly reduces the air and noise pollution in the city.

An electric car being charged
(Image courtesy: Frankh, http://commons.wikimedia.org/wiki/File:Reva_charging.jpg)

The electric car seems to be an ideal solution, but there is a catch. If the electricity that charges the batteries comes from a conventional thermal power plant, then we have only transferred the emission problem to the power plant. To produce the extra power needed for charging, the power plant puts out more emissions. Thus, the electric car can be considered to be clean, only if the electricity comes from a renewable source. The disposal of the discarded battery also poses an environmental problem.

A hybrid car is a petrol-and-electricity driven vehicle. It starts using the petrol engine, but switches automatically to the electric motor at low speeds or while idling. At normal speeds both engines contribute power. When the car slows down, the wheels run the generator to charge the batteries. Several carmakers have introduced hybrid models.

A car running on liquid hydrogen would be extremely clean, the only waste being water. In such a car, fuel cells (Chapter 8) combine hydrogen with oxygen in the air to produce electricity. The hydrogen car has no emissions and gives better performance since there is no waste during idling.

Where is the catch? As we saw in Chapter 8, hydrogen has to be first produced and that process consumes energy. If the hydrogen is made using non-renewable energy, then we are back to square one. The hydrogen car will make sense only if we use renewables like solar energy to obtain the hydrogen.

Experiments have been done to run cars with other less-polluting fuels like methane and biodiesel. It is, however, unlikely that the zero-emission wonder car running on low-cost, abundant, and renewable energy will soon

> **KEY IDEA**
> It is necessary to design and use automobiles that pollute much less than what current models do.

arrive. Well before that happens, we will be forced to cut down on the number of cars on the road due to oil shortages, the reality of global warming, mounting solid waste, lack of space, and other problems.

How are automobile emissions regulated in India?

The Indian government began regulating automobile emissions in 1991. In the year 2000, the government introduced Bharat emission norms modelled on the basic Euro norms of the European Union.

Tightening the limits stage by stage, Bharat-III norms for new passenger cars came into effect nationwide from April 2010. At the same time, Bharat-IV norms were introduced in 12 cities—Bangalore, Delhi, Mumbai, Kolkata, Chennai, Hyderabad, Ahmedabad, Pune, Surat, Kanpur, Sholapur, and Agra. For 2–and 3–wheelers, Bharat-III became applicable from April 2010. In addition, the National Auto Fuel Policy introduced certain emission requirements for interstate buses.

The new Bharat-III petrol cars would be emitting 28 per cent lower emission than Bharat-II cars and 89 per cent lower than cars manufactured in 1991. Similarly there would be almost 30 per cent emission reduction in diesel cars in the Bharat-III cars compared to Bharat-II ones. Compared to 1992 diesel cars the emission reduction would be 72 per cent.

> **KEY IDEA**
> India has been introducing stringent norms for vehicle emissions.

Lead has been phased out of automobile fuel with effect from February 2000. Petrol and diesel conforming to Bharat norms are now available.

What are the causes and effects of indoor air pollution?

We give importance and attention to outdoor air pollution, but we do not realise that indoor pollution can be equally damaging.

Pesticides, mosquito repellents, cleaning agents, etc., used in urban households can cause toxic conditions. Building materials like asbestos, glass fibre, paints, glues, and varnishes are all health hazards. They can cause irritation of the eyes and skin, respiratory ailments and cancer.

Air-conditioned rooms and offices cause a broad spectrum of health complaints, because the sealed space accumulates various contaminants. Cigarette smoke affects both smokers and non-smokers (Box 11.5). The concentration of pollutants indoors may be five times more than outdoors.

BOX 11.5

The story of smoking: A grave matter

It is a major cause of suffering and death among adults and it takes about 500 people every single hour to an early grave. What is shocking is that these deaths are completely preventable, if only people would stop smoking.

According to the World Health Organization (WHO), cigarette smoking causes the premature death of 4 million people every year and this figure is expected to reach 10 million by 2030. Most of this increase will occur in the developing countries,

Contd

Box 11.5 Contd

China in particular. India is losing 800,000 to 900,000 lives every year due to tobacco. Worldwide cost of treating smoking-related illnesses is about US$ 200 billion per year.

Cigarette smoke is a mixture of hydrocarbons, carbon dioxide, carbon monoxide, cyanide, and particulate matter. In addition, it contains a small amount of radioactive material from the fertilizer used for the tobacco plant. All these substances are dangerous when the smoke is inhaled regularly. Nicotine in cigarettes is so addictive that only 10 per cent of smokers who want to quit the habit actually succeed in doing so.

The connection between smoking and lung cancer has been well established. Smoking also leads to heart diseases and cancer of the bladder, mouth, throat, pancreas, kidney, stomach, voice box, and oesophagus.

Passive smoking, the chronic breathing of smoke from the cigarettes of others, also increases the risk of cancer, besides causing respiratory problems. Passive smoking is particularly harmful to infants, young children, pregnant women, seniors, and those with lung disease.

Smoking has declined in the US, Japan, and Europe. The tobacco companies are now aggressively exporting the habit to the developing countries. Smoking is on the increase in many of the poorer countries including India.

The Indian government has taken several steps to curb the advertisement and sale of tobacco products. From October 2, 2008, smoking has been banned in all public places.

The most common pollutants in urban interiors are cigarette smoke, gases from stoves, formaldehyde (from carpets and furniture), pesticides, cleaning solvents, and ozone (from photocopiers). Organisms like viruses, bacteria, fungi, dust mites and pollens also thrive in the many ducts found in office buildings.

Urban indoor pollution results in ailments like colds, influenza, and upset stomachs. Since these are common ailments, the connection with indoor pollution is often missed. Indoor pollution can also cause eye irritations, nausea, depression, etc., collectively called the 'Sick Building Syndrome'.

How bad is indoor air pollution in India?

According to WHO, annually 400,000 to 2,000,000 premature deaths are attributable to indoor air pollution in India with a majority of deaths occurring in children under five due to acute respiratory infection.

In rural areas, indoor pollution is taking a toll on the health of women. Traditional stoves that use wood, coal, or animal dung spew out poisons that women inhale directly. This is equivalent to smoking 100 cigarettes a day! Many deaths take place in North India during winters when the doors and windows are closed shut and the poisonous smoke from the stove is not ventilated.

KEY IDEA

Indoor air pollution is as damaging as outdoor pollution.

There have been campaigns to substitute these inefficient and polluting stoves with smokeless chulhas. The effort, however, has failed to make an adequate dent on this huge problem. We will return to this issue in Chapter 17 (Women and Child Welfare).

From air pollution let us move to noise pollution.

What is noise pollution and what are its sources?

Noise is defined as unwanted sound and it is an irritant and a source of stress. Most of the noise one hears originates from human activities. The main sources are:

- Transport sector: aircraft, trains, trucks, tractors, cars, three-wheelers, and motorcycles contribute the maximum noise.
- Industrial and construction machinery: factory equipment, generators, pile drivers, pneumatic drills, road rollers, and similar machinery.
- Special events: high-volume sound from loudspeakers during pop music performances, marriage receptions, religious festivals, public meetings, etc.

An aircraft flying over a residential area

Noise pollution is increasing in industrial societies and in cities everywhere.

How is sound measured? Sound is measured in decibels (db). It is not a linear, but a logarithmic scale. For example, a change from 40 db to 80 db represents a 10,000-fold increase in loudness. When the sound level reaches 140 db, you will start feeling pain in the ears. However, long exposure to noise even at 85 db can cause hearing loss.

Apart from loudness, the frequency or pitch of the noise also determines whether it is harmful or not. A modified scale called decibel-A (dbA) takes pitch into account. Hearing loss begins if a person is exposed more than 8 hours a day to a noise level of 80–90 dbA. A level of 140 dbA is painful and 180 dbA could kill. Table 11.1 gives the typical intensity levels of common sources of sound.

Table 11.1 Typical Average Decibel Levels (dbA) of Some Common Sounds
(Where necessary, the distance of the source in metres is specified.)

Source	dbA	Source	dbA
Threshold of hearing	0	Motorcycle (10 m)	88
Rustling leaves	20	Food blender (1 m)	90
Quiet whisper (1 m)	30	Subway (inside)	94
Quiet home	40	Diesel truck (10 m)	100
Quiet street	50	Power mower (1 m)	107
Normal conversation	60	Pneumatic riveter (1 m)	115
Inside a car	70	Chainsaw (1 m)	117
Loud singing (1 m)	75	Amplified Rock and Roll (2 m)	120
Automobile (8 m)	80	Jet plane (30 m)	130

What are the effects of noise pollution?

Noise can do physiological or psychological damage if the volume is high or if the exposure is prolonged. Loud, high-pitched noise damages the fine hair cells in the cochlea of the ear. The vibration of these hair cells in response to sound is transmitted to the brain by the auditory nerve. Since the body does not replace damaged hair cells, permanent hearing impairment is caused by prolonged exposure to loud noise.

Noise can also produce other effects like heart palpitation, pupil dilation, or muscle contraction. Migraine headaches, nausea, dizziness, gastric ulcers, and constriction of blood vessels are some of the other possible outcomes.

Noise can cause serious damage to wildlife, especially in remote regions, where the normal noise level is low. Ways in which animals are adversely affected by noise pollution include
- hearing loss, affecting their ability to avoid predators,
- masking, which is the inability to hear important environmental cues and animal signals,
- non-auditory physiological effects such as increased heart rate and respiration and general stress reaction and
- behavioural effects, which could result in the abandonment of territory and lost reproduction.

What are the control measures against noise pollution?   Producing less noise is the best method of reducing this pollution. Almost all machinery can be redesigned to reduce noise. Another way is to provide shields and noise-absorbing material. Earplugs and earphones can shield the receiver from noise.

What is the level of noise pollution in India?

In urban as well as rural areas, noise pollution is on the increase. Public meetings, festivals, marriage receptions, sound of televisions, automobile horns, general traffic movement, etc., have all become louder.

In the 1980s and 1990s, there were several court judgements in India restricting the generation of noise by industries, fire crackers, electric horns, etc. Finally, in 2000, the Indian government notified the Noise Regulation Rules (Box 11.6).

> **KEY IDEA**
> Noise pollution is on the increase in India and it has many adverse effects. We now have laws to control noise pollution.

BOX 11.6

Noise regulation rules

In 2000, the Indian government notified the Noise Regulation Rules under the Environment (Protection) Act of 1986. Two types of noise standards are prescribed: ambient noise level standards and noise limits for designated types of machinery, appliances and fire crackers.

The rules regulate noise levels in industrial (75 db), commercial (65 db) and residential zones (55 db), and also establish zones of silence (100 m) near schools, courts, hospitals, etc.

The rules specify that no permission could be granted by any authority for use of public address (PA) system in the open after 10.00 pm and before 6.00 am. After permission has been procured the sound must fall within the sound limits prescribed in the Noise Rules.

Contd

Box 11.6 Contd

An amendment to the Rules, made in January 2010, addresses the following issues:

1. Stress has been laid on making the night peaceful. The 'night time' has been defined (10.00 pm to 6.00 am) and restrictions have been imposed on the use of horns, sound emitting construction equipments and bursting of fire crackers during night time.
2. 'Public place' has been defined and the occupant of a public place has to restrict the volume of PA system, etc., so that the noise emitting from its activity would not exceed the noise limit more than 10 dbA.
3. Similarly, the occupant of a private place has to restrict the volume of music system, etc., so that the noise emitting from its activity would not exceed the noise limit by more than 5 dbA.
4. State Governments must specify in advance the number and particulars of days, not exceeding fifteen in a year, on which 2 hours exemption (10.00 pm to 12.00 midnight) would be operative for the use of PA system.

These amendments are in line with the Supreme Court orders from time to time. A National Ambient Noise Monitoring Network is also being set up.

REVIEW: A SUMMARY OF THE KEY POINTS

- While there are some natural sources of air pollution, most of the pollution today is caused by human activities.
- Burning fossil fuels in automobiles and industry is the major source of air pollution.
- Air pollution has many adverse effects on human health.
- Technologies are available to reduce automobile and industrial emissions.
- The zero-emission wonder car running on low-cost, abundant, and renewable energy is still a dream

- The world will be forced to cut down on the number of cars on the road due to a variety of reasons.
- Indoor air pollution can be as damaging as outdoor pollution.
- As the number of automobiles increases rapidly in India, air pollution is becoming a serious problem. In particular, it is taking a heavy toll on the health of urban poor children.
- Spurred on by the courts, the Indian Government is introducing stringent rules to reduce emissions.
- Noise pollution can have very damaging effects and the best way is to curb the generation of noise.

EXERCISES

Objective-type questions

In each question below, choose the best out of the given choices:

1. Which of the following statements is **not** true with regard to air pollution?
   (a) Air pollution is caused only by human activities.
   (b) Urban areas have high air pollution.
   (c) A burning forest produces air pollution.
   (d) Air pollution is caused by volcanoes.

2. Which of the following is **not** a primary air pollutant?
   (a) Methane
   (b) Sulphur dioxide
   (c) Ozone
   (d) Asbestos

3. Which of the following is an occasional cause of air pollution?
   (a) Mining
   (b) Driving automobiles

(c) Cooking

(d) Celebrating a festival

4. Which of the following statements is true?

   (a) Hybrid cars run on petrol and diesel.

   (b) The only emission from a hydrogen-powered vehicle will be oxygen.

   (c) An electric car has to be charged from the grid.

   (d) A diesel vehicle pollutes less than a petrol vehicle.

5. Which of the following statements is true with regard to noise and noise pollution?

   (a) Decibel is a linear scale of noise measurement.

   (b) A jet plane is one of the high-decibel sources of noise.

   (c) Noise will not affect the heart.

   (d) Noise cannot be shielded.

Short-answer questions

1. What are primary and secondary air pollutants? Give examples.

2. What are the sources of outdoor air pollution?

3. What are the effects of outdoor air pollution?

4. How can outdoor air pollution reduced or controlled?

5. What are the causes and effects of indoor air pollution?

6. What are the sources and effects of noise pollution?

7. Give an account of the rules framed by the government to control noise pollution.

Long-answer questions

1. 'The automobile is one of the worst inventions made by humankind.' Write an essay supporting this statement. Focus on the environmental impact of the automobile. Comment on the possible impact of the rapid increase of the number of cars in India and China. Review the approaches for making cleaner cars.

2. Describe the state of urban air pollution in India. What is its impact on health, especially on that of children? What are the measures the government is taking to reduce vehicle emissions? How did the quality of air improve in Delhi?

Think critically: Deeper questions for reflection and discussion

What is the psychological basis for the great attraction of the personal car? How can that need be satisfied through public transport? How can cycling be promoted (even as the Chinese are giving up this healthy and ecofriendly habit)?

SOMETHING DIFFERENT FOR A CHANGE

The children's book *The Lorax* by Dr Seuss is a great environmental story and you may like it for it message and its wacky verse. Here is an extract from the book:

Then again he came back! I was fixing some pipes
when that old nuisance Lorax came back with more
gripes.
I am the Lorax, he coughed and he whiffed.
He sneezed and he snuffled. He snarggled. He sniffed.
Once-ler! he cried with a cruffulous croak.
Once-ler! You're making such smogulous smoke!

My poor Swomee-Swans...why, they can't sing a note!
No one can sing who has smog in his throat.

And so, said the Lorax,
—please pardon my cough—
they cannot live here.
So I'm sending them off.
Where will they go?...
I don't hopefully know.
They may have to fly for a month...or a year...
To escape from the smog you've smogged-up around
here

ACTIVITIES

Act: What you can do to minimize air and noise pollution

1. Discourage your friends or neighbours from lighting bonfires. Bonfire smoke is dangerous, containing highly toxic, and possibly carcinogenic, chemicals.

Never burn tyres or plastics, which release deadly dioxins and poisonous gases. Join the police and NGOs to discourage people from lighting such fires during festivals like Bhogi in Tamil Nadu.

2. If you must light a bonfire, burn diseased cuttings and branches. If you are at a bonfire, do not inhale the smoke.
3. If any group creates too much noise in your neighbourhood, especially between 10 pm and 6 am, try to persuade them to stop or reduce the volume. If they do not respond, feel free to go the police.

Learn by doing: Case study/Project

Volunteer your services to the Central Pollution Control Board for its programme of monitoring the air quality in the cities. Work with the monitoring unit for two or three weeks and write a report on your experience. Include in your report a description of the measuring equipment, the parameters that are measured, how the parameters changed over the period you were involved, etc.

Organize together: Eco-club activities and projects

Observe Car Free Day on September 22. Over 1100 cities across the world observe the Car Free Day. There is also the UN Car Free Days Programme, which provides information and supports the observance of the Day in all countries.

Try to organise a Car Free Day in your city by bringing together the concerned citizens' groups and organizations. Get the traffic police, the local mayor and some politicians to join. Some possible activities are:

- Get cars banned in busy shopping areas on that day
- Set up stalls on the road to put up posters regarding air pollution, effects of traffic jams, importance of public transport, oil shortage, global warming, etc.
- Demonstrate ecofriendly vehicles like electric cars and scooters
- Launch a campaign for pedestrian zones, better public transport, non-polluting vehicles, etc.
- Arrange a bicycle rally to create awareness of the problems of increasing car use.

For more information, access the websites: www. 22september.org, www.uncfd.org

LEARN MORE

Book

Brown, Lester R., Janet Larsen, and Bernie Fischlowitz-Roberts 2002, *The Earth Policy Reader*, Earth Policy Institute, Indian Edition, Orient Longman, Hyderabad.

Articles

Bell, Ruth Greenspan, Kuldip Mathur, Urvashi Narain, and David Simpson 2004, 'Clearing the Air: How Delhi Broke the Logjam on Air Quality Reforms', *Environment*, Vol. 46, No. 3, April, pp. 22–39.

Mahapatra, Richard 2002, 'Consigned to Flames: Central and State Authorities Fiddle While Jharia Burns', *Down To Earth*, Vol. 11, No. 13, November 30, pp. 25–29.

Varshney, Vibha 2004, 'Out of Breath', *Down To Earth*, Vol. 12, No. 20, March 15, pp. 27–34. (on juvenile asthma)

Film

Battling the Epidemic, a documentary on the anti-smoking campaign undertaken by Justice Narayana Kurup.

CHAPTER **12**

Water, Soil, and Marine Pollution

As we watch the sun go down, evening after evening,
through the smog across the poisoned waters of our native earth,
we must ask ourselves seriously whether we really wish
some future universal historian on another planet to say about us:
'With all their genius and with all their skill,
they ran out of foresight and air and food and water and ideas,' or,
'They went on playing politics until their world collapsed around them.'

U Thant
(1909–1974)
Third Secretary-General of the United Nations

THIS CHAPTER IS ABOUT...

Water pollution, water purification, sanitation, soil pollution and soil treatment, marine and coastal pollution, initiatives for controlling marine pollution

THE KEYWORDS AND PHRASES ARE...

algal bloom	ecological sanitation	eutrophication	fluorosis
reverse osmosis	sludge	biomagnification	biological oxygen demand
bioremediation	persistent organic pollutants (pops)		

THE STORY OF FLUORIDE CONTAMINATION: CANNOT LIVE, CANNOT DIE!

In Jharana Khurd village, 20 km from Jaipur, Rajasthan, there are no youth. All the 1,200 inhabitants, irrespective of age, look old. Their shoulders, hips, and ankles are swollen and ache all the time. All have cracked teeth.

The people of Jharana Khurd are not alone. The story is similar in Baroli Aheer in Uttar Pradesh, Chukru in Jharkand, Kachariadih in Bihar, Annaparti in Andhra Pradesh, and thousands of other villages across the country. The people of all these villages suffer from fluorosis, caused by an excess of fluoride in water.

Excess intake of fluoride leads to fluorosis: dental, skeletal, or non-skeletal. Dental fluorosis results in blackened, mottled, or cracked teeth. Skeletal fluorosis means permanent and severe bone and joint deformities. Non-skeletal fluorosis leads to gastro-intestinal and neurological problems.

High fluoride concentration in groundwater occurs naturally in a number of countries. While fluorosis is most severe and widespread in India and China, it is endemic in at least 25 countries across the globe. The Indian geology is such that the bedrock contains minerals with high fluoride content. When the bedrock weathers, the fluoride leaches into the water and soil.

In India, fluorosis has wiped out the economy of whole villages by disabling most of the inhabitants. To women, the disease brings social stigma. Normally, the disease does not lead to death, but to extreme suffering. As someone put it, 'It neither allows a person to live nor to die.'

Why has fluorosis become a problem in recent years? Excessive extraction of groundwater has led to deeper and deeper borewells, which draw water from aquifers containing high fluoride concentrations. There is no fluoride problem if one drinks water from an open well or pond.

Fluorosis is now endemic in 19 Indian states, affecting 65 million people, including 6 million children. At least 60,000 villages have high fluoride levels. As India digs deeper and deeper to get water, the fluoride problem will become more widespread and more acute.

Until now, state and national level initiatives to combat fluorosis have been weak. There is no regular monitoring and testing of groundwater. Technologies are available for defluoridation, but the plants are expensive and involve significant maintenance costs.

UNICEF (UN Children's Fund) has introduced domestic de-fluoridation filter units, which can be used in homes to remove excess fluoride from drinking water. This easy-to-use device, where contaminated water poured into the upper chamber gets filtered and collects in the lower one, reduces the fluoride content to acceptable levels. Another solution is to use rainwater in place of the contaminated water (Box 12.5).

What do we learn from the fluorosis story?

Under normal use of water resources, the fluoride problem would not have become such a widespread issue. Fluoride contamination began only when we went deeper and deeper into the ground to extract increasing amounts of water. It is once again a case of exceeding the limits of nature to satisfy our needs and paying a heavy price for it.

In this chapter, we will find out how water, soil, and the ocean are being polluted largely due to human activities.

What is water pollution and what is the scale of water pollution in the world?

Water pollution is the contamination of water sources including ponds, lakes, rivers, groundwater, and the ocean. Water pollution occurs when pollutants are discharged directly or indirectly into water bodies without removing harmful compounds. Water pollution affects plants and organisms living in these bodies of water as well as human communities that use the polluted water.

Here are some UN statistics on water pollution:

- Every day, 2 million tons of human waste are disposed of in water bodies.
- In developing countries, 70 per cent of industrial wastes are dumped untreated into waters where they pollute the usable water supply.

Water pollution due to untreated waste

- Projected increases in fertilizer use for food production and in wastewater effluents over the next three decades suggest there will be a 10–20 per cent global increase in river nitrogen flows to coastal ecosystems.
- Half of the world's wetlands, which act as natural filters, have been lost since 1900.

Which are the pollutants of freshwater and what are the effects?

Most of the freshwater sources in the world like rivers, lakes, and groundwater are already polluted. This is true even of remote places like the Polar Regions. Most of the pollution that ultimately reaches the ocean contaminates freshwater sources on the way.

The main categories of water pollutants and their effects are:

Sediments   Excessive amounts of soil particles carried by flowing water, when there is severe soil erosion. Sediments cloud the water and reduce photosynthesis, clog reservoirs and channels, smother coral reefs, destroy feeding grounds of fish, and disrupt aquatic food webs.

Oxygen-demanding wastes   Organic waste such as animal manure and plant debris that are decomposed by bacteria, from sewage, animal feedlots, paper mills, and food processing facilities. Bacteria that decompose these wastes deplete the oxygen and cause the death of fish and other aquatic organisms.

Infectious microorganisms   Parasitic worms, viruses and bacteria from infected organisms as well as human and animal wastes. They are responsible for water-borne diseases that kill thousands of adults and children, primarily in the developing countries.

Organic compounds   Synthetic chemicals containing carbon from industrial effluents, surface runoff, and cleaning agents. These chemicals cause many health problems for humans and harm fish and wildlife.

Inorganic nutrients   Substances like nitrogen and phosphorus from animal waste, plant residues, and fertilizer runoff. The nutrients can cause eutrophication (explained below) and can affect infants and unborn babies.

Inorganic chemicals   Acids, salts, and heavy metals like lead and mercury from industrial effluents, surface runoff, and household cleaning agents. They make water unfit for drinking or irrigation, harm fish and other aquatic organisms, cause many health problems for humans, and lower crop yields.

Radioactive substances   Wastes from nuclear power plants, nuclear weapons production, mining and refining uranium and other ores. Such substances cause cancers, birth defects, miscarriages, etc.

> **KEY IDEA**
> Many kinds of pollutants, mostly from human activities, contaminate water sources and cause adverse effects.

Thermal pollution   Hot water from industrial processes. The heat lowers oxygen levels and makes aquatic organisms more vulnerable to disease, parasites and toxic chemicals. When the hot water is let in, the sudden increase in temperature produces thermal shock in aquatic organisms.

Where do the water pollutants come from?

Water pollutants come from point sources and nonpoint sources. Specific places like sewage treatment plants and factories are point sources that discharge pollutants through pipes, sewers, or ditches. Point sources can be regulated through laws and rules.

Where pollutants enter the water over large areas than at a single point, we have nonpoint sources. This is the case when rainwater flows along the soil, picks up pollutants, and carries them into the water bodies. Nonpoint sources include surface runoff, mining wastes, municipal wastes, construction sediments, acid rain, and soil erosion. Nonpoint sources are difficult to control.

What is eutrophication of lakes?

A lake or a pond that has clear water contains minimal levels of nutrients and supports small populations of aquatic organisms. Eutrophication is the enrichment of such a standing water body by nutrients such as phosphorus and nitrogen. It occurs when sewage and fertilizer runoff bring large amounts of nutrients to the water body.

In eutrophic lakes, there is increased photosynthetic activity. This results in cloudy water covered by a slimy and smelly mat of algae and cyanobacteria. When the excessive numbers of algae die, they fall to the bottom of the lake and get decomposed. Since this process uses up a lot of the dissolved oxygen, some fish species die. They are replaced by other species that can tolerate lesser amounts of oxygen.

Eutrophication is not desirable, since it changes the species mix and also covers the surface. Reducing phosphorus and nitrogen input is the best way of controlling eutrophication.

How does groundwater get polluted?

About two billion people, approximately one-third of the world's population, depend on groundwater for their daily needs. About 600 to 700 cubic km of groundwater is withdrawn every year, mostly from shallow aquifers.

It was believed for long that water that slowly seeps or infiltrates into the ground would be thoroughly filtered by the soil and hence groundwater would be free of pollutants. We know now that this is not necessarily true. The filtering capacity of soil varies greatly from place to place. Further, there is also a limit to the amount of pollutants the soil can filter.

Excessive extraction leads to the natural pollution of groundwater. Examples are the fluoride concentration described at the beginning of this chapter and the arsenic contamination discussed in Box 12.1. In coastal areas, when water tables drop due to excessive extraction, there is intrusion of salt water and this is often an irreversible process.

BOX 12.1

The story of arsenic poisoning

Arsenic contamination of groundwater was first reported in 1983 from the 24–parganas district of West Bengal. Later, it was found that almost the whole of Bangladesh was affected by this problem. Arsenic is an element found in combination with oxygen, chlorine, hydrogen, mercury, gold, and iron. The effect of arsenic in the body starts showing after 2–5 years of consuming the contaminated water. The skin develops spots, then hard nodules, leading later to gangrene and cancer. It also brings many other complications like blindness, liver, and heart problems, diabetes, and goitre.

Arsenic contamination has been worsening steadily in West Bengal, Bihar, and Bangladesh.

Contd

Box 12.1 Contd

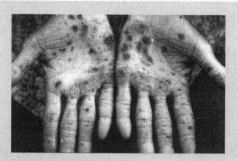

Arsenic poisoning

Almost 330 million people may be at risk in the two countries. In Bangladesh, 1.5 million tubewells are now heavily contaminated with arsenic. Some scientists believe that all this is only the tip of the iceberg. Many future generations could be at grave risk from this poisoning. This is perhaps the largest mass poisoning in history.

Where does the arsenic come from? One theory is that it originated in the Himalayan headwaters of the Ganga and the Brahmaputra and had been below the deltas of the region for thousands of years.

Over a long period this arsenic has contaminated the deep wells.

The other theory is that arsenic deposits are present in aquifers. When the rate of groundwater extraction is very high, the water level goes below the deposits, and arsenic is released. When the aquifer gets recharged, the arsenic contaminates the water.

Until now national and international initiatives to tackle the problem have been tentative and ineffective. Testing for arsenic is a complex, difficult, and expensive process. There is also lack of basic knowledge about the movement of groundwater and the location of arsenic in the water sources.

The Berkeley Arsenic Alleviation Group, a multidisciplinary team from the University of California, Berkeley and Jadavpur University, Kolkata, is trying to solve the arsenic crisis. They are testing two inexpensive methods: Electro-Chemical Arsenic Remediation (ECAR) and Arsenic Removal Using Bottom Ash (ARUBA).

Groundwater receives pollutants from septic tanks, landfills, hazardous waste dumps, and underground tanks containing petrol, oil, chemicals, etc. Substances like paint thinners and motor oil that we pour on the ground ultimately reaches the groundwater.

KEY IDEA

The world's groundwater, on which millions of people depend, are now polluted in many places.

Groundwater pollution is long lasting because it does not get flushed or decomposed away. The flow of groundwater is very slow, decomposing bacteria are few in number, and the cold temperatures slow down the decomposing process. As a result, even degradable waste stays in the water for hundreds to thousands of years. In any case, nondegradable waste like lead, arsenic and fluoride remain in groundwater permanently.

What is biomagnification?

Biomagnification is the increase in concentration of a substance, such as the pesticide, that occurs in a food chain. The pollutant enters the first organism in a food chain. When the second organism in the chain consumes the first one, the pollutant too moves into the second organism.

We know that, as we go up the levels of the ecological pyramid (Chapter 2), there is energy loss. Hence, at each succeeding level, the predator consumes more of the prey. As a result, the organisms at higher levels have greater concentrations of the pollutant. This is called biomagnification.

For example, mercury is only present in small amounts in seawater. It is absorbed by algae. Plankton consume a lot of algae and get higher doses of mercury. Through biomagnification, mercury level increases in each further link of the food chain: small fish and then larger fish.

Anything, which eats these fish, also consumes the higher level of mercury the fish have accumulated. Hence, swordfish, sharks, and birds like osprey and eagles have high concentrations of mercury in their bodies. We also take in high levels of mercury, when we eat fish.

Let us now look at some aspects of water pollution in India.

What do we know about water pollution in India?

It is estimated that almost 70 per cent of India's surface water resources and many of its groundwater reserves are already contaminated by a variety of pollutants. In many cases, these water sources have been rendered unsafe for human consumption as well as for other activities such as irrigation and industrial needs. This has reduced the supply of freshwater.

Water pollution

What is the state of rivers in India?   While the major rivers retain their pristine quality at the headwaters stage, they become polluted once they reach the plains. Agricultural runoff, industrial effluents, and domestic sewage find their way into most rivers. The rivers are stressed in the middle stretches where both extraction rates and pollution levels are high.

Tests of the river waters near or in cities show that in most cases the water is unfit for drinking. This is the case with the Yamuna near Delhi, Sabarmati in Ahmedabad, Gomti in Lucknow, Adyar in Chennai, Vaigai at Madurai, and Sutlej near Ludhiana.

According to the World Health Organization, 1.1 million litres of raw sewage is dumped into the Ganga every minute. Note that one gram of faeces in untreated water may contain 10 million viruses, one million bacteria, 1000 parasite cysts and 100 worm eggs. Read more about Ganga's pollution in Chapter 20.

How severe is pesticide contamination of freshwater in India?

Since the beginning of the Green Revolution, large amounts of pesticide have been used (and continue to be used) in agriculture and other sectors. It is not surprising that pesticide residues have contaminated many water sources.

KEY IDEA
Water pollution is severe in India and many of our rivers are polluted and unsafe for use.

We have reached the stage where we cannot be sure of the quality of any water source in the country. Even bottled water samples have shown the presence of pesticide residues (Box 12.2). This is also the case with soft drinks, which use the same sources of water.

BOX 12.2

The story of bottled water: Poisons in packages

A decade ago, bottled water was sold only in expensive hotels. Today, bottles and pouches of water are found everywhere, even in small towns and villages, railway stations and bus stands. People in cities no longer get enough water in their taps and they do not trust the quality of the little amount they get. Their borewells give only brackish water. As a result, most middle class urban residents buy drinking water.

When you go to a hotel or travel by train, you are very likely to order a bottle of water as you do not trust the quality of water served by the hotel or the water from the railway tap. You believe that the bottled water is safe. Well, some tests have shown that bottled water could contain pesticide residues above acceptable limits.

In 2002, the Centre for Science and Environment (CSE) in Delhi tested 34 common brands of bottled water for the presence of pesticides. The tests were conducted in their laboratory using methodology approved by the US Environment Protection Agency. The results were compared to the norms set by the European Union (EU).

Pesticide residues were found in all the samples except in one imported brand. The residues included deadly pesticides like lindane, DDT, and malathion and the amounts were well above the EU norms.

The CSE team traced the pesticides to the sources of water, mostly borewells. The water sources contained even higher levels of pesticides. The bottling plants used chemical and filtration techniques in the purification process, but they could remove only a part of the pesticide residues.

There are Indian standards for packaged water and, since March 2001, certification by the Bureau of Indian Standards is mandatory. However, for limits on pesticide presence, the standards refer to the Prevention of Food Adulteration Act, which only says that pesticides should be 'below detectable limits'.

Thousands of bottles of water are consumed in India every day. If they contain deadly pesticides, why are people not dropping dead on the streets? The reason is that, while the levels may be above EU norms, they are not so high as to cause immediate symptoms of poisoning. Over a period, however, the pesticides will show their adverse effects on the health.

In July 2003, the Union Ministry of Health and Family Welfare notified new standards for pesticide residues in bottled water. The Bureau of Indian Standards has notified standards for bottled water and Courts have ruled that BIS certification was necessary for any packaged water.

How do we measure water quality?

Here are some ways in which water quality is measured:

Biological Oxygen Demand (BOD) This parameter measures the degree of water pollution from oxygen-demanding wastes and plant nutrients. BOD is the amount of dissolved oxygen needed by the decomposers to break down the organic material in specified conditions. It is measured in parts per million or ppm. Table 12.1 shows the connection between BOD level and water quality.

Table 12.1 BOD and Water Quality

BOD level (parts per million)	Water quality	Description
1–2	Very good	Not much organic waste present
3–5	Moderately clean	
6–9	Somewhat polluted	Bacteria decomposing organic matter present
100 or greater	Very polluted	

Total Dissolved Solids (TDS)   This is a measure of the combined content of all inorganic and organic substances contained in a liquid. TDS is measured for freshwater systems such as streams, rivers and lakes. TDS is not generally considered a primary pollutant, but it is used as an overall indicator of the presence of a broad array of chemical contaminants. TDS is also measured in ppm.

Presence of disease-causing organisms   The number of colonies of coliform bacteria present in a 100 millilitre (ml) sample of water is one measure. There should be no coliform colonies in drinking water, while water in a swimming pool could have up to 200 colonies per 100 ml.

Chemical analysis   The presence of chemicals like pesticides can be measured by analysis.

How are polluted water and sewage treated?

The first step in freshwater purification is to use a chemical to make the suspended particles settle down. The water is then filtered and disinfected. The most common disinfectant is chlorine, though there is concern about the hazard of consuming low doses of chlorine over long periods.

Wastewater, including sewage, goes through several stages of treatment. The primary treatment removes suspended particles by screening and settling. The secondary treatment uses microorganisms to decompose the organic material in the wastewater. After several hours, the particles and the bacteria are allowed to settle down as secondary sludge. The tertiary treatment is a complex biological and chemical process that removes the remaining pollutants like minerals, metals, organic compounds, and viruses.

KEY IDEA
We can treat wastewater, but we end up with toxic sludge at the end.

The major problem with sewage and wastewater treatment is the disposal of the sludge. The sludge is often toxic, since people tend to dump all kinds of waste into drains. Treating the sludge is a costly and time-consuming process. Cities in industrialized countries do not know how to get rid of the sludge and so they export it to the developing countries (Read a discussion on this issue in Chapter 13).

What can be done about industrial pollution of freshwater?

Every litre of wastewater discharged by an industry pollutes on an average eight litres of freshwater. The total amount of water polluted in this manner is more than all the water in the largest river basins.

There are ways of reducing industrial pollution of freshwater:
- Improving process technology to reduce water demand
- Using the same water in series for two or more successive stages in the process
- Recirculating process water indefinitely, making up only for unavoidable losses
- Rainwater harvesting to meet as many of the requirements as possible

Governments could take the following steps to regulate the use of water by industries:
- Ensure that they withdraw water from downstream of their own discharge, forcing them to clean their discharges
- Establish specific and total load-based effluent standards
- Fix a quota for total freshwater withdrawal for each industry in a watershed
- Specify mandatory recycling percentage
- Restrict groundwater withdrawal where levels are low
- Make rainwater harvesting compulsory
- Price the water properly: charge high for an industry that can reuse water, charge for groundwater use, and increase unit price with increasing use
- Introduce pollution charges, high enough to be an incentive to reduce pollution
- Impose stiff penalties for non-compliance of regulations.

What are the methods of purifying water?

Some of the purification methods are described below:

Reverse osmosis or RO method   This process was discovered in the late 1950's and was slow to catch on but now it enjoys patronage worldwide. In the RO method, water is forced through a semi-permeable membrane. This filters unwanted substances, producing clear, fresh-tasting drinking water. RO uses no chemicals and can also be used to desalinate seawater. The membranes, however, need to be manufactured and later disposed off.

The UV method   Ultraviolet radiation is directed through clear, pre-filtered, particle-free water. The UV light is extremely effective in killing and eliminating bacteria, viruses, fungi, and certain harmful organisms. It is mainly used in industry and hospitals to treat water. The method must be used in conjunction with sediment and carbon filters.

Distillation method   Water is boiled to create steam and when this steam cools, it condenses to form water droplets, which in turn are deposited in a container. The residual water contains the contaminants and is discarded. The resultant is pure mineral free water. When used in conjunction with other filter mediums such as carbon you can get very pure water.

Planted filter method   This can be used even to purify sewage water. The wastewater first goes through a septic tank and a baffle reactor, in which all the particulate and organic matter are removed. Next the water is sent through an open horizontal planted gravel filter containing pebbles with plants like reeds, which absorb many of the impurities. Finally, the water moves through an open polishing pond. The output is good enough for gardening and irrigation.

Water supply and sanitation are closely connected and it is time to review the global sanitation crisis.

What is the status of the world's sanitation?

According to the World Health Organization (WHO), sanitation generally refers to the provision of facilities and services for the safe disposal of human urine and faeces. Inadequate sanitation is a major cause of disease worldwide and improving sanitation is known to have a significant beneficial impact on health both in households and across communities. The word 'sanitation' also refers to the maintenance of hygienic conditions, through services such as garbage collection and wastewater disposal.

In 2008, around 2.6 billion people lacked access to adequate sanitation globally. The regions with the lowest coverage were sub-Saharan Africa (37 per cent), southern Asia (38 per cent) and eastern Asia (45 per cent). 5,000 children die every day in the world from diarrhoeal diseases, mostly due to poor sanitation. Other estimates show that 2.7 billion people managed with only basic pit latrines and 0.8 billion with dysfunctional flush sanitation. Just 300 million people (with relatively high incomes) had proper flush sanitation.

According to the Census of India 2001, 108 million rural households and 14 million urban households had no sanitation facilities. The 2011 Census is bound to show worse figures. India is the second worst case in sanitation after China.

Sanitation coverage in rural areas is less than half that in urban settings, even though 80 per cent of those lacking adequate sanitation (2 billion people) live in rural areas. These figures are all the more shocking because they reflect the results of at least twenty years of concerted effort and publicity to improve coverage. The situation will get worse with the projected steep increase in the urban populations of Latin America, Africa and Asia.

The UN Millennium Development Goal was to reduce by one-half the proportion of people without access to hygienic sanitation facilities by 2015. To achieve this target in Africa, Asia and Latin America and the Caribbean alone, an additional 2.2 billion people will need access to sanitation. At the current rate of progress, many countries are likely meet the target only by 2025.

What has been the approach of governments and municipalities for providing sanitation facilities to the population?   The cities of the world have tended to set up centralised systems with pipes carrying the waste to sewage treatment plants. Such systems are expensive to build and maintain and they cannot keep pace with the rapid expansion of the extent and population of cities. Centralised systems are in any case impractical in rural areas.

Why can't we provide everyone with flush toilets?   Some environmentalists rate the flush toilet as being one of worst inventions of humankind, comparable to the automobile. In the flush system, the water is utilized not just to clean the toilet bowl, but also to transport the excreta. A family of five would need more than 150 thousand litres of water to transport 250 litres of excrement in just one year.

Given the worsening water scarcity, shortage of funds to build large sewage plants, and increasing population, we will never solve the sanitation problem with the current approaches. The only way is to adopt ecological sanitation.

What is ecological sanitation?

Ecological sanitation (EcoSan) represents a shift in thinking about and acting upon human excreta. The faeces are composted close to the place of excretion, and the composted organic matter is applied to the soil to improve its structure, water-holding capacity and fertility.

EcoSan is a sustainable closed-loop system and its main features are:

- EcoSan regards human excreta as a resource to be recycled rather than as a waste to be disposed of.
- EcoSan uses dry composting toilets, which is a practical, hygienic and cost-effective solution to human waste disposal.
- EcoSan separates urine from faecal matter and uses it as fertilizer.
- Recycling of human waste prevents direct pollution caused by sewage, returns it as nutrients to soil and plants, and reduces the need for chemical fertilisers.
- EcoSan does not use water to carry away the solid waste. It is thus very appropriate for areas with water shortages or irregular water supplies.
- EcoSan is applicable for rural and urban areas, and for rich and poor alike.

Hundreds of EcoSan toilets have been built in Kerala, Tamil Nadu, Sri Lanka, and elsewhere. Read Box 12.3 for an account of the EcoSan toilet.

BOX 12.3

The story of EcoSan: The sweet smell of compost

It is now an almost dry, crumbly, black stuff that smells light, pleasant and earthy. Six months ago, however, it was fresh human waste. Sounds unbelievable? This is the magic of ecological sanitation or EcoSan, for short.

Paul Calvert, a British engineer and a pioneer in ecological sanitation, has set up EcoSan toilets in numerous homes in rural Kerala. These are dry, composting toilets. One model consists of a slab constructed over two vaults. The slab has a hole over each vault for the faeces to drop in and a funnel for the urine to collect. While one hole is used, the other is kept closed. Washing is done separately so that wash water does not mix with the solid waste.

Before use, the vault is covered with straw to facilitate decomposition. After each use some ash or saw dust is sprinkled on the faeces. The urine is collected separately, diluted, and used as fertilizer. After six months, the first hole is closed and the

second one is put into use. The faecal matter in the first hole begins to decompose and in six more months the fertilizer is ready for collection.

Calvert identifies three basic benefits of EcoSan:

- It prevents diseases by removing pathogen-rich excreta from the immediate environment.
- It does not contaminate groundwater or use up scarce water resources.
- It creates a valuable resource that can be recycled back into the environment.

Calvert spends much of his time demonstrating and promoting the ecological sanitation approach among communities, government and non-government organisations. He has also designed EcoSan toilets for urban areas. He says: 'If everyone harvested rainwater, used an ecological toilet, planted a tree, and helped their neighbour, India would surely be a land of plenty.' Is anyone listening?

KEY IDEA
There is a world crisis in sanitation and we are unable to cover even for half the deprived population. Given this fact and the water scarcity, ecological sanitation seems to be the only way out.

To change to EcoSan needs a change in the mindset. In India, we find anything to do with human faeces disgusting, degrading or polluting. We end up pretending that they don't exist and so expose ourselves much more to the danger of infection.

Let us now take a brief look at soil pollution.

How does soil become polluted?

Soil pollution is any physical or chemical change in the soil conditions that may adversely affect the growth of plants and other organisms living in or on it.

Soil pollution and water pollution are closely connected. Acid rain and excessive use of chemical fertilisers result in the soil becoming unable to hold nutrients. This in turn allows toxic pesticides or atmospheric fallout seep rapidly into groundwater or runoff into rivers and coastal waters. Some of the persistent pollutants remain in the soil and degrade it.

Most soil pollutants are agricultural chemicals, primarily fertilizers and pesticides. It is now known that these chemicals attach themselves to soil particles and persist for long, continuously releasing contaminants into the surface water, groundwater, and the topsoil. Dumping of waste including garbage, untreated sewage, industrial effluents, nuclear waste, and mining waste pollute the soil by leaking the dangerous substances.

Salts tend to accumulate in the soils of arid and semi-arid regions. The little precipitation that falls evaporates quickly leaving the salts behind. Salinization can also occur in any region due to continued application of irrigation water containing some salts.

Why are plants unable to tolerate saline soil?   Water always moves from an area of higher concentration to one of lower concentration. Normally, plants have a lower concentration than the surrounding soil and water flows into the plants. Saline soil, however, has often a lower concentration of water than plants. Consequently, water starts flowing out of the plant into the soil.

How can soil condition be restored?   Dilution is one way of removing pollutants from the soil. It involves running large quantities of water though the soil to leach out the pollutants. This works only if the soil has good drainage properties. Even then, disposing off the water carrying the pollutants poses a problem. The method also requires lots of water.

In vapour extraction, air is injected into the soil to remove organic compounds that evaporate quickly. Bioremediation uses bacteria and other microorganisms to clean up the soil. In phytoremediation, we use plants, whose roots absorb pollutants and store them in their stems and leaves.

From water and soil, we now move to marine pollution.

How does marine pollution occur?

Since the ocean forms 71 per cent of the earth's surface, most of the pollutants in the atmosphere fall on it. In recent decades, however, there is in addition a huge amount of direct marine pollution caused by human activities.

Dead fish on a beach

Industrial discharges and agricultural run-off (about 70 trillion litres a year) containing pesticides, fertilisers, and various toxic chemicals find their way to the ocean. Treated and untreated human and other domestic waste (about 6 million tons a year) end up in the ocean with all their contaminants. In fact, sewage remains the largest source of contamination of the coastal and marine environment.

The oil industry contributes deadly pollution through leaks, spills, and cleaning of tankers. The impact of oil discharges into the ocean and the remedial measures are discussed in Chapter 14.

Nitrogen input into the ocean has been rapidly increasing due to agricultural runoff, atmospheric deposition, and loss of natural interceptors like coastal wetlands, coral reefs, and mangroves. The result is greater marine and coastal eutrophication. Blooms of toxic or otherwise undesirable phytoplankton are increasing in frequency, intensity, and geographic distribution. Such blooms or red tides greatly affect fisheries, aquaculture, and tourism (Box 12.4).

BOX 12.4

The story of the red tides: Bloom that kills

It is an explosion of colour on the ocean—orange, red, or brown. Beautiful to look at perhaps, but they are deadly for humans and animals. They are called red tides or algal blooms.

Blooms occur when some pigmented marine algae experience population explosion. Some of these algal species produce toxins that attack the nervous system of fishes, leading to massive fish kills. When this fish is eaten by water birds, they too die. The toxins get into the food web and end up killing marine mammals and affecting fish-eating humans.

Even if the bloom is non-toxic, it still causes problems by shading aquatic vegetation and upsetting food webs. Algal blooms are dangerous even after they die. They then sink to the bottom where they reduce the oxygen supply and kill bottom-dwelling organisms like crabs, oysters, and clams.

Algal blooms are becoming more common and more severe. What triggers them off? We do not know for sure, but scientists blame costal pollution. Wastewater and agricultural runoff into coastal waters contain increasing amounts of nitrogen and phosphorus, both of which can stimulate algal growth. A higher ocean temperature due to global warming is another possible cause.

How can we prevent blooms from occurring or end them when they do occur? Again, we do not know, but we are able to predict the conditions that are likely to stimulate them.

Persistent Organic Pollutants (POPs), which spread through the atmosphere, are found everywhere in the ocean. POPs cause reproductive, immunological, and neurological problems in marine organisms and possibly in humans. Another concern is the increasing amounts of nonbiodegradable waste like plastic articles and nets that float in the ocean. Large numbers of birds, turtles, and mammals are killed by entanglement in or ingestion of such waste.

Human activities have changed sediment flows into coasts and the ocean. Areas like deltas that need sediments do not get enough, whereas coral reefs are smothered by them.

How bad is coastal pollution?

With the inexorable movement of the world's population towards the coastal areas, the pollution of the ocean nearer the shores has reached alarming proportions. Thousands of tons of sewage and industrial effluents are directly discharged into the ocean in many parts of the world.

A few years ago, shrimp aquaculture was taken up on a large scale on the Indian coast. This industry requires freshwater as well as seawater and uses heavy doses of antibiotics. Within a short time, the effluents from the shrimp farms polluted large areas. The local soil and groundwater were affected. Ultimately, diseases and court orders put a stop to coastal aquaculture, but the industry flourishes in inland areas.

KEY IDEA

Coastal and marine pollution has reached alarming proportions.

It is no wonder that the marine pollution finds its way into the fish that we catch. For example, three major shrimp species harvested off Mumbai's coastal waters have tested positive for lead and cadmium. The fish catch itself is declining in these waters, probably due to marine pollution.

What are the international initiatives to control marine pollution?

Since 1972, a number international agreements and programmes have focused on controlling marine and coastal pollution:

The 1972 London Dumping Convention The purpose of this Convention is to control all sources of marine pollution and prevent pollution of the sea through regulation of dumping into the sea of waste materials. It prohibits all dumping, incineration of wastes at sea, and the export of wastes.

The 1989 Basel Convention on the Control of Transboundary Movement of Hazardous Wastes and their Disposal Until 1999, the Convention was principally devoted to setting up a framework for controlling the movement of hazardous wastes across international frontiers. It has now expanded its scope to include the active promotion and use of cleaner technologies and production methods and the prevention and monitoring of illegal traffic.

Convention on the Prevention of Pollution from Ships (MARPOL) It is the main international convention covering prevention of pollution of the marine environment by ships from operational or accidental causes.

Global Programme of Action for the Protection of the Marine Environment from Land-based Activities (GPA-LBA) This programme was adopted in 1995 by over 100 countries. The aim is to control contaminants like sewage, persistent organic pollutants, radioactive substances, heavy metals, oils, nutrients, sediments, and litter that enter the ocean from land.

The UNEP Regional Seas Programme This programme has fostered regional cooperation on behalf of the marine and coastal environment. It has stimulated the creation of Action Plans for sound environmental management in each region. India, Bangladesh, Maldives, Pakistan and Sri Lanka are partners in the South Asian Seas Programme.

India is a party to all these agreements and programmes.

Ending on a hopeful note: Positive stories

Rainwater harvesting is being successfully used in India to tackle the problem of fluoride contamination (Box 12.5)

BOX 12.5

Rainwater harvesting tackles fluoride problem

We saw in the lead story of the chapter how widespread was the fluoride contamination of water. One successful solution is to use rainwater in place of the contaminated water. Here are two examples:

1. The village of Balisana in Gujarat had been affected both by drought and fluoride contamination of water. With the help of the NGO Utthan, the villagers diverted rainwater into an old tank. From the tank, the rainwater was led to a recharge well. The water has recharged the local aquifer and the local wells now have potable water.

2. Many villages in Tumkur, Kolar, and Gadag districts of Karnataka have been suffering from fluoride contamination of groundwater. In 60 of these villages, a joint project of the NGO BAIF and the state government now provides potable water to over 5,500 families. The main approach is to harvest rainwater from roofs and artificial catchment areas and use that water for domestic purposes. Other activities include excavating farm ponds as well as recharging borewells and aquifers directly with rainwater. The project has been implemented with the active involvement of the local communities.

REVIEW: A SUMMARY OF THE KEY POINTS

- Most of the freshwater sources in the world like rivers, lakes, and groundwater including those in remote regions are already polluted. The pollutants come from a variety of sources, mostly due to human activities.
- Excessive extraction of groundwater in India and Bangladesh is leading to increasing contamination with fluoride and arsenic. This has extremely serious effects on the health of the people who consume the water.
- There are several ways of treating and purifying water and sewage. Disposing off the toxic sludge that results is a major problem.
- Most of the Indian rivers are polluted and the National River Conservation Authority has launched Action Plans for several rivers.

- Pesticide residues have been found in bottled water and soft drinks.
- Two-fifths of the world's population, mostly in Asia and Africa, lacks sanitation facilities.
- The adoption of ecological sanitation or composting toilets seems to be the only way to solve the sanitation problem of the world.
- The world's soil is becoming polluted with agricultural chemicals and hence getting degraded.
- Human activities are responsible for heavy pollution of the ocean and the coastal zone; many international initiatives have been taken to control this pollution.
- The future looks grim with respect to water, soil, and marine pollution and this calls for urgent steps.

EXERCISES

Objective-type questions

For each question below, choose the best answer out of the given choices.

1. Which of the following is a nonpoint source of water pollution?
   (a) Oil spill
   (b) Sewage treatment plant
   (c) Open cast mine
   (d) Deep borewell

2. What does BOD stand for?
   (a) Biological Oxygen Demand
   (b) Basic Oxygen Dissolved
   (c) Biological Oxygen Decomposition
   (d) Biological Organic Demand

3. Which of the following statements is true with regard to wastewater treatment?
   (a) Wastewater can be completely converted into fresh water.
   (b) Wastewater can be treated, but some sludge will remain.
   (c) Primary wastewater treatment makes use of microorganisms.
   (d) Any sludge that remains after treatment can be easily processed.

4. Which of the following statements is **not** a method of purifying water?
   (a) Reverse Osmosis
   (b) Ultraviolet Radiation
   (c) Distillation
   (d) Evaporation from a pond

5. Which of the following statements is **not** true with regard to global sanitation?
   (a) The number of people lacking sanitation is more than those not having access to drinking water.
   (b) Asia contains the largest population without sanitation.
   (c) Inadequate sanitation is a major cause of disease worldwide.
   (d) China is the worst country in sanitation coverage and India is the second.

6. Which of the following statements is true with regard to Ecological sanitation or EcoSan?
   (a) EcoSan toilet uses water to carry away the solid waste.
   (b) Ecosan considers human excreta as waste.
   (c) EcoSan increases the load on sewage plants.
   (d) EcoSan gives us pleasant-smelling compost.

Short-answer questions

1. How did the groundwater in many places in India become contaminated with fluoride and arsenic?
2. How do fluoride and arsenic contamination of water affect the health?
3. Give any five major categories of water pollutants, their sources, and their effects.
4. Explain point and nonpoint sources of water pollution.
5. What is meant by eutrophication of lakes?
6. Describe three measures of water quality.
7. What is the status of sanitation in the world?
8. How can we provide sanitation facilities to the maximum number of people in the world?
9. How does soil become polluted and how can it be remedied?
10. What are the main sources of marine and coastal pollution?

Long-answer questions

1. Write an essay on the various international conventions and agreements concerning water resources, both freshwater and marine waters. Use the information given in this chapter as well as in Chapters 4 and 7.
2. Describe the various ways of treating and purifying water and sewage.

Think critically: Deeper questions for reflection and discussion

How can we make people aware of the fact that any pollution that we create ultimately comes back to us? How can we encourage people to avoid polluting water and soil—though regulation or education?

SOMETHING DIFFERENT FOR A CHANGE

At the end of Chapter 6, there was a poem by the British poet Gerard Manley Hopkins (1844–1889). Here is one more from him:

Wild air, world-mothering air,
Nestling me everywhere,
That each eyelash or hair
Girdles; goes home betwixt
The fleeciest, frailest-flixed
Snowflake; that is fairly mixed

With riddles, and is rife
In every least thing's life,
This needful, never spent,
And nursing element;
My more than meat and drink,
My meal at every wink;
This air, which, by life's law,
My lung must draw and draw
Now but to breathe its praise......

ACTIVITIES

Act: What you can do to conserve water and soil pollution

1. Many household items like naphthalene balls, drain cleaners, paint thinners, etc., are very toxic. Try to use safer alternatives like ammonia, bleaching powder, baking soda, mineral oil, and vinegar.
2. Do not throw unwanted medicines or motor oil down the drain. If the medicines have not expired, donate them to any charitable hospital or voluntary organization that accepts them. There is a thriving industry in cities that recycles motor oil. If there are genuine recyclers in your city, collect all the oil in your neighbourhood and give it to them.

3. Replace lawns by trees and shrubs that need little fertilizer and are drought-resistant.
4. Use fertilizer sparingly, never near a body of water

Learn by doing: Case study / Project

Approach the National River Conservation Authority and volunteer your services. Join a team that is implementing an Action Plan for a river in your state or in a neighbouring one. Spend at least three weeks working with the team or any ecologist in the team. Write a report describing the state of the river, the sources of pollution, the Action Plan, methods used for field-level implementation, problems encountered, results achieved, etc.

LEARN MORE

Book

Calvert, Paul 2006, *Ecological Solutions to Flush Toilet Failures,* Eco-solutions, Thiruvananthapuram.

Articles

DTE 2003, 'Gulp: Bottled Water Has Pesticide Residues', *Down To Earth,* Vol. 11, No. 18, February 15, pp. 27–34.

Jamwal, Nidhi and D.B.Manisha 2003, 'The Dark Zone', *Down To Earth,* Vol. 11. No. 22, April 15, pp. 27–41.

Vörösmarty, C.J. 2010, 'Global Threats to Human Water Security and River Biodiversity', *Nature* 467, 30 September, pp. 555–561.

For articles on pesticides in soft drinks, read the issue of *Down To Earth,* Vol. 12, No. 6, August 15, 2003.

For an account of ecological sanitation, read *Gobartimes,* a supplement to *Down To Earth,* May 1999.

Websites

Ecosan: www.eco-solutions.org (Paul Calvert), www.ecosanres.org

Fluoride poisoning in India: www.fluoridealert.org/fluorosis-india.htm; www.rainwaterharvesting.org/rural/Balisana1.htm

Water pollution: http://en.wikipedia.org/wiki/Water_pollution

Water pollution: http://www.unwater.org/statistics_pollu.html

Film

The Story of Bottled Water, a documentary by Annie Leonard on the packaged water industry (download from www.storyofstuff.org)

CHAPTER 13

Solid Waste Management

And Man created the plastic bag and the tin and aluminium can
and the cellophane wrapper and the paper plate, and
this was good because Man could then take his automobile and
buy all his food in one place and
He could save that which was good to eat in the refrigerator and
throw away that which had no further use.
And soon the earth was covered with plastic bags and aluminium cans and paper plates
and disposable bottles and
there was nowhere to sit down or walk, and
Man shook his head and cried: 'Look at this Godawful mess.'

Art Buchwald
(1925–2007)
American humourist

THIS CHAPTER IS ABOUT...

Waste and its management, hazardous waste, ship-breaking and its impact, waste problem in India, recycling waste

THE KEYWORDS AND PHRASES ARE...

Biomedical waste   common effluent treatment plant   e-waste   landfill   sanitary landfill

THE STORY OF ALANG: TOXIC SHIPS, HAZARDOUS WASTE

There is a constant clang of metal. Dust and toxic fumes are everywhere. Huge metal monsters are ripped apart and become mountains of scrap. Welcome to Alang, the famous ship-breaking yard!

Alang is located in the Gulf of Kambhat on the Gujarat coast, 56 km south of Bhavnagar city. The unique geographical features of high tidal range and wide continental shelf, coupled with a mud-free coast, allow very heavy ships to reach the coast easily during high tide. It is ideal for ship-breaking.

The necklace-shaped Alang ship-breaking yard is said to be the largest in the world. With 184 ship-breaking plots, it dismantles about 300 ships every year and has a turnover of Rs 6,000 crores. The yard employs 40,000 people directly and 100,000 more indirectly.

The workers, mostly migrants from Orissa, Uttar Pradesh, and Bihar, toil under extremely hazardous conditions in a toxic atmosphere. Given the nature of the job, lack of training, and the absence of protective gear, accidents are common. The workers have no medical facilities, sanitation, housing or safe drinking water. Accidents and related deaths are common.

They reside in rented shanties in different villages around the yard in relative poverty. The huge influx of migrant labourers, with languages and cultures very different from the local ones, has also created social tensions in the area.

Most of the ships that come to Alang carry toxic waste, which cause environmental and health problems. In addition, the cost of clean-up falls on the Gujarat government.

Greenpeace and other organizations have been campaigning for the adoption of an environmentally-

A ship waiting at Alang

safe approach to ship-breaking and for improving the conditions in the ship-breaking yards. Thanks to the directives issued by the Supreme Court and the Greenpeace campaign, some improvements have been made in the working conditions at Alang.

The main problem, however, remains: How do we ensure that the ships are decontaminated before they arrive at Alang or any of the other yards?

What is the message that the story of Alang carries for us?

Building huge ships may be a technological feat. The bigger problem, however, arises when their lives are over. How do we dispose off the solid waste, the huge hulk of metal with tons of stuff inside? The Alang case shows the complex nature of hazardous waste disposal.

In the previous two chapters, we discussed the pollution of air, soil, freshwater and ocean. We also covered noise pollution. What remains of the pollution problem is discussed in this chapter. We will also return to the ship-breaking case. Though the title is 'solid waste management', we will be considering liquid waste too.

What is waste and why does it require management?

Waste is any material that is not needed by the owner, producer, or processor. Humans, animals, other organisms, and all processes of production and consumption produce waste. It has always been a part of the earth's ecosystem, but its nature and scale were such that the ecosystem could use waste in its many cycles. In fact, there is no real waste in nature. The apparent waste from one process becomes input to another.

It is the exponential growth (Chapter 1) of human activities that has made waste a problem to be managed. We are simply producing much more waste than nature can handle.

It is far better to prevent generation of waste than to produce waste and then try to 'manage' it. We cannot simply throw away waste. As they say, 'There is no away in throw away.' What we dispose off remains in the ecosystem and causes some form of pollution. This pollution can have an impact far away from the point of generation and far removed in time too.

The composition, quantity, and disposal of waste determine the environmental problems it creates. To minimise the adverse effects of any waste, it has to be recycled, isolated permanently in storage, allowed to decompose and degrade into a harmless state, or treated to remove any toxicity it may have.

Gaseous waste, which is caused mainly by emissions from vehicles and other sources and carries fine particles of matter, leads to air pollution and smog (Chapter 11). When gaseous waste is deposited on land as acid rain, it pollutes the soil and water (Chapter 12).

Most disposable wastes are in the form of solids, liquids, or slurries. The main categories of such wastes are the following:

Domestic waste   Sewage, waste water contaminated by detergents, dirt, or grease, household garbage, and bulky waste including packaging material, appliances, furniture, office equipment, and used cars.

Factory waste   Solids and effluents from factories of all types; the worst polluters are slaughterhouses, breweries, tanneries, textile, paper and steel mills and most chemical industries; power plants discharge heated coolant water causing thermal pollution.

Waste from the oil industry   Oil spills, oil leaks, water used for cleaning tankers, etc.

Construction waste   Materials from buildings that are demolished or renovated and materials discarded after completing a building

Waste from the extractive industries   Mining, quarrying, and dredging create solid waste (during extraction) and slurries (during processing).

Plastic waste   Thousands of different goods made of plastic (including the carry bag), thrown away after use, are everywhere on land and sea. (Box 13.1)

Agricultural waste   Mostly organic waste from plants and animals; irrigation water from farms containing fertilisers and pesticides

Waste from food processing   Organic solid and liquid waste from discarded food material

Biomedical waste   Originates mainly from hospitals and clinics and includes blood, diseased organs, poisonous medicines, etc.

E-waste   A more recent form of waste from discarded electronic equipment (Box 13.2)

Nuclear waste: Radioactive waste from nuclear power plants and the manufacture of nuclear weapons; remains active and dangerous for thousands of years.

Apart from these regular sources, waste also comes from special events:

Waste from natural disasters   Rubble from earthquakes, slag and ash from volcanoes, wastes left behind by floods, cyclones, and typhoons

Waste from wars and conflicts   Apart from dead bodies and destroyed buildings, wars leave behind exploded and live shells, landmines, etc. In some cases, deadly war material has effects lasting decades. Agent Orange in Vietnam and depleted uranium in the 1991 Gulf war are examples.

It is very difficult to assess the effects of all the types of waste on the environment. We do not know the total amounts, composition, and dispersal of waste. Nor do we have enough scientific knowledge of the long-term impact of most substances that form part of waste. What is considered non-hazardous today may be declared dangerous tomorrow. In fact, environmentalists feel that we must follow the precautionary principle and treat every chemical or waste as being potentially harmful unless proved otherwise.

KEY IDEA
There are many kinds of waste with known and unknown impact on health and environment.

BOX 13.1

Pollution by plastic

Developed in the 1860s, plastic has become an indispensable part of our lives. Longevity is its main characteristic, but this very quality has also become a major problem. It is the non-biodegradable nature of plastic that is causing a massive environmental problem. It simply does not 'go away' after use.

Plastic bags and bottles are found discarded everywhere. They now form an increasing proportion of municipal waste and cause many environmental problems. They clog sewage lines and canals and litter public places, gardens, wildlife reserves, and forests. Animals and birds consume plastic items and even die as a result. Disposing of plastic by burning only creates more toxic fumes. The worst offender is the thin carry bag that easily gets airborne when thrown away.

The plastic carry bag has become a common item all over the world, both in the poor and rich countries. In 2002 alone, 4–5 trillion bags were produced, almost all of it being the non-biodegradable variety. About 100 billion bags are thrown away in the US every year.

Certain plastics can be recycled. Many household articles like water containers and buckets are made of recycled plastic. Non-reusable items include carry bags, cups, plates, and magazine wrappers. Even in these cases, ecofriendly plastics are available as options.

Plastic bottles in a trash can

There are strong views for and against plastic. The plastics industry cites the advantages of convenience, low cost, employment potential, recycling possibilities, etc. Environmentalists point out the problems listed above and also add in the difficulty of separating the recyclable plastic items in landfills.

Some countries have banned plastic bags. In India, several states and local bodies have enforced various degrees of banning, mostly on thin bags. The Government of India has banned carrybags made of plastic films of thickness less than 20 micrometers. But this rule is not being implemented seriously. Some Indian towns, however, have strictly banned such bags.

BOX 13.2

E-waste

It is an industry that thrives on obsolescence. New gadgets and new models appear almost daily and the old ones are discarded as junk. The waste is mounting in the electronic and computer industries.

These industries ensure their continued and rapid growth by making the products obsolete as fast as possible. The old ones may still be in good working condition, but they cannot be used because spare parts are not available. About 1.5 million PCs

become obsolete in India every year and this figure will keep increasing.

The net result is a rapid increase in e-waste or electronic waste that results from discarded devices like computers, televisions, telephones, music systems, and so on. The city of Bangalore alone generates 600 tons of e-waste every year.

E-waste contains many hazardous materials like lead, copper, zinc, and aluminium, flame retardants,

Contd

Box 13.2 Contd

E-waste

plastic casings, cables, etc., which can have harmful effects on the environment, if burnt or buried.

Some countries have begun exporting e-waste to developing countries. China and India import such waste and it is recycled carelessly in crowded areas of the cities like Delhi. This has undesirable consequences for health and environment. There are, however, companies that accept and recycle e-waste in a responsible way.

How are wastes managed?

In the industrialized countries, household waste is separated into categories like organic material, paper, glass, other containers, etc. The separation is often done at the home itself, using different bins. In the developing countries, all the waste is collected together, though some cities are trying to persuade the public to separate the waste.

The simplest and most common method used in the cities is to collect and dump the waste in a landfill. These landfills are located just outside the city. There are now thousands of landfills in the world with huge piles of waste. In the industrialized countries, you can also see separate mountains of used cars and tyres. Many countries and cities have run out of space for landfills.

In the poorer countries, rag pickers sift through the waste, collect the reusable and recyclable material, and sell it to the scrap traders. They, in turn, take the material to the recycling units.

The rag pickers, the majority of whom are women and children, work under extremely unhygienic conditions and yet provide a great ecological service by manually separating thousands of tons of recyclable waste from the garbage dumps. (Read the story of women scrap collectors in Chapter 17).

Often, the waste in a landfill is burnt away. While this reduces the volume of the garbage, it releases deadly dioxins. Proper incineration of waste needs modern technology and proper management.

What is a sanitary landfill?

Sanitary landfills are sites where waste is isolated from the environment until it is safe. Waste is deposited in thin layers (up to 1 m thick) and immediately compacted by heavy machinery. Several such layers are placed and compacted on top of each other to form a refuse cell (up to 3 m thick). At the end of each day the refuse cell is covered with a layer of compacted soil to prevent odours and windblown debris.

There are several requirements for a proper sanitary landfill:

- It should be located above the water table.
- The area should not be geologically active.
- It should not be very near residential communities.
- The land must be inexpensive to make the cost of operating the landfill worthwhile.
- It must be accessible to roads so that garbage can be delivered easily.
- Trained staff should be based at the landfill to supervise site preparation and construction, the depositing of waste and the regular operation and maintenance.

> **KEY IDEA**
> Dumping waste on open landfills is very common. Setting up safer sanitary landfills is more uncommon and difficult.

As the matter inside the sanitary landfill breaks down, it generates gases including methane. Some landfills simply vent these gases, while others collect and use them as fuel. Often, sanitary landfills are reclaimed once they are full. The area on top is used to make sports fields, parks, office parks, and so forth.

How is liquid waste managed?

Sewage and industrial effluents are in most cases released directly into water bodies—rivers, lakes, or the ocean. Very often they are not treated before release.

The 1972 London Convention (Chapter 12) prohibits the ocean dumping of hazardous waste. The ocean, however, is still not safe, since the Convention is not observed by all the countries. Further, thousands of tons of toxic substances (including nuclear waste), dumped into the ocean before the Convention came into force, are still present in the ocean and silently polluting the marine environment.

With increasing amounts being generated, management of waste is becoming difficult and expensive. The industrialised countries have found an easier and less expensive method: export the waste to other countries!

Why are hazardous and toxic wastes exported?

Many of the industrialized countries have a waste management problem. Since their economies are based on constant growth, development, and consumption, wastes are mounting up and they are running out of suitable space for landfills or dump yards. At the same time, these countries have strict environmental regulations that make waste management expensive.

The most attractive option for the industrialized countries is to export the waste to developing countries, where disposal is cheap and environmental regulations are lax. The latter need the money and the former want to get rid of the waste. Developing countries do have more space for disposal, but their tropical ecosystems are more vulnerable to the damaging effects of the waste. There are many cases of environmental damage caused in the developing countries due to improper management of imported toxic waste.

At any time, there are a number of ships carrying toxic waste prowling on the high seas, ready to dump the waste on an unsuspecting poor country. Alternately, they just dump the cargo somewhere in the middle of the vast ocean (Box 13.3).

BOX 13.3

The story of *Khian Sea*: Around the world in 16 years

The ship left the US in 1989 loaded with 14,000 tons of toxic flyash from Philadelphia's municipal waste incinerator. 16 years later, 2,500 tons of that very flyash came back to Philadelphia's garbage dump! In between, the original ship travelled to 11 countries in 4 continents, was sold once, changed its name twice, nearly had a mutiny, had its engineer jailed, was twice turned away from ports at gunpoint, and even disappeared for a time. It is a story fit for a Bollywood movie!

In the mid-1980s, the city of Philadelphia had no space to dump the ash from its trash incinerators. The city signed a contract with a shipping company and the cargo ship *Khian Sea* headed for the Bahamas with the ash.

Even before the ship reached Bahamas, their government refused to take the load. The ship then began a remarkable journey round the world looking for a place to dump the ash. The environmental organization Greenpeace had been alerting countries and no port would allow it to unload the deadly stuff. After two years, it obtained permission from Haiti to unload the cargo as fertilizer.

The crew has hardly unloaded 4,000 tons on the Haiti shore, when public protests forced the ship to leave with the rest of its cargo. It then disappeared from the public gaze, but turned up in Singapore in November 1998—without the ash!

The story did not end there. Spurred on by Greenpeace, the Haitians kept up pressure on the US to take back the ash from their beach. This campaign continued through two changes of government in Haiti. Finally, the US agreed to the demand.

In 2000, the ash came back to the US and landed in Florida. At least five states and the Cherokee Nation (Native Americans) refused to accept the ash. As the ash waited on a barge in Florida, two full trees grew on it! Finally, in July 2002, what was left of the ash came back to a landfill in Philadelphia.

It was surely a long journey in time and distance. There is, however, an unanswered question: Where are the missing 10,000 tons of the ash? In which part of the ocean were they dumped and with what consequences?

An even more important question: How many other ships with deadly cargo are on the prowl?

KEY IDEA

Industrialized countries often export their hazardous waste to other countries legally and illegally.

Waste management has become an international industry and even some industrialised countries like the UK import waste and make money on it. 90 per cent of the hazardous waste generated in the US is exported to Canada.

The 1989 Basel Convention (Chapter 12) aims to minimize the creation of hazardous wastes, reduce transboundary movements of such wastes, and prohibit their shipment to countries lacking the capacity to dispose them off in an environmentally sound manner.

How is municipal waste handled in Indian cities and towns?

It is difficult to estimate the amount of municipal waste produced in Indian cities. According to the Central Pollution Control Board, the daily per capita generation of municipal solid waste in India ranges from 100 g in small towns to 500 g in large towns. (The real figures are likely to be higher.) The recyclable content is said to be 13–20 per cent. The total amount of solid waste generated annually in Indian cities is about 40 million tons. Waste collection efficiency ranges from 50 per cent to 90 per cent.

It is clear that the amount of solid waste is growing faster than the population. For example, during 1981–1991, Mumbai's population increased from 8.2 to 12.3 million (49 per cent), while the daily municipal waste generation grew from 3,200 to 5,355 tons a day (67 per cent). Now, Mumbai generates over 7,000 tons every day and this is expected to reach 10,000 tons by 2025.

70 per cent of Indian cities do not have adequate waste transportation facilities. Out of the total municipal waste collected, on an average 94 per cent is dumped on land and 5 per cent is composted. As a result, streets piled with garbage, choked drains, and stinking canals are common features of most cities. The garbage that is transported in polluting old trucks is just dumped on sites in low-lying areas on the outskirts of cities. The choice of the site is more a matter of availability than suitability.

A dangerous practice is disposing off biomedical waste (from hospitals and clinics) along with municipal waste in dumpsites. The biomedical waste could turn the entire yard infectious. Further, biomedical waste also contains sharp objects like scalpels, needles, broken ampoules, etc., which could injure or infect rag pickers and municipal workers.

According to a study by the Indian Institute of Management, Lucknow, we generate about 4.2 lakh tons of biomedical waste per day. Of this, only 2.4 lakh tons are treated in any way.

KEY IDEA

Our cities are drowning in increasing mounds of waste and there is no easy solution.

In most cities, the solid wastes lie unattended in the dumpsites and attract birds, rodents, insects, and other organisms. As the waste decays, it releases odour and airborne pathogens. Further, the practice of burning the waste creates toxic fumes and spreads the hazardous substances in the air.

Zero-waste systems are being attempted in Indian cities such as Vellore (Box 13.4). Sanitary landfills are also coming up near Delhi.

BOX 13.4

The story of Vellore Srinivasan: Waste to gold

Srinivasan, a concerned citizen of Vellore, had first initiated a project to green the barren hills surrounding the town. Through this work, he came face to face with the environmental problems of the town. A major problem was that of garbage. There was almost no open space left in the town where waste could be dumped. As a result, garbage was being burnt or left to rot in the open all over town.

With the support of UNICEF and the NGO Exnora Green Cross, Srinivasan started a Community Composting Project, in which waste from five neighbourhoods was recycled and successfully processed. Later, Srinivasan turned the Vellore Fish Market into a clean and bustling place by collecting all the biodegradable waste from there and composting it at another location. Many more such projects followed and, even as Srinivasan refined his approaches, his work also came to be recognized.

Through his work, Srinivasan has evolved a zero waste management (ZWM) model, which he has been implementing in many places. The features of ZWM are:

- Separation of garbage at the source, be it at households, farms, villages, wards, municipalities, educational institutions, hospitals, jails or temples.
- Separate collection (where possible) of each kind of waste -kitchen waste, toilet waste, cattle waste, temple waste, hotel and shop waste, plastics, metal, tyres, hair, etc.

Contd

Box 13.4 Contd

- Segregation of waste into different categories and selling the recyclable items to appropriate buyers. Paper is sorted into categories like newspaper, cardboard, and wet paper and sent to third-party recycling facilities. Glass is dealt with in a similar manner. Hair is sold to wig companies.
- Composting of organic waste using cow dung and earthworms and selling the compost.
- Involvement of the community in all activities.
- Livelihood for the local poor through selling recyclable items and making and selling compost.

ZWM is financed by user fees and by the sales it makes to recycling plants. Each month, each household pays a nominal fee for joining the refuse collection program. ZWM also helps society by providing employment. The disabled or aged help sort garbage, while the young collect and transport waste.

Srinivasan now advises many cities and organizations on dealing with waste in the ZWM way.

Which are the major polluting industries of India?

Here are some examples of polluting industries in India and the possible measures to mitigate the problems:

- 2500 tanneries discharge about 24 million cubic metres of wastewater containing high levels of dissolved solids and 400,000 tons of hazardous solid wastes per year.
- About 300 distilleries discharge 26 million kilolitres of spent wash per year containing many pollutants.
- Thermal power plants discharge 100 million tons of flyash and this figure is expected to reach 175 million soon. Flyash contains silicon, aluminium, iron, and calcium oxides and is said to cause silicosis, fibrosis of the lungs, cancer, and bronchitis. Flyash, however, is being utilised in many ways: making bricks, blending with cement, building roads and embankments, adding micronutrients to soil, etc.

India continues to produce several pesticides banned or restricted in other countries. Examples are DDT, Malathion, and Endosulfan. One-sixth of the total pesticides used in India are those banned elsewhere. The bulk of the production is from small units that have no technology to treat the toxic and non-biodegradable pollutants generated during the manufacturing process. 50 per cent of the pesticides used in India are for cotton.

Industrialised states like Gujarat, Maharashtra, Tamil Nadu and Andhra Pradesh face major problems of toxic and hazardous waste disposal. For example, the Ahmedabad-Vadodara-Surat industrial belt houses 2,000 industrial units and more than 63,000 small scale units manufacturing chemicals like soda ash, dyes, yarns, and fertilizers. Most of the units dump their wastes in low-lying areas within a radius of two km. A major illegal dump yard has sprung up on the banks of the river Daman Ganga. During the monsoon, the hazardous substances are washed into the river. There are many such cases across the country.

The Ministry of Environment and Forests estimates that 7.2 million tons of hazardous waste is generated annually in India. In addition, industries discharge about 150 million tons of high volume—low hazard wastes every year, which is mostly dumped on open, low-lying land.

Are hazardous wastes dumped in India?

Huge amounts of wastes, particularly scrap metal, are imported into India. According to the Basel Convention as well as India's Hazardous Wastes (Management and Handling) Amendment Rules 2003, scrap metal is hazardous. Import of such waste is not banned in India, but prior permission is needed from the respective state pollution control boards and the Ministry of Environment and Forests.

Customs authorities do not have the required personnel and the equipment needed to check each consignment of imported waste for explosive material or toxics. They only check if the seals are okay.

Another major concern is the hazardous waste that is released and generated during ship-breaking.

What are the environmental consequences of ship-breaking?

Ship-breaking has become a big industry today. The huge vessels, which have served their lives and have been decommissioned, are sent to yards for recycling the parts to the extent possible. India, Taiwan, China, and Bangladesh have large ship-breaking facilities.

Most of the ships sent to the yards contain hazardous material such as asbestos, toxic paints, and fuel residues. However, as we saw in the case of Alang yard at the beginning of this chapter, ship-breaking is not just a solid waste problem. It has many dimensions: the export of hazardous waste to the developing countries, the environmental problems of handling toxic waste, the safety and health issues of the workers, the social tensions the enterprise creates, the role of the government, and so on.

Ship-breaking results in the following kinds of pollution:

- Discharge of oil into the ocean damages marine organisms and birds and destroys their natural habitats.
- Wastes like blasting residue and paint chips contaminate the soil and surface water.
- Improper storage and disposal of scrap metal and other wastes cause lead contamination.
- Cutting the metal parts with a blowtorch generates smoke, hazardous fumes, and particulates of manganese nickel, chromium, iron, asbestos, and lead.

Responding to a public interest petition, the Supreme Court of India issued a number of directives in 2003 with regard to the ship-breaking industry. Some of the important directives are:

- The owners should properly decontaminate the ship before the breaking operation. They should also submit a complete inventory of hazardous waste on board.
- The Maritime Board and the Pollution Control Board of the concerned state should monitor all ship-breaking operations.
- The industry should be allowed to operate only if it has facilities for disposal of waste in an environmentally sound manner.
- Waste generated during the process should be classified into hazardous and non-hazardous categories and the details made know to the State Maritime Board.

> **KEY IDEA**
> Ship-breaking is big business in India, but it is also a very dirty business, since the ships often contain toxic waste.

From October 2004, decommissioned ships are also covered under the Basel Convention. Consequently, countries exporting ships for recycling should seek the informed prior consent of the importing countries. This decision would encourage the industrialized countries to set up domestic ship recycling facilities. Alternately, they would have to carry out some level of decontamination of ships before sending them abroad for recycling.

What are common effluent treatment plants?

A small-scale industry cannot afford to clean up all its effluents. One solution to this problem is to collect the waste of several units from an industrial estate and treat it in a common location. The state pollution control boards in India are now compelling specific polluting industries in an area to set up common effluent treatment plants (CETPs).

CETPs are cost-effective, perhaps the ideal, solution to control pollution. Half the cost is met by the industries and a quarter each by the state and central governments. Each unit also contributes towards the running of the plant.

The first CETPs were set up to treat tannery wastes in Tamil Nadu, textile wastes in Rajasthan and industrial waste in Andhra Pradesh. There are more than 100 CETPs in the country.

CETPs have run into many problems. In many cases, reliable information is not available on the amounts and types of waste expected to reach the CETP. As a result, the design may not be the appropriate one. Further, a cocktail of different chemicals can be far more toxic than the individual chemicals themselves.

There are also problems in fixing the charges and getting the users to pay them. Questions also remain about the management and proper functioning of the CETPs. For example, who should be held responsible if the treatment is poor and the CETP itself becomes a polluter?

How can solid waste be recycled?

A good way of dealing with the solid waste problem is recycling, which is the processing of a used item or any waste into a usable form. There is a large recycling industry in the world. In India, we have a thriving, unorganised recycling industry, thanks to the itinerant collector, who buys your old newspaper, bottles, used clothes, utensils, scrap, motor oil, etc.

Recycling brings multiple benefits:

- By taking away some of the waste, it reduces environmental degradation.
- As against expenditure incurred on disposing off the waste, we now make money out of the waste material.
- We save energy that would have gone into waste handling and the making of products.
  Some specific examples of savings through recycling are:
- When aluminium is resmelted, there is considerable savings in cost. The recycling process, however, is energy-intensive.
- Making paper from waste pulp rather than virgin pulp saves 50 per cent energy.
- Every ton of recycled glass saves energy equal to 100 litres of oil.

Safe and profitable technologies for recycling paper, glass, metals, and some forms of plastic are available. Biogas can be produced from landfill waste. Paper factories can certainly recycle their waste.

Recycling is not a solution for all waste material. In many cases, the technologies are not available or unsafe. In other cases, the cost of recycling is too high.

What is the way out of the waste problem?

We have to move from waste management to waste prevention. That is, we should design clean production technologies or zero-discharge systems that use minimum amounts of raw materials, energy, and water and do not generate any wastes.

The life cycle of a product should be such that at no stage is any natural ecosystem adversely affected. This should apply to raw material extraction, design, manufacture, material transport, actual use, and disposal. Clean production technologies do exist and they will be cost-effective if the true environmental costs are taken into account.

> **KEY IDEA**
> Waste prevention is far better than waste management.

Even as we move to clean technologies, there is another way out of the industrial waste problem. If the industries in an area cooperate, they could design a system in which the waste from one industry becomes the input for one or more industries in the neighbourhood. A good example is the Kalundborg industrial ecosystem in Denmark (Box 13.5).

BOX 13.5

The story of Kalundborg: Zero waste, more profits!

Suppose industries in an area begin exchanging their outputs that are normally considered as wastes. What is waste for one could be an input or raw material for another. If we are lucky, we could evolve an almost closed system in which matter and energy circulate within the system.

Ten units in the small town of Kalundborg in Denmark work together to produce almost zero waste and make more profits in the bargain. What began as one-to-one exchanges evolved over ten years as a zero-discharge system.

The Kalundborg system comprises five core partners:

- Asnæs Power Station, Denmark's largest coal-fired power station with a capacity of 1,500 MW
- Statoil Refinery, Denmark's largest, with a capacity of 4.8 m tons per year
- Gyproc, a plasterboard factory
- Novo Nordisk, an international biotechnological company
- The City of Kalundborg that supplies heating to the 20,000 residents, as well as water to the homes and industries.

The other partners are a cement plant, a producer of sulphuric acid, local farmers, greenhouses, and a fish farm.

The power station supplies its waste heat to the other four partners as well as to the fish farm. The surplus natural gas from Statoil goes to the power plant and to Gyproc. The flyash from the power plant becomes an input to the cement plant.

Statoil first removes the sulphur from the natural gas and sells it to the acid plant. The power plant is required to remove sulphur from its coal smoke and this goes to Gyproc as a cheaper substitute for gypsum. The farmers buy the sludge from the fish farm and Novo Nordisk as fertilizer.

This web of recycling and reuse has generated new revenues and cost savings for the companies involved and reduced pollution to air, water, and land in the area. The partners have reduced their water and energy consumptions. In ecological terms, Kalundborg exhibits the characteristics of a simple food web: organisms consume each other's waste materials and energy, thereby becoming interdependent with each other.

The Kalundborg model, an example of 'industrial symbiosis', will work only if the industries are of the right mix, are located near one another, and share an attitude of openness.

Ending on a hopeful note: Positive story

Read the story of the inspiring work in waste management being done Vellore Srinivasan (Box 13.4).

REVIEW: A SUMMARY OF THE KEY POINTS

- Waste has always been a part of the earth's ecosystem, but human activities now generate so much waste that it needs proper 'management'.
- Human activities generate many categories of wastes, each with its own characteristics and disposal problems.
- Hazardous and toxic wastes generated in the industrialized countries are often exported for disposal in the developing countries, where environmental regulations are lax.
- Hazardous wastes are imported into India and cause many problems.
- Disposing off decommissioned ships is a complex task, since it involves handling large amounts of toxic waste.
- Tanneries, distilleries, and thermal power plants are some of the polluting industries in India.
- The widespread use of plastics is a problem because many plastics are nondegradable, persist for long, and cause many environmental problems.
- Indian cities face huge problems in managing municipal waste and sewage, though some amount of recycling is done.
- The only way out of the waste problem is to prevent or minimize the generation of waste.

EXERCISES

Objective-type questions

For each question below, choose the best answer out of the given choices.

1. Which of the following statements is true with regard to waste and its management?
   (a) There is no real waste in nature.
   (b) Waste can always be fully reused.
   (c) Nature can handle our waste.
   (d) We can always handle waste by throwing it away.

2. What is the most serious issue with ship-breaking?
   (a) Lack of facilities for workers
   (b) Toxic content of ships
   (c) Marine pollution
   (d) Air pollution

3. Which of the following is the most dangerous and long-lasting?
   (a) Biomedical waste
   (b) Ash from volcano
   (c) Mining waste
   (d) Nuclear waste

4. What is the precautionary principle?
   (a) We can assess the effects of all types of waste on the environment.
   (b) We must take precautions while managing waste.
   (c) Any waste is potentially harmful unless proved otherwise.
   (d) We do not know the long-term effect of waste.

5. Which of the following statements is **not** true with regard to landfills?
   (a) Finding space for landfills is becoming difficult.
   (b) Rag-pickers work on landfills.
   (c) Waste in a landfill is often burnt.
   (d) Landfills are often outside the city.

6. What is the best way of managing hazardous waste?
   (a) Export it to another country.
   (b) Burn it away.
   (c) Import it and make money.
   (d) Dispose it off in an environmentally sound manner.

7. Which of the following statements is **not** true with regard to normal plastic waste?
   (a) It lasts long.
   (b) It clogs sewage pipes.
   (c) It can be composted.
   (d) Burning it produces toxic fumes.

8. Which of the following statements is **not** true with regard to recycling waste?
   (a) Recycling is a solution for all waste material.
   (b) Paper can be recycled.
   (c) Recycling brings in money.
   (d) Recycling saves energy.

Short-answer questions

1. What is ship-breaking and why is it a complex task?
2. Why has waste become a major problem in the world?
3. List any five categories of waste and give their sources.
4. What are the ways of managing waste?
5. List the major polluting industries in India and describe the scale of their pollution.
6. What are the effects of plastic waste?
7. What are common effluent treatment plants?
8. How are Indian cities handling the increasing amounts of municipal wastes?
9. How can solid waste be recycled?

Long-answer question

Write an essay on the export of hazardous and toxic wastes from one country to another? Why are the wastes exported? What are the environmental and social issues involved? Which international agreements cover the case of such movement and disposal of waste? What are the recent developments in this regard?

Think critically: Deeper questions for reflection and discussion

Can a country shift its environmental problems to another country? Should the export of hazardous wastes be banned? What then will be the consequences in the developing countries, where thousands of people are employed in handling foreign waste (as in Alang, for example)?

SOMETHING DIFFERENT FOR A CHANGE

1. A poem for reflection written by Fuad Rifka of Syria:

   A Vision

   *All day long
   in the sky this bird,
   Where to rest?
   'On the tree'
   Where is the tree?
   'In the field'
   Where is the field?
   'North at the wood'
   Where is the wood?
   'East of the mountain
   'Where is the mountain?*

   *'There you blind man, don't you see?'
   Oh, yes, I see,
   I see mountains of refuse, its smoke smells of fields and trees.
   (a voice from the end of the 20th century):
   'Signs are imminent winds. In the stars,
   On that day,
   the mother will not recall her infant,
   Nor the sky its stars,
   And between the seasons
   No time for making the crossing'*

2. Read the book *Trash: On Ragpicker Children and Recycling* by Gita Wolf, Anushka Ravishankar, and Orijit Sen (Tara Publishing, Chennai, 1999)

ACTIVITIES

Act: What you can do to minimize waste and manage it better

Examine every item of waste that is generated in your home. Find out where it came from and where it is headed. In each case, try to prevent the generation of that waste item. If it cannot be prevented, can it be reused or recycled in any way? Is there an alternative to throwing it in the garbage bin?

Some practical steps you can take:

- Minimize packaging waste by taking your own cotton bags to the market and the grocery store. Do not buy pre-packaged items. Buy reusable or refillable containers. Avoid supermarkets and if you do shop in them, take your own bag. Refuse the large plastic carry bag offered by the shop. Even better, support the small store, which uses old newspaper to pack groceries.
- Do not throw away toxic material like batteries, thermometers, and insecticides into garbage. Find out if the manufacturers will take them back or if any one would recycle them. Otherwise, encase them in something like concrete before burying them.
- Avoid buying dangerous substances like mosquito repellents, insect sprays, chemical cleaners, detergents, etc. Use as far as possible natural or organic alternatives.
- Reuse every possible item at home—paper, plastic bags, cards, envelopes, wood, etc. You can make artistic items out of waste.
- Donate old clothes, books, etc., to NGOs for redistribution

- Try to persuade supermarkets in your area to offer a small discount to shoppers who bring their own bags; tell them that they can benefit by spending less on bags and advertising their 'green' concerns.
- Buy recycled products (paper, stationery items, etc.)
- Buy rechargeable batteries if you can afford them.

Learn by doing: Case study / Project

Trace the path of the waste that you dump in your street bin. Interview conservancy workers, municipal officials, rag-pickers, waste dealers, etc. Write a report answering questions such as:

- Where does the truck take the waste?
- Is it treated in any way or is it just dumped on land?
- What do the rag-pickers collect, how much, and where do they sell it? How can we assess the role of this unorganised sector in waste management?
- Does the waste contaminate soil, water, and air?
- How much of the waste is recycled and what are the processes used? Is there a waste from recycling?
- What is the economics of the recycling trade?

LEARN MORE

Book

Dengel, Lucas et al. 2001, *The Gita of Waste*, Auroville Health Centre, Auroville, Tamil Nadu.

Articles

Bavadam, Lyla 2004, 'In Troubled Waters', *Frontline*, Vol. 21, No. 1, January 16, pp. 112–113. (on Alang)

Beans, Bruce E. 2002, 'The Waste That Didn't Make Haste', *Washington Post*, 17 July. (on the voyage of *Khian Sea*)

Chowdhury, Namrata 2004, 'Ship-breaking Industry: Need for Global Solutions', *The Hindu Survey of the Environment 2004*, The Hindu, Chennai, pp. 125–129.

Jamwal, Nidhi 2003, 'e-Waste', *Down To Earth*, Vol. 12, No. 12, November 15, pp. 50–51.

Websites

Kalundborg: www.symbiosis.dk and www.uneptie.org/pc/ind-estates/casestudies/kalundborg.html

Srinivasan's Zero Waste Management: http://zerowastemanagement.org/

Films

Garbage to Gold, a documentary by UNICEF on the work down by Vellore Srinivasan. (http://video.yahoo.com/)

On the Road to Alang, a documentary film by Peter Knego on the Alang ship-breaking yard (2004).

Shipbreakers, a documentary film by Michael Kot on the Alang ship-breaking yard (2006).

CHAPTER 14

Disaster Management

*It wasn't the Exxon Valdez captain's driving
that caused the Alaskan oil spill.
It was yours.*

**Banner of the environmental organization
Greenpeace**

THIS CHAPTER IS ABOUT...

Natural and human-induced disasters, disaster management

THE KEYWORDS AND PHRASES ARE...

Richter Scale	seismograph	earthquake	tsunami
tailings	nuclear waste	oil spill	disaster mitigation

THE STORY OF THE ORISSA SUPERCYCLONE: WHEN THE MANGROVES WERE GONE ...

Will it or won't it? That was the all-important question in Bhubaneswar, Orissa's capital, on the night of October 28, 1999. Will the severe cyclonic storm that had developed in the Bay of Bengal hit the Orissa coast, or move away towards West Bengal and Bangladesh?

Just 12 days earlier, a cyclone had struck Ganjam District in the state, killing 100 people and destroying the town of Berhampore. As cyclone warnings began sounding again from October 25, there was more disbelief than alarm. How can two cyclones strike the same coast in such quick succession? The administration made only feeble preparations hoping that the cyclone would go away. It is even said that the Chief Minister consulted his astrologers, who assured him that Orissa would be spared.

The second cyclone, however, beat the odds and struck the coast. Not only that, it struck with a fury that made the Ganjam one seem like a gentle breeze. A gale with winds of up to 300 km per hour and tidal waves eight metres high attacked the coast from Puri to Balasore, covering six districts. It lasted for nearly two days.

What was the cyclone's toll? The cyclone caused heavy damage to life and property in 18,000 villages, affecting a population of nearly 20 million. More than 10,000 people were killed, 15 million rendered homeless, half a million livestock lost, 1.8 million hectares of agricultural land damaged, 90 million trees uprooted, and significant damage caused to infrastructure. The impact on the ecosystem was threefold: physical impact by strong winds; resulting storm surge and flash floods; and saline inundation.

Previously forests had formed a 5 km wide buffer zone against strong winds and flash floods. However, large tracts of Orissa's mangroves had been cleared to make way for shrimp farms and the coast had lost its natural protective shield. When the cyclone came it had an unfettered path and travelled as much as 100 km inland. Wherever mangroves were still intact,

however, they absorbed a part of the shock, and the damage was less. An area near Paradeep where the forests were intact was largely saved from the ravage caused by the cyclone.

The two cyclones uprooted practically all the tree cover in the immediate vicinity of the coast and caused much damage to trees tens of kilometres inland. This continues to affect the microclimate. The lack of protective forest cover also made it possible for the floods to inundate large areas and cause so much destruction.

What are the lessons of the Orissa supercyclone?

The first and most important lesson from the Orissa cyclone is that we should restore and conserve coastal mangroves. Second, weather patterns are changing and we should expect the unexpected.

How can disasters be classified?

Disasters can be classified as below:
- Natural disasters (Table 14.1)
- Human-induced or technological disasters (Table 14.2)

Table 14.1   Types of Natural Disasters

Type and definition	Event	Major example(s)
Geophysical: Events originating from solid earth	Earthquake, volcano, tsunami	2004: Asian tsunami (Box 14.2)
Meteorological: Events caused by short-term atmospheric processes	Cyclone, hurricane, typhoon, tornado	1999: Orissa Supercyclone
Hydrological: Events caused by deviations in the normal water cycle and/or overflow of bodies of water	Flood, landslide	2010: Floods in Pakistan
Climatological: Events caused by long-term processes	Extreme temperature, drought, wildfire	2003: European heat wave 2009: Bushfires in Australia
Biological: Disaster caused by the exposure of living organisms to germs and toxic substances	Epidemic, insect infestation	2006: Chikungunya in many Indian states

Table 14.2   Types of Human-induced Disasters

Type	Major example(s)
Industrial accidents	1984: Bhopal Gas Tragedy (Chapter 16)
Nuclear accidents	1986: Chernobyl (Box 14.3)
Nuclear testing	1946–1958: US nuclear tests on Bikini Atoll, Marshall Islands
Oil spill	2010: Deepwater Horizon spill in the Gulf of Mexico (Box 14.6)
Disasters caused by conflicts and wars	1945: Dropping of atom bomb over Hiroshima and Nagasaki 1962–1970: Spraying of Agent Orange in Vietnam by the US Army (Chapter 16, Box 16.2)

We should remember, however, that natural disasters could also be due to human activities. Landslides occur when mountainsides are deforested, extreme weather could be caused by global warming induced by greenhouse gas emissions, an earthquake could occur due to a large reservoir of water, and so on.

There are also disasters waiting to happen. The mounting nuclear wastes, the accumulation of nuclear and biological weapons, and the offshore oil drilling are examples.

We think of disasters as swift events, but they can also develop slowly over a period of time. Radioactive contamination from nuclear power plants, uranium mines, and stored nuclear waste, arsenic poisoning by groundwater, and washing of oil tankers at sea are examples.

What is the natural disaster scene in the world?

Natural disasters seem to be on the increase in the world (Table 1).

Table 14.3   Natural Disaster Events (1980–2009)

Decade	Number of disaster events
1980–1989	1690
1990–1999	2580
1999–2009	3850

The events counted here include droughts, floods, storms, extreme temperatures and wildfires, as well as mass movements such as landslides, volcanoes, earthquakes, and tsunami. Such disasters during 1999–2009 killed more than 780,000 people and affected more than two billion others. The economic losses were more than US$ 960 billion. In terms of human losses, Asia accounts for 85 per cent of all fatalities.

KEY IDEA

Natural disasters are on the increase in the world.

90 per cent of natural disasters and 95 per cent of all deaths in such disasters occur in the developing countries. In fact, the Asia-Pacific Region is very prone to natural disasters. The average annual population affected is highest in China (90 million), followed by India (56.6 million) and Bangladesh (18.5 million).

What are geophysical disasters?

These are events originating from solid earth and they include earthquakes, volcanoes, and tsunamis.

How are earthquakes caused and how are they measured? Earthquakes are violent upheavals of the earth's surface due to stresses occurring deep below the surface. When a weak point gives way under the stresses, huge masses of underground rock begin to shift, and energy is released as shock waves. These waves move outward from the earthquake's focus and reach the surface.

Table 14.4 Richter Scale

Value on Richter scale	Earthquake level
4.0–4.9	Minor
5.0–5.9	Moderate
6.0–6.9	Severe
7.0–7.9	Very severe
8.0–8.9	Extremely severe

The severity of an earthquake is measured on the modified Richter scale (Table 14.4). It is a measure of the amount of energy released, which is indicated by the vibrations in a seismograph.

Note that each unit on the Richter scale represents an amplitude 10 times greater than the next smaller unit. Thus, a 5.0 quake is 10 times more severe than a 4.0 quake.

Mild earthquakes occur all the time, mostly under the oceans. Every year, about twenty serious earthquakes occur, about half of them in built areas. An earthquake is often followed by aftershocks that gradually fade over several months. Accurate prediction of earthquakes is still difficult.

What is the impact of earthquakes? The primary effect of an earthquake is the shaking and possible displacement of the ground. This results in damages to buildings, roads, dams, pipelines, etc. and causes loss of life and property. The secondary effects include flooding caused by subsidence of land, fires, epidemics, aftershocks, etc. The damage and fatalities resulting from secondary effects can be as great, if not greater, than the impact of the main earthquake.

KEY IDEA
Earthquakes have been claiming many lives and causing heavy damage in recent years.

Five earthquakes since 2000 have claimed lives in excess of 10,000: Over 13,000 dead in Gujarat in 2001 (Box 14.1), 26,000 in Iran in 2003, 74,000 in Kashmir in 2005, 68,000 in Sichuan in 2008, and 230,000 in Haiti in 2010.

BOX 14.1

The story of the Gujarat earthquake: Only the town tower remained!

It was Republic Day, 2001. 12-year-young Nancy Takkar of Anjar in Gujarat had reached school well before time for the celebration. A few minutes later, at 8.45 a.m., the earth started shaking violently, tossing the children around the school building. For Nancy and her friends in the Anjar School it was just the beginning. Within a few seconds the school building collapsed with 200 children crushed beneath it. Nancy was the lone survivor.

A severe earthquake with a magnitude of 6.9 on the Richter scale had hit Gujarat near the town of Bhuj in Kachch. The shock was felt in most parts

Contd

Box 14.1 Contd

(Image courtesy: Gabriel N.; http://commons.
wikimedia.org/wiki/File:Gujarat_Earthquake_
Relief_by_RSS_Volunteers.jpg)

of the country. The districts of Kachch, Bhavnagar, Surendranagar, Rajkot, and Ahmedabad districts were devastated.

It was the most severe earthquake in the last fifty years in India, with 20,000 to 30,000 dead, 150,000 injured, and 15.9 million affected. The total economic loss was estimated to be Rs 225 billion.

Bhuj was the worst affected town with about 10,000 people killed. Almost half of its structures had been levelled. Amazingly, its historic tower was still standing. This was the case in other places too, with many old buildings remaining intact, while new buildings had collapsed.

As in the case of the Orissa cyclone, the state government was grossly unprepared to meet such an emergency. In many places help arrived too late to save people trapped in the debris.

How can the effects of earthquakes be mitigated? We can locate fault zones and map them, so that their presence is considered while planning settlements, irrigation projects, siting of nuclear establishments, etc. Building codes have been established for appropriate design of structures in earthquake-prone areas.

Tsunami

What is a tsunami?

Tsunami refers to a series of tall waves that hit the shore with great energy. A tsunami, however, is not a tidal wave and is not caused by winds or the gravitational pull of the moon or the sun. Most tsunamis are caused by undersea earthquakes that set off waves in water.

A tsunami moves silently but rapidly across the ocean and when it hits the coast, it un-expectedly rises as destructive high waves. These waves may last just minutes, but can cause widespread devastation along the coast.

Most tsunamis occur in the Pacific Ocean. During the 1990s, 82 tsunamis occurred worldwide, many more than the historical average of 57 a decade. They are relatively rare in the Indian Ocean but not unprecedented. The 2004 Asian tsunami was the biggest ever in history (Box 14.2).

> **KEY IDEA**
> Tsunamis are caused by undersea earthquakes that set off waves in water. The Asian tsunami of 2004 was the biggest in history.

BOX 14.2

The story of the Asian tsunami

The tsunami that hit South-east and South Asia on December 26, 2004, was the biggest ever in history. It was triggered by a massive undersea earthquake measuring nearly 9.0 on the Richter scale that occurred in Sumatra. The resulting series of tsunamis moved with a speed of about 900 kmph and hit the Indian Ocean coasts with waves up to 30 m high. It caused the entire earth to vibrate as much as 1 cm and triggered other earthquakes as far away as Alaska.

The tsunami killed over 230,000 people in fourteen countries: Indonesia was the hardest hit (170,000 dead), followed by Sri Lanka, India, and Thailand. The powerful waves destroyed houses and other infrastructure in the coastal areas. Fishing communities lost 100,000 boats and 1.7 million units of fishing gear.

The environmental impact included the following:

- Coastal erosion
- Contamination of groundwater and soil with salt water and sewage
- Damage to coral reefs and mangroves
- Adverse effect on habitats of coastal species.

The tsunami once again demonstrated the importance of coastal mangroves and forests. In all the affected countries, areas with natural coastal protection suffered less damage.

The tsunami hit the Andaman and Nicobar Islands barely an hour after the quake occurred. Car Nicobar, Cuddalore, and Nagapattinam were the worst affected places in India. Over 10,000 people died, 7,000 were injured, and 5,600 went missing. Thousands of people, particularly fisherfolk, lost their homes and livelihoods. In India too, the damage was less in those parts of the coast that had natural barriers like mangroves and casuarina trees.

What are meteorological disasters?

These events are caused by short-term atmospheric processes and they include the following:

Tornado (often called a twister) A violent, rotating column of air that is in contact with both the surface of the earth and a cloud. It is in the form of a visible condensation funnel, whose narrow end touches the earth.

Hurricanes and typhoons They are the same—violent storms with very strong winds that form over water. Hurricanes happen in the Atlantic and typhoons occur in the Pacific.

Cyclone A strong tropical storm that occurs off the coast of India and in which strong winds move in a circle. It often brings large amounts of rainfall with it.

What are hydrological and climatological disasters?

Hydrological disasters are events caused by deviations in the normal water cycle and/or overflow of bodies of water caused by wind set-up. They include floods (river flood, flash flood, storm surge/coastal flood), and wet mass movement (rock fall).

Climatological disasters are events caused by long-term processes in the spectrum from intra-seasonal to multi-decadal climate variability. They include extreme temperature (heat waves, cold waves and extreme winter conditions such as freezing rain and avalanche), drought, and wildfire (forest fires and land fires).

Why is India classified as a country prone to natural disasters?

India's size, geographical position, and the behaviour of monsoons make it one of the most disaster-prone in the world. The subcontinent is highly vulnerable to droughts, floods, cyclones, and earthquakes. In addition, the Himalayan region experiences landslides, avalanches, and bush fires. However, volcanoes are uncommon in India, with just two active ones in the Andamans.

During the 30-year period 1980–2009, India experienced over 400 disaster events that killed 142,000 people and affected more than 10 times that number. The economic losses were estimated to be US$ 50 billion.

In India, the number of people affected is highest in earthquakes, cyclones, and floods, followed by droughts. The areas prone to different types of natural disasters are as follows:

Cyclones: The eastern coastline and the islands of Lakshadweep, Andaman and Nicobar

Floods: Eight major river valleys

Earthquakes: 56 per cent of the land area

> **KEY IDEA**
> India is prone to natural disasters.

Droughts: 16 per cent of land area spread over 16 states

Landslides: Himalayan region and Western Ghats

Fires: Bihar, West Bengal, Orissa, and the north-eastern states

How do floods occur in India?

Floods are a result of the peculiar rainfall pattern in most of the country. 75 per cent of the total annual rainfall occurs over three to four months. This leads to very heavy discharge from the rivers, flooding large areas.

Of all the natural disasters that occur in India, the most frequent and devastating are river floods. The Ganga-Brahmaputra-Meghna basin, which carries 60 per cent of the total river flow, is most susceptible to floods. The rivers Brahmaputra, Ganga and their tributaries carry tons of debris and water throughout the year and during monsoon the water flow exceeds the capacity of the rivers, breaks the man-made ridges and floods whole areas.

A flooded locality
(Image courtesy: S. Koilraj, http://commons.wikimedia.org/wiki/File:Kaliamman_1.JPG)

The states most affected by floods are Assam, Bihar, and Uttar Pradesh. About 40 million hectares of land in the country are flood-prone. Every year, an average of 19 million hectares of land become flooded.

Siltation too plays a role in increasing storm surges and resultant floods. The major rivers of India and Bangladesh, including Ganga, Yamuna and Brahmaputra, flow into the Bay of Bengal. Due to deforestation and soil erosion, the rivers bring vast amounts of silt. When the silt is deposited in the Bay, the areas around the deltas become shallower. This creates ideal conditions for high tidal waves and storm surges. Infrastructure development on the coast prevents the seawater from receding, thus aggravating floods.

What about cyclones in India?

The Indian Ocean is one of the six major cyclone prone regions of the world. India is exposed to tropical cyclones arising in the Bay of Bengal and the Arabian Sea. On an average, four out of five cyclones are generated in the Bay of Bengal and have an impact on the eastern coast.

Are cyclones and hurricanes increasing in frequency and severity?

Many scientists and environmentalists are certain that global warming (Chapter 19) is occurring and as a result natural disasters like cyclones and hurricanes are increasing in frequency and severity. We cannot as yet establish conclusively a connection between any individual weather event and global warming. However, there is considerable evidence to believe that climate change is having an overall impact on the pattern of extreme weather events.

A statistical analysis of 98 years of data (1891–1988) reveals that there is an increasing frequency of pre- and post-monsoon cyclones in the North Indian Ocean. Storms have become more frequent especially during the past four decades. On the other hand cyclones have become less frequent during the summer monsoon.

Let us now turn to human-induced disasters. In this book, we cover industrial accidents (such as the Bhopal Gas Tragedy) in Chapter 16 under Environmental Health. The other main human-induced disasters are discussed below.

How do nuclear accidents occur?

A nuclear power station
(Image courtesy: Rahm Emanuael, http://commons.wikimedia.org/wiki/File:Nuclear_power.JPG)

Scientists and administrators had assured us that nuclear power was safe, given all the foolproof features of reactors. Yet, accidents, big and small, have occurred in nuclear establishments all over the world.

Nuclear power stations do have many safety features. However, the accidents have shown that such features can never be a total defence against human errors and unforeseen technical problems.

The worst nuclear accident to date is the one that occurred in Chernobyl in 1986 (Box 14.3). Accidents also happened in the Sellafield nuclear complex in UK (1957), Hanford Nuclear Complex, US (1973), and Three Mile Island Power Plant, US (1979). Several minor accidents have also been reported from Japan, which has a large number of nuclear power stations.

BOX 14.3

The story of Chernobyl disaster: The giant wheel does not turn

There is a giant wheel meant for the amusement of children in the town of Pripyat, Ukraine. Since 1986, the wheel has not moved. No children come there. In fact, Pripyat is a ghost town and nobody lives there any more.

The giant wheel is a reminder of the life of the city, which was specially built for the workers of the nuclear power station in nearby Chernobyl. In the early hours of April 26, 1986, Reactor No.4 at the nuclear power complex exploded with terrible and long-lasting consequences. It remains the biggest nuclear accident in the world.

The Chernobyl plant in Ukraine (then a part of the Soviet Union) was considered to be one of the most efficient in the country and had been operating without problems since it was commissioned in 1983. What happened on the fateful day?

The operators were conducting an experiment and had switched off the reactor's automatic shutdown mechanism. The experiment went wrong and caused runaway chain reactions. There was a massive steam explosion, which blew off the roof. Radioactive gases and debris went high into the air. More than 30 fires were set off in the complex.

It took ten days for hundreds of firemen to control the fires. Helicopters dropped 5,000 tons of lead, boron, and other materials on the core to smother the radioactive gases. Over the next six months, the reactor was entombed in a giant steel and concrete building.

Land was contaminated for 1,000 sq km around the complex. About 60,000 buildings had to be decontaminated. 135,000 people along with 80,000 animals were evacuated from the area over the next ten days.

The radioactive clouds travelled across Europe and deposited the dust at random depending on weather conditions. Eventually radioactivity even reached Siberia, Saudi Arabia, and North America.

The actual damage caused by the radioactivity will never be known due to lack of monitoring and the long time spans of radioactive decay and cancer growth. Many areas in Europe will remain contaminated well into the 22nd century or even longer.

Chernobyl radically undermined public faith in the safety of nuclear reactors. Public memory, however, is short and many governments, including India, go ahead with more nuclear power projects. In spite of all the assurances given by the nuclear establishment, there will surely be more Chernobyls.

What is nuclear waste and why is it a problem?

Radioactive waste being transported

There are three types of radioactive waste: low-level, intermediate-level and high-level. Hospitals, laboratories, and other buildings where radioactive technology is used emit low-level radiation, which is not considered a health hazard.

Intermediate-level waste consists of substances from nuclear power stations like cleaning agents and sludge. This material is bulky and decays slowly. Hence it is encased in bitumen or concrete before being stored. Until 1980, this kind of waste was just dumped in the ocean. Since then it is being stored in deep landfill sites because of an international convention against ocean dumping.

High-level nuclear waste is extremely dangerous and must be isolated for thousands of years. This is mostly spent nuclear fuel that comes from nuclear reprocessing plants. There is no definitely safe method of storing this waste. Tons of this hazardous waste is piling up all over the world (Box 14.4).

BOX 14.4

The story of nuclear waste: 'Chernobyl would be small potatoes'

By 2035, there will be 100,000 tons of the deadly stuff to be stored and secured. It will ultimately become safe to handle, but it will take 10,000 years!

This is the story of spent nuclear fuel in the US. More than 100 nuclear reactors produce 20 per cent of the energy in that country. The nuclear waste that the reactors generate needs permanent and safe storage facility. For years, the US has been looking for such a central site for all the waste.

Every nuclear complex has the facility to store the spent fuel on site. The problem is that local communities object to such storage and the states place limits on the amount of on-site storage. Further, many units are running out of space and some aging reactors have to be closed down.

In 1985, the US Department of Energy chose the Yucca Mountain desert region in Nevada for building a permanent underground storage facility.

It was to cost US$ 58 billion, to be financed by a tax on nuclear power.

Citizens and scientists oppose the plan for several reasons: the area is a seismic zone, there is an active volcano nearby, rock fractures could allow water to leak in and corrode the storage casks. One geologist has said that if water were to flood the site, the resulting explosion could be so large that 'Chernobyl would be small potatoes.'

To transport all the waste from the power stations to Yucca would need six shipments a day for 30 years, passing through 109 populated cities. At the end, there will still be the same amount of waste in the plants, since they will be producing new wastes as fast as they ship out the old ones.

Despite all the objections, the US Congress approved the plan in July 2002. However, it will be ten years before Yucca is ready to accept waste.

Though nuclear bombs have been used only once so far (by the US on Hiroshima and Nagasaki in 1945), innumerable nuclear tests have been conducted since then by a number of countries, including India and Pakistan. During the first two decades, the tests were conducted above ground and thousands of unsuspecting people and many habitations were exposed to dangerous levels of radiation. Bikini Atoll in the Marshall Islands, and some desert regions of Australia and US were the worst affected. Since 1963, the tests are conducted underground, but the there is still contamination of air, soil, and water.

KEY IDEA

Nuclear accidents and disposal of nuclear waste are major problems.

Exposure to low-level radiation over long periods can have damaging effects on the human body. Such contamination could occur in nuclear power plants and near uranium mines (Box 14.5). On the whole, there is a need for constant vigilance.

BOX 14.5

The story of Jadugoda: Mining in 'Magic Land'

Once the Lippis and the Peos, beautiful birds with sweet voices, were abundant here. Beautiful girls used to be named after these birds. Now the birds have gone. Mainas, hariyals, and owls have declined, so have monkeys and honeybees.

The people have been falling ill with fatigue, lack of appetite, and respiratory illnesses. There is an unusual variety and prevalence of problems including miscarriages, birth defects, cancer, tuberculosis, and so on.

What black magic has been happening in Jadugoda (literally meaning 'Magic land') in Singhbhum District of Jharkhand? Is it the effect of uranium mining that has been going on here for over 30 years? This is an unresolved controversy.

Since 1964, the public sector Uranium Corporation of India Limited (UCIL) has been extracting uranium ore from three underground mines in Jadugoda. The waste products that come out of the initial processing of the ore are called 'tailings'. In Jadugoda the tailings are stored in three ponds, which are in reality small-sized dams.

The waste in the tailing ponds is radioactive and is supposed to be isolated. In Jadugoda, however, the isolation has never been strict. People move freely in and out of the tailings area with their cattle, and children used to play there. What is worse, the tailings have been used to construct roads, schools, playgrounds, and other tailing dams.

Water in the wells near the tailing dams have turned black and salty. During monsoon, water from the tailing dams overflows and reaches the local river. On the whole, the tailings have not been protected well.

Committees set up by the Atomic Energy authorities, however, have concluded that there was no abnormally high level of radioactivity in the area and that the local disease patterns could not be ascribed to radioactive exposure.

There is, however, considerable circumstantial evidence that things are not all right with the people of Jadugoda. There have been protests by citizens' groups, intervention by the Bihar Assembly, and petitions in court. Meanwhile we need nuclear energy, we need the uranium, and the mining goes on. But the doubts linger.

From nuclear contamination, we now move to the problem of oil spills.

Are oil spills common?

Oil spills result from tanker accidents and blowouts at offshore drilling rigs. They occur quite often and the spill sizes vary greatly. Some notable oil spills are:

Smoke from controlled burns in the Gulf of Mexico

- 2010 Deepwater Horizon spill in the Gulf of Mexico: Largest accidental spill in history, probably leaked 650,000 tons of oil (Box 14.6).
- 1989 spill from the *Exxon Valdez* that struck Bligh Reef, in Alaska: Leaked only 30,000 tons, but its environmental impact was huge (Box 14.7).
- 1991 Gulf War oil spill: Iraqi armed forces opened valves at the Sea Island oil terminal and let out oil from tankers into the Gulf waters in order to stall the US Marines from advancing. The spilled oil (1,360,000–1,500,000 tons) destroyed the marine ecosystem and killed thousand of birds, besides causing billions of dollars in monetary losses.

BOX 14.6

The story of Gulf of Mexico oil spill

On April 20, 2010, an explosion occurred on an off-shore oil drilling rig located in the Gulf of Mexico. The rig, called Deepwater Horizon and owned by the oil firm BP, was drilling 1.5 km below the surface. 11 workers were killed and 17 others injured. The ship burned for about 36 hours and sank. The oil started gushing into the ocean, making it the largest accidental spill in history.

The well continued to leak for three months even while various efforts to plug the leak failed. The well was finally capped in July, but it was fully sealed off only on September 20, 2010.

Meanwhile, about 5 million barrels of oil had flowed into the Gulf and the oil had spread to the shores of Mississippi, Alabama, and Florida. Very little of the leaked oil could be captured and there is still a huge plume of dispersed oil deep in the Gulf of Mexico.

The spill had disastrous effects: local fisheries closed in some areas, many pelicans, turtles, birds, etc., killed or coated with oil. The dispersed oil might pose a threat to wildlife for months or even years. In addition, there is also concern about the impact of the chemical dispersants used to combat the spill.

The response to the accident was marked by a lack of preparation, organization, urgency, and clear lines of authority among federal, state and local officials, as well as BP. The government repeatedly underestimated how much oil was flowing into the Gulf. BP too deliberately gave very low figures for the leak.

The spill perhaps could have been avoided. Several workers on the platform had expressed their concerns regarding the well months before, but no action was ever really taken. Many key components including safety systems had not been fully inspected since 2000.

The Obama administration imposed a moratorium on deepwater drilling after the oil spill, but lifted it in October 2010. The government claimed that new rules now put in place would prevent another such disaster.

BOX 14.7

The story of *Exxon Valdez* disaster: How to kill 22 whales and a million birds without trying?

It was around 9 pm on March 23, 1989 and Gregory Cousins, Third Mate of the oil tanker *Exxon Valdez*, was piloting the tanker through the icebergs near Prince William Sound in Alaska. Around midnight, the ship ran aground on Bligh Reef.

After the oil tanker hit the reef, it spewed 38,800 tons of crude oil into the sea. The spill contaminated 2000 km of shoreline, four national wildlife refuges, three national parks, and a national forest. The containment work was poor and the spill ended up affecting 4000 km of the coast.

There have been many bigger oil spills since then. However, *Exxon Valdez* is the number one spill in terms of damage to the environment. The timing of the spill, the remote and spectacular location, the thousands of miles of rugged and wild shoreline, and the abundance of wildlife in the region combined to make it a huge environmental disaster.

The victims included 250,000 seabirds, 2,800 sea otters, 300 harbour seals, 250 bald eagles, up to 22 killer whales, and billions of salmon and herring eggs. Some estimates talk about the death of three million birds.

Exxon, the tanker's owners, spent US$ 1.8 billion in a controversial cleanup operation. Some of the methods used by them damaged more wildlife. More than 150 cases were filed against the company.

Exxon agreed to pay US$ 900 million to restore natural and other resources that suffered a substantial loss or decline as a result of the oil spill. The

Contd

Box 14.7 Contd

Exxon Valdez Oil Spill Trustee Council was formed to oversee restoration of the injured ecosystem through the use of these funds.

The disaster created tremendous awareness of environmental issues in the US. The Congress set up a US$ one billion cleanup fund and blocked several new offshore drilling operations. At the international level, many new regulations came into being for oil transport.

Even 20 years later, huge quantities of oil still coat Alaska's shores with a toxic glaze. Oil is found even 700 km away from the spill site. The spill continues to harm wildlife and the livelihoods of local people.

Substantial amount of oil is also discharged into the ocean by the normal drilling operation, cleaning of tankers, and leaks from pipelines and storage tanks. Oil pollution of the ocean comes from the land too. Waste oil of all kinds from industries, automobile workshops, and homes ultimately reach the ocean.

What are the environmental effects of oil spills and oil leaks?

Chemicals in oil kill many marine organisms and coral reefs. Other chemicals form a black layer on the surface that coat the feathers of birds and fur of marine mammals. They die or drown, unless rescued and treated. Heavier components sink to the bottom and kill organisms like crabs and mussels or make them unfit for human consumption. When the oil spill reaches the coast, it destroys fishing activities and tourism.

> **KEY IDEA**
> Oil spills occur regularly and have huge environmental and economic impacts.

Can the environment be restored after an oil spill? About 10–15 per cent of an oil spill can be removed through mechanical and chemical means. The rest remains in the water. Many marine organisms recover in about three to ten years. Beaches covered with oil slicks may take several years before they become clean and usable again. It has been found that ocean processes in general can absorb oil spills and break down hydrocarbons.

What is disaster management?

With so many natural and man-made disasters occurring, there is need for proper disaster management. The objectives of disaster management and mitigation are:

• Reduce, or avoid, losses from disasters
• Assure prompt assistance to victims
• Achieve rapid and effective recovery

The cycle of activities in disaster management consists of four phases:

Before any disaster occurs:

1. Mitigation: Minimizing the possible effects of a disaster
2. Preparedness: Planning how to respond to a disaster

After a disaster occurs:

3. Response: Taking immediate measures to save life and property, providing medical relief, etc.
4. Recovery: Returning the community to normal conditions

These four phases usually overlap. For example, even as we respond to a disaster like an earthquake, we have to prepare for more shocks that may follow.

Disaster prevention, mitigation, and preparedness are far better than disaster response and recovery. Let us now consider each of the phases in some detail.

What is disaster mitigation?

The aim of mitigation is to eliminate or reduce the probability of disaster occurrence, or reduce the effects of unavoidable disasters. Mitigation measures include the following:

- Establishing and enforcing codes for the construction and use of buildings:
  Examples: provision of fire escapes, entrances, staircases, etc., for quick evacuation, earthquake-resistant design of buildings in quake-prone areas, provision of fire extinguishers and fire hydrants
- Carrying out vulnerability analysis:
  Examples: study of vulnerability of areas for disasters, preparing vulnerability maps for use by government agencies
- Zoning and land use management:
  Examples: Rules for location of industries (for example, not allowing hazardous industries in crowded urban areas), rules for using the coastal zone (for example, protecting mangroves and prohibiting construction close to the shore)
- Preventive health care:
  Examples: vaccination campaigns against expected epidemics, campaigns for preventive steps at home
- Public education:
  Examples: awareness creation through advertisements and training programmes, including disaster management in school curriculum

What is disaster preparedness?

The aim of disaster preparedness programmes is to become ready to respond to a disaster. Preparedness measures include the following:

- Working on preparedness plans to save lives, minimize disaster damage, and enhance disaster response operations
- Preparing evacuations plans
- Conducting emergency exercises and training by simulating a disaster
- Setting up early warning systems using satellites, remote sensing, floating instruments in the ocean, etc.
- Setting up emergency communications systems like community radio
- Creating strategic reserves of food, equipment, water, medicines, and other essentials
- Preparing lists of emergency personnel and contact
- Informing and involving the public in preparedness measures, conducting training and awareness programmes in schools

How should we respond to a disaster?

The aim of disaster response is to provide immediate assistance to the affected population. The focus in this phase is on meeting the basic needs of the people until more permanent and sustainable solutions can be found. The activities include the following:
- Organizing search and rescue missions to save lives and attend to the injured
- Providing food, clothes, blankets, etc., to the people
- Arranging transport for moving the injured to the hospitals and other people to safer areas,
- Building temporary shelters and semi-permanent settlements for the people who have lost their homes
- Repairing damaged infrastructure (like roads) and communication facilities (like telephone lines)

What can we do to recover from a disaster?

The aim of disaster recovery is to help the community return to its normal life as quickly as possible. Such measures include the following:

KEY IDEA

Disaster mitigation, preparedness, response, and recovery are the main phases of disaster management. Mitigation and preparedness are far better than having to carry out response and recovery.

- Restoring livelihoods or creating alternate livelihoods
- Helping the affected people receive government relief and insurance payments
- Building permanent homes
- Rebuilding infrastructure like roads, communication facilities, schools, etc.
- Arranging for long-term medical care
- Counselling individuals who are deeply affected by the disaster (shock, loss of family members, etc.)
- Providing foster homes for children orphaned by the disaster

What is the status of disaster management in India?

In recent years, there has been a shift of focus in India from post-disaster management to preparedness and mitigation. Forecasting and monitoring systems are now in place for earthquakes, droughts, floods, and cyclones.

The National Policy on Disaster Management proposes the following:
- A holistic, and proactive approach towards prevention, mitigation, and preparedness
- Each ministry and department of the central and state governments should set apart adequate funds for vulnerability reduction and preparedness.
- Mitigation measures should be built into ongoing schemes and programmes.

KEY IDEA

India has a National Policy on Disaster management and an active implementation programme.

- Each project in a hazard-prone area should include mitigation measures and vulnerability reduction.
- A national disaster management law should be enacted covering all the existing mechanisms.

A districtwise vulnerability atlas has been prepared and is available for use by development planners, decision makers, professionals and ordinary citizens.

Are we ready to meet disasters?

KEY IDEA

Since we can expect the frequency and severity of disasters to increase, we should be better prepared to meet them. But we do not learn from disasters and tend to forget them.

Since we can expect the frequency and severity of natural disasters to increase, we should be better prepared to meet disasters. The public and the government respond when disasters strike, but forget the whole issue after a while. Immediate relief arrives, but funds for long-term projects for better preparedness are rarely received.

After the supercyclone in Orissa, 500 cyclone shelters were planned so that every village would have access to one within a distance of 2.5 km. A year later, not a single one had come up. A crucial satellite communication system had been recommended, but not a single phone had been set up. This is a story repeated in many disaster-prone areas.

Ending on a hopeful note: Positive stories

- After the Gujarat earthquake of 2001, the Gujarat State Disaster Management Authority (GSDMA) and national NGO SEEDS took up the Gujarat School Safety Initiative in 25 districts. The project promotes preparedness amongst school children, teachers and parents to reduce disaster risk in schools and to make them act appropriately in an emergency. It also trains teachers in disaster management so that they are able to impart disaster education to children more effectively.
- Forest departments in the coastal states of India are planting mangroves and casuarinas trees on the coast as a protection against cyclones and tsunamis.

REVIEW: A SUMMARY OF THE KEY POINTS

- It is vitally important to maintain mangrove cover on the coasts in order to reduce the impact of cyclones.
- Natural disasters in the world are increasing in severity and frequency.
- Most of the natural disasters and maximum damage occur in the developing countries.
- India is a disaster-prone country with occasional earthquakes and regular floods, cyclones, and droughts.
- Earthquakes have caused major damages in India.
- Nuclear accidents do occur due to human errors and unforeseen technical problems.

- While the Chernobyl accident has been the worst so far, several others have occurred in different parts of the world.
- The safekeeping of deadly nuclear waste from reactors is posing a major problem.
- Large oil spills cause great damage to the marine and coastal environment. We cannot easily and quickly clean up a spill and restore the environment.
- With increasing natural and human-induced disasters, proper disaster management is necessary.

EXERCISES

Objective-type questions

For each question below, choose the best answer out of the given choices.

1. Which of the following is an effective protection against cyclones and tsunamis?
   (a) Disaster management
   (b) Mangrove forests
   (c) Shrimp farms
   (d) Prior cyclone

2. Which of the following is **not** an example of natural disaster?
   (a) Nuclear accident
   (b) Tsunami
   (c) Heat wave
   (d) Epidemic

3. Which of the following is an example of natural disaster?
   (a) Bhopal Gas Tragedy
   (b) Chernobyl accident
   (c) Exxon Valdez spill
   (d) Bush fire

4. Which of the following statements is true with regard to natural disasters?
   (a) Asia accounts for all deaths from natural disasters.
   (b) Natural disasters are on the increase.
   (c) The average annual population affected by natural diasters is highest in India.
   (d) Natural disasters were maximum during the 1990s.

5. What is the severity level of an earthquake that measures 7.8 on the Richter Scale?
   (a) Very severe
   (b) Moderate
   (c) Severe
   (d) Extremely severe

6. Which of the following statements is true with regard to tsunami?
   (a) It moves very fast in the ocean.
   (b) It is a tidal wave.
   (c) It is caused by the moon's gravitation.
   (d) It is caused by an undersea earthquake.

7. Which of the following statements is **not** true with regard to meteorological disasters?
   (a) A tornado touches the earth.
   (b) Hurricane and typhoon are the same.
   (c) Cyclone occurs off the Indian coast.
   (d) Cyclone brings rain, but no wind.

8. Which of the following statements is **not** true with regard to nuclear waste?
   (a) There is a safe method of storing any nuclear waste.
   (b) High-level nuclear waste is extremely dangerous.
   (c) Nuclear waste is encased in bitumen or concrete before being stored.
   (d) High-level nuclear waste must be isolated for thousands of years.

9. Which of the following statements is **not** true with regard to oil spills?
   (a) Chemicals in oil kill many marine organisms.
   (b) Most of the oil is collected and disposed off.
   (c) The oil has long-term effects on the ecosystem.
   (d) Oil is also discharged into the ocean by the cleaning of tankers.

10. What is meant by disaster mitigation?
    (a) Planning how to respond to a disaster
    (b) Returning the community to normal conditions
    (c) Taking immediate measures to save life and property
    (d) Minimizing the possible effects of a disaster

Short-answer questions

1. What role do mangroves play in the event of a cyclone?
2. List the various types of natural, human-induced, and slow-acting disasters.
3. What is the scale of damage that occurs due to natural disasters in the world and in India?
4. Where do most floods in India occur and why?
5. Why have the cyclones on the eastern coast become more severe in their impact?
6. Give a brief account of the Gujarat earthquake of 2001.
7. List the main features of the draft National Policy on Disaster Management.
8. In what ways does oil find its way to the ocean?
9. List three major oil spills. Describe in brief the Exxon Valdez or the Deepwater Horizon accident.
10. How is an oil spill cleaned up?

Long-answer questions

Write an essay on the environmental health problems created by nuclear power plants through accidents and the generation of radioactive waste. Include an account of the major nuclear accidents and their effects. Why do such accidents occur? What are the issues concerning the storage of nuclear waste? What is the impact of uranium mining?

Think critically: Deeper questions for reflection and discussion

Given the risks of accidents and the problem of storing deadly waste for thousands of years, should we persist with nuclear power? Is it really clean as its proponents say?

SOMETHING DIFFERENT FOR A CHANGE

Seeking a breath of fresh air in the middle of that fateful night, Lyubov Sirota (1956–) went out on to her balcony in the city of Pripyat and watched the Chernobyl nuclear reactor explode in front of her. After this exposure, she and her son grew gravely ill from heavy doses of radioactive contamination. To express her grief and rage, she turned to writing poems. Here is the first stanza of one of her poems:

To Pripyat

We can neither expiate nor rectify
the mistakes and misery of that April.
The bowed shoulders of a conscience awakened
must bear the burden of torment for life.
It's impossible, believe me,

to overpower
or overhaul
our pain for the lost home.
Pain will endure in the beating hearts
stamped by the memory of fear.
There,
surrounded by prickly bitterness,
our puzzled town asks:
since it loves us
and forgives everything,
why was it abandoned forever?

The poems of Lyubov Sirota are available on the website: http://www.wsu.edu/~brians/chernobyl_poems/chernobyl_index.html

ACTIVITIES

Act: What you can do to participate in disaster management

You can play a role in disaster management in several ways:

1. Arrange and take active part in disaster preparedness programmes in the college
2. Ensure that the college is at a high level of disaster preparedness
3. Create awareness about disaster management among the parents and the public through exhibitions, plays, discussions, etc.
4. Volunteer help to the affected people when disaster occurs in the area

Learn by doing: Case study / Project

Visit a place where a disaster had struck recently. Study the environmental consequences of the disaster and write a report. What were the remedial measures attempted? How far has the environment been restored? What can still be done?

Organize together: Eco-club activities and projects

1. Observe National Disaster Reduction Day: October 29, the day the supercyclone hit Orissa in 1999, is observed every year in India as the National Day of Disaster Reduction. The activities are conducted during the fortnight ending October 29. You can organise events to highlight the major disasters that have occurred in India, their impact, mitigation measures, lessons learnt for the future, etc.

   If you live in a disaster-prone area, you should focus on preparedness and explain to the people how they should meet disasters, what kind of protective measures they should take, where to turn to for help if a disaster strikes, etc.

2. Alternately, you can observe the International Day for Natural Disaster Reduction: The UN and its agencies have been observing the Day on the second Wednesday of October. Each year a theme is also announced. For more information, access the website www.unisdr.org.

LEARN MORE

Books

Banerjee, Ruben 2001, *The Orissa Tragedy: A Cyclone's Year of Calamity*, Books Today, New Delhi.

UNEP 2001, *India: State of the Environment 2001*, United Nations Environment Programme, Regional Resource Centre for Asia and the Pacific, Thailand.

Articles

Bhatia, Bela 2001, 'Jadugoda: Fighting an Invisible Enemy', *The Hindu Survey of Environment 2001*, The Hindu, Chennai, pp. 129–135.

Swami, Praveen, Parvathi Menon, and Lyla Bavadam 2001, 'The Aftershocks', *Frontline*, Vol. 18, No. 4, March 2, pp. 4–20.

Venkatesan, V. and Praveen Swami 2001, 'The Killer Earthquake', *Frontline*, Vol. 18, No. 3, February 16, pp. 4–16.

Websites

Chernobyl disaster: www.chernobyl.info

Disaster Management Information System, an initiative of SRISTI (Society for Research and Initiatives for Sustainable Technologies and Institutions): www.sristi.org/dmis/

Exxon Valdez Oil Spill Trustee Council: www.evostc.state.ak.us

Gujarat earthquake: http://gujarat-earthquake.gov.in/

International Disaster Database: www.emdat.be

Jadugoda: www.wise-uranium.org/umopjdg.html

Natural Disaster Management Division, Government of India: www.ndmindia.nic.in/

Orissa Supercyclone: www.nic.in/cycloneorissa, www.oras.net

Module 6

Human Population and the Environment

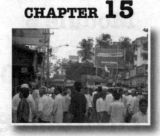

CHAPTER 15

Population Growth

Too many people brings suffering to the land, and the land returns its suffering to the people.

Otto Soemarwato
(1926–2008)
Indonesian biologist and environmentalist

THIS CHAPTER IS ABOUT...

Population explosion, population growth and distribution, measuring population growth, population trends in India, urbanization, growth of cities

THE KEYWORDS AND PHRASES ARE...

crude birth rate   crude death rate   population growth rate   ecological architecture

THE STORY OF DHARAVI: DEPRIVATION AND DESPERATION, ENERGY AND ENTERPRISE!

Dharavi is a slum spread over 175 hectares in the centre of Mumbai. Within the congested city, Dharavi has the highest density of population, an unbelievable 45,000 persons per hectare. The residents come from many parts of India, driven to the city from their villages by drought, discrimination, or deprivation. There are potters from Kumbharvada in Saurashtra, dhobis from Gujarat, and tanners form Tamil Nadu. Many began as workers and ended up as owners of small factories. Many of the old timers even live in two-storey houses. All of them, however, are 'illegal' occupants!

Living in Dharavi is not easy. Everywhere there are open drains, piles of uncleared garbage, filth and pitiful shacks. Water supply and sanitation were once

Dharavi Slum

nonexistent, now poor. The people suffer incredible hardships during the monsoon, with flooded lanes and rivers of sewage.

There are around 5,000 small industries in the area with a total turnover of Rs 20 billion. The industries include plastic recycling, garment-making, printing, zari making, leather products, and pottery. Leather products made here are exported to France and Germany. Every day, about 200 tons of snacks are produced in over 1,000 units.

When the migrants were banished to Dharavi years ago, it was a swamp outside the city. Now, it finds itself in the heart of the vastly expanded city in a strategic location between the two main railway lines. And so the land has become extremely valuable!

Over the years, unsuccessful attempts were made 'to develop' Dharavi. In early 2004, however, the state government announced a Rs 56 billion project to completely transform the area. A Dharavi Develop-

ment Authority has been set up. According to the original plans, Dharavi would be divided into sectors, allocating space for residential, commercial, industrial, and recreational use. Every resident, who had come there before 1st January 2000 would be eligible for a free home of 270 sq ft. The space released would be given to builders for commercial development.

The residents and NGOs have opposed the project. The original plans are being revised, but serious doubts about the idea itself still remain. Will the scheme work at all? What will happen to the large number of residents not covered by the scheme? Where is the space to build transit camps for at least 600,000 people during the construction phase? Will new slums be created in the process of redevelopment? What will happen to the thousands of illegal, polluting, but flourishing businesses?

The Dharavi Redevelopment Project had not taken off even in 2010, but we have wait for further news.

What does the story of Dharavi tell us?

Managing the urban population is becoming a bigger and more complex problem every day. In particular, how do we treat the poor, who arrive in the cities by thousands each day? More than a billion people (a third of the urban dwellers) live in slums. Can we provide jobs, food, shelter, water and sanitation for all of them? Such questions are likely to become more pressing in the coming decades.

This chapter looks at issues of population and urbanization with reference to environmental problems.

What is meant by population explosion?

About 10,000 years ago, there were about five million people on earth, all hunter-gatherers. Then came agriculture and settlements, the population started growing, and by the 14th century the figure had reached 500 million. Thereafter it remained steady for about 500 years, until the Scientific and Industrial Revolutions took place in Europe.

Between 1850 and 1950, the world population doubled to a figure of 2 billion. By that time, exponential growth had set in and the five billion mark was reached in 1987 and the six billion mark in 1999.

> **KEY IDEA**
> World population increases by a billion every 12 years.

We now add one billion to the population every 12 years or so. The world population is projected to cross 7 billion in early 2011 and reach about 8.1 billion by 2025. Such growth is perhaps beyond the earth's capacity to support.

How is the population distributed in the world?

The land area covers only 30 per cent of the earth's surface and, of that area, 80 per cent is not conducive to human settlement. This includes deserts, the Polar Regions, tropical rainforests, tundra, and the like.

Most of the population lives in coastal areas, river basins and cities. At least 40 per cent of the world's population lives within 100 km of the coast. By 2025, this figure is likely to double. Again, many of the megacities of the world are on the coast.

There is a stark difference in the population growth pattern between the developing and the industrialized nations. Nearly 99 per cent of all population increase now takes place in developing countries, while the population size is static or declining in the industrialized nations. Among the major industrialized nations, only the US has significant population growth, mainly because of immigration.

The low birth rates in industrialized countries are beginning to challenge the health and financial security of their senior citizens. On the other hand, the developing countries add over 80 million to the population every year and the poorest of those countries add 20 million. This worsens poverty levels and threatens the environment.

KEY IDEA
While birth rates are falling in the industrialized countries, they are very high in many developing countries.

Table 15.1 lists the ten most populous countries and shows how the list is likely to change between 2010 and 2050. Of the three industrialized countries in the list now, only the US is expected to remain in 2050.

Table 15.1   The Ten Most Populous Countries: 2010 Status and 2050 Estimates
(Source: Population Reference Bureau, 2010 Report)

2010 Status			2050 Projections		
Rank	Country	Population (millions)	Rank	Country	Population (millions)
1	China	1338	1	India	1748
2	India	1189	2	China	1437
3	US	310	3	US	423
4	Indonesia	235	4	Pakistan	335
5	Brazil	193	5	Nigeria	326
6	Pakistan	185	6	Indonesia	309
7	Bangladesh	164	7	Bangladesh	222
8	Nigeria	158	8	Brazil	215
9	Russia	142	9	Ethiopia	174
10	Japan	127	10	Congo	166

Note that, by 2050, India is expected to be well ahead of China. Obviously, China is doing a better job of controlling its population (Box 15.1). Since Pakistan and Bangladesh are also growing in population, China and the Indian sub-continent together could be home to about 40 per cent of the world's population by mid-century.

BOX 15.1

The story of China: Carrot and stick for fewer births

China has 21 per cent of the world's population, but only 7 per cent of the global freshwater and cropland, 3 per cent of forests, and 2 per cent of the soil. Desertification and soil erosion are serious problems (Refer to Box 11.3).

China introduced birth control measures in 1971, persuading young people to marry late, space out children, and have not more than two children. From 1979, the government introduced a more aggressive plan offering incentives for late marriages and having just one child. While the child was assured of free medical care, schooling, and preferential employment, the family would get cash bonuses, preferential housing, and retirement funds. If a second child were to arrive, however, all the incentives would be withdrawn and penalties would be levied.

This policy was controversial and unpopular, but it produced impressive and rapid results. Between 1972 and 2000, the crude birth rate fell by 50 per cent and the average number of births per woman came down from 5.8 to 1.8. It is said that 81 per cent of women use contraceptive devices.

One problem that China is facing is that disproportionately more male babies are being born. It is not clear whether female babies are aborted or female infanticide is practised (as in India). By the middle of the 21st century, marriageable males will be one million more than females.

In 1984, the one-child policy was relaxed in rural China. Now family planning is promoted more through education and publicity and there are fewer penalties.

How is population growth measured?

The common measures of population growth are:
- Crude birth rate: The number of live births per 1,000 people in a population in a given year
- Crude death rate: The number of deaths per 1,000 people in a population in a given year

- Annual population growth rate $= \dfrac{\text{crude birth rate—crude death rate}}{1{,}000} \times 100$

Table 15.2 gives the birth and death rates in different areas of the world as of 2010.

Table 15.2   Average Crude Birth and Death Rates (2010 estimates)
(Source: CIA World Factbook)

Area/Country	Crude birth rate	Crude death rate	Growth rate per cent
World	19.86	8.37	1.13
India	21.72	7.60	1.41
China	14.00	7.06	0.66
US	13.83	8.38	0.98
Germany	8.18	10.9	−0.05

What is the scale of urbanisation in the world?

The UN Report on World Urbanization Prospects (2009 Revision) provides the following key findings:

- With more than half the population living in cities, the world has now become more urban rather than rural. China, India and the US account for 36 per cent of the world urban population. Globally, the level of urbanization is expected to rise from 50 per cent in 2009 to 69 per cent in 2050.
- The world urban population is expected to increase by 84 per cent by 2050, from 3.4 billion in 2009 to 6.3 billion in 2050. Virtually all of the expected growth in the world population will be concentrated in the urban areas of the less developed regions,
- 21 megacities (population more than 10 m each) accounted for 4.7 per cent of the population in 2009. That is, just about one in every twenty people on earth lived in megacities. The number of megacities is projected to increase to 29 in 2025, at which time they are expected to account for 10.3 per cent of the world urban population.

A crowded Mumbai street

- Tokyo, the capital of Japan, is today the most populous urban agglomeration with 36.5 m people. It comprises Tokyo and 87 surrounding cities, including Yokohama, Kawasaki and Chiba. Following Tokyo, the next largest urban agglomerations are Delhi in India with 22 million inhabitants, São Paulo in Brazil and Bombay in India, each with 20 million inhabitants.

KEY IDEA
The world is now more urban than rural. By 2050, 69 per cent of the population will be in the cities.

- In 2009, Asia was home to about half of the urban population in the world. Over the next four decades, Asia will experience a marked increase in its urban populations. By mid-century, most of the urban population of the world will be concentrated in Asia (54 per cent) and Africa (20 per cent).

How are the world's large cities growing?

Table 15.3 lists the ten largest cities in 1950 and 2009. It also gives the expected list in 2025.

Table 15.3   Ten Largest Cities of the World
(Source: UN World Urbanization Prospects: 2009 Revision)

Rank	City	1950 Pop. (million)	City	2009 Pop. (million)	City	2025 Pop. (million) (Estimate)
1	New York	12.3	Tokyo	36.5	Tokyo	37.1
2	London	8.7	Delhi	21.7	Delhi	28.6
3	Tokyo	6.9	Sao Paulo	20.0	Mumbai	25.8
4	Paris	5.4	Mumbai	19.7	Sao Paulo	21.7
5	Moscow	5.4	Mexico City	19.3	Dhaka	20.9
6	Shanghai	5.3	New York	19.3	Mexico City	20.7
7	Essen	5.3	Shanghai	16.3	New York	20.6
8	Buenos Aires	5.0	Kolkata	15.3	Kolkata	20.1
9	Chicago	4.9	Dhaka	14.3	Shanghai	20.0
10	Calcutta	4.4	Buenos Aires	13.0	Karachi	18.7

KEY IDEA

Delhi, Mumbai, and Kolkata are among the ten largest cities of the world.

We can see the rapid growth of the cities of the developing world between 1950 and 2009. Note that the three largest metros of India are in the 2025 list.

BOX 15.2

The story of Mechai Viravaidya: Asian success!

The population growth rate of the country was 3.2 per cent in 1971 and the average number of children per family was 6.4. By 2000, the figures were down to 1.6 per cent and 1.9 children! The current population of the country is about 64 million. This figure would have been reached 15 years ago, had the 1971 growth rate continued!

Thailand is a rare case of effective population control in Asia. How was this miracle achieved? A major part of the credit should go to Mechai Viravaidya (born 1941), who founded the NGO, Population and Communication Development Association (PCDA) in 1974 to make family planning a national goal.

Viravaidya introduced some innovative ideas in family planning. Participants in the programme were offered loans for building toilets and water resources. The loan funds allotted to a village would increase with higher use of contraceptives. He also organized the distribution of contraceptives at festivals, movies, and even traffic jams!

Between 1971 and 2000, the percentage of women using birth control went up from 15 to 70. A figure of 50 per cent is considered good for developing countries.

Thailand's success is attributed to several factors:
- The creativity of Mechai's programmes
- High literacy rate (90 per cent) among women
- Good health care for women and children
- Openness of the people to new ideas
- Support from religious leaders
- Government's readiness to allot funds and to work with NGOs like PCDA

Mechai now devotes his efforts towards youth philanthropy and education through the Mechai Viravaidya Foundation.

What is driving urbanisation and what is its implication?

For the poor rural inhabitant facing problems of drought, discrimination, and deprivation, the city offers what the person desperately needs—employment. Most of the world's economic activities take place in cities and even a person without any skills can almost always find something to do in a city. The city also offers the hope of a better life with comforts not available in most rural areas.

Increasing urbanisation, however, places enormous pressure on the local resources of the city. As the city grows, its ecological footprint (Chapter 1) grows even faster. Environmental problems increase: water scarcity intensifies, more and more waste piles up, the air quality drops, public transport gets overloaded, traffic jams increase, and so on.

Governments and civic bodies are finding it increasingly difficult to provide and maintain adequate water supply, sanitation, sewage systems, housing, roads, transportation, power supply, and other infrastructure for the citizens. Things get much worse when disasters like monsoon floods and epidemics strike the city.

✎ What are the environmental implications of the population growth and urbanization?

Population growth and urbanization will place greater pressures on the natural resources, but there are ecofriendly alternative measures that would mitigate the problems:

Land   There will be increasing takeover of land for human settlements. Expanding cities will encroach into the surrounding areas, converting any kind of land, including fertile fields. Land will also be needed for infrastructure like roads, highways, industries, tourist facilities, and educational complexes. Better land-use planning, creation of satellite towns, and similar measures are necessary.

Food   Even as the number of mouths to feed keeps increasing, our ability to produce enough food is being tested. Unless there is a second Green Revolution, which does not demand high inputs as the first one did, it will be difficult to feed all the millions.

Forests   We can expect increasing encroachment of forest areas and exploitation of forest resources. It will become increasingly difficult to protect reserved forests and national parks. The only way is to make the local people partners in conservation.

Water supply and sanitation   Water scarcity will become more severe and sanitation targets will not be met unless water conservation measures and ecological sanitation are aggressively implemented.

Energy resources   Fuelwood and conventional energy sources will have problems of scarcity and higher prices, unless wood plantations are encouraged and renewable energy sources are promoted.

Housing   The shortage of housing, which is already a problem, will become severe in the future. There is a need to implement mass housing using the principles of ecological architecture (Box 15.3 and Box 15.4).

BOX 15.3

Ecological architecture

Brick and concrete houses (that are hot in summer and cold in winter) with Malaysian wood, Italian marble, and German bathroom fittings—that is the architecture in our cities and even smaller towns. The ecological footprints of such buildings are enormous and this approach is clearly not sustainable in the long run. What is the way out? Ecological architecture!

Ecological architecture, also called 'green architecture' or 'sustainable architecture', seeks to minimize the ecological footprint of the house, building, or complex that is being designed and constructed.

The primary objective of green architecture is not to reduce cost, but to minimize the burden that the unit imposes on nature. There is likely to be a saving in cost, but that should be seen as a bonus. Often, green architecture involves more labour than mainstream architecture does, but that is desirable in a country like India.

In practice, ecological architecture follows principles such as the following:

- The ecological footprint of the house, that is, the area from which the unit draws all its building requirements, should be as small as possible. Use material available nearby, in the same town, state or at worst in the country; do not in any case use imported material, even if it is less expensive.
- When there is a choice, use material that can be reused when the building is demolished.
- Minimize use of material like burnt bricks, cement and steel that consume energy during

Contd

Box 15.3 Contd

- manufacture; replace them with natural materials like mud; earth blocks can be made on site using the soil from the foundation, if appropriate for block-making.
- Use of wood may be unavoidable, but choose the wood of a tree that you can plant to repay your debt to nature.
- Minimize finishing work that costs time and money without adding real value: plastering, whitewashing, sandpapering, polishing, painting, etc. Use natural herbal mixtures for protection against termites, etc.

- Wherever possible, use or dispose off waste material in the construction: For example, fix broken tiles on bathroom walls, bury plastic bags from the neighbourhood under the foundation, use discarded styrofoam sheets or even computer keyboards as fillers in concrete slabs
- Use options that would save energy: examples are skylights to allow more natural light into the building, compact fluorescent lamps, solar lamps, solar water heaters, etc.
- Recycle wastewater and use ecological sanitation.

There are now many architects in India who practice green architecture.

BOX 15.4

The story of Laurie Baker: The man who built for the people

Born in England, he worked during the War in an ambulance unit in China, Japan, and Burma. Some time in the early 1940's he had a chance encounter with Mahatma Gandhi, which changed his life. In 1945, he came to India to design buildings for leprosy missions. He stayed here the rest of his life.

Laurie Baker, a British Architect, undertook a wide range of projects in India from fishermen's villages to institutional complexes and very low-cost mud-housing schemes to low-cost cathedrals. Most of his work was in Kerala and he lived in Thiruvananthapuram.

He designed more than 1000 houses, over 40 churches, school buildings, institutions (like the Centre for Development Studies), hospitals and low-cost housing schemes. He also helped in designing and building new houses in quake-ravaged Latur.

When he first came to work in India, Baker and his Indian wife Elizabeth, lived among the poor in Pithoragarh for 16 years. During this period, the simple, efficient and inexpensive methods used by the poor people to construct their homes

had a profound influence on him. His realised the importance of using local materials, taking into account local climate patterns and accommodating the local social pattern of living. He worked with and learnt from mountain tribes and village masons using indigenous materials for building. He built schools, hospitals and community buildings and developed the unique Baker style of architecture.

In 1963, Baker moved to Kerala, where he evolved methods for using mud, employing discarded Mangalore tiles for reducing the amount of concrete in roofs, avoiding plastering of walls etc.

Baker was awarded the Padmashri in 1990. He set up an organization called COSTFORD (Centre of Science and Technology for Rural Development) for spreading awareness for low cost housing. Laurie Baker died on April 1, 2007.

As one writer puts it, 'Nature is transcendent in his work. He uses it to create stunning effects. A pool of water, a patch of shade, sunlight marooned in shadows, a clump of bushes, a wild tree—it is all grist for his mill'.

What are the international initiatives in population-related issues?

A major UN initiative was the International Conference on Population and Development (ICPD) held in Cairo in 1994. It was agreed in Cairo that:
- population policies should address social development beyond family planning;
- family planning should be provided as part of a broader package of reproductive health care; and,
- if we improve the status and health of women and protect their rights, lower fertility and slower population growth will follow.

The Cairo Conference set the following goals for the period 1995–2015:
- Provide universal access to a full range of safe and reliable family planning methods and related reproductive health services.
- Reduce infant mortality rates to below 35 infant deaths per 1,000 live births and under-5 mortality rates to below 45 deaths of children under age 5 per 1,000 live births.
- Close the gap in maternal mortality between developing and developed countries. Aim to achieve a maternal mortality rate below 60 deaths per 100,000 live births.
- Increase life expectancy at birth to more than 75 years. In countries with the highest mortality, aim to increase life expectancy at birth to more than 70 years.
- Achieve universal access to and completion of primary education; ensure the widest and earliest possible access by girls and women to secondary and higher levels of education.

Since 1994, there has been uneven progress in the implementation of these goals. Many countries that have made attempts could not marshal the resources and organizational capacity necessary for addressing such a wide range of health and social concerns.

Enough funding has not come from donor agencies to support these changes. The US has stopped funding family planning programmes. Meanwhile, another UN Conference is being planned for 2015 or so.

What has been the growth pattern of India's population?

Table 15.4 shows how India's population has grown since 1901.

Table 15.4   Growth of India's Population
(Source: Raghunathan 1999, Census of India 2001)

Year	Population (millions)	Annual growth percentage	Density per sq km
1901	238		77
1911	252	0.56	82
1921	251	-	81
1931	279	1.04	90
1941	319	1.33	103
1951	361	1.25	117
1961	439	1.96	142
1971	548	2.20	177
1981	683	2.22	216
1991	844	2.11	267
2001	1027	1.93	324

India's population was about 1.2 billion in 2010, but we will get the correct figure when the 2011 Census is completed.

We can see four phases in the growth of the population in India:

- 1901–1921: Stagnant population
- 1921–1951: Steady growth
- 1951–1981: Rapid high growth
- 1981–2001: High growth (with some signs of slowing down)

Some features of India's population (according to the 2001 census) are:

- Almost 40 per cent of Indians are younger than 15 years of age.
- About 70 per cent of the people live in more than 550,000 villages.
- The remaining 30 per cent live in more than 200 towns and cities.
- According to Census 2001 nine states showed a definite decline in the population growth rate, while eight states (mostly in the north) showed a high growth rate.
- Between 1991 and 2001, the overall literacy rate improved from 51.6 per cent to 65.4 per cent (an increase of 13.75 per cent). The male literacy rate went up from 64.1 per cent to 75.8 per cent, while the female literacy rate improved from 39.3 per cent to 54.2 per cent in 2001.

> **KEY IDEA**
> India has about 16 per cent of the world's population, but only 2.3 per cent of the land and 1.7 per cent of forests.

We have about 16 per cent of the world's population, but only 2.3 per cent of the land and 1.7 per cent of forests. As we have discussed in previous chapters, Indian agriculture faces problems like soil degradation, water scarcity, and decreasing biodiversity. We have enough food, but millions go hungry every day because of poverty.

What has been India's response to the population growth?

India was the first country in the world to start a family planning programme. It was launched in 1952, when our population was about 400 million. Fifty years and many programmes later, we have more than one billion people. By 2050, we will be the most populous country in the world.

Successive Five-Year Plans reflected a broadening of the family planning programme to provide comprehensive maternal, child and reproductive health care. In 1976, when forced sterilizations were attempted, there was resistance.

The next government shifted the emphasis to voluntary family planning and its integration with overall maternal and child health programmes. The Eighth Five Year Plan (1992–1997) launched the Child Survival and Safe Motherhood Programme. Efforts were made to provide

People waiting to get into the local train in Mumbai
(Image courtesy: Rakesh Krishna Kumar, http://commons.wikimedia.org/wiki/
File:Borivali_station_peak_hours.jpg)

antenatal, intra-natal, and post-natal care to women. It is clear, however, the goal of stabilizing the population is still far away.

Poverty, low literacy and education levels among women, lack of consistent support from the government, poor planning, and bureaucratic inefficiency are some of the reasons why the family planning programme has not been a big success. Poverty drives many people to have more children so that there will be more working members in the family. The desire to have male children is also a factor in increasing the family size. Though 90 per cent of all couples know of at least one birth control method, less than 50 per cent actually use one.

What lies ahead?

India and many other developing countries will face the prospect of unmanageable numbers unless urgent steps are taken to reduce the birth rate. Even if the birth rates are reduced now, it will take decades before the population growth starts slowing down.

We began the chapter with the case of Dharavi. There are hundreds of slums in Indian cities, most of them in much worse condition than Dharavi. According to estimates, 20 to 25 per cent of India's urban families live in slums, squatter settlements or refugee colonies. How do we handle the unceasing migration of the rural poor into cities? How can we improve the conditions in the villages so that people do not migrate at all? How do we find space to live and provide basic facilities for those who do come to the cities? Such questions will become increasingly pressing in the coming years.

Ending on a hopeful note: Positive stories

- The inspiring work of Mechai Viravaidya in Thailand (Box 15.2)
- Ecological architecture (Box 15.3) and the inspiring story of Laurie Baker (Box 15.4)
- The post-plague transformation of Surat in Gujarat (Box 15.5)
- Curitiba, the ecocity of Brazil (Box 15.6)

BOX 15.5

The story of S.R. Rao: Transforming a city

In 1994, the city of Surat in Gujarat (with a population of two million) was struck by pneumonic plague. During the heavy monsoon that year, there was flooding and waterlogging in low-lying areas. Hundreds of animals died. In September, the whole system gave way, inviting the plague.

Surat was known for its diamond business and also for its filth. Despite being one of the richest civic bodies in the country, the Surat Municipal Corporation (SMC) had failed to provide basic sanitation and clean drinking water to a majority of the city's population.

When the plague struck, Surat became a shunned city and 60 per cent of the citizens fled. The economy was devastated and export of food grains from Surat was banned. Gradually, however, the plague subsided and normalcy began to return. The strange fact was that the plague did not change matters much. A miracle was to happen, however.

In May 1995, S.R. Rao, IAS, took over as the Municipal Commissioner of Surat. Faced with a city traumatised by the plague, Rao set to work. When he left Surat two years later, it was ranked as the second cleanest city in India, after Chandigarh.

Contd

Box 15.5 Contd

This is what Rao did:

- Formed a team to work together on policy and implementation and delegated powers down the line
- Launched a 'Surat First' programme to involve citizens, companies, and institutions in working for the city's welfare
- Built water and sanitation facilities in the slums and improved the living conditions of the sanitation workers
- Demolished illegal structures, even those built by powerful people
- Enforced cleanliness in all eating places
- Set up a night cleansing system: Every street was scrubbed at night and garbage bins cleared so that the people awoke to a clean city each morning

- Established 275 surveillance centres for monitoring public health

The level of sanitation improved from 35 to 95 per cent, while solid waste removal increased from 40 to 97 per cent. Disease rate went down by 70 per cent.

Rao himself and his officers went to the filthiest of slums. The initial scepticism of the citizens gave place to a spirit of cooperation, when they saw that the Corporation meant business.

The most important thing Rao did was to put a system in place. He made the civic staff realise how a proper use of their powers would earn them respect. Later, it became a matter of prestige for the staff to continue the work that was started after the plague.

BOX 15.6

The story of Curitiba: Ecocity in Brazil

Would you like to live in a city set amidst greenery, where the streets are clean, the air is breathable, the public transportation is excellent, there are no traffic jams, the citizens are happy and are fully involved in running the city? Then, head for Curitiba in Brazil!

Curitiba's transformation into an ecocity (2.5 million population) is due to the ideas and efforts of Jaime Lerner, architect and the city's Mayor. Lerner set out to establish a municipal government that would find simple, innovative, and inexpensive solutions to the city's problems. He wanted an accountable, transparent, and honest government. It should be ready to take risks and also correct itself. It should be above all an environment friendly city.

Lerner introduced innovations in many aspects of the city's working:

Greenery He planted 1.5 million trees and created a series of interconnected parks crisscrossed with bicycle paths.

Transportation The city has perhaps the world's best public transport, with clean and efficient buses carrying 1.9 million passengers every day at low

A bus stop in Curitiba

cost. The buses run on high-speed dedicated lanes and the bus stops are connected to the bicycle paths. The population has doubled since 1974, but the traffic has reduced by 33 per cent.

City planning High-density development is restricted to areas along the bus routes, where low-income groups are housed. Every high-rise block

Contd

Box 15.6 Contd

includes two floors of shops, reducing the need to travel far for shopping. The city centre is a large pedestrian zone connected to the bus stations, parks, and bicycle paths.

Welfare Slums do exist, but each poor family can build its own home. A family gets a plot of land, building materials, two trees and a one-hour consultation with an architect. The poor receive free medical aid and childcare and infant mortality has reduced by 60 per cent since 1977. There are 40 feeding centres for street children.

Waste management There is a labour-intensive garbage purchase programme. 700,000 poor people collect and deliver garbage-filled bags in exchange for bus tokens, surplus food or school notebooks. The city recycles 70 per cent of paper and 60 per cent of metal, glass, and plastic. The recovered material is sold to the city's 500 units in an industrial park.

Industries The city developed an industrial park with services, housing, schools, etc., so that the workers can cycle or walk to work. There are strict pollution control laws.

Education All the children study ecology, while adults have special environmental courses. The older children are given training and apprenticeship in environment-related areas like forestry, water pollution, and ecorestoration.

All this has happened even as the population grew from 300,000 in 1950 to 2.2 million in 1999, as rural people flocked to the city. The city expects to grow by another million by 2020.

REVIEW: A SUMMARY OF THE KEY POINTS

- The unceasing migration from villages into cities and the lack of space and housing for the urban poor leads to slums like Dharavi.
- The slum development schemes of governments have generally failed.
- Innovative and transparent approaches like the ones used in Surat and Curitiba can mitigate urban problems.
- The world's population has been rapidly increasing, though there are now signs of slower growth.
- Most of the population growth now occurs in the developing countries.

- India is very likely to overtake China in population.
- India's efforts in family planning have not produced the expected results. China and Thailand have done better in this regard.
- Half the world's population now lives in cities.
- By 2015, India's three largest metros will be among the ten largest cities of the world.
- Ecological architecture is one way of providing sustainable housing.
- The Cairo International Conference on Population and Development held in 1994 set many progressive goals, but the implementation has been poor.

EXERCISES

Objective-type questions

For each question below, choose the best answer out of the given choices.

1. Which of the statements below in true with regard to world population?
   (a) The population increases by about a billion every year.
   (b) The population is levelling off in the developing countries.
   (c) Half the world's population lives in the cities.
   (d) The population size is increasing in the industrial-ized nations.

2. Which of the statements below in true with regard to the population of India and China?
   (a) China will always be the country with the largest population.
   (b) China is now the country with the largest population.

(c) India has just now overtaken China in population.

(d) China has just now overtaken India in population.

3. Which country is expected to have the largest population by 2050?

(a) India

(b) China

(c) US

(d) Asia

4. What is the trend in urbanization?

(a) More and more people are moving into cities.

(b) People are leaving the cities because of unemployment.

(c) Cities in the industrialized countries are getting bigger all the time.

(d) Number of megacities is going down.

5. Which of the following has **not** been a success story?

(a) Planning of Curitiba

(b) Family planning in Thailand

(c) Cleaning up Surat

(d) Family planning in India

Short-answer questions

1. What are the problems that a resident of an urban slum faces?

2. What do we mean by the term population explosion?

3. What is the most disturbing fact about population growth in the world?

4. Compare the family planning programmes of India, China, and Thailand.

5. List the important features of India's population figures.

6. Trace the process of urbanisation in the world. How are the large cities growing?

7. Why are people ceaselessly migrating to the cities?

8. What is ecological architecture?

9. What were the main goals set by the 1994 Cairo Conference on Population and Development?

Long-answer question

Write an essay on the environmental and social problems facing any large city in India (with a population of more than one million). Do many migrants come into the city and end up in slums? What are the problems faced by the poor residents of the city? What is the situation with regard to water supply, sanitation, power supply, public transport, and other infrastructure? Are the residents, especially the poor, involved in city planning? How are citizens' difficulties redressed?

Think critically: Deeper questions for reflection and discussion

Should the Indian Government introduce strict measures of family planning (as was done in China) to control the population growth? Or should we stick to just creation of awareness and improving the status of women?

SOMETHING DIFFERENT FOR A CHANGE

Here is a poem on Dharavi by Imtiaz Dharker, a poet, artist and filmmaker. She was born in Pakistan but now lives in India.

Blessing

The skin cracks like a pod.
There never is enough water.

Imagine the drip of it,
the small splash, echo
in a tin mug,
the voice of a kindly god.

Sometimes, the sudden rush
of fortune. The municipal pipe bursts,
silver crashes to the ground

and the flow has found
a roar of tongues. From the huts,
a congregation: every man woman
child for streets around
butts in, with pots,
brass, copper, aluminium,
plastic buckets,
frantic hands,

and naked children
screaming in the liquid sun,
their highlights polished to perfection,
flashing light,
as the blessing sings
over their small bones.

ACTIVITIES

Learn by doing: Case study/Project

Volunteer your services to any NGO working in a slum in your city. Spend about three weeks working with them and write a report on your experience. What are the social and environmental problems the slum dwellers are facing? Is the city government trying to solve them? What is the NGO's contribution? What are your recommendations?

Organize together: Eco-club activities and projects

1. Observe July 11 as the World Population Day: The Day was inaugurated in 1988 by the United Nations Population Fund (UNFPA) to mark July 11, 1987, when the world's population hit five billion. The Day seeks to focus attention on the urgency and importance of population issues, particularly in the context of overall development plans and programmes, and the need to find solutions for these issues. For more details, access the website www.unfpa.org/

2. Observe World Habitat Day: Every year, since 1985, World Habitat Day has been celebrated on the first Monday in October. This day has been set aside by the UN for the world to reflect on the state of human settlements and the basic right to adequate shelter and to remind the world of its collective responsibility for the future of the human habitat. Every year a theme is announced. For more details, access the website www.unhabitat.org/

LEARN MORE

Books

Bhatia, Gautam 1991, *Laurie Baker: Life, Work, Writings,* Viking Penguin, New Delhi.

Raghunathan, Meena, and Mamata Pandya 1999, *The Green Reader: An Introduction to Environmental Concerns and Issues,* Centre for Environmental Education, Ahmedabad.

Sharma, Kalpana 2000, *Rediscovering Dharavi,* Penguin India, New Delhi.

Article

Singh, Joginder and Shrinivas Warkhandkar 2003, 'Laurie Baker's Creative Journey', *Frontline,* Vol. 20, Issue 05, March 01–14.

Websites

Census of India: www.censusindia.net.

CIA World Factbook: https://www.cia.gov/library/publications/the-world-factbook/index.html

Curitiba: www.dismantle.org/curitiba.htm; http://thecityfix.com/keepin-up-with-curitiba/

Dharavi: www.dharavi.org; http://projectdharavi.blogspot.com/

Laurie Baker: http://lauriebaker.net/

Mechai Viravaidya Foundation: www.mechaifoundation.org

Population Reference Bureau, US: www.prb.org

UN documents on the population reaching six billion: www.un.org/esa/population/publications/sixbillion/sixbillion.htm

Films

Blessed by the Plague, a documentary on Surat made by Setu Films.

Dharavi, Slum for Sale, a documentary on Dharavi and its redevelopment, made by Lutz Konermann (2010)

A Convenient Truth: Urban Solutions from Curitiba, Brazil, a documentary on Curitiba by Giovanni Vaz Del Bello (2007)

CHAPTER **16**

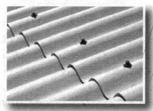

Environment and Human Health

The poor shall inherit the earth…
and all the toxic waste thereof.

Greenpeace slogan

THIS CHAPTER IS ABOUT…

Environmental health, hazardous chemicals and their effects, industrial disasters, international agreements

THE KEYWORDS AND PHRASES ARE…

Agent Orange	DDT, dioxin	endosulfan	electromagnetic fields
environmental health	PCBs	persistent organic pollutant	

THE STORY OF THE BHOPAL GAS TRAGEDY: THE LUCKY ONES DIED THAT NIGHT

It was five minutes past midnight in Bhopal on December 2, 1984. The congested city was asleep and the winter air was heavy. Many had gone to sleep late after watching the Sunday movie on television. It seemed quiet and peaceful, but the city was to change forever.

Suddenly, 27 tons of lethal gases including methyl isocyanate (MIC) started leaking from Union Carbide's pesticide factory. The deadly cloud of gases rapidly blanketed the city. It turned out to be the world's worst industrial disaster.

More than 8,000 people died in the few days following the disaster. 70,000 people were evacuated from the area after the accident and 200,000 more fled in panic. The gas affected more than 500,000 people over an area of 100 sq km. The worst affected

were poor people living in the slums that surrounded the factory.

Today, at least 150,000 people, including children born to gas exposed parents, continue to suffer health problems such as headaches, breathlessness, giddiness, numb limbs, body aches, fevers, nausea, anxiety attacks, neurological damage, cancers, depression, and mental illness. The death toll rose to more than 20,000, and at least 30 people continue to die every month due to exposure related illnesses.

How did the accident occur? Most probably water entered the storage tank and caused a runaway chemical reaction that led to an increase in temperature, which converted the liquid MIC into gas. The safety systems did not work.

Union Carbide accepted only moral responsibility for the disaster and not any liability. The Government of India filed a case against the company for US$ 3 billion compensation, but strangely accepted US$ 470 million as settlement in 1989. Nearly 95 per cent of the survivors have received just Rs 25,000 for lifelong injury and loss of livelihood. That works out to less than Rs 4 a day for more than 20 years of unimaginable suffering.

The story did not end with the disaster. When Union Carbide finally quit Bhopal in 1998, it left behind around 5,000 tons of deadly waste. The toxins have since leached into the soil and water in and around the factory. 20,000 local people, 70 per cent of them gas affected, are facing soil and water contamination. Dow Chemical, which purchased Union Carbide, has refused to clean up the site, provide safe drinking water, or compensate the victims.

Even the small amount given by Union Carbide to the Indian Government was not fully disbursed. In 2004, the Supreme Court of India ordered the government to distribute the balance of Rs 15 billion in the compensation fund among the 572,000 victims.

In June 2010, a Bhopal court convicted former Union Carbide India Chairman Keshub Mahindra and seven others and awarded them a maximum of two years imprisonment. The sentence was criticised by the victims and NGOs as being too light. Responding to a petition by the Central Bureau of Investigation, the Supreme Court reopened the case in August 2010. Earlier in 2010, the Prime Minister had set up a Group of Ministers to go into all aspects of the Bhopal case. And so the process goes on, with no end in sight and no sign of proper justice.

For over 25 years, the survivors and their families have refused to give up their fight for justice, proper compensation, economic rehabilitation, and adequate health care. Their struggle goes on.

What are the lessons from the Bhopal tragedy?

Protesters in Bhopal
(Image courtesy: Yann, http://commons.wikimedia.org/wiki/File:Dow_Chemical_banner,_Bhopal.jpg)

The tragedy showed that poor communities are disproportionately affected by toxic materials discharged into the air, land and water. When a crisis occurs or an accident happens, these people cannot easily get justice from the polluters or from the governments. The poor often do not know how dangerous their workplaces or neighbourhoods are.

As we will see in Chapter 20, the Bhopal tragedy triggered the passing of several environmental laws in India. But the laws are not being implemented strictly.

This chapter takes up the question of environmental health, especially in the context of hazardous chemicals.

What is the connection between environment and human health?

Humans have always been affected by the natural environment. Changes in climate and any extreme weather conditions affect us. A change in the season brings more pollen in the air and causes respiratory problems in susceptible people.

KEY IDEA

Human health is now affected by a wide range of environmental factors.

Sometimes, harmful substances and organisms like viruses and bacteria get into the body and cause discomfort or disease. They enter the body through the air, food, or water. Normally, the body's immune system handles the invading organisms. When the health is weak, or the invading organism is strong, the body succumbs to the disease.

Since the beginning of the scientific and industrial revolutions, however, human activities have been affecting human health in a big way. We have seen a number of examples in the previous chapters.

The World Health Organization (WHO) defines environmental health as comprising those aspects of human health that are determined by physical, chemical, biological, social, and psychosocial factors in the environment. The term also refers to the theory and practice of assessing, correcting, controlling, and preventing those factors in the environment that can potentially affect the health of present and future generations.

The areas covered by environmental health include:

- Water and sewage pollution (Chapter 12)
- Indoor and outdoor air pollution (Chapter 11)
- Noise pollution (Chapter 11)
- Radioactive contamination (Chapter 14)
- Electromagnetic fields: In recent years, there has been concern about the impact of electromagnetic fields (EMF). Television receivers, computer monitors, overhead electric lines, and mobile phones are examples of EMF sources. Such fields of all frequencies represent one of the most common and fastest growing environmental influences. Humans are now exposed to varying degrees of EMF and the levels will continue to increase as technology advances. There is still inadequate knowledge of the effects of EMF on the human body.
- Contamination caused by hazardous substances: We covered oil spills in Chapter 14. Some of the main hazardous chemicals are discussed below.

What are the common hazardous chemicals?

In modern societies, synthetic chemicals dominate the lives of people. Textiles, plastic goods, detergents, cleaners, toiletries, batteries, packaging material, vehicles, daily newspapers, medicines, computers—almost every item that you use has either gone through chemical processes or contains some chemicals.

Pesticide

Most of the chemicals used by humankind are hazardous to some part of or to the entire biosphere. Some chemicals affect all species, while others affect only a few. Some cause only minor problems, some can kill instantly. Some are dangerous only when the exposure is long, while others are toxic only in high concentrations. We do not have complete information about the effects of many of the chemicals on humans and other organisms.

There are broadly two categories of hazardous chemicals that can significantly affect humans and the environment:

KEY IDEA

Most of the chemicals created and used by humankind are hazardous to some part of or to the entire biosphere. We have incomplete information about their effects.

- Pesticides and herbicides that are deliberately introduced into the environment: Beginning with DDT, a large number of chemicals have been used for killing pests and unwanted weeds.
- Industrial chemicals that are disposed off as waste or discharged accidentally into the environment: These include organic solvents, waste oil, polychlorinated biphenyls (PCBs), paints, glues, preservatives, and metal residues.

The use and impact of some of these chemicals and substances like asbestos, lead and mercury are discussed below.

What are the chemicals used as pesticides and what is their impact?

Pesticide is a general term for any chemical that is used to kill unwanted organisms. It includes insecticides, herbicides, fungicides, and other chemicals (that kill spiders, mites, worms, and rodents). Modern agriculture and sanitation depend heavily on pesticides. Pesticides have saved millions of lives by killing disease-carrying insects. They have also increased our crop yields by eliminating pests that attack plants.

Until the middle of the last century, most pesticides in common use were simple naturally occurring substances like arsenic and nicotine. Then came new chemical compounds like DDT that were much more effective against crop pests and disease-carrying insects. The new chemical pesticides, however, remain in the environment for much longer than the natural ones. Many are also toxic to humans.

WHO estimates that every year there were 3 million cases of pesticide poisoning worldwide, resulting in over 250,000 deaths. According to another WHO Report, 25 million farm workers in the developing countries suffer from pesticide poisoning. When farmers in countries like India are driven to commit suicide, they often do so by drinking pesticide.

WHO also notes that the majority of pesticide poisonings go unreported, and that 99 per cent of the deaths from pesticide poisonings occur in developing countries. A recent example of pesticide poisoning in India is the Endosulfan case in Kerala (Box 16.1).

BOX 16.1

The story of Endosulfan: Poison from the sky?

Mohana Kumar, a doctor practising for a decade in Padre village in Kasaragod District of Kerala, was a puzzled man. Among the patients coming just from two wards of the Panchayat, he found very high incidence of cancer, psychiatric problems, mental retardation, epilepsy, congenital anomalies, to name a few. Surprisingly, almost all the ailments were restricted to people under the age of 25 and all were difficult to cure. In addition, cows in the area started giving birth to deformed calves.

Dr Kumar kept detailed records and felt that the effects could be due to the pesticide Endosulfan. This pesticide is effective against a variety of pests that attack crops of cereals, coffee, potato, tea, and vegetables. But it is easily absorbed by the stomach and lungs and through the skin. Being anywhere near the area of use is enough to get contaminated. It is highly toxic to humans, birds, and animals. The US, Canada, and many other countries have banned it, while others have restricted its use. Endosulfan is

Contd

Box 16.1 Contd

covered by the Stockholm Convention on Persistent Organic Pollutants or POPs (See end of chapter).

Since 1976, the government-owned Plantation Corporation of Kerala (PCK) had been carrying out aerial spraying of Endosulfan over cashew plantations in an area of nearly 4,700 acres in Kasaragod including the hills around Padre. The pesticide residues settled on the soil and got washed away into drinking water streams below.

Dr Kumar and journalist Shree Padre found enough published evidence to connect Endosulfan with the ailments. Samples of blood, fruits, and animal tissues from Padre were tested at the Indian Institute of Technology Kanpur and found to contain extremely high levels of the pesticide.

Kumar and Padre began holding public meetings to explain their findings to the public. PCK and pesticide manufacturers denied the role of Endosulfan in causing the ailments. The Kerala Government, however, banned the aerial spraying of Endosulfan.

Since then, studies have been done and committees set up on the issue. A study by the National Institute of Occupational Health showed that Endosulfan was the causative factor in the incidence of illnesses in Padre. There were counter studies too absolving Endosulfan. The pesticide industry was quick to declare that Endosulfan had nothing to do with the health problems.

In December 2004, on the basis of a Kerala High Court Order, the State Pollution Control Board banned the use of Endosulfan. The Kerala government has since asked the Centre to ban the manufacture, sale, and use of the pesticide all over the country. Further, the POP Review Committee under the Stockholm Convention, which met in October 2010, recommended a global ban on Endosulfan. The Indian government opposed this move, while most other countries supported it.

The last word on this controversy has not been said yet. However, what about the people of Padre? Who is going to help them or compensate them?

The chemical pesticides also kill non-target species, including the predators of the very organisms they are supposed to eliminate. When pesticides are overused, many pests are able to develop resistance to the chemicals. This leads to the use of even greater amounts of the chemical or more powerful chemicals, resulting in more problems. The only way out of this vicious cycle is to shift to organic pesticides and biological control.

There is a great risk in the manufacture and storage of large amounts of pesticides. Several disasters have already occurred, the Bhopal Tragedy being the worst case.

Many of the new pesticides have been banned in the industrialised countries. However, the same countries continue to manufacture and sell the banned pesticides to the poorer countries, where regulations and enforcement are often lax. The US is the world's largest exporter of pesticides, followed by Germany and the UK. Often, whole pesticide factories are shifted or sold to the poorer countries to avoid environmental regulations.

It is not that the populations of the developing countries alone suffer from pesticide poisoning. With freer and increasing global trade, the pesticides come back to the industrialised countries in the imported food products and in other ways (known as the 'boomerang effect').

Herbicides have also been used in wars with disastrous effects. An example is the use of Agent Orange in Vietnam (Box 16.2).

BOX 16.2

The story of Agent Orange: The deadly double agent

The assignment given to Agent Orange was to clear the countryside of all vegetation, thus denying cover for the guerrilla forces. The agent did the job only too well. Not only was the vegetation destroyed, so was the health of thousands and thousands of people for years afterwards. In fact, it was a case of double agent: the soldiers on the agent's side were also affected.

Agent Orange was not the codename for a spy. It was a compound herbicide, a defoliant used extensively by the US Army in the Vietnam War. As admitted by US, 72 million of litres of Agent Orange were sprayed over parts of Vietnam (between 1962 and 1970) to defoliate the jungle and flush out the Vietcong. The name derives from orange markings on the drums the chemical was shipped in.

The herbicide, however, contained one of the most virulent poisons known to man, a strain of dioxin called TCCD. A small 80-gram tin of TCCD would destroy New York City. The US dropped 170 kilograms of it in Vietnam!

After stripping the jungle bare, the dioxin spread its toxic reach gradually to the food chain. This has had serious effects on the health of the Vietnamese people as well as the US soldiers: defective births, Down's syndrome, skin diseases, liver cancer, mental disorders, and so on.

About three million Vietnamese were exposed to the chemical during the war. Today, there are 150,000 Vietnamese children, whose birth defects can be traced back to their parents' exposure to Agent Orange during the war. At least one million suffer serious health problems today.

In the early 1980s, 2.5 million US war veterans filed compensation claims against the US government and the manufacturers of Agent Orange. The companies paid out US$180 million as an out of court settlement, but never admitted any liability. American victims of Agent Orange get up to US$1500 a month. However most Vietnamese families affected receive around 80,000 Dong a month (just over US$5) in government support for each disabled child.

The US government has denied any moral or legal responsibility for the toxic legacy said to have been caused by Agent Orange in Vietnam. In January 2004, three Vietnamese filed in a US Court cases against Monsanto Corporation, Dow Chemicals and eight other companies that manufactured Agent Orange and other defoliants used in Vietnam. The cases were, however, dismissed by the Courts.

How long will the Vietnamese continue to suffer? How many US war veterans have been victims of their own Agent Orange? To what purpose?

What is special about DDT?   DDT (Dichloro-diphenol-trichloroethane) is an insecticide introduced first in the US in the 1940s and later in many parts of the world to protect crops and human beings from insects. It is cheap, easy to make, and chemically stable.

The spraying of DDT has been a very important part of the Green Revolution package (Chapter 12). It is effective against a wide spectrum of insects in agriculture, body lice that carry typhus, and mosquitoes that transmit malaria and yellow fever.

DDT is initially very effective against pests, but over a period of time, the insects develop resistance to the chemical. It is now recognized as a dangerous pollutant and a suspected carcinogen (cancer-causing substance). It is highly toxic to vertebrate mammals and some species of fish and birds and is passed along the food chain. It affects the breeding patterns of some predatory birds.

DDT was banned in the US in 1973, thanks primarily to the book *Silent Spring* by Rachel Carson. Many other industrialized countries have followed suit. In most developing countries, however, DDT continues to be used against malaria. In India, it is banned for agricultural use, but allowed for eradicating malaria.

What are the alternatives to pesticides from the chemical industry?   In the long run, chemical pesticides will only ruin the soils and the health of nations. The only alternative is to promote first the responsible use of pesticides and then shift to the use of traditional organic practices. We have covered this topic in Chapter 10.

What are PCBs?

PCBs are polychlorinated biphenyls, chemical compounds that are very stable, have good insulation qualities, are fire resistant, and have low electrical conductivity. They are widely used in electrical capacitors, transformers, hydraulic systems, fluorescent lamps, etc.

PCBs persist for long in the environment and are extremely toxic. They can cause cancers in animals and liver and nervous disorders in humans. When burnt, they leave a toxic ash and when buried, they leach into the groundwater. Rainfall deposits PCBs in the atmosphere into rivers and seas.

PCBs are found in high concentration levels in many marine mammals. They have a serious effect on the reproductive capacity of these animals and this could lead to the extinction of many species.

Humans who mainly consume fish are at risk from PCBs. These chemicals are said to have caused defects in children in the Great Lakes area of Canada. Surprisingly, PCBs have been found in the breast milk of Arctic women.

PCBs have been banned in the industrialised countries. Yet, thousands of tons of PCBs are still present in storage, landfills, or abandoned electrical equipment. A substantial part is in the developing countries with high risk of contamination.

What are dioxins?

Dioxins are a group of chemical compounds that occur accidentally as contaminants in a number of industrial processes and products. They are highly toxic to humans and animals and are carcinogens.

Dioxins are formed during the incomplete incineration of waste and the burning of plastics, coal or cigarettes. When fuel is partly burnt in a vehicle, dioxins are released. Dioxins are deposited on plants, soil, and water and thereby enter the food chain.

Dioxins are also produced during the manufacture of paper. The pearly white colour of the paper comes from bleaching, which uses highly toxic chemicals. Bleaching uses chlorine, which produces toxins including dioxins. Ultimately the toxic effluents from the paper factory end up in water bodies everywhere.

What are persistent organic pollutants?

Chemicals such as PCBs, DDT, dioxins, and Endosulfan belong to a group called persistent organic pollutants (POPs). Most POPs are created during human activities, either intentionally or as by-products. They remain in the environment for long, travel far, accumulate in the body, and are not easily detectable. They can cause severe health problems.

Many POPs are (or were) used as pesticides. Others are used in industrial processes and in the production of a range of goods such as solvents, PVC, and pharmaceuticals.

POPs are now covered by three international agreements (Read below).

How dangerous is contamination by lead or mercury?

Lead is an extremely poisonous metal that accumulates in organisms. Large doses of lead can cause paralysis, blindness, and even death in humans. If a pregnant woman carries even a small amount of lead in her body, the mental development of the baby could be affected. Lead in the atmosphere contaminates leafy vegetables and fruits.

The lead that we breathe in comes mostly from vehicle exhausts. For long, lead has been added to petrol to prevent the knocking of the engine. Lead-free petrol is now available in India and is mandatory for most new cars. Lead is also found in batteries, paints, bullets, and some alloys. There is a global move to phase out lead from products and processes.

Mercury is a liquid metal that is dangerous to humans and animals. While small doses cause headaches, large ones could lead to death. If inhaled, swallowed, or absorbed through the skin, mercury can damage the human nervous system. It accumulates easily in the body and is non-excretable.

Chemical and plastics industries use large amounts of mercury and release it with the effluents into rivers, lakes, and seas or dump it on land as waste. This has led to poisoning of fish and people. (Read Box 16.3 on the Minamata case)

BOX 16.3

The story of Minamata: The dancing cats

It started out in the 1950s quite simply, but somewhat strangely: cats were found 'dancing' on the street and sometimes collapsing and dying. Friends or family members occasionally shouted uncontrollably, slurred their speech, or dropped their chopsticks at dinner. When such scattered, apparently unconnected, and mildly mysterious events began to haunt the fishing town of Minamata, Japan, the people did not realise that they were the first signs of one of the most dramatic and emotionally moving cases of industrial pollution in history.

A chemical plant of the Chisso Corporation had been dumping mercury into the Minamata Bay. Between 1953 and 1983, 300 inhabitants of Minamata died by eating fish contaminated with methyl mercury. Hundreds of others suffered from blindness, convulsions, and brain damage. Children of victims were born with the disease.

Minamata is an extraordinary tragedy with environmental, social, and political aspects:

- Chisso persistently denied any connection between the mercury discharge and the disease and the government went on supporting the company. By 1959 Chisso knew the connection, but withheld the information.
- The dumping of mercury went on for a long time, even after the strange disease started spreading among the fisherfolk. Neither the company, nor the local and central governments acted to stop the discharge of mercury.
- Chisso was very much a part of the town, providing employment and bringing prosperity. The loyal workers refused to blame the company for

Contd

Box 16.3 Contd

causing the disease. In fact, the company doctor who discovered the connection revealed it only on his deathbed.

- Since it was a strange disease, the sufferers were stigmatised by their neighbours, until of course the latter too caught the disease.
- Denying any responsibility, the company paid token compensation only to those victims who signed away their right to further legal action. Many victims took the company to court, but they had to wait long for justice. The first damages were awarded only in 1973. In fact, the Japanese government officially accepted mercury discharge as the cause of the disease only in 1983!
- About 3,000 people were recognized as victims of mercury poisoning, making them eligible for a variety of health benefits, but over 16,000 were refused recognition.

- A persistent group of sufferers kept up pressure on Chisso through continued petitioning, recruiting of grass-roots support across Japan, months of sit-ins at Chisso headquarters, etc. They got some justice ultimately, but it required enormous amounts of patience and effort.
- Nearly fifty years passed before they scored a moral victory: In October 2004, Japan's Supreme Court held the government responsible for the spread of the disease. Giving its judgement in the last pending case, the Court awarded a compensation of US$ 650,000 to 37 victims.

One fish in Minamata, one night on a Bhopal street, or one breath of air near Chernobyl was enough for a lifetime of suffering for generations. How can we still continue to support the use of toxic pesticides or nuclear power?

Even small amounts of mercury used in thermometers and scientific and medical equipment can cause poisoning, if they are leaked under warm conditions. (Read the Kodaikanal mercury case in Chapter 20.)

What is the problem with asbestos?

Asbestos is a fibrous silicate mineral. The fibres are woven into a cloth, a binder like cement is added, and the resulting rigid material shaped in many forms. It is a noncorrosive, nonflammable, and nonconducting material and is inexpensive.

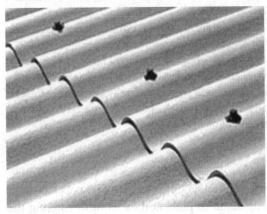

Asbestos roof
(Image courtesy; ELRiK http://upload.wikimedia.org/wikipedia/commons/2/2f/Roofing_slate_asbestos.jpeg)

Asbestos is widely used in construction, most commonly as corrugated roof and sometimes also as door or partition. Asbestos wool is used as insulation.

Asbestos is very dangerous to health when the fibres are inhaled. They can be as short as 0.0000025 cm in length and lodge themselves in the lungs and bronchial tubes. This causes a disease called *asbestosis*, which affects the respiratory tissues. Chronic shortage of breath and sometimes premature death are the results. The fibres can also cause lung and intestinal cancer. Diseases from asbestos exposure take a long time to develop. Most cases of lung cancer or asbestosis in asbestos workers occur 15 or more years after initial exposure to asbestos.

KEY IDEA

We are now constantly exposed to a large number of pesticides, industrial chemicals, and substances such as lead, mercury, and asbestos that adversely affect our health.

There is now a worldwide movement against the use of asbestos. Many conferences have called for a ban on asbestos and for providing assistance and compensation to those suffering from asbestos-related diseases.

There is still an active and large asbestos industry in India. Out of 125,000 tons of asbestos used in India, 100,000 tons are imported, mainly from Russia and Canada. Efforts to ban at least some forms of asbestos in India have not succeeded so far.

What were the major industrial disasters in the world?

In Chapter 14, we covered nuclear accidents and oil spills. Of the many other industrial disasters that have occurred since the middle of the last century, the following three are described in this chapter:

- Bhopal Gas Tragedy, 1984
- Minamata Case, Japan, 1950s: Mercury poisoning (Box 16.3)
- Love Canal Case, US, 1977: Leak from toxic dump (Box 16.4)

BOX 16.4

The story of Love Canal: Dump and disappear!

In the 1880s, William Love began digging a canal from the Niagara River to divert water for a power plant. The canal was never completed, but a small part remained unused. Between 1942 and 1952, Hooker Chemical Corporation bought the Canal and used it as a dump for toxic waste packed in barrels. The company covered the dump with a clay cap and soil.

In 1952, when Niagara falls wanted land for building homes and a school, Hooker sold it to the city and left. About 950 homes, a school and playfields were built on the site.

In the late 1950s, the barrels started leaking, children playing in the school ground suffered burns. Gradually, things got worse. Trees lost bark, gardens died, and smelly pools of toxins welled up. In the 1970s, home basements were flooded with thick black sludge. Many health problems surfaced and finally the residents realised they had a serious problem on their hands.

Tests of the water, soil, and air showed 82 different contaminants, most of them carcinogens. There was a public outcry, the canal was fenced off and several hundred families were evacuated. Ultimately, all but 72 of the owners moved out of the area. President Carter declared it a disaster area.

The cleanup began in 1987 and, by 1995, the state and federal governments had spent US$ 272 million for cleanup, relocation of families, compensation, etc. The site was covered with a new clay cap and surrounded by a drainage system. The families started coming back, but the long-term effects remain unknown.

Some of the other major industrial disasters were:

- Seveso, Italy, 1976: Due to the release of dioxins into the atmosphere, 3,000 pets and farm animals died. Later, 70,000 animals were slaughtered to prevent dioxins from entering the food chain.

- Basel, Switzerland, 1980: Fire at the Sandoz chemical plant. 1200 tons of pesticides were burnt and 30 tons of highly toxic chemicals were washed away into the River Rhine.
- Nigeria, 1998: Pipeline at Jesse Nigeria exploded, instantly killing more than 500 people and severely burning hundreds more. Up to 2,000 people had been lining up with buckets and bottles to scoop up oil. The fire spread and engulfed the nearby villages, killing farmers and villagers sleeping in their homes.

There have been many accidents in mines all over the world.

Industrial accidents continue to occur in India. The International Disaster Database (EM-DAT) lists a large number of industrial accidents in India. Since the Bhopal gas tragedy, over 50 accidents have killed more than 250 people, not counting the deaths in mining accidents. Several of the accidents took place in chemical or gas factories.

What are the international initiatives on hazardous chemicals and wastes?

There are three major international conventions that promote the proper use of hazardous chemicals and waste:

- *The Basel Convention on the Control of Transboundary Movements of Hazardous Wastes and their Disposal* was adopted in 1989 in response to concerns about toxic waste from industrialized countries being dumped in developing countries. The Convention focuses on:

  ☐ controls on the movement of such wastes across international frontiers

  ☐ promotion of environmentally sound management of hazardous wastes

  ☐ minimization of hazardous waste generation.

  The Convention covers hazardous wastes that are explosive, flammable, poisonous, infectious, corrosive, toxic, or ecotoxic.

- *The Rotterdam Convention on the Prior Informed Consent Procedure for Certain Hazardous Chemicals and Pesticides in International Trade* was adopted in 1998. Dramatic growth in chemicals production and trade had highlighted the potential risks posed by hazardous chemicals and pesticides. The Convention established a mandatory Prior Informed Consent (PIC) procedure for 30 hazardous pesticides. The exporters of such items must provide importers with information on their potential health and environmental effects.

- *The Stockholm Convention on Persistent Organic Pollutants* was adopted in 2001 in response to the urgent need for global action to protect human health and the environment from POPs. The Convention seeks the elimination or restriction of production and use of all intentionally produced POPs (i.e. industrial chemicals and pesticides). It also seeks the continuing minimization and, where feasible, ultimate elimination of the releases unintentionally produced POPs such as dioxins and furans. Stockpiles must be managed and disposed of in a safe, efficient and environmentally sound manner. The Convention imposes certain trade restrictions.

KEY IDEA
Several industrial disasters have left a lasting legacy of death and suffering to people and other beings.

Together, the Basel, Rotterdam and Stockholm Conventions cover key elements of 'cradle-to-grave' management of hazardous chemicals.

BOX 16.5

The story of Lois Gibbs: Mother of Superfund

In 1977, she was a young housewife with two children living near Love Canal (Box 16.4). She had no experience in environmental or social work— until she became concerned when her children began experiencing unexplained illnesses. She began investigating the cause, became an activist and ultimately a national figure.

When Lois discovered that toxic chemicals from the Love Canal dumpsite were causing the problems, she organized her neighbourhood into the Love Canal Homeowners Association. Apart from fighting for the residents' rights and safety, Lois raised the hazardous waste question into a national debate. She campaigned ceaselessly and wrote books on the issue. Her persistence led President Carter to establish a federal Superfund for cleaning up hazardous waste sites.

Later, Lois moved to Washington, D.C., and set up the Center for Health, Environment, and Justice (CHEJ). This organization has helped over 7,000 communities to protect themselves from hazardous wastes.

Lois has become a symbol of what happens when citizens, provoked by injustice and emboldened by outrage, stand up for themselves and their families. Her story has become a legend because of her relentless demand for the truth opened the eyes of an entire nation. Her actions, and the actions of her neighbours who formed the Love Canal Homeowner's Association, demonstrate how one committed person or one committed community can change the course of history.

Lois continues to work for a safe environment and there are new battles to be fought. President George Bush closed the Superfund Program and CHEJ, Sierra Club and others are together campaigning for reinstating it. With hundreds of toxic waste sites in US still in need of cleanup, Lois and others have more than enough to do!

Ending on a hopeful note: Positive stories

In many of the industrial disasters, there have been inspiring stories of individuals who went to great lengths to help the victims. Some individuals have also led the struggles for justice, compensation, and government action to prevent such events in the future. Examples are Lois Gibbs in Love Canal (Box 16.5) and Rashida Bee and Champa Devi Shukla in Bhopal (Chapter 17, Box 17.4).

REVIEW: A SUMMARY OF THE KEY POINTS

- While pesticides and industrial chemicals have brought benefits, they have also inflicted damage to humans and other organisms, immediately and over a long period.
- Effect of chemicals on humans can extend to succeeding generations.
- Given the nature of the chemicals we use, serious accidents will continue to occur.

- It is difficult to hold chemical companies responsible and liable for the industrial disasters caused by their negligence or operations and governments for lack of appropriate and timely action.
- Poor people are disproportionately affected by industrial accidents and often do not receive proper compensation and justice.

EXERCISES

Objective-type questions

For each question below, choose the best answer out of the given choices.

1. Which of the following statements is **not** true with regard to the Bhopal Gas Tragedy?
   (a) The pesticide company accepted responsibility.
   (b) The safety systems did not work.
   (c) The company left behind toxic waste.
   (d) The victims got speedy justice and compensation.

2. Which of the following statements is **not** true with regard to chemicals that we use?
   (a) There are thousands of synthetic chemicals in use.
   (b) We know all the effects of the chemicals we use.
   (c) Some chemicals affect all species, while others affect only a few.
   (d) Some chemicals cause only minor problems, some can kill instantly.

3. Which of the following statements is **not** true with regard to chemical pesticides?
   (a) Chemical pesticides may kill the pests and also their predators.
   (b) When pesticides are used in excess, the pests can develop resistance to the chemicals.
   (c) Pesticides often poison the farmers and farm workers.
   (d) Pesticides can always be stored safely.

4. Which of the following chemicals is least harmful to human beings?
   (a) DDT
   (b) PCB
   (c) Sodium chloride
   (d) Dioxin

5. Which of the following is **not** a quality of asbestos?
   (a) It is noncorrosive.
   (b) It is nonflammable.
   (c) Its fibres are good for health.
   (d) It is nonconducting.

Short-answer questions

1. What is meant by environmental health?
2. Explain through examples how pesticides and industrial chemicals have positive and negative impacts on society.
3. Discuss the health issues in connection with the use of or contamination by any two of the following substances: DDT, Endosulfan, PCBs, lead, mercury, asbestos.
4. Why are Persistent Organic Pollutants so called?

Long-answer question

Discuss the issue of responsibility and liability in the case of industrial accidents, pesticide poisoning, and chemical warfare. Using the case studies described in this chapter, explain why it is difficult for the victims, especially the poor, to get timely and adequate compensation and long-term support. How have the governments responded in these cases?

Think critically: Deeper questions for reflection and discussion

Is it possible to get rid of all factory-made pesticides and go back to organic and natural pesticides? How do we balance the need to produce more food with the desire to avoid chemical inputs in agriculture?

SOMETHING DIFFERENT FOR A CHANGE

1. Read what a Bhopal survivor has to say:

   ### Torture Me

   torture me.
   aim a blowtorch at my eyes
   pour acid down my throat
   strip the tissue from my lungs.
   drown me in my own blood.

   choke my baby to death in front of me.
   make me watch her struggles as she dies.
   cripple my children.
   let pain be their daily and their only playmate.
   spare me nothing. wreck my health
   so I can no longer feed my family.
   watch us starve. say it's nothing to do with you.
   don't ever say sorry.

poison our water. cause monsters
to be born among us. make us curse God.
stunt our living children's growth.
for seventeen years ignore our cries.
teach me that my rage is as useless as my tears.
prove to me beyond all doubt
that there is no justice in the world.
you are a wealthy american corporation
and I am a gas victim of Bhopal.

2. Read *Animal's People* by Indra Sinha, a novel with the backdrop of the Bhopal Gas Tragedy.
3. Watch the feature film *Bhopal Express,* directed by Mahesh Mathai, based on the Gas Tragedy. The cast includes Naseeruddin Shah and Zeenat Aman. You can watch it online: http://film.bhopal.net/bhopal-express/

ACTIVITIES

Act: What you can do to minimize the impact of toxic chemicals

1. Examine every item you use at home and try to find out if it contains hazardous chemicals or if it has been processed using such chemicals. If the answer is yes, try to replace the item with a more ecofriendly and safer product.
2. Avoid the use of chemical mosquito repellents in your home and in those of your friends. Chemicals like allethrin used in mosquito coils, mats, and liquids are toxic to the body. Covering windows with nets and using a mosquito net are far safer methods of protection against mosquitoes. If you must use a repellent, choose natural substances like lemongrass (citronella) oil available in the market.

Learn by doing: Case study / Project

Identify a case of industrial accident, pesticide or chemical poisoning, dumping of toxic waste, or water/soil contamination reported in your area. Study the incident and write a report on the causes, impact, relief and compensation to victims, concerned rules and regulations, steps taken for the future, etc.

Organize together: Eco-club activities and projects

Observe December 3 as the Global Day of Action Against Corporate Crime. The International Campaign for Justice in Bhopal (ICJB) initiated this observance. Many NGOs like Greenpeace and the Sierra Club have joined the worldwide observance of this Day.

Besides coordinating protests against Dow-Union Carbide facilities worldwide, the ICJB invites all groups fighting corporate crime to take action on December 3 against the human, environmental, consumer and labour rights violations by private or public corporations.

The Day is observed through protests at Dow Chemical facilities and offices worldwide as well as other events. You can use the Day to get students thinking about polluting and dangerous industries, finding out about industries in their locality, what they produce, raw materials used and disposal of waste, etc. For more information, access the website www.studentsforbhopal.org.

LEARN MORE

Books

Gibbs, Lois Marie 1982, *Love Canal: My Story,* State University of New York Press, New York.

Gibbs, Lois Marie 1995, *Dying from Dioxin,* South End Press, Boston.

Lapierre, Dominique and Javier Moro 2001, *It Was Five Past Midnight in Bhopal,* Indian Edition, Full Circle Publishing, New Delhi.

Mukherjee, Swaroopa 2002, *Bhopal Gas Tragedy: The Worst Industrial Disaster in Human History,* Tulika Publishers, Chennai.

Articles

Joshi, Sopan 2001, 'Children of Endosulfan', *Down To Earth,* Vol. 9, No. 19, February 28, pp. 28–35.

Yadav, Kushal P.S. 2003, 'Dubiously Acquitted: Evidence Ignored as Endosulfan is Declared Not Guilty', *Down To Earth,* Vol. 11, No. 23, April 30, pp. 7–8.

Yadav, Kushal P.S. and S.S.Jeevan 2002, 'Endosulfan Conspiracy', *Down To Earth,* Vol. 11, No. 4, July 15, pp. 25–34.

For articles on various aspects of the Bhopal Tragedy, read *Seminar,* No.544, December 2004. This issue was devoted to Bhopal under the title *Elusive Justice.*

Websites

Basel Convention: www.basel.int

Bhopal Gas Tragedy and the International Campaign for Justice in Bhopal: www.bhopal.net; www.studentsforbhopal.org

Campaign for asbestos ban in India: http://banasbestosindia.blogspot.com/

Endosulfan case: www.indiatogether.org/

International Disaster Database: www.emdat.be

Lois Gibbs: http://arts.envirolink.org/arts_and_activism/LoisGibbs.html

Major industrial disasters: http://en.wikipedia.org/wiki/List_of_industrial_disasters

Minamata Case: www1.umn.edu/ships/ethics/minamata.htm

Rotterdam Convention: www.pic.int

Stockholm Convention: www.pops.int

Films

Lois Gibbs: The Love Canal, a documentary made by the US television channel CBS.

For some documentaries on Bhopal, go to the website: http://film.bhopal.net/documentaries/

CHAPTER 17

Women and Child Welfare

*You can tell the condition of a nation
by looking at the status of its women.*

Jawaharlal Nehru

THIS CHAPTER IS ABOUT...

Women and environmental degradation, cookstove pollution, child labour, HIV and AIDS

THE KEYWORDS AND PHRASES ARE...

AIDS   HIV   opportunistic infection

THE STORY OF PHULMAI PHULO: BILLION-DOLLAR BUSINESS, MILLIONS OF POOR WOMEN

She is up at 3 a.m., cooks for her family of five, and feeds her cow. By 5 a.m., she is in the forest collecting fuelwood. She looks for dry branches and cuts them almost in equal size before making a neat bundle. She continues this search and collection for two hours, walking about a kilometre inside the forest.

She pays Rs 5 as bribe to the forest guard and walks a long distance to the market carrying the 30–35 kg load. She has to sell the bundles the same day, at whatever price she can get. At the end of the day, after buying some food, she is left with Rs 15. She herself never uses fuelwood or kerosene, only twigs and leaves.

35-year-old Phulmai Phulo of Chauda Village in Jharkhand has been following this routine for 15 years. Her lifeline is a patch of the Khellari Forest, where 30–40 other women do the same thing. These

are among the millions of headloaders of India—all women.

How did Phulmai end up as a headloader? It took just three successive droughts and lack of irrigation to make her one-acre plot barren. Headloading was the only option. Her husband migrated to Gorakhpur in search of a job and she hardly hears from him. In fact, there has been a mass migration of men from the area, leaving the women to fend for themselves.

During monsoon, the headloaders do less business and many starve. In years of drought, more women join the activity, and everyone earns less. With more people collecting from the same area, there are also conflicts.

Women headloaders are often portrayed as environmental villains who were illegally destroying forests. Their story, however, is different. They say they are driven to this work only because agriculture was destroyed. They do not cut whole trees, only dry branches. They have to bribe the forest guards, panchayat officials, bus and train conductors, and finally they sell the bundles to middlemen at throwaway prices.

India is the world's largest consumer of fuelwood. It is, in fact, a multi-billion-rupee business and the headloader is the foundation of this economy. Why then do Phulmai and millions of other women walk long distances every day, work hard, and yet earn so little? Why are they considered to be the destroyers of the forest?

What is the significance of the Phulmai case?

We discussed fuelwood collection in Chapter 8 with reference to energy sources. The return to the topic here was necessary, since we cannot emphasise enough the impact of environmental degradation on women and their role in environmental conservation.

What is the impact of environmental degradation on women and children?

Women feel the adverse effects of environmental and occupational problems much more than men do. This is especially true in relation to inadequate fuel, water supply and sanitation. The main reason is their role in society as determined by the social, economic, and political structures. At the same time, women often do a much better job than men when it comes to environmental conservation or fighting for environmental justice. In this chapter, we will see examples of both these aspects.

Children too are very vulnerable to the consequences of environmental degradation. Toxicity in the mother's body can result in birth defects among children. Children are also affected easily by pollution. Recall for example, the case of juvenile asthma due to air pollution (Chapter 11).

Women and children are also the prime sufferers in wars and conflicts and from their environmental consequences. For example, according to a study made by the Johns Hopkins University, most of the 100,000 civilians who died in the Iraq War in 2003–2004 were women and children.

The topic of women/children and environment is a vast one with many ramifications. We will confine ourselves to the following aspects:

- Collection and burning of household fuel by women
- Women's special problems with regard to water supply and sanitation, especially in urban areas
- Women and children in hazardous occupations
- HIV/AIDS situation with regard to women and children
- Women in the movement for environmental conservation and justice

KEY IDEA
Women and children suffer more from environmental degradation than men do.

⬛ **What are the women's issues related to collection and burning of fuel?**

Millions of women like Basumati Tirkey (Chapter 8) and Phulmai Phulo in the developing countries make a living out of collecting and fuelwood. Millions of other women spend substantial amounts of time and effort every day to collect fuelwood for their own use (Box 17.1).

BOX 17.1

The story of women scrap collectors: Toiling for an invisible economy

Janakibai Salve's life is similar to that of Phulmai Phulo, whom we met in the beginning of this chapter. Janakibai too wakes up at 4 a.m., completes all the household chores, and gets out for her daily work—collecting garbage from the dustbins of upmarket neighbourhoods of Mumbai.

By noon, Janakibai is ready to sort the garbage and salvage the scrap. She carries the scrap (15 kg or more) to the trader's shop 4 km away. She makes about Rs 50 on which she, her husband, and three children manage to live.

Chandrakala Adagale, Janakibai's neighbour, is also a scrap collector. Every day she goes to one of the municipal garbage dumping grounds. Chandrakala and hundreds of other women and children wait for the garbage trucks to arrive from the city. For six hours, she walks around in the dump, braving the glass and sharp metals, breathing in toxic fumes, just for collecting paper. When she delivers the load to the trader, she too gets Rs 50.

From the trader upwards, dealing in scrap is a lucrative business. Very few scrap traders pay sales tax or income tax. It is an invisible economy, whose only visible face is that of the woman collector standing in knee-deep garbage!

There are about 50,000 scrap collectors in Mumbai, a large number of them women and children. They are mostly dalit migrants from the drought-prone areas of Maharashtra, Karnataka, and Tamil Nadu.

Scrap collection is an unhealthy and hazardous occupation. Women develop respiratory problems or meet with accidents. Most collectors do not have any footwear or any protective gear. They have no social security like pension even if they deal with the same trader for generations. If a scrap collector falls sick, her children take over the job. They are ignored or even shunned by the society and there are no labour laws to protect them. On top of all this, they are often harassed by the police. When garbage disposal is privatised (some municipalities have done so), the collectors lose their occupation.

The ecosystem services provided by the scrap collectors is tremendous. They are in fact giving a free waste separation and removal service to the municipal waste management system. Further, the urban recycling industry for paper, board, glass, plastic, metal, etc., is heavily dependent on them. A significant part of the recycling process is over by the time the collector hands over the material to the trader. A large number of small industries use the scrap to reduce their cost of production.

Ideally, the scrap collectors should be formally involved in implementing a waste management system for the city. An example is the Zero Waste Management method promoted by Vellore Srinivasan (Chapter 13, Box 13.5).

The women's problem does not stop with the collection of fuelwood. When they burn the wood or any biomass in their cookstoves, they inhale poison. Through cookstove pollution, a typical rural woman in India inhales every day carcinogens equivalent to smoking 100 cigarettes!

Urban outdoor air pollution is all too visible and affects the health of all who breathe the air. Yet, in the rural areas of developing countries, indoor air pollution can be much worse than the pollution levels in big cities. It accounts for much ill health and well over a million deaths annually. In India alone, 400,000 to 550,000 women and children die prematurely every year because of indoor air pollution.

World Health Organization (WHO) has ranked various risk factors in terms of the percentage of ill health accounted for by each of them in the developing countries. In this list, indoor air pollution ranks fifth, behind malnutrition, AIDS, tobacco, and poor water/sanitation. The estimate is that there are more than 1.6 million premature deaths every year due to cookstove pollution. Despite such data, it does not attract much public attention. It is a quiet killer, affecting mostly poor women and young children.

Why is the problem of cookstove pollution so widespread and severe?

Nearly half of the world's households use unprocessed biomass fuels like wood, animal dung, crop residues, and grasses for cooking and heating. In the developing countries of South Asia and sub-Saharan Africa, 80 per cent of all homes cook with biomass fuels.

Pollution from cookstoves is serious because of the following reasons:

- Burning biomass fuels in simple indoor cookstoves releases large amounts of pollutants like fine particles of matter (that can get into the lungs), carbon monoxide, nitrogen oxides, formaldehyde, and dozens of toxic hydrocarbons. A study in Gujarat showed that women were exposed to total suspended particulates of 7,000 microgram per cu.m in each cooking period. The safe limit for outdoor air is 140 microgram per cu.m.
- The problem is aggravated when cooking areas are inadequately ventilated and the dwelling lacks a separate kitchen.
- Even when the cookstoves are used outdoors, they can raise pollution levels in the surrounding neighborhood to unhealthy levels.
- Fires from biomass fuels require more or less continual feeding, resulting in extended exposure to their smoke. Many people are exposed for three to seven hours daily, and even longer in winter months when houses must also be heated. Every winter, deaths occur in North India when people close all openings and let the smoke circulate within the dwelling.

Inhaling the deadly smoke leads to a host of respiratory diseases, including acute respiratory infections, chronic bronchitis, asthma, and tuberculosis. It has also been linked to lung cancer, adverse pregnancy outcomes, cataract, and blindness.

What can be done to solve the problem of cookstove pollution?

The obvious strategy would be to reduce the inhalation of smoke through:

- Creating awareness about the risks of exposure to cookstove smoke
- Providing more efficient and better ventilated cookstoves: For over 50 years, universities and research establishments in India have designed many 'smokeless chulhas', but the programmes for promoting the use of such stoves have never fully succeeded. The most successful cookstove programme has been in China, where some 200 million improved stoves have been introduced in recent decades.

KEY IDEA
Cookstove pollution is a major, but silent, killer of poor women in India and elsewhere.

- Promoting use of cleaner fuels: When urban India gets subsidized LPG (Liquefied Petroleum Gas), there is no reason why villages should not get the same in small cylinders. There are other ecofriendly options too, like biogas.

What are the women's issues concerning water supply and sanitation?

In Chapter 7 we covered the issue of water scarcity and in Chapter 12 we noted the severe shortfall in providing sanitation facilities to the people of the developing countries.

In these countries, it is typically women who collect and manage water. In rural areas, they have to walk long distances to the water sources and walk back with heavy loads of water. In urban areas, they have to queue up for long periods at the water point. In the process, they have to get up very early or go to bed late.

It is the women again who have to manage the inadequate supply of water, using it carefully for washing, cleaning, and cooking. Often they have to take greater trouble to collect drinking water separately.

Lack of sanitation facilities affects women much more than men. There is a severe shortage of toilets in the slums and the poorer areas of cities. In the rural areas, men use the open fields, but the women have to wait for darkness to provide cover. The suppression of natural urges for long hours causes serious health problems.

> **KEY IDEA**
> The poor women of the world face daily struggles with regard to water and sanitation.

The daily struggle for water and toilet facilities in crowded urban slums is perhaps the worst burden for women to bear. The first-person accounts of their experience can be very moving (Box 17.2).

BOX 17.2

Women and water

In 2003, the UN Human Settlements Programme (UN-HABITAT) published a Report entitled *Water and Sanitation in the World's Cities*. The Report carries first-person accounts on water and sanitation from women of Dharavi, the slum in Mumbai that we described in Chapter 15. These are the voices of some of the women:

Paliniamma:
I have been here for 15–20 years. We have a lot of problems. There is no outlet for the drains. We dig holes near our houses and collect our washing water in it. The building says no water should come out on the path, so we collect the dirty water in drums and we take the drums and throw the water in the drain along the road. Children ask us when we will get the house. The other day I filled some containers with water and it was stinking. I could not drink any water at night after my food.

Kalyani:
I have been here for the past 39 years, since I got married. I came here before the highway was built. There
was no toilet, no drains. There was no water. We had to go and beg for water. We would not bathe because there was no water. If we had to go to the toilet there were just two toilets, one for men and one for women. Once we went in the other people in the queue would shout and we had to come out in two minutes. At night we would go across the road.

Bhagwati:
I have been here for the past 18 years. 18 years ago we had to go to the Ganesh temple for water. We went at 4 a.m. and stood in line until 6 a.m. and got two containers of water. We had to leave the children at home. My child once fell into the drain and I thought he had died, but the neighbours picked him up and bathed him and he was okay. Five years back we put in a tap, but when they put in the borewell they broke the pipe. Now the water is dirty and we can only wash clothes in it.

The stories speak for themselves. No comments are needed.

How widespread is the child labour in hazardous occupations?

A child labourer
(Image courtesy: Shanjoy, http://commons.wikimedia.
org/wiki/File:Child_labor_Bangladesh.jpg)

The International Labour Organization (ILO) has estimated that, in the developing countries, 250 million children in the 5–14 age group work for wages. At least 120 million of them are employed on a full time basis. Over 60 per cent of the child workers are in Asia, 32 per cent in Africa, and 7 per cent in Latin America.

Most working children in rural areas are found in agriculture; urban children work as domestic help or in trade and services, with fewer in manufacturing and construction. In general, they work for too many hours and too many days, for too little, or sometimes no pay. They are subject often to physical abuse, exposed to dangerous chemicals and polluted environments, and made to work with dangerous tools.

Most child workers are denied education and a normal childhood. Some are confined and beaten or reduced to slavery. Others are denied the right to leave the workplace and go home to their families. Some are abducted and forced to work.

Child labour has consequences for the adults too. Poverty is one of the causes of child labour but is also one of the consequences. Because it is so cheap it causes adult unemployment and wage suppression.

The worst form of child labour occurs when a family hands a child over to an employer in return for a small, but urgently needed, loan. In most cases the child cannot work off the debt, nor can the family raise enough money to buy the child back. The workplace is often structured so that 'expenses' and/or 'interest' are deducted from a child's earnings in such amounts that it is almost impossible for a child to repay the debt. In some cases, the labour is generational, that is, each generation provides the employer with a new worker, often with no pay at all.

There has been international public awareness of the high incidence of child servitude in the carpet industry of South Asia. The Western public now associate child labour with the image of small children chained to carpet looms, slaving away to make expensive carpets for the wealthy. In particular, the case of bonded children in the Pakistani carpet industry caught the media attention (Box 17.3).

BOX 17.3

The story of Iqbal Masih: One million knots, one carpet, one child

On April 16, 1995, Iqbal Masih, a Pakistani boy, was shot to death while visiting relatives. He was only thirteen, but he had already become famous the world over.

Iqbal was one of the 500,000 or more children between the ages of four and fourteen who work full-time as carpet weavers. UNICEF estimates that children make up 90 per cent of Pakistan's carpet industry. Boys aged seven to ten are preferred for their dexterity and endurance. They earn one-quarter to one-third the salary of adult weavers, and they are obedient. They are from Pakistan's poorest families, sold by their parents.

Contd

Box 17.3 Contd

The children work for 14 hours a day, six days a week, often chained to their looms. They make beautifully intricate carpets by tying thousands of knots with fingers gnarled and callused from years of work. A single carpet may have a million knots.

They work in a polluted atmosphere and often have difficulty breathing due to cotton dust, and many contract tuberculosis. They are thin, malnourished, and small for their age. Their backs are curved from lack of exercise and from bending over the looms. Their hands are scarred from the repetitive work. The monotony of tying thousands of knots is torture, like a death sentence, which it is for many of them.

Though the Government of Pakistan passed a law in 1992 prohibiting the bonded labour system, it does not enforce the law. Moved by the children's' plight, Ehsan Ulla Khan set up the Bonded Labour Liberation Front (BLLF). This NGO has liberated 30,000 adults and children from brick kilns, farms,

tanneries, and carpet factories. In addition, the BLLF has established its own primary schools and has placed more than 11,000 children in them.

Iqbal Masih was one of those freed from slavery by the BLLF. He proved to be a special child, became a BLLF worker, and freed many other children. Under Ehsan Khan's guidance, Iqbal became a spokesman for the bonded children of Pakistan, and travelled to the US and Europe to convince customers against buying Pakistani carpets. As a result, Pakistani carpet sales started falling.

Iqbal won the Reebok Human Rights Youth in Action Award 1994. The very next year, however, Iqbal was allegedly killed by the 'carpet mafia', who were keen on maintaining bonded child labour in their factories. Iqbal's killers were never brought to justice. In fact, BLLF was raided and Ehsan Khan was hounded, until he fled to Europe. What is the price of a carpet?

What about child labour in India?

India has the largest number of working children in the world, the estimate ranging between 60 and 115 million. Most of them work in agriculture, while the rest pick rags, make bricks, polish gemstones, roll beedis, pack firecrackers, work as domestics, and weave silk saris and carpets. More than half of them remain illiterate. Many of them have been working since the age of four or five, and by the time they reach adulthood they are likely to be irrevocably sick or deformed. They will be old at the age of forty, likely to be dead by fifty.

Some of the worst cases of child labour in India can be found in the silk industry in Karnataka and Tamil Nadu, matches and firecracker units in Sivakasi in Tamil Nadu, and carpet weaving in Uttar Pradesh. Tamil Nadu has identified more bonded labourers than any other state.

There are many Indian laws against bonded and child labour, but enforcement is poor. In December 1996 the Supreme Court of India issued a groundbreaking decision outlining a detailed framework for punishing employers of children in hazardous occupations and for rehabilitating the children. In 1997 the Court ordered India's National Human Rights Commission (NHRC) to supervise states' implementation of the bonded labour law.

NHRC then began appointing special officers who applied pressure in certain regions and industries. State governments were obliged to conduct surveys on bonded labour and child labour, although the numbers reported seemed to be gross underestimates. A few of the employers were prosecuted, but almost no employer actually went to prison.

The children and women of the world, however, now face a much bigger threat—the HIV/AIDS epidemic. Here again, women face greater challenges than men.

KEY IDEA

Child labour is rampant in the developing countries with horrible consequences for the young.

What are AIDS and HIV?

AIDS stands for Acquired Immune Deficiency Syndrome. It is a condition in which the body's immune system is weakened and therefore less able to fight certain infections and diseases. It is caused by infection with HIV, or the Human Immunodeficiency Virus.

When the immune system breaks down the body is attacked by 'opportunistic infections'. When a person dies of AIDS, it is in fact the opportunistic infection, which causes the fatality. AIDS, in itself, is not in fact what kills its victims. Again, of the people with HIV, only some will develop AIDS as a result of their infection.

It is still not known from where HIV came, but the earliest known case was probably that of a man in the Democratic Republic of Congo in 1959. Genetic analysis of his blood sample suggested that HIV might have stemmed from a single virus in the late 1940s or early 1950s. We know that the virus has existed in the US since at least the mid-1970s. The term AIDS has been in use since 1982.

The virus is passed from one person to another through blood-to-blood and sexual contact. In addition, infected pregnant women can pass HIV to their babies during pregnancy or delivery, as well as through breastfeeding.

HIV spreads rapidly when many people use the same needle to inject drugs into their bodies. In this way, just one infected person spreads HIV to many others. When drug users share contaminated equipment, needles or syringes, they receive a mini blood transfusion—injecting in their bodies, along with the drugs, leftover blood from previous users. A single act of exposure through injecting drug use has a 1 per cent chance of causing HIV infection, compared with a 0.2 per cent chance through unprotected heterosexual sex. If each person used his or her own injecting equipment, HIV transmission would not take place.

HIV is not transmitted by day-to-day contact in any social setting. It is not passed by shaking hands, hugging, etc. One cannot become infected from a toilet seat, dishes, drinking glasses, food, or pets. HIV is not an air-borne or food-borne virus, and it does not live long outside the body.

KEY IDEA
The AIDS epidemic is a major killer in the world. It spreads through sexual contact, blood transfusion, and the sharing of injecting needles and syringed by drug users.

What is the current status of the AIDS epidemic?

HIV AIDS is perhaps the biggest epidemic in human history, but it seems to have peaked. However, AIDS-related illnesses remain one of the leading causes of death and are projected to continue as a significant global cause of premature mortality for many years to come.

The data on HIV AIDS given below have been taken from the following UN reports:
- AIDS Outlook Report 2010
- AIDS Annual Report 2009
- AIDS Epidemic Annual Update 2009
  Here are some global facts on HIV AIDS:
- Since the beginning of the epidemic, almost 60 million people have been infected with HIV.
- About 7,400 new infections occur every day. For every 2 people on HIV treatment, 5 are becoming newly infected.

- Even though the treatment (antiretroviral therapy) has beneficial effects, the continued high rates of new HIV infections has resulted in the continuing rise in the population of people living with HIV.
- 25 million people have died of HIV-related causes. However, yearly AIDS-related deaths appear to have peaked in 2004 at 2.2 million.
- Every day, about 5,500 persons die from AIDS, mostly because of inadequate access to HIV prevention care and treatment services.
- The spread of HIV appears to have peaked in 1996, when 3.5 million new infections occurred. New HIV infections worldwide have dropped by 17 per cent since 2001.
- The epidemic appears to have stabilized in most regions. However, its prevalence continues to increase in eastern Europe and central Asia, due to a high rate of new HIV infections. In these areas, injecting drug use is the primary route of transmission of HIV.
- Sub-Saharan Africa remains the most heavily affected region, accounting for 70 per cent of all new HIV infections.
- Differences are apparent in all regions, with some national epidemics continuing to expand even as the overall regional HIV incidence stabilizes.

KEY IDEA

Every day, 7400 more people get HIV infection and 5500 AIDS patients die. However, the spread of HIV appears to have peaked and the epidemic appears to have stabilized in most regions except in Asia.

Table 17.1 presents the key figures from the UN AIDS Epidemic Update December 2009.

Table 17.1 World AIDS Status 2008
(Source: www.unaids.org)

Category	Number living with AIDS in 2008 (Millions)	Number newly infected in 2008 (Millions)	AIDS deaths in 2008 (Millions)
Men	15.6		
Women	15.7		
Total adults	31.3	2.30	1.70
Children under 15 years	2.1	0.43	0.28
Total	33.4	2.73	1.98

How is AIDS spreading among women? The most disturbing aspect of the AIDS scene is that the epidemic is affecting women and girls in increasing numbers:

- 50 per cent of the 33.4 million adults living with HIV are women—up from 35 per cent in 1985.
- Women and girls make up almost 57 per cent of all people infected with HIV in sub-Saharan Africa, where a striking 76 per cent of young people (aged 15–24 years) living with HIV are female.
- Women constitute 35 per cent of all adult HIV infections in Asia—up from 17 per cent in 1990.

- In most other regions, women and girls represent an increasing proportion of people living with HIV.
- AIDS is the leading cause of death for African-American women ages 25–34.
- Adolescent girls face HIV-infection rates up to 5 to 6 times higher than those of boys.

Many women are dangerously unaware of the risks of HIV infection and of the ways to protect themselves from it. Upto 60 per cent of young women in high-prevalence countries did not know the basic facts about AIDS. Generally, women also lack adequate access to prevention services and methods.

Young women are especially vulnerable to HIV for both biological and social reasons. Only 38 per cent of young women have accurate and comprehensive knowledge of HIV. They are also physically more susceptible to infection than men are and they often lack the self-confidence to resist sexual advances.

The vulnerability of women and girls to HIV infection, however, arises more from gender inequality than from just ignorance. Most women around the world become HIV-infected through their partners' high-risk behaviour, over which they have almost no control. This is particularly true of Asia, where more than 90 per cent of the 1.7 million women living with HIV became infected by their husbands.

Further, in many countries, gender discrimination means that the treatment needs of males often come first. Families are also hesitant to send women to clinics for fear of disrupting the 'care economy' that these women provide through their household duties. Often, these duties include taking care of other family members with AIDS.

Just as in family planning, better education and greater empowerment of women are the key necessities in AIDS prevention. We have to safeguard women's legal rights and provide them with equal access to health care.

How are children affected by AIDS?

Roughly 17.5 million children under the age of 18 have lost one or both parents to AIDS, including nearly 14.1 million children in sub-Saharan Africa. Millions more have been affected, with a vastly increased risk of poverty, homelessness, school dropout, discrimination, and loss of life opportunities. These hardships include illness and death. Of the estimated 1.98 million people who died of AIDS-related illnesses in 2008, 280,000 were children under 15 years old.

Orphans and vulnerable children are at higher risk of missing out on schooling, live in households with less food security, suffer anxiety and depression, and are in greater danger of exposure to HIV. In many places, children suffer the adverse effects of HIV/AIDS long before they are orphaned. Millions live in households with sick and dying family members. Many children or adolescents whose families are affected by AIDS, especially girls, are forced to drop out of school in order to work or care for their sick parents or younger siblings. They face an increased risk of engaging in hazardous labour and of being otherwise exploited.

KEY IDEA

Women and children are much more vulnerable than men to AIDS and its consequences.

Grandparents are increasingly shouldering the burden of care for orphans. Families that have taken in orphans become poorer because the household income will have to sustain more dependents. Hence, the children may be required to work and help sustain the families.

AIDS is also destroying the protective network of adults in children's lives. Many teachers, health workers, and other adults on whom children rely are also dying. Because of the time lag between HIV infection and death from AIDS, the crisis will worsen for many years to come.

What is the AIDS situation in India?

Although India is considered a low-prevalence country, it has the world's third largest HIV burden, behind South Africa and Nigeria. 60 per cent of the 2.2 million people living with HIV in the country are concentrated in six high prevalence states—Andhra Pradesh, Karnataka, Maharashtra, Tamil Nadu, Manipur, and Nagaland.

India's epidemic is largely driven by sexual transmission. However, injecting drug use is the main mode of HIV transmission in the north-eastern part of the country. The growth in HIV infections among women over the years is especially striking.

Stigma and discrimination towards people living with HIV and populations at higher risk, both at the community level and within the health sector itself, continue to pose a significant barrier to accessing services. Despite these trends, progress is being made on the prevention and treatment fronts.

In India, people in the age group of 15–29 years comprise about 25 per cent of the country's population; however, they account for 31 per cent of AIDS burden. This clearly indicates that young people are at high risk of contracting HIV infection.

KEY IDEA
India has the third largest number of people with HIV.

Over the past few years, India has strengthened its AIDS response by expanding prevention, treatment and care programmes for populations at higher risk, increasing services for HIV-positive pregnant mothers and scaling up HIV testing and counselling services. Access to antiretroviral therapy rose from 32 per cent in 2008 to 45 per cent in 2009.

Where can hope spring from for the women and children of the world?

We can perhaps draw some hope from the fact that a number of women activists and environmentalists have joined the struggle for conserving the environment and preventing human-induced disasters and accidents. They are also trying to hold the polluters responsible for the consequences.

In the previous chapters, we reviewed the contribution of some better-known environmentalists:

• Wangari Maathai, who founded the Green Belt Movement in Kenya (Chapter 9, Box 9.6)
• Julia Butterfly Hill, who did a tree sit-in for two years, to save the California redwoods (Chapter 9, Box 9.8)
• Lois Marie Gibbs, who raised the issue of toxic dumps to the national level in the US (Chapter 16, Box 16.5)

We also discovered how ordinary and poor women made remarkable contributions, like the Chipko activists in Tehri-Garhwal (Chapter 9, Box 9.5) and Thimmakka, the tree planter (Chapter 9, Box 9.7). There are of course many other women environmentalists in India and abroad.

Ending on a hopeful note: Positive stories

- Rashida Bee and Champa Devi Shukla have been fighting for justice in the Bhopal Case (Box 17.4).
- Launched in 2007, India's Red Ribbon Express is the region's largest mass mobilization effort against HIV. The train stops at 180 stations across the country each year and is expected to reach 6.2 million people in more than 50,000 villages with critical information on HIV prevention. HIV testing and general health check-ups are provided to the villagers. Six performing teams disembark the train on a fleet of bicycles to visit dozens of villages during each station stop, staging plays and skits about preventing HIV infection and fighting HIV-related stigma and discrimination.

BOX 17.4

The story of Rashida Bee and Champa Devi: Two women take on big business

The two women first met as employees at a stationery factory in 1986 where they founded an independent union to fight for better labour conditions and wages (traditionally male-dominated unions would not accept them). In 1989, they led a 750 km march to New Delhi, presented a petition to the Prime Minister, and won a wage raise and other important concessions. Rashida Bee and Champa Devi Shukla, however, were destined to fight a much bigger battle—to seek justice for the Bhopal gas victims.

Bee and Shukla are themselves survivors of the tragedy. Since 1984, Bee has lost six family members to cancer. Shukla, who has one grandchild born with congenital deformities, lost her husband and her health.

Buoyed by their success with the labour union, the two women decided to join the Bhopal struggle. The long-suffering victims have found new hope in Bee and Shukla. They have ignited the international campaign to seek justice for the survivors.

The two have drawn poor and illiterate women like themselves from the margins of society to the centre of an unequal struggle. The aim is to hold Union Carbide and Dow Chemical accountable for the disaster, bring the executives to trial, get them to provide long-term health care and economic support to survivors and their children, and to clean up the site.

In 2002 Bee and Shukla organized a 19–day hunger strike in New Delhi to press their demands. In 2003, they confronted Dow officials at their offices in Mumbai and the Netherlands with hand-delivered samples of toxic waste. They also toured more than 10 cities across the US ending with a passionate protest at Dow's shareholder meeting in Michigan and a 12–day hunger strike on New York's Wall Street. They are also party to the case against Union Carbide filed in US by the survivors.

Their leadership has energized the International Campaign for Justice in Bhopal and catapulted the issue onto the global stage once more. In their journey, Bee and Shukla have had to overcome poverty, their status as women in a male-dominated society, and, in Bee's case, illiteracy. They have also had to struggle with chronic health problems.

The two women have worked together in a complementary way. Bee's oratory ability and Shukla's quiet diligence and strength have together made a powerful combination. For their selfless contribution to the cause of Bhopal survivors, they were awarded the Goldman Environmental Prize in 2004.

REVIEW: A SUMMARY OF THE KEY POINTS

- Environmental degradation has a greater impact on women than on men.
- Compared to men, women share a greater burden of the household work and toil for longer hours.
- Rural women are exposed to dangerous levels of indoor pollution from burning biomass fuels in traditional cookstoves and this problem has not been addressed adequately.
- Million of rural women collect and sell fuelwood. They get very little benefit, though the trade is worth billions of rupees.
- Scarcity of water and lack of sanitation facilities place women under particular stress, especially in urban slums.

- Though more and more women are joining the workforce, real socio-economic empowerment eludes them.
- There are 250 million child workers in the world, with the largest number found in India. Many work as bonded labour.
- HIV/AIDS is affecting women and children in increasing numbers.
- Many women activists have been making great contributions to environmental conservation and justice.

EXERCISES

Objective-type questions

For each question below, choose the best answer out of the given choices.

1. What is the most serious problem with regard to the use of cookstoves that burn wood?
   (a) Wood needs to be collected.
   (b) Consumes a lot of time.
   (c) Men have to find time.
   (d) Women inhale the toxic smoke.

2. Which of the following statements is **not** true with regard to the use of cookstoves that burn wood?
   (a) Toxic pollutants are released.
   (b) Requires continual feeding with wood.
   (c) Safe smokless chulhas are widely used.
   (d) Outdoor pollution may also be increased.

3. Which of the following statements is **not** true with regard to child labour?
   (a) Most child workers are provided with education.
   (b) Children could be in bonded labour.
   (c) Children often do not get proper wages.
   (d) Children work for long hours.

4. In which way does HIV **not** spread?
   (a) By sexual contact.
   (b) By blood transfusion.
   (c) By sharing food with an infected person.
   (d) By sharing injection needles.

5. Which of the following statements is **not** true with regard to the status of HIV AIDS?
   (a) Antiretroviral therapy has no beneficial effects.
   (b) The spread of HIV appears to have peaked.
   (c) The epidemic is affecting women and girls in increasing numbers.
   (d) Millions of children have become orphans.

Short-answer questions

1. How does the fuelwood business work in India and what is the role of women in it?
2. What is the cause of high levels of indoor pollution in rural households and what is its effect on women?
3. Describe the problems faced by a child working as bonded labour in one of the hazardous industries.
4. What are the problems faced by children who are either AIDS victims or live in AIDS-affected families?
5. Describe the current status of the AIDS epidemic with particular reference to women and children.
6. Describe the work of any two women activists working for environmental conservation and justice.

Long-answer questions

Write an essay on the challenges faced by poor (rural and urban) women in India. What is their role in the household? How do environmental problems affect them? Where do they find employment and what are the hazards they face in their work? How does the HIV/AIDS epidemic affect them?

Think critically: Deeper questions for reflection and discussion

What is it that drives the business owners to mistreat and abuse children (for example, the way Iqbal Masih and others were treated in the carpet units)? How can we begin to change the situation?

SOMETHING DIFFERENT FOR A CHANGE

Here is a poem by Stephanie Ray, who was born in 1986 with AIDS, not just infected with HIV. Her mother, who contracted the disease from a transfusion, passed it to her and died in 1992. Doctors expected Stephanie would survive only to age 2 or 3. Stephanie not only survived, but became a young advocate for people with AIDS. This poem was taken from the website: http://earthrenewal.org/children.htm.

Listen to my heart speak....
Please look at me and see
I a.m. just a child
Trying to live with aids/hiv

It was given to me by my
Mother passed on to me
At birth and now I'm trying
To live my life giving it my
Best while here on earth

Listen to my heart speak
To those who are afraid
Showing kindness touching
And hugging me will not
Give you hiv or aids

I know what it feels like to live
With pain when people I love
Are sick and go away
Smiling and laughing
Sometimes can be a strain

Listen to my heart speak
Please, please hear
What I say let us love one
Another for I, like you
May be here just for today.

ACTIVITIES

Act: What you can do to promote the welfare of women and children

1. Find out more about child labour in India in occupations like carpet weaving, silk industry, matchbox and firecracker units. Beginning with yourself, campaign for a boycott of products that come out of child labour. Join groups that campaign against firecrackers from the environmental and child labour angles.
2. Connect with the global AIDS response through AIDSspace.org. This is an online community for the people living with HIV and the millions who are part of the AIDS response. AIDSspace.org was created to expand both informal and established

networks in order to help maximize resources for a stronger response to the epidemic. Through AIDSspace members can meet and connect with other members to: learn from their work; exchange ideas and discover new networks; post and share key policies, best practices, multimedia materials, reports and other essential resources; and access and post jobs, consultancies and requests for proposals and become a service provider.

Learn by doing: Case study / Project

1. Offer your services as a volunteer to an organization that is working either in eradicating child labour or helping AIDS patients. Study the problems faced by

the target group, the attempts to help the group or solve the problems, any preventive actions that are being taken, and so on. Write a report on your work.

2. Visit an organization that has been promoting 'smokeless chulha'. Study the different designs that have been tried. What were the difficulties faced in promoting the use of efficient cookstoves? What is the feedback from the women who use them? What can be done to popularise such stove sin a big way? Write a report on your study.

Organize together: Eco-club activities and projects

1. Observe the International Women's Day on March 8
2. Observe the National Children's Day on November 14
3. Observe World AIDS Day on December 1: Since 1988, December 1 is being observed as the World AIDS Day. It is the only international day of coordinated action against AIDS. The Day celebrates progress made in the battle against the epidemic and brings into

focus remaining challenges. In the process, it creates greater awareness of AIDS among the people. Each year, a theme is chosen for the Day to highlight the ways in which HIV affects different groups of people. Information on the year's theme, posters, etc., can be seen on the website www.worldaidsday.org/

4. Form a Red Ribbon Club in your college. It is a voluntary on-campus intervention programme for students in educational institutions. It is initiated and supported by the State AIDS Prevention and Control Societies and implemented through multi-sectoral collaboration, particularly using the services of cadre officers of the State's NSS. The club will provide youth with access to information on HIV/AIDS and voluntary blood donation. The club also works towards promotion of life skills to bring about behavioural change among the youth. For more information, access the website www.nacoonline.org/Quick_Links/Youth/.

LEARN MORE

Books

Mishra, Vinod, Robert D. Retherford and Kirk R.Smith 2002, *Indoor Air Pollution: The Quiet Killer,* East West Center, Hawaii.

Whiteside, Alan 2008, *HIV/AIDS: A Very Short Introduction,* Oxford University Press, New York.

UN-HABITAT 2003, *Water and Sanitation in the World's Cities: Local Action for Global Goals,* U.N. Human Settlements Programme, Earthscan, London.

Articles

Katakam, Anupama 2001, 'On the Scrap Heap', *Frontline,* Vol. 18, No. 15, August 3, pp. 89–92.

Mahapatra, Richard 2002, 'Phulmai's Walk', *Down To Earth,* Vol. 11, No. 14, December 15, pp. 25–34. (on women headloaders)

Narain, Sunita 2003, 'Killing the High-End Killer', *Down To Earth,* Vol. 12, No. 4, July 15, p. 5. (on cookstove pollution)

Websites

Child labour (Human Rights Watch): www.hrw.org/children/labor/

Children with AIDS: http://earthrenewal.org/children.htm

India's National AIDS Control Organization: www.nacoonline.org

Iqbal Masih: www.mirrorimage.com/iqbal/, en.wikipedia.org/wiki/Iqbal_Masih

Rashida Bee and Champa Devi Shukla: www.goldmanprize.org/

State of the World Population (with focus on women and youth: www.unfpa.org/swp/

UN AIDS Programme: www.unaids.org

World's Women 2010—Trends and Statistics: http://unstats.un.org/unsd/demographic/products/Worldswomen/WW2010pub.htm

Module 7

Social Issues and the Environment

CHAPTER 18

Sustainable Development

You tell us to take land in Gujarat. You tell us to take compensation. For losing our lands, our fields, for the trees along our fields.
But how are you going to compensate us for our forest?
How will you compensate us for our river—for her fish, her water,
for the vegetables that grow along her banks,
for the joy of living beside her?
What is the price for this?
Our gods, and the support of our kin—what price do you put on that? Our adivasi life—
what price do you put on that?

Excerpt from a letter written in 1994 by **Bava Mahalia of Jalsindhi,** one of the
Narmada Dam-affected villages, to the Chief Minister of Madhya Pradesh

THIS CHAPTER IS ABOUT...

Displacement, resettlement and rehabilitation of people, impact of dams on people, sustainable
development, green economy

THE KEYWORDS AND PHRASES ARE...

green economy   green business

THE STORY OF MANIBELI: DISPLACEMENT AND RESISTANCE

'*My children will never till the hill slopes. It is unthinkable. My father tilled here. I walked by his side as a child, knowing that I would be doing the same when I grow older. I cannot give my children these assurances. I cannot give them anything because whatever I have is suddenly not mine,*' said Jatrabhai, a 70-year-old resident of Manibeli village in the north of Maharashtra.

Manibeli, with 140 residents, was the first village to be affected by the Sardar Sarovar Dam project on the River Narmada. For the tribal people of Manibeli it had been a long struggle. The authorities had tried to resettle these villagers right from 1983. About 100–odd families were moved to Parveta. The land offered to them as compensation was in a very bad condition and the monetary compensation was less than half of what was promised.

Meanwhile, the Narmada Bachao Andolan (NBA) had been formed and the fight for proper resettlement and rehabilitation had begun. Manibeli became famous during the satyagraha undertaken by the people in June 1991. With the waters steadily rising, the first batch of the NBA's Samarpit Dal ('drowning squad') sat in dharna in a hut at the lowest level. This hut became the NBA headquarters in July 1991. On August 3, district police raided Manibeli and arrested 63 people.

By March 1992, hundreds of policemen virtually laid siege to the village. There were forcible evictions and a number of other atrocities. During July-September 1992, the second Manibeli satyagraha was organised. Rains lashed the area and the water level began to rise in the hut where the satyagrahis sat. But they did not move. In December, the authorities served fresh eviction notices, which were challenged in the courts.

The final siege of Manibeli by the police occurred in May-June 1993, when only 14 families were left in the village. Their demand for adequate compensation had not been met and they would not compromise.

On July 16, 1993, the river rose rapidly and submerged the huts of the 14 villagers. Manibeli, which had become synonymous with the NBA's struggle against the Sardar Sarovar Project (SSP), disappeared along with the 1,000-year-old Shurpaneshwar temple.

The remaining villagers shifted to a higher level. As the height of the dam increased, the waters rose higher up the hill slope. When the water level reached too close for comfort, the villagers would dismantle their homes and move further up the hill. In this way, the residents relocated their homes and fields thrice.

Once they reached the very top of the hill, they had literally nowhere to go. In August 2006, the river fully encircled and covered the Manibeli hill. It was the end of a saga.

Manibeli, however, lives on as the symbol of resistance and struggle. On October 3, 1994, over 2,000 NGOs from 44 countries issued the Manibeli Declaration calling for a moratorium on World Bank funding of large dam projects.

What are the lessons of the Narmada case?

The story of displacement and distress is common to many of the affected villages of Narmada Valley. Nobody knows exactly how many families are affected by the project. Estimates are 35,000 in Madhya Pradesh and about 5,000 each in Gujarat and Maharashtra, but the real numbers are likely to be much more. Further, the numbers keep going up as the dam height is increased. The numbers also do not tell the story of repeated relocation of some families. In general, the resettlement and rehabilitation process has been incomplete and unsatisfactory.

The story highlights the displacement aspect of the Narmada Project and illustrates the problems faced by poor people who are displaced by development projects. Such stories are common to many large projects in different parts of the world. There are many other aspects of dams like the high costs, loss of biodiversity, radical changes in the ecosystem, siltation, impact on fishing, etc. There are also the possible benefits like generation of power, supply of water for drinking and irrigation, and promotion of tourism.

In this chapter, we will consider the issues of displacement, resettlement, and rehabilitation. We will then raise the question whether this kind of development could ever be sustainable. That will lead us to alternative concepts such as new economics and green economy.

What are reasons for displacement of populations?

Millions of people have had to leave their homes and move to other places, cities, or foreign countries for a variety of reasons:

- Conflicts like wars between countries, civil wars, ethnic conflicts, and religious persecution
- Natural disasters like cyclones, hurricanes, tsunamis, floods, earthquakes, volcano eruptions, and drought
- Environmental disasters like industrial mishaps, nuclear accidents, pollution of water bodies, toxic contamination of sites, and oil spills
- Development projects in various sectors:
  - Water supply (dams, reservoirs, irrigation)
  - Urban infrastructure (roads, flyovers, beach resorts, etc.)
  - Transportation (roads, highways, canals)
  - Energy (mining, power plants, oil exploration and extraction, pipelines)
  - Agricultural expansion
  - Forests (conversion into national parks and reserves)
- Economic needs (in search of a livelihood or for improving the quality of life)
- Forcible relocation by the government under population redistribution schemes as it happened in South Africa under apartheid, China during the Cultural Revolution and the Soviet Union in the Stalinist era.

The reasons for displacement are often interconnected. For example, a family displaced by the construction of a dam loses its livelihood and hence moves to another place for economic reasons.

When people leave an area, they may leave behind environmental problems like abandoned agricultural land. Their migration also poses environmental problems in the area into which they move. There are large refugee camps in the world that have become permanent settlements lacking in basic amenities. In other cases, the refugee group upsets the balance of the area by making unsustainable demands on the natural resources.

The UN High Commission for Refugees predicts that economic and environmental refugees will continue to make up a significant percentage of the total refugee populations around the world, and that the number will only increase as more damage is done to the environment and as more countries become globalized and offer better opportunities than their host countries.

What are the displacement problems created by development projects?

People who are forced to flee from a disaster or conflict usually receive sympathetic attention and international aid. The same cannot be said about the millions of people worldwide who have been displaced by development, even though the consequences they face may be every bit as grave as those faced by people displaced by other forces.

In the past, the dominant view was that large-scale development projects accelerated the pace toward a brighter and better future. If people were displaced along the way, that was deemed a necessary evil.

In recent times, however, a new development paradigm has been articulated, one that promotes poverty reduction, environmental protection, social justice, and human rights. In this paradigm, development is seen as both bringing benefits and imposing costs. Among its greatest costs has been the displacement of millions of vulnerable people.

The World Bank estimates that every year since 1990, roughly 10 million people worldwide have been displaced by development projects for a variety of reasons. During the last 50 years,

KEY IDEA

Millions of people in the world have been displaced from their homes and lands due to development projects and environmental changes.

development projects have displaced 25 million people in India and 40 million in China (of whom, 13.6 million were displaced in the 1990s alone). Read about China's Three Gorges Dam in Box 18.1.

The displaced people may not have crossed a border and may not be considered to be in 'refugee-like' circumstances within their own country. Nevertheless, they have been evicted from their homes or places of habitual residence, had their lives and livelihoods disrupted, and face the uncertainties of resettling in unfamiliar and often inhospitable locations.

BOX 18.1

The story of the Three Gorges Dam: A dragon tamed by technology?

Until recently, Huang Zongjin was a poor farmer cultivating rice and vegetables on the banks of the Yangtze river near Wushan town in China. One day, his world changed, suddenly and totally. He has now become Huang the boatman, ferrying tourists up the Yangtze.

The Government had decided to build a dam on the Yangtze (known in China as 'the dragon'), just downstream from the place known as Three Gorges. Huang and more than 700,000 others were asked to move leaving their homes and fields, which were to be submerged in water.

If completed, the Three Gorges Dam on the Yangtze will be the largest hydroelectric dam in the world. It will stretch nearly 1.5 km across and tower 200 m above the world's third longest river. Construction began in 1994 and is scheduled to take 20 years and cost over US$ 24 billion. The river is no longer seen as an unstoppable force, but as a dragon, which can be tamed by technology.

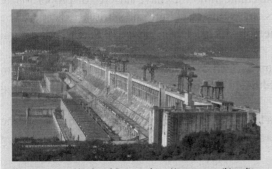

(Image courtesy: Le Grand Portage, http://commons.wikimedia.org/wikiFile:ThreeGorgesDam- China2009.jpg)

The expected benefits of the dam include the prevention of the devastating Yangtze basin floods, which have killed millions of people, and the generation of 18,200 MW of electricity, supplying a tenth of China's needs. The power generated would be equivalent to operating more than a dozen nuclear power plants or burning 50 million tons of coal. It is a remarkable feat of engineering.

Outside China, the project has been strongly criticised for the corruption, secrecy, financial incompetence, human rights violations, and possible environmental consequences. The reservoir will partially or completely inundate 2 cities, 11 counties, 140 towns, 326 townships, and 1,351 villages.

Between one and two million people will have to be resettled, accounting for about one third of the project's cost. Many critics believe resettlement would fail and create reservoir refugees. The forced migration would raise social unrest. Many of the residents to be resettled are peasants. They would be forced to move from fertile farmland to much less desirable areas.

By October 2003, the second stage was over, the water had risen, 700,000 people had been relocated, and the dam was finally producing electricity. The Dam reached its maximum reservoir water level of 175 m in October 2010. It should now be able to generate full power.

Most of the people seem to be either positive or fatalistic about the dam. Huang Zongjin used his compensation money to buy the dilapidated boat. The government has built the family a new, far bigger, hillside home, but as yet it has no running

Contd

Box 18.1 Contd

water or electricity. The land is too steep to be cultivated.

Huang, however, is sanguine. 'I may float over my old home every day, but I never think about it. What's the point?' he says. 'We can't change anything. And besides, life is better now. We have a new home, more space and more money. The dam has been good for us.'

Is it good for everybody? Is it good for the environment? Will the dam surprise everybody one day with its secrets?

What are the special problems with regard to displacement by dams?

After a multi-year study, the World Commission on Dams listed the following social impacts of dams in its report published in 2000:

- Dams have physically displaced some 40–80 million people worldwide.
- Millions of people living downstream from dams—particularly those reliant on natural floodplain function and fisheries—have also suffered serious harm to their livelihoods and the future productivity of their resources has been put at risk.
- Many of the displaced were not recognised (or enumerated) as such, and therefore were not resettled or compensated.
- Where compensation was provided it was often inadequate, and where the physically displaced were enumerated, many were not included in resettlement programmes.
- Those who were resettled rarely had their livelihoods restored, as resettlement programmes have focused on physical relocation rather than the economic and social development of the displaced.
- The larger the magnitude of displacement, the less likely it is that even the livelihoods of affected communities can be restored.
- Even in the 1990s, impacts on downstream livelihoods were, in many cases, not adequately assessed or addressed in the planning and design of large dams.

The WCD report noted that the poor, other vulnerable groups and future generations were likely to bear a disproportionate share of the social and environmental costs of large dam projects without gaining a commensurate share of the economic benefits:

- Indigenous and tribal peoples and vulnerable ethnic minorities have suffered disproportionate levels of displacement and negative impacts on livelihood, culture and spiritual existence. The outcomes have included assetlessness, unemployment, debt-bondage, hunger, and cultural disintegration.
- Affected populations living near reservoirs as well as displaced people and downstream communities have often faced adverse health and livelihood outcomes from environmental change and social disruption.
- Among affected communities, gender gaps have widened and women have frequently borne a disproportionate share of the social costs and were often discriminated against in the sharing of benefits.

The Report concluded, 'impoverishment and disempowerment have been the rule rather than the exception with respect to resettled people around the world.' The Report gave specific recommendations to national government, NGOs, affected people's organisations, private sector, aid agencies, and development banks on all aspects including displacement and resettlement.

What are the issues concerning the resettlement and rehabilitation of displaced groups?

The majority of displacement and resettlement programmes involving large populations has occurred in the developing countries. The reasons are the massive development projects financed by foreign aid and international agencies and high densities of population.

Some of the problems faced by the displaced people are the following:

- The compensation for the lost land is often not paid or delayed, and even if paid, the amounts are pitifully small. The oustees are rarely able to start new lives with the compensation. To add to the problem, agents and corrupt officials deprive the poor of the full compensation.
- Generally, the new land that is offered is of poor quality and the refugees are unable to make a living.
- Basic infrastructure and amenities are not provided in the new area. Very often, temporary camps become permanent settlements.
- When tribal groups are displaced, they do not get any compensation, since they have no legal title to the land.
- Ethnic and caste differences make it difficult for the refugees to live peacefully with the communities already living in the area.

In India, we are in the process of rapid economic development. Poor people are being increasingly displaced from their homes and lands to make way for a variety of projects: mines, large industries, Special Economic Zones, highways, airports, power plants, educational institutions, dams, canals, national parks, reserve forests, and so on. We have to ask ourselves: Is this unceasing development, displacement of people, and exploitation of natural resources sustainable? What are their real costs?

> **KEY IDEA**
> Resettlement and rehabilitation of displaced people has generally been unsatisfactory.

Is sustainable development still a meaningful concept?

In Chapter 1, we introduced the concept of sustainable development. This concept seems to be a contradiction in terms. If we continue with the current model of economic growth and development, we cannot sustain it indefinitely. If we use the natural resources in a sustainable way, we cannot show continuous economic growth.

While the term 'sustainable development' continues to be used, newer concepts such as New Economics, Green Economy, Green Business, Sustainable Business, and Eco-economy are gaining currency. They are often projected as answers to the challenge posed by Global warming and Climate Change (Chapter 19).

The alternative approaches raise and try to answer questions such as the following:

- In the face of the environmental devastation being caused by current economic systems, how can we move to more sustainable economic models?
- What do the concepts of ecological sustainability and sustainable development really mean and how can they be achieved?
- Can the value of an environment be measured?
- Is GDP the appropriate measure of 'growth'? What is the real 'growth' of a society we should aim at?
- What tools for change exist within the current system?

- How can we make the transition from a global to a local economy, from efficiency to sufficiency?

The objectives that seem to be common to many of these alternative models are to:

- achieve full employment by providing an ongoing means of livelihood for all job seekers.
- protect and restore the environment for present and future generations.
- ensure healthy communities based on the sustainable use of local resources for local consumption and regional trade, the availability of meaningful work and the opportunity for creative, diverse cultural expression.
- measure the success of the economy by the improvement in the well-being of all people and the development of healthy, vibrant, diverse communities, rather than by the total monetary value of economic activity.

We can 'green' the economy by modifying our businesses and infrastructure such that we get proper returns on our natural, human and economic investments, while at the same time reducing greenhouse gas emissions, extracting and using less natural resources, creating less waste and reducing social disparities.

A green economy would focus on areas such as:

- Promoting renewable energies including wind, solar, geothermal and biomass
- Working towards sustainable transport options including hybrid vehicles, high speed rail and bus rapid transit systems
- Restoring and conserving the planet's ecological infrastructure, including freshwaters, forests, soils and coral reefs
- Supporting sustainable agriculture, including organic farming.
- Improving the energy efficiency of old and new buildings

Is Green Economy being promoted in any way?

There are Green Economy initiatives being taken by international agencies, countries, corporate associations, and companies. Here are some examples:

UNEP Green Economy Initiative (GEI) It is designed to assist governments in 'greening' their economies by reshaping and refocusing policies, investments and spending towards a range of sectors, such as clean technologies, renewable energies, water services, green transportation, waste management, green buildings and sustainable agriculture and forests. GEI activities include providing advisory services to countries and regions; producing research reports and engaging in partnerships to effectively promote and implement green economy strategies.

UN ESCAP Green Growth Initiative With the support of the UN Economic and Social Commission for Asia and the Pacific (UN ESCAP), the Governments in the Asian and Pacific region have unanimously agreed to respond to the challenges of simultaneously improving people's lives and conserving natural resources through the promising path of environmentally sustainable economic growth, or 'Green Growth'. This is a strategy to foster creative sustainability responses for the region. Green Growth proposes to harness the power of economic growth while guiding it in a way that will enhance the immense possibilities provided by innovative technologies and industries, so that progress can be registered in more than gross domestic product increases alone.

Country Initiatives   Here are some examples:

- Denmark is moving away from fossil fuels (Chapter 8, Box 8.2)
- Iceland is working towards a hydrogen economy (Chapter 8, Box 8.3)
- South Africa, after holding a Green Economy Summit held in May 2010, is developing a Green Economy Plan. The country is investing on 'green' jobs, railways, energy efficient buildings, and water and waste management.
- Kenya is implementing a US$ 99 million restoration of the entire Mau Forest Complex, the largest closed-canopy forest ecosystem in Kenya covering over 400,000 hectares. The country has committed to go totally green by 2017 and to restore the forest cover to 10 per cent by 2020. Currently, the government has launched a green energy campaign and mobilized $1 billion to construct a 280 MW geothermal power plant.
- Rwanda, Uganda, and other African countries are investing in green economic sectors such as renewable energies and energy efficiency improvements, sustainable agriculture, and better management of water and waste.
- India announced in 2008 a National Action Plan on Climate Change (Chapter 19, Box 19.4). This Plan has many features of a green economy.
- Many developing countries report success stories described in the UNEP Green Economy Report:
  - Renewable energy in China
  - Feed-in tariffs in Kenya (attractive options for generating renewable energy and feeding it into the electricity grid)
  - Organic agriculture in Uganda
  - Sustainable urban planning in Brazil
  - Rural ecological infrastructure in India (through the National Rural Employment Guarantee Scheme)
  - Forest management in Nepal
  - Ecosystem services in Ecuador (water users contribute to a fund that promotes upstream watershed management)
  - Solar energy in Tunisia

UNEP believes that such green investments and policies, if scaled up and integrated into a comprehensive strategy, could offer an alternative development pathway, one that is pro-nature, pro-jobs and pro-poor.

BOX 18.2

The Ceres Principles: Greening the corporation

Ceres offers the following principles as a comprehensive statement of environmental values for businesses within any industry sector. They are intended to help companies formalize their dedication to environmental awareness and accountability, and actively commit to an on-going process of continuous improvement in environmental performance, dialogue, and comprehensive, systematic reporting.

The ten Ceres principles:

- Protection of the Biosphere: We will reduce and make continual progress toward eliminating the release of any substance that may cause environmental damage to the air, water, or the earth

Contd

Box 18.2 Contd

or its inhabitants. We will safeguard all habitats affected by our operations and will protect open spaces and wilderness, while preserving biodiversity.

- Sustainable Use of Natural Resources: We will make sustainable use of renewable natural resources, such as water, soils and forests. We will conserve non-renewable natural resources through efficient use and careful planning.
- Reduction and Disposal of Wastes: We will reduce and where possible eliminate waste through source reduction and recycling. All waste will be handled and disposed of through safe and responsible methods.
- Energy Conservation: We will conserve energy and improve the energy efficiency of our internal operations and of the goods and services we sell. We will make every effort to use environmentally safe and sustainable energy sources.
- Risk Reduction: We will strive to minimize the environmental, health and safety risks to our employees and the communities in which we operate through safe technologies, facilities and operating procedures, and by being prepared for emergencies.
- Safe Products and Services: We will reduce and where possible eliminate the use, manufacture or sale of products and services that cause environmental damage or health or safety hazards. We will inform our customers of the environmental impacts of our products or services and try to correct unsafe use.
- Environmental Restoration: We will promptly and responsibly correct conditions we have caused that endanger health, safety or the environment. To the extent feasible, we will redress injuries we have caused to persons or damage we have caused to the environment and will restore the environment.
- Informing the Public: We will inform in a timely manner everyone who may be affected by conditions caused by our company that might endanger health, safety or the environment. We will regularly seek advice and counsel through dialogue with persons in communities near our facilities. We will not take any action against employees for reporting dangerous incidents or conditions to management or to appropriate authorities.
- Management Commitment: We will implement these Principles and sustain a process that ensures that the Board of Directors and Chief Executive Officer are fully informed about pertinent environmental issues and are fully responsible for environmental policy. In selecting our Board of Directors, we will consider demonstrated environmental commitment as a factor.
- Audits and Reports: We will conduct an annual self-evaluation of our progress in implementing these Principles. We will support the timely creation of generally accepted environmental audit procedures. We will annually complete the Ceres Report, which will be made available to the public.

Ceres   Ceres (pronounced 'series') is a network of investors, environmental organizations and other public interest groups working with companies and investors to address sustainability challenges such as global climate change. The mission of Ceres is to integrate sustainability into capital markets for the health of the planet and its people.

The Ceres coalition of investor groups, environmental organizations, and investment funds engages directly with companies on environmental and social issues. Ceres companies seek to attain long-term business value and to improve management quality through stakeholder engagement, public disclosure and performance improvements. In 2010, there were about 80 Ceres companies.

In 1989, Ceres announced the creation of the Ceres Principles, a ten-point code of corporate environmental conduct to be publicly endorsed by companies as an environmental mission statement or ethic (Box 18.2). Over 50 companies have endorsed the Ceres Principles.

By endorsing the Ceres Principles or adopting their own comparable code, companies not only formalize their dedication to environmental awareness and accountability, but also actively commit to an ongoing process of continuous improvement, dialogue and comprehensive, systematic public reporting.

In 1997, Ceres, in partnership with UNEP, established the Global Reporting Initiative (GRI) with the mission of developing globally applicable guidelines for reporting on the economic, environmental, and social performance of corporations, governments and non-governmental organizations (NGOs). GRI incorporates the active participation of corporations, NGOs, accountancy organizations, business associations and other stakeholders from around the world.

GRI has become the defacto international standard in sustainability reporting and currently, more than 1,500 companies and organizations worldwide issue GRI-based sustainability reports.

Interface   Ray Anderson is the Chairman and founder of Interface, the world's largest manufacturer of commercial carpets, located in the US. The way he is turning Interface into a totally sustainable corporation is a remarkable story (Box 18.3). More companies are following the path of sustainability.

BOX 18.3

The story of Ray Anderson: Building a sustainable corporation

Ray Anderson is the Chairman and founder of Interface, the world's largest commercial carpet manufacturer. The company has 26 factories in 6 countries. In 1994, Anderson realized that, as the head of a company, he was 'plundering' the natural resources of the world. He decided to convert Interface into a totally sustainable green corporation. What he did has now become a legend.

Anderson came up with Ecosense, a vision for 2020. He wanted Interface to become totally sustainable by 2020 and also to help others to become sustainable. He planned the following steps:

- Reduce, reuse, reclaim, redesign
- Adopt best practices, share them
- Develop sustainable technologies
- Challenge suppliers to follow

Since his change of heart, Anderson has implemented hundreds of projects in the company with these objectives in mind:

- Zero waste generation
- Minimum energy use
- Eventual zero use of fossil fuels

Interface now leases out carpets instead of selling them. For a monthly charge, the company installs, cleans, and maintains the carpets. It repairs worn-out tiles and recycles old carpets into new ones.

The company has developed a new carpet material called Solenium, which can be completely recycled. It requires 40 per cent less raw material and energy, generates very little waste, and lasts much longer.

By 2009, Interface had reached a sound position:

- It was halfway towards the goal of total sustainability.
- It has sharply reduced energy use and waste generation and saved millions of dollars.
- The products were the best they have ever been.

Contd

Box 18.3 Contd

- Its people were galvanized around a shared higher purpose.
- The company's goodwill in the marketplace was far better than what any amount of advertisement could have brought.

Interface was ranked number one in the Sustainability Survey, a survey of global sustainability thought leaders conducted by GlobeScan.

Anderson himself gave up his luxury car for a hybrid car and built a home without a grid connection. He was named one of TIME International's 'Heroes of the Environment' in 2007. He's a sought-after speaker and was co-chairman of the President's Council on Sustainable Development and as an architect of the Presidential Climate Action Plan, a 100–day action plan on climate that was presented to the Obama Administration.

The company is a model to follow, because, even as it moved towards sustainability, it tripled its profits. Green business can also be good business.

What can India to promote a Green Economy and green jobs?

Lack of employment is the main source of poverty in India. A study by the Centre for Science and Environment, New Delhi, suggests that the key to generating employment lies in promoting productive and sustainable livelihoods based on natural resources. We should renew and revive the key livelihood areas of agriculture, forestry, livestock, fishing, and horticulture, by promoting sustainable occupations in these sectors. The existing impediments to such development should be removed.

Some examples of such green livelihoods that would generate employment and income and at the same time conserve the environment are:

Bamboo
(Image courtesy: Michele Buzzi, http://commons.
wikimedia.org/wiki/File:Bamboo_DSCN2465.jpg)

Bamboo   It is an exceptionally versatile plant with about 1,500 uses, including as a building material and for making paper, handicrafts, and agricultural appliances. It generates 10 million jobs now and can provide 8.6 million jobs more. The main hurdle is that it remains a monopoly of the forest department. It should be declared as an agricultural item, permitting people to cultivate, harvest, process, and sell it in various forms.

Fuelwood   Wood plantations on degraded land can be promoted and managed by the women headloaders (Chapter 8 and Chapter 17) or the community and fuelwood trade can be legitimised. Apart from generating huge employment, we will also be promoting renewable energy in a big way. The plantations will also give timber for homes and village industries and help regenerate the soil.

Silk   From rearing silkworms to making the fabric, the sector employs about 8 million people in 26 states. At least 3 million more can be employed in this activity if the technology is improved, quality silkworms are made available, and use of non-mulberry sources in forests is allowed.

Sal leaf trade   The sal leaf is collected from the forests of Orissa and other places, processed into disposable cups and plates and sold all over the country. It is an unorganised and yet a profitable multimillion business, employing 1.2 million people in Orissa alone. If the forest laws are rationalised and the business is organised, it can employ five million people for 100 days a year in Orissa alone.

> **KEY IDEA**
> There are attempts in different parts of the world by different groups to move towards a more sustainable 'green' economy.

Tree plantations for pulp and paper sector   An area of about one million hectares can produce the five million tons of raw material the industry needs every year. This could generate employment for 550,000 families.

For such green livelihoods to succeed, changes in laws and policies are needed. There should be a shift from conservation to sustainable utilisation of natural resources. Laws that prohibit the growing, transporting, and marketing of trees like the bamboo should be repealed or modified.

Ending on a hopeful note: Positive stories

While the general rehabilitation scene is depressing, there are some success stories too, like that of Tawa Matsya Sangh in Madhya Pradesh. Even here, the initial success has been followed by problems later (Box 18.4).

BOX 18.4

The story of Tawa Matsya Sangh: From forests to fisheries

Most people displaced by development projects end up losing everything—their lands, livelihood, and shelter. In most cases they do not get any compensation for their lands and even if they do, the amount is grossly inadequate. This story, from Madhya Pradesh, however, is one of hope.

A dam on the River Tawa, a tributary of Narmada, submerged 20,000 hectares and displaced over 4,000 adivasi families in 44 villages. More than half the villages were on forestland and hence the people got no compensation at all.

Normally these oustees would have migrated to other villages or towns in search of livelihoods. This group, however, campaigned for and secured fishing rights in the reservoir created by the dam. The adivasis learnt how to spread nets, use boats, and do the fishing operations.

They formed the Tawa Matsya Sangh (TMS), a federation of primary fishermen's cooperative societies with 1,200 members. In 1996, TMS was given a 5-year lease by the government. TMS was in charge of overall management and was responsible for stocking the reservoir with fish. It also took care

of transport and sale of fish, regulatory measures for conservation, and members' welfare.

The former hunter-gatherers became good fishermen and the harvest was good. TMS made profits and shared it with the members. It even paid wages to them during the lean season, between June and August when there was an agreed ban

Contd

Box 18.4 Contd

fishing. TMS was also able to pay the agreed royalty to the government.

It was a rare case of dam oustees doing well in a new occupation, but troubles were ahead. When the lease was renewed the government steeply increased the royalty amount. In return, however, the government agency did little to improve the infrastructure. Even the promised ice factory was not built. Under the new terms, TMS was also subject to greater government control. In fact, the government appointed a review committee to evaluate the performance of TMS, but did not share the report with them. In December 2006, TMS lost its licence.

Difficult times are ahead for a group that has achieved success against great odds!

REVIEW: A SUMMARY OF THE KEY POINTS

- There is increasing displacement of populations due to a variety of reasons.
- The resettlement and rehabilitation of displaced people have been poor in most projects.
- New concepts such as Green Economy and Green Business have emerged in our search for sustainability.
- Green Economy initiatives are being taken by international agencies, countries, corporate associations, and companies.
- India can follow its own path in developing a Green Economy.

EXERCISES

Objective-type questions

For each question below, choose the best answer out of the given choices:

1. What is the importance of the village Manibeli?
   (a) It is in Maharashtra part of the Narmada Dam project.
   (b) The villagers had to leave Manibeli in 2003.
   (c) It was submerged in the waters in 2006.
   (d) It has become a symbol of resistance and struggle against displacement and lack of proper resettlement.

2. Which of the following may **not** be a case of displacement due to development projects?
   (a) Dam oustees moving to another area.
   (b) Forest tribals resettled outside the forest.
   (c) Poor people coming to cities every day looking for work.
   (d) People leaving an area due to the coming of a new airport.

3. Which of the following statements is **not** true with regard to people displaced due the construction of dams?

   (a) They are always resettled and rehabilitated well.
   (b) The compensation is often poor or not paid.
   (c) The new land that is offered is often of poor quality.
   (d) Very often, temporary camps become permanent settlements.

4. Which of the following **cannot** be a valid and meaningful approach for the world?
   (a) Being sustainable.
   (b) Consume less.
   (c) Exploit nature without limit.
   (d) Respect nature.

5. Which of the following activities would **not** be acceptable in a green economy?
   (a) Generating solar energy
   (b) Organic agriculture
   (c) Burning LPG
   (d) Promoting public transport

Short-answer questions

1. Explain the reasons for the displacement of populations and its impact.

2. Describe the special problems of displacement caused by dams.
3. Discuss the issues concerning the resettlement and rehabilitation of displaced groups.
4. What are the questions raised by those who propose alternate models of economy?
5. Describe any two Green Economy initiatives.
6. Give two examples of green livelihoods that would generate employment and income and at the same time conserve the environment in India.

Long-answer questions

Write an essay on the impact of dams on people. What are the usual expected benefits? What are the negative impacts on people? What does the World Commission on Dams say on the topic? What do the cases of Narmada and the Three Gorges dams illustrate?

Think critically: Deeper questions for reflection and discussion

If constant economic growth is neither possible nor desirable, what kid of 'growth' should a society aim for? Is Mahatma Gandhi's ideas relevant to this question?

SOMETHING DIFFERENT FOR A CHANGE

A poem by the American educator, economist, and peace activist Kenneth Boulding (1910–1993), American economist, systems scientist, peace activist, and poet:

A Conservationist's Lament

The world is finite, resources are scarce,
Things are bad and will be worse,
Coal is burned and gas exploded,
Forests cut and soils eroded.
Wells are dry and air's polluted,
Dust is blowing, trees uprooted.

Oil is going, ores depleted,
Drains receive what is excreted.
Land is sinking, seas are rising,
Man is far too enterprising.
Fire will rage with Man to fan it,
Soon we'll have a plundered planet.
People breed like fertile rabbits,
People have disgusting habits.

Moral: The evolutionary plan went astray by evolving Man.

ACTIVITIES

Learn by doing: Case study / Project

Visit the site of any project that has displaced people. Study the project documents and examine the plans and reports regarding resettlement and rehabilitation. Interview some of the oustees and record their experiences. Write a report outlining what was promised and what was delivered as far as resettlement and rehabilitation were concerned. What are your recommendations?

Organize together: Eco-club activities and projects

Participate in any Green Jobs Fair that may be organized in your area. Even better, organize one in your college. Invite students, young people looking for green jobs, entrepreneurs, companies, NGO's, etc. The Fair could have exhibition stalls and meetings. Exhibitors would promote potential green careers within their organisation. The meetings would cover green careers, need for appropriate environmental education and training, etc.

LEARN MORE

Books

Anderson, Ray 1999, *Mid-Course Correction: Toward a Sustainable Enterprise—The Interface Model,* Peregrinzilla Press, Atlanta.

Anderson, Ray 2009, *Confessions of a Radical Industrialist: Profits, People, Purpose—Doing Business by Respecting the Earth,* St.Martin's Press, New York.

McCully Patrick 1996, *Silenced Rivers: The Ecology and Politics of Large Dams*, Zed Books, London.

Articles

Bavadam, Lyla 2004, 'Sardar Sarovar Project: Rehabilitation Realities', *Frontline,* 29 January, pp. 43–44.

Bavadam, Lyla 2004b, 'Sardar Sarovar Project: Flood of Fears', *Frontline*, August 13, pp. 94–95.

Sethi, Nitin and Vikas Parashar 2004, 'Officially Bankrupt', *Down To Earth*, Vol. 13, No. 5, July 31, pp. 22–35.

Barik, Satyasundar, Ranjan Panda, Deepa Kozhisseri and Mahesh L. 2004, 'The Job Queue', *Down To Earth*, Vol. 13, No. 13. November 30, pp. 26–34. (on green livelihoods)

Menon, Meena 2003, 'Development or Displacement?', *The Hindu*, 9 November. (on Narmada Dam)

Menon, Meena 2002, 'Tawa Matsya Sangh: Fishing for their Lives', *The Hindu Survey of Environment 2002*, The Hindu, Chennai, pp. 99–103.

Websites

Ceres: www.ceres.org

Displacement issues: www.displacement.net

Global Reporting Initiative: www.globalreporting.org

Green Economy: www.neweconomics.org; www.greeneconomics.net

Three Gorges Dam: www.hrw.org; www.irn.org/programs/threeg/

UNEP Green Economy Initiative: www.unep.org/greeneconomy/ (includes the reports *Green Jobs: Towards Decent Work in a Sustainable, Low-Carbon World* and *Green Economy: Developing Countries Success Stories*)

UN ESCAP Green Growth Initiative: www.greengrowth.org

World Commission on Dams: www.dams.org.

Films

A Narmada Diary, a documentary on Sardar Sarovar Dam and the Narmada Bachao Andolan, by Anand Patwardhan

Up the Yangtze, a documentary on the Three Gorges Dam and its impact on the people, by Yung Chang

CHAPTER 19

Global Warming, Acid Rain, and Ozone Depletion

For the first time in history,
my community has had to use air conditioners.
Imagine that, air conditioners in the Arctic.

Sheila Watt-Cloutier
Inuit leader
March 2007

THIS CHAPTER IS ABOUT...

Acid rain, ozone depletion, global warming, climate change, international agreements

THE KEYWORDS AND PHRASES ARE...

acid rain	ozone layer	global warming
greenhouse gas	climate change	Montreal protocol
Kyoto protocol	IPCC	chlorofluorocarbon (CFC)
ozone depleting substance (ODS)	ozone depleting potential (ODP)	

THE STORY OF TUVALU: RISING SEA, SINKING ISLANDS

'I feel sad and angry at the same time, sad that eventually we will have to move, and angry because this is not our doing, but because of doings of others who don't care, who are looking after their own needs and not at the bigger picture.'

That was Paani Laupepa, the Assistant Secretary for the Environment, Tuvalu. He was referring to the soon-to-come evacuation of Tuvalu before it disappears into the ocean as the world's first casualty of global warming.

Tuvalu is a chain of nine coral islands in the South Pacific with a total area of 25 sq km and a population of 11,000. It is one of the smallest and most remote countries, halfway between Hawaii and Australia. It is now a paradise with chalk-white beaches and coconut palms. Soon, however, it will be a paradise lost!

Sea level rise, caused by global warming, is already a fact in Tuvalu. The islands are made of porous fossil coral and water has started flowing up through holes in the ground. The tides are higher and the storms are more frequent and severe.

Waves wash over the island's main roads. Coconut trees stand partly submerged. The small patches of cropland have been rendered unusable because of encroaching saltwater.

Thousands of journalists, researchers and curious onlookers now come to Tuvalu during high-tide months to see the big waves. These visitors bring valuable income to the country. They also spread awareness about global warming when they return their countries.

The people, who survive on agriculture and fishing, are not giving up yet. They may, however, be forced to evacuate the islands within the next 50 years. While Australia does not want them, New Zealand is ready to take half the population and give them farm jobs.

Tuvalu is not alone. Rising sea level threatens also the other Pacific island nations such as Kiribati, Vanuatu, the Marshall Islands, the Cook Islands, Fiji and the Solomon Islands. They have larger populations and where will they all go?

Tuvaluans feel that they are being punished for no fault of theirs. The reckless burning of fossil fuels by the rich countries has resulted in global warming and sea level rise. They have even threatened to filecases against countries like the US and Australia at the International Court of Justice.

Tuvalu may well become the first nation in the world to disappear due to global warming. When the Tuvaluans leave their homes, who will compensate them for the loss of their culture, language, and way of life?

(Image courtesy: Stefan Lins, http://commons.wikimedia. org/wiki/File:Tuvalu_Funafuti_atoll_beach.jpg)

What should the world learn from the story of Tuvalu?

The Tuvalu story shows how interconnected the world's ecosystems are. The effects of environmental degradation are worldwide. Anything we do—driving a car in the US, cutting down a rainforest in Amazonia, or conducting a nuclear test in India—has an impact on the rest of the world.

The story also shows that the people worst affected by global warming will be the poor of the world. They are not causing the environmental damage, but they will pay the price first.

In this chapter, we will look at the causes and consequences of major environmental effects like acid rain, depletion of the ozone layer, and global warming.

What is acid rain?

When atmospheric water droplets combine with a range of man-made chemical air pollutants, acidic rain is formed. It could also be in the form of acidic mist or snow.

The main pollutants involved are oxides of nitrogen and sulphur. In nature, volcanoes, fires, and decomposing matter emit these substances in small amounts. However, since the advent of the Industrial Revolution, human activities have been releasing such pollutants in large quantities. Such emissions are very high in the major industrial centres and have been increasing rapidly since mid-twentieth century.

Automobiles and coal- and oil-fired power stations are major sources of acid-forming compounds. In fact, any burning of coal, oil, and (to a lesser extent) natural gas produces them.

The acid rain ultimately falls on the ground, sometimes hundreds of kilometres from the area in which it formed and generally one to four days later. The effects are quite damaging.

What is the effect of acid rain?

When soil is acidified, it leads to loss of productivity. The acidification damages plant roots and they are not able to draw in enough nutrients to survive and grow.

When trees, particularly conifers, are exposed to acid rain for several years, they lose their leaves and die. This is one of the several causes for the decline of forests in Europe, North America, and Japan. Plants like orchids, lichen, and moss are also very sensitive to acid.

Effect of acid rain on trees

Acid rain falling on lakes and rivers leaves them clear and lifeless. Thousands of lakes in Sweden, Norway, and Canada, for example, have been permanently affected by acid. Fish populations have died and so did species like otters, amphibians, and birds that depended on fish for their food.

Acid rain harms people directly when they breathe in the acidic air. Acid rain can also harm people indirectly, when they eat fish caught in affected lakes or rivers.

Old buildings are also threatened by acid rain; the famous St Paul's Cathedral in London has decayed more in the last fifty years than in the previous two centuries. Some famous statues, such as the Lincoln Memorial and Michaelangelo's statue of Marcus Aurelius, have started deteriorating because of acid rain. The same is true of many historic buildings in Europe.

The Taj Mahal was also threatened by acid rain caused by factories in Agra. Thanks to the orders of the Supreme Court some of these industries have been shifted or closed down.

A side effect of acid rain is the leaching of aluminium out of the soil into water bodies. Aluminium is very toxic to fish and the birds that prey on the fish. Sometimes acidification leads to the leaching of cadmium and this can affect animals.

> **KEY IDEA**
>
> Acid rain is formed when atmospheric water droplets combine with a range of man-made chemical air pollutants. Acid rain had adverse effects on trees, fish populations, human beings, buildings, etc.

What can be done about acid rain?

Acid rain occurring in a place could be caused by emissions from far away. In most cases, acid rain formed in one country falls on some other country. It is also difficult to prove that a particular country or a factory was responsible, or to quantify the amount of contributing pollution from a source.

Pouring powdered limestone into water bodies is a rapid, but short-lived, method of reducing acidity. A more permanent, but slow and expensive, method is the liming of surrounding soils.

Some technologies for reducing emissions are flue gas desulphurisation in power stations and catalytic converters and engine modifications in automobiles. The best way, of course, is to reduce emissions.

What is the problem of ozone layer depletion?

Ozone is a poisonous gas made up of molecules consisting of three oxygen atoms. This gas is extremely rare in the atmosphere, representing just three out of every 10 million molecules. 90 per cent of ozone exists in the upper atmosphere, or stratosphere, between 10 and 50 km above the earth.

The ozone layer in the atmosphere absorbs most of the harmful ultraviolet-B (UV-B) radiation from the sun. It also completely screens out the deadly UV-C radiation. The ozone shield is thus essential to protect life.

Depleting the ozone layer allows more UV-B to reach the earth. The result would be an increase in skin cancers, eye cataracts, weakened immune systems, reduced plant yields, damage to ocean ecosystems and reduced fishing yields, and adverse effects on animals.

In the 1970s, scientists discovered that when CFCs (chlorofluorocarbons, used as refrigerants and aerosol propellants), finally break apart in the atmosphere and release chlorine atoms, they cause ozone depletion. Bromine atoms released by halons (used in fire extinguishers) have the same effect. These are called ozone depleting substances (ODS).

KEY IDEA

The ozone layer over the earth depletes due the human use of certain chemicals. The depletion of the ozone layer has several harmful effects on human beings and ecosystems.

When measurements started in the early 1980s, scientists noticed that the ozone layer over the Antarctic was weakening. The land area under the ozone-depleted atmosphere increased steadily to more than 20 million sq km in the early 1990s and has varied between 20 and 29 million sq. km since then. In 2000, the area of the ozone hole reached a record 29 million sq. km.

While no hole has appeared elsewhere, the Arctic spring has seen the ozone layer over the North Pole thin by up to 30 per cent. The depletion over Europe and other high latitudes varied between 5 per cent and 30 per cent.

What are the international initiatives against the depletion of the ozone layer?

Inter-governmental negotiations for an international agreement to phase out ozone-depleting substances started in 1981 and concluded with the adoption of the Vienna Convention for the Protection of the Ozone Layer in March 1985.

The Vienna Convention encouraged intergovernmental cooperation on research, systematic observation of the ozone layer, monitoring of CFC production, and the exchange of information. The Convention committed the signatories to take general measures to protect human health and the environment against human activities that modify the ozone layer. The Vienna Convention was a framework agreement and did not contain legally binding controls or targets.

The Vienna Convention set an important precedent. For the first time nations agreed in principle to tackle a global environmental problem before its effects were felt, or even scientifically proven.

In May 1985, British scientists published their discovery of severe ozone depletion over the Antarctic. Their findings were confirmed by American satellite observations and offered the first proof of severe ozone depletion. The discovery of the ozone 'hole' shocked the world. It is regarded as one of the major environmental disasters of the 20th century.

The governments now recognized the need for stronger measures to reduce the production and consumption of a number of CFCs and several halons. As a result, the Montreal Protocol on Substances that Deplete the Ozone Layer was adopted in September 1987.

Ninety-six chemicals are presently controlled by the Montreal Protocol and phase-out schedules. The Protocol was designed so that these schedules could be revised on the basis of periodic scientific and technological assessments.

In 2009 the Montreal Protocol became the first UN treaty to achieve universal ratification (that is, by all the member countries), demonstrating the world's commitment to ozone protection, and more broadly, to global environmental conservation.

What have been the results so far?

The Montreal Protocol has been an outstanding success and the 2009 status was as follows:

- As of the end of 2009, the Parties to the Protocol had phased out the consumption of 98 per cent of all of the chemicals controlled by the Protocol.
- There was strong evidence that global ODS concentrations were decreasing and that the global stratosphere had already experienced its highest levels of ozone depletion from man-made halocarbons.
- Outside the Polar Regions the ozone layer has shown some initial signs of recovery. Assuming continued compliance with the Protocol, global ozone levels are estimated to recover to the pre-1980 values around 2050.
- Polar ozone loss will remain large and highly variable in the coming decades. Assuming continued compliance with the Protocol, Arctic ozone levels are expected to return to pre-1980 levels before 2050, while Antarctic ozone is expected to do so in 2060–2075.

It is estimated that without the Protocol, by the year 2050 ozone depletion would have risen to at least 50 per cent in the northern hemisphere's mid latitudes and 70 per cent in the southern mid latitudes, about 10 times worse than current levels. The result would have been a doubling of the UV-B radiation reaching the earth in the highly populated northern mid latitudes and a quadrupling in the southern latitudes.

The amount of ODS in the atmosphere would then have been five times greater. The implications of this would have been horrendous, and have been estimated to include: 20 million more cases of cancer, and 130 million more cases of eye cataracts, if there had been no Montreal Protocol.

In 1986 the total consumption of CFCs worldwide was about 1.1 million ODP (Ozone Depleting Potential) tonnes; by 2006 this had come down to about 35,000 tonnes. The bulk of the 1986 total, or about 0.9 million tones weighted in terms of ODP, was consumed in developed countries, but this figure declined to about 1,000 tonnes in 2006.

We saw that the Montreal Protocol has resulted in the phasing out of over 98 per cent of all ozone-depleting substances. As most of these substances are also potent greenhouse gases, the Protocol has delivered substantial climate benefits too. It is estimated that the reduction in ozone depleting substances between the peak levels in the 1990s and the year 2000 has yielded a net integrated reduction of approximately 25 billion tonnes of global greenhouse gases.

KEY IDEA

The Montreal Protocol has been a great success and, as a result, the ozone layer could recover before the end of the century.

The success of ozone protection has been possible because science and industry were able to develop and commercialise alternatives to ozone-depleting chemicals. Developed countries ended the use of CFCs faster and with less cost than was originally anticipated.

What have been the lessons of the Montreal Protocol?

The efforts of the world community to protect the ozone layer are a fascinating example of how humanity can act as one to face a common danger. The Protocol offers many lessons that could be applied to solving other global environmental issues:

- Adhere to the 'precautionary principle' because waiting for complete scientific proof can delay action to the point where the damage will become irreversible.
- Send consistent and credible signals to industry (e.g., by adopting legally binding phase-out schedules) so that they have an incentive to develop new and cost-effective alternative technologies.
- Ensure that improved scientific understanding can be incorporated quickly into decisions about the provisions of a treaty.
- Promote universal participation by recognizing the 'common but differentiated responsibility' of developing and developed countries and ensuring the necessary financial and technological support to developing countries.
- Base control measures on an integrated assessment of science, economics, and technology.

Is the global climate changing?

Weather is the condition of the atmosphere at a particular place and time, such as the temperature, humidity, rain, wind, etc. Climate is the long-term pattern of weather conditions for a given area.

Until the middle of the 20th century, the earth's climate was generally regarded as unchanging, but it is now known to be in a continuous and delicate state of flux. Relatively small changes in climate could have major effect on our resources like food, energy, and water.

The factors that influence global climate are the flow of solar energy, the condition of the atmosphere, the shape and rotation of the earth, and the currents and other processes of the ocean.

What is global warming and how does it occur?

Recall the way the carbon cycle works (Chapter 2). During photosynthesis, plants absorb carbon dioxide and release oxygen. Organisms breathe in this oxygen, and give out carbon dioxide, which goes back to the plants. This is the carbon cycle in brief.

Normally, carbon dioxide and other gases that surround the planet let the radiation from the sun reach the earth, but prevent some of the heat from being reflected back out again. Without these greenhouse gases, the earth would be far colder, largely covered in ice. The problem comes when the amount of gases exceeds a limit.

By burning large amounts of fossil fuels, we release huge quantities of carbon dioxide into the atmosphere. Concurrently, deforestation also releases carbon trapped in the tissues of the trees. At the same time, loss of trees reduces the earth's capacity to absorb carbon dioxide through photosynthesis. Natural processes like volcano eruptions and earthquake-induced fires also contribute carbon dioxide emissions.

Due to the factors listed above, the carbon dioxide concentration in the atmosphere has been rapidly increasing (Table 19.1).

Table 19.1 Carbon Dioxide in the Atmosphere
(Unit: Parts per million or ppm)

Period/Year	Average CO2 ppm
During the ice ages	180–220
Between ice ages	260–280
1750	280
1958	315
1992	355
2010	389

Some of the other greenhouse gases are far more effective than carbon dioxide in trapping heat. CFCs are an example, but their role is greater in the depletion of the ozone layer. Methane, released from swamps, human and animal waste, and garbage dumps, is also a greenhouse gas and its concentration is increasing. Similarly, human activities are causing the rapid increase in the amounts of thirty other greenhouse gases.

The abnormal increase in the concentration of these gases leads to higher temperatures and global warming. The average temperatures around the world have risen by about 0.5°C since the beginning of the 20th century. If emissions continue at the current rate, a temperature rise of 1.5–4.5°C is likely by 2030.

From which countries do the human-induced greenhouse gas emissions come? Most of the gas emissions come from the northern hemisphere, the US being the highest contributor. Russia is also a major source. The European countries produce substantial amounts, but they are also trying to reduce them. Developing countries are catching up fast. In 2006, China overtook the US to become the largest emitter of greenhouse gases.

Between 1900 and 2004, the whole of Africa was responsible for just 2.5 per cent of cumulative carbon dioxide emissions whilst the US accounted for 29.5 per cent. India's current per capita carbon dioxide emissions are 1.5 tonnes per annum against 6.1 tonnes in China and 20 tonnes in the US.

> **KEY IDEA**
> Excessive burning of fossil fuels releases huge amounts of greenhouse gases, which leads to global warming.

These statistics, combined with our knowledge that carbon dioxide absorbed by the atmosphere remains to exert a greenhouse effect for many decades, illustrate how the countries most seriously affected by climate change are those which carry the least responsibility.

In addition to ecological footprint (Chapter 1) and water footprint (Chapter 7), we also have the concept of carbon footprint (Box 19.1).

What the likely effects of global warming?

Accurate predictions are difficult, but all computer models indicate an average rise of 3°C by 2100. An increase of just 1.5°C in the mean global temperature could cause a major change in the climate. The change is likely to be greater than anything experienced during the last 10,000 years.

Global warming is likely to have a wide variety of effects on the following:

- Climate
- Ocean and coasts
- Glaciers, ice caps, and permafrost
- Water, agriculture, and food
- Animal and plant species

These effects are interconnected. In fact, climate change causes many of the other effects.

Climate change

Regional and seasonal weather patterns will change, with longer summers and shorter winters. Extreme weather conditions like floods and droughts are likely to occur more often. Across the world the effects may be even contradictory, due to the interconnectedness of the ocean, land, and atmosphere.

Many believe that such climate change is already noticeable. Since the 1960s, each decade has been warmer than the previous one. In the 1990s, there were an unprecedented number of natural disasters. During that decade, the weather-related damage was five times greater than in the 1980s.

Box 19.2 gives examples of extreme weather conditions in recent years, based on data from the US National Oceanic and Atmospheric Administration.

BOX 19.1

Carbon Footprint

The carbon footprint measures the total greenhouse gas emissions caused directly and indirectly by a person, organisation, event, product, or country.

Unlike ecological footprint, carbon footprint is not measured in area, but in tonnes of carbon-dioxide equivalent (tCO_2e). The footprint of a country does not just measure emissions that occur on its territory. Similar to water footprint, it includes emissions that occur in the production of all goods and services consumed in a country. It also includes international transport (ocean freight and aviation).

The table below gives the carbon footprint of selected countries.

Country	Carbon Footprint (tCO_2e)
US	28.6
Singapore	24.1
Canada	19.6
Germany	15.1
Japan	13.8
South Africa	6.0
China	3.1
India	1.8
Bangladesh	1.1
Global Average	**5.1**

You can also calculate your personal carbon footprint.

BOX 19.2

Some exceptional climate events (2007–2009)

Year 2007
- Arctic Sea-Ice: All-time lowest extent on record in September. Surpassed previous record set in 2005 by 23 per cent
- Bangladesh: Tropical Cyclone Sidr, worst storm since 1991. More than 8.5 million people affected and over 3,000 killed.

Year 2008
- US: One of the top 10 years for tornado-related fatalities since 1953.
- United Kingdom: One of 10 wettest summers on record and coldest winter since 1996/1997.
- Spain and Portugal: Worst drought for over a decade

Contd

Box 19.2 Contd

- Portugal: Worst drought winter since 1917
- Cuba: Hurricane Gustav, worst storm to hit Cuba in 5 decades
- Brazil: Heavy rain and flooding affected 1.5 million people.
- Iran: Heaviest snowfall in more than a decade
- Iraq: First snowfall in living memory in Baghdad
- China: Worst severe winter weather in 5 decades affecting over 78 million people
- India: Heaviest rainfall in 7 years in Mumbai

Year 2009

- US: Worst wildfire in South California since 30 years scorched nearly 8,100 hectares.
- Mexico: Worst drought in 70 years, affecting about 3.5 million farmers, with 80 per cent of water reservoirs less than half full and 17 million acres of cropland wiped out.

- Argentina, Paraguay, and Uruguay: Worst drought in over 50 years in some areas.
- Central Europe: flooding, worst natural disaster since 2002.
- India: Intense heat wave resulted in nearly 100 fatalities as temperatures soared past 40 °C.
- Bangladesh: Dhaka received 290 mm, the largest rainfall in a single day since 1949, leaving 12 million stranded
- Philippines: Torrential downpours caused flash floods and landslides, forcing 200,000 to evacuate.
- Kenya: Worst drought in almost two decades affecting 10 million people and causing crop failure.
- Philippines: Typhoon Kujira triggered floods and major landslides, affecting over 246,000 people.
- Australia: Warmest January and driest May, drought conditions for over a decade in some parts

Ocean and coasts

The ocean has become warmer and sea levels are rising. The melting of polar ice caps is adding to the problem. Small islands like those of the Maldives and the South Pacific are threatened. Tuvalu may be the first country to go off the world map. Islands in the Sundarbans have also been affected. If sea-level rise continues, coastal areas will be flooded in places like the Netherlands, Egypt, Bangladesh, and Indonesia, necessitating the evacuation of large populations.

Coral reefs are already dying all over the world due to human activities. A warmer ocean will accelerate this process. Corals are home to 9 million different kinds of marine plants and animals. Their death will have a devastating effect on marine life and fisheries.

Melting of glaciers, ice caps, and permafrost

The most dramatic evidence of global warming is the melting of the Arctic (Box 19.3).

BOX 19.3

The story of the Arctic: Melting ice, hungry bears

The Arctic is the area around the North Pole. It is a vast ocean covered with ice and surrounded by treeless, frozen ground. The Arctic region is one of the last remaining areas of unspoilt nature.

The Arctic is full of organisms living in the ice: fish and marine mammals, birds, and land animals, besides human settlements. Its biological diversity is very valuable. The natural resources include oil, gas, minerals, forest, and fish.

The Arctic sea ice keeps the polar regions cool and helps moderate global climate. Sea ice has a bright surface, so 80 per cent of the sunlight that strikes it is reflected back into space. As sea ice melts in the summer, it exposes the dark ocean surface. Instead

Contd

Box 19.3 Contd

of reflecting 80 per cent of the sunlight, the ocean absorbs 90 per cent of the sunlight. The oceans heat up, and Arctic temperatures rise further.

A small temperature increase at the poles leads to still greater warming over time, making the poles the most sensitive regions to climate change on earth. According to scientific data, both the thickness and summer sea ice extent in the Arctic have shown a dramatic decline over the past thirty years. The sea ice extent has decreased from about 8.5 million sq km in 1978 to 6 million sq km in 2010. This is consistent with observations of a warming Arctic. The loss of sea ice also has the potential to accelerate global warming trends and to change climate patterns.

A melting Arctic has many adverse effects in the region:

- The indigenous people of the Arctic have never seen such weather before. They have to travel far over the dangerous thin ice to hunt seals.

They have even had to use boats! Accidents are increasing due to unusual conditions, resulting in injuries and death, loss of valuable equipment, and expensive rescues.

- Severe storms and coastal erosion are happening.
- Marine habitats are shrinking for ice-dependent seals, polar bears, and some seabirds. This may push some species to extinction.
- Polar bears need ice for protective cover and for a platform to hunt seals. During the summer, they eat very little while they wait for the ocean to freeze. They are moving to land earlier in the season as sea ice melts earlier in the spring, which means they do not have enough fat reserves to survive the ice-free season. Changing ice conditions have already reduced the number of polar bears over the last 20 years, and the number of live births and the health of adult bears have declined.

Water, agriculture, and food

Extreme floods and droughts are likely to have serious effects on water resources, agriculture, and food security:

- Loss of top soil, erosion of soil, and desertification
- Overflow of sewage systems and resulting water pollution and epidemics
- Amount and location of fresh water affected by changing rainfall, melting ice, and more evaporation
- Warmer water attracting more organisms and getting contaminated
- Sea level rise bringing salt water into coastal marshes and aquifers
- Drying up of fresh water sources: For example, if the Himalayan glaciers are gone, there will be no water for 500 million people

Animals, plant species, and human beings

Thousands of animal and plant species will go extinct, unable to adjust quickly enough to the new conditions. Polar species may be the first to go, followed by those in the coastal zones everywhere. Polar bears, which depend on ice, are in big trouble and could go extinct by 2050. Animals and birds will change their migration patterns.

Warming will increase photosynthesis activity leading to faster growth of plants and trees. Initially, the yields will be more, but too much heat will kill the crops.

Extreme weather will increase human migration. There will be many millions more of environmental refugees. People living on the coasts will suffer extensive damage due to sea-level rise and cyclones.

What is the likely impact of global warming on India?

India is already being affected by global warming and its impact will be stronger in the coming years. Apart from sea-level rise, the meltdown of Himalayan glaciers is another effect of global warming.

Global warming has already affected our monsoon patterns and climate. Since 1951, instances of very heavy rains every year have gone up. Spells of moderate rain are going down. This changing trend of the monsoon has made us more vulnerable to disasters such as floods and landslides.

> **KEY IDEA**
>
> Global warming is likely to result in massive changes in climate, natural disasters, biodiversity loss, and sea level rise. Climate change, bought about by global warming is perhaps the biggest environmental challenge faced by the world.

In future, global warming could change the climate in ways we have never before experienced. Frequencies and intensities of tropical cyclones in Bay of Bengal could increase particularly in the post-monsoon period. Low-lying coastal areas could be flooded, displacing millions of people. Mumbai and other coastal cities could suffer severe losses.

Some states are likely get very heavy rains, .while other states could experience severe droughts. The meltdown of glaciers would ultimately lead to water scarcity and severe fall in food production.

In 2008, Prime Minister Manmohan Singh unveiled the National Action Plan on Climate Change (Box 19.4).

BOX 19.4

India's National Action Plan on Climate Change

On June 30, 2008, Prime Minister Manmohan Singh released India's first National Action Plan on Climate Change (NAPCC) outlining existing and future policies and programs addressing climate mitigation and adaptation. The plan identified eight core 'national missions' running through 2017 and directed the ministries to submit detailed implementation plans to the Prime Minister's Council on Climate Change.

Emphasizing the overriding priority of maintaining high economic growth rates to raise living standards, the plan identified 'measures that promote our development objectives while also yielding co-benefits for addressing climate change effectively.' It said these national measures would be more successful with assistance from developed countries, and pledged that India's per capita greenhouse gas emissions 'will at no point exceed that of developed countries even as we pursue our development objectives.'

National Missions

National Solar Mission   The Plan aims to promote the development and use of solar energy for power generation and other uses with the ultimate objective of making solar competitive with fossil-based energy options. The plan includes:

- Specific goals for increasing use of solar thermal technologies in urban areas, industry, and commercial establishments;
- A goal of increasing production of photovoltaics to 1,000 MW/year; and
- A goal of deploying at least 1,000 MW of solar thermal power generation.

Other objectives include the establishment of a solar research center, increased international collaboration on technology development, strengthening of domestic manufacturing capacity, and increased government funding and international support.

Contd

Box 19.4 Contd

National Mission for Enhanced Energy Efficiency
Current initiatives are expected to yield savings of 10,000 MW by 2012. Building on the Energy Conservation Act 2001, the plan recommends:

- Mandating specific energy consumption decreases in large energy-consuming industries, with a system for companies to trade energy-savings certificates;
- Energy incentives, including reduced taxes on energy-efficient appliances; and
- Financing for public-private partnerships to reduce energy consumption through demand-side management programs in the municipal, buildings and agricultural sectors.

National Mission on Sustainable Habitat To promote energy efficiency as a core component of urban planning, the plan calls for:

- Extending the existing Energy Conservation Building Code;
- A greater emphasis on urban waste management and recycling, including power production from waste;
- Strengthening the enforcement of automotive fuel economy standards and using pricing measures to encourage the purchase of efficient vehicles; and
- Incentives for the use of public transportation.

National Water Mission With water scarcity projected to worsen as a result of climate change, the plan sets a goal of a 20 per cent improvement in water use efficiency through pricing and other measures.

National Mission for Sustaining the Himalayan Ecosystem: The plan aims to conserve biodiversity, forest cover, and other ecological values in the Himalayan region, where glaciers that are a major source of India's water supply are projected to recede as a result of global warming.

National Mission for a 'Green India' Goals include the afforestation of 6 million hectares of degraded forest lands and expanding forest cover from 23 per cent to 33 per cent of India's territory.

National Mission for Sustainable Agriculture The plan aims to support climate adaptation in agriculture through the development of climate-resilient crops, expansion of weather insurance mechanisms, and agricultural practices.

National Mission on Strategic Knowledge for Climate Change To gain a better understanding of climate science, impacts and challenges, the plan envisions a new Climate Science Research Fund, improved climate modeling, and increased international collaboration. It also encourages private sector initiatives to develop adaptation and mitigation technologies through venture capital funds.

Other Programmes
The NAPCC also described other ongoing initiatives, including:

- *Power Generation:* The government is mandating the retirement of inefficient coal-fired power plants and supporting the research and development of IGCC and supercritical technologies.
- *Renewable Energy:* Under the Electricity Act 2003 and the National Tariff Policy 2006, the central and the state electricity regulatory commissions must purchase a certain percentage of grid-based power from renewable sources.
- *Energy Efficiency:* Under the Energy Conservation Act 2001, large energy-consuming industries are required to undertake energy audits and an energy labeling program for appliances has been introduced.

Implementation
Ministries with lead responsibility for each of the missions were directed to develop objectives, implementation strategies, timelines, and monitoring and evaluation criteria, to be submitted to the Prime Minister's Council on Climate Change. The Council will also be responsible for periodically reviewing and reporting on each mission's progress. To be able to quantify progress, appropriate indicators and methodologies will be developed to assess both avoided emissions and adaptation benefits.

How did climate change become a global issue and what were the international initiatives?

There is no dispute about the increased accumulation of greenhouse gases in the atmosphere. There is, however, a minority who believe that our understanding of climate is not sufficient to make any prediction of global warming. Most scientists agree with the environmentalists that the unchecked increase in greenhouse gases is too great a risk to take. Meanwhile, more and more studies confirm that global warming is a reality.

Even in the 1960s and '70s, scientists were finding hard evidence that concentrations of carbon dioxide in the atmosphere were increasing. By the early 1990s, it was clear to many scientists that global warming was a serious issue.

The petroleum and automobile industries, however, tried to cast doubts over global warming. They were against any move to cut carbon emissions. They did not want any steps that would affect their businesses and profits. The US government too supported them. They did not want the economy to be hit or the citizens' lifestyles to be changed.

It took years before the international community responded properly to the threat of climate change. In 1988, the World Meteorological Organization and UNEP together created the Intergovernmental Panel on Climate Change (IPCC), a task force of climate scientists from nearly 100 countries. This group issued a first assessment report in 1990, which reflected the views of 400 scientists. The report stated that global warming was real and urged that something be done about it.

The IPCC findings spurred governments to create the UN Framework Convention on Climate Change (UNFCCC), which came into force in 1994. The Convention sets an overall framework for intergovernmental efforts to tackle the challenge posed by climate change. It recognizes that the climate system is a shared resource whose stability can be affected by industrial and other emissions of carbon dioxide and other greenhouse gases.

The IPCC now has a well-established role. It does not conduct its own scientific inquiries, but reviews worldwide research, issues regular assessment reports (there have now been four), and compiles special reports and technical papers.

Over the years, the IPCC Reports have become increasingly strong in stressing the seriousness of global warming and the need for action. The IPCC said clearly in its 1995 Report that global warming was indeed happening. This Report, with 78 lead authors and 400 contributors from 26 countries, came to the following serious conclusions:

- Global warming was happening.
- Human activity was causing it.
- Warming was likely to unleash unnatural, devastating storms, floods, heat waves, droughts, etc.
- Carbon dioxide emissions must be cut, particularly in the industrialized nations.

Many other studies came to similar conclusions. In November 2004, new evidence of global warming came from the Arctic Climate Impact Assessment. It predicted that greenhouse gases from human activities were likely to contribute an additional warming of 3–9°C over the next 100 years.

The Arctic Region is an indicator of global climate change and provides early warning of events worldwide. It is certainly getting warmer at the Poles (Box 19.3) and glaciers are melting in many parts of the world.

KEY IDEA

According to the IPCC, emissions must start declining by 2015, if we wanted to prevent temperatures from rising more than 2 degrees C over pre-industrialisation levels.

The IPCC Report of February 2007 said that global temperatures could rise up to 6°C by 2100, triggering disaster for billions of people. In its May 2007 Report, the IPCC stated that emissions must start declining by 2015, if we wanted to prevent temperatures from rising more than 2°C over pre-industrialisation levels.

IPCC reports are frequently used as the basis for decisions made under the UNFCCC, and they played a major role in the negotiations leading to the Kyoto protocol, a far-reaching international treaty on climate change.

What is the Kyoto Protocol?

The Kyoto protocol is an international agreement to reduce the greenhouse gas emissions. It was negotiated under the UNFCCC during a meeting held Kyoto, Japan, in 1997. The major distinction between the Protocol and UNFCCC is that, while the Convention encouraged industrialised countries to stabilize GHG emissions, the Protocol commits them to do so. The Protocol came into force in 2005.

The Kyoto Protocol is a legally binding agreement under which industrialized countries will reduce their collective emissions of greenhouse gases by 5.2 per cent compared to the year 1990. Note that, compared to the emissions levels of 2010 without the Protocol, this target represents a 29 per cent cut.

The goal is to lower overall emissions from six greenhouse gases— carbon dioxide, methane, nitrous oxide, sulphur hexafluoride, hydrofluorocarbons, and perfluorocarbons—calculated as an average over the five-year period of 2008–12. National targets range from 8 per cent reductions for the European Union and some others to 7 per cent for the US, 6 per cent for Japan, 0 per cent for Russia, and permitted increases of 8 per cent for Australia and 10 per cent for Iceland.

Note that, even if the Kyoto Pact were to be fully implemented, it would do very little to solve the problem of carbon dioxide emissions. The IPCC had stated in its reports that the emissions had to be cut by 60–80 per cent if the climate had to be stabilised.

Developing countries were not legally bound to emissions reduction targets initially, because these countries had historically been responsible for only a small portion of the global greenhouse gas emissions.

Under the Treaty, countries must meet their targets primarily through national measures. However, it offers them an additional means of meeting their targets by way of market-based mechanisms.

The two important Kyoto mechanisms are:

Emissions trading   This mechanism allows countries that have emission units to spare—emissions permitted them but not 'used'—to sell this excess capacity to countries that are over their targets. Thus, a new commodity was created in the form of emission reductions or removals. Since carbon dioxide is the principal greenhouse gas, people speak simply of trading in carbon. Carbon is now traded like any other commodity. This is known as 'the carbon market'.

Clean Development Mechanism (CDM)   This mechanism allows a country with an emission-reduction commitment to implement an emission-reduction project in developing countries. Such projects can earn saleable certified emission reduction credits, each equivalent to one tonne of CO_2, which can be counted towards meeting Kyoto targets. A CDM project activity might involve, for example, a rural electrification project using solar panels or the installation of more energy-efficient boilers.

Many countries including India ratified the Protocol. Most countries, however, have not met the targets for emission reductions. Hence, the Protocol's impact on the rising trend in global emissions has been very small.

KEY IDEA

The Kyoto Protocol was a welcome agreement to cut greenhouse gas emissions, but the targets set were woefully inadequate and even those targets were not met.

The CDM has so far registered more than a 1000 projects, with another 4,000 in the pipeline. Projects range from wind turbines in India to capturing and using methane from landfills in Brazil to geothermal plants in Central America. But there has been concern that, while a few countries (China, India, Brazil and Mexico, in particular) have attracted the major share of projects under this mechanism, the least developed nations—particularly in Africa—have been left out. There is also concern that too many projects deliver few real cuts in emissions.

What was the outcome of the 2009 Copenhagen meeting of the UNFCCC?

With the Kyoto Protocol set to expire in 2012, the UNFCCC Conference in Copenhagen in 2009 was expected to come up with a better agreement. The Conference attracted unprecedented participation:

- Attendance by 120 Heads of State, including US President Obama and Indian PM Manmohan Singh
- Record numbers of participants including 10,500 delegates and 13,500 observers
- Many parallel meetings and protests by NGOs and activists.

At the Conference, the focus was on ethics and justice aspects of climate change and adaptation needs. The developing countries wanted the richer ones to commit to reduce emissions to required levels and to fund adaptation programmes in the poorer countries. In spite of intense negotiations, the issues remained unresolved. Finally, the Copenhagen Accord was noted, but not adopted. Hence, it is not a legally binding agreement.

Drafted by China, India, Brazil, South Africa and US, countries strongly opposed to legally binding commitments, the Accord included the following:

- *Long-term goal*: Limit global average temperature increase to 1.5–2°C
- *Emissions reduction*: Countries asked to set voluntary targets
- *Financing for poor nations*: Call to raise US$ 100 billion a year by 2020

The Accord has been widely criticised as a failure of global leadership. The UN is pursuing a compromise text to unite the 'Kyoto track' with the Copenhagen Accord, which could then become legally binding at the next major UNFCCC conference in Mexico in November 2010.

And so the meetings go on, even as the planet is getting warmer and the climate crazier!

Why do we disagree about climate change and not take much action?

Views on global warming and climate change vary widely in the world. The poor millions of the world, of course, have no idea what is hitting them. Even among the educated and the prosperous, the views differ.

In a survey conducted in the US in 2008, the Yale Project on Climate Change Communication found that there were six groups of Americans with regard to opinions on climate change:

- The Alarmed (18 per cent) were fully convinced of the reality and seriousness of climate change and were already taking individual, consumer, and political action to address it.
- The Concerned (33 per cent)—the largest of the six groups—were also convinced that global warming was happening and a serious problem, but had not yet engaged the issue personally.
- The Cautious (19 per cent), the Disengaged (12 per cent), and the Doubtful (11 per cent) represented different stages of understanding and acceptance of the problem, and none were actively involved.
- The Dismissive (7 per cent) were very sure it was not happening and were actively involved as opponents of a national effort to reduce greenhouse gas emissions.

Public perceptions also change over time. For example, another survey by the Yale Project in late 2009 found that public concern about global warming had dropped sharply since 2008. Only 50 per cent of Americans said they were 'somewhat' or 'very worried' about global warming, a 13–point decrease since a year ago. The percentage of Americans who thought global warming was happening had declined 14 points, to 57 per cent.

The percentage of Americans who thought global warming was caused mostly by human activities dropped 10 points, to 47 per cent. In line with these shifting beliefs, there was an increase in the number of Americans who thought global warming would never harm people or other species in the US or elsewhere.

Such studies are important because the Americans' energy use, consumer choices, and support for policies to reduce greenhouse gas emissions will largely influence the success—or failure—of global efforts to limit human-induced climate change.

Why do we disagree about climate change, especially about the action to be taken to mitigate its impact? Why are individuals, communities and governments unwilling to commit themselves to action?

Alarmist messages of impending chaos and catastrophe due to climate change seem to be counter-productive. They only generate a feeling of helplessness and apathy. They do not lead to behavioural change among the citizens.

Some of the reasons why we (the people and governments of the world) disagree on climate change are:

- We receive multiple and conflicting messages about climate change and interpret them in different ways.
- We understand science and scientific knowledge in different ways.
- Our political ideologies and our 'development' priorities are different.
- We value things (activities, people, assets, resources) differently.
- We believe different things about ourselves, the universe, and our place in the universe.
- We fear that the suggested or required actions would affect our daily lives adversely or we would have to make some sacrifices. We may lose some of our comforts, we may even lose our jobs, etc.

Perhaps we should respond to climate change or the other major environmental problems not by trying to 'solve' them, but in creative ways. For example, we should examine closely the long-term implications of our short-term actions. We could also ask what we really want for ourselves and humanity.

What is climate justice?

The concept of climate justice seeks to restore equity in two ways:

- The richer countries should repay their climate debt by agreeing to and implementing severe cuts in their emissions, thus reserving 'atmospheric space' for the growing emissions of poorer countries.
- The poorer countries should receive funds for meeting the costs of transition to low carbon economies and of adaptation to the damaging effects of climate change.

Climate change should really be addressed in human rights terms. Its impact on essential food and water supplies represents a violation of social and economic rights.

REVIEW: A SUMMARY OF THE KEY POINTS

- Acid rain is formed by the emission of pollutants from human activities. Acid rain has a number of adverse effects on the environment and living beings.
- The ozone layer in the atmosphere is getting depleted and an ozone hole has developed over the Antarctic
- The depletion of the ozone layer has adverse effects on life.
- The Montreal Protocol on Substances that Deplete the Ozone Layer has been successful in reducing the production and consumption of such substances. The ozone hole is now closing.
- There is clear evidence that global warming is occurring due emissions from human activities.
- Global warming will have serious effects on the environment and human society.
- The Kyoto Protocol set modest targets for the reduction of greenhouse gases, but the targets were not met.
- The 2009 Copenhagen meeting failed to agree on a new agreement in place of the Kyoto Protocol.

EXERCISES

Objective-type questions

For each question below, choose the best answer out of the given choices:

1. Acid rain is formed when
   (a) an acid mixes with rain.
   (b) man-made chemical air pollutants combine with atmospheric water droplets.
   (c) factories let out gases.
   (d) matter decomposes

2. Which of the following is **not** an effect of acid rain?
   (a) Death of trees
   (b) Plants lose productivity.
   (c) Soil turns alkaline.
   (d) Lakes turn lifeless.

3. Which of the following statements is **not** true with regard to the ozone layer?
   (a) It absorbs most of the UV-B radiation.

   (b) It screens out the UV-C radiation.
   (c) Its depletion leads to more cancers.
   (d) It has now recovered fully.

4. Which of the following is the successful international agreement on ozone layer depletion?
   (a) Montreal Protocol
   (b) Kyoto Protocol
   (c) Vienna Convention
   (d) Copenhagen Accord

5. What is the main cause of global warming?
   (a) Photosynthesis
   (b) Climate change
   (c) Burning fossil fuels
   (d) Carbon cycle

6. Your carbon footprint measures the
   (a) amount of carbon you consume
   (b) land you need for sustaining yourself indefinitely

(c) greenhouse gas emissions caused by you

(d) the amount of travel you do

7. Which of the following statements is **not** true with regard to the Kyoto Protocol?

(a) It commits countries to specified reductions in emissions.

(b) It has not been implemented seriously.

(c) It concerns specified greenhouse gases.

(d) It has a uniform emission reduction target for all.

8. Which of the following statements is **not** true with regard to the Intergovernmental Panel on Climate Change (IPCC)?

(a) It conducts research.

(b) It comes out with periodical assessment reports.

(c) It consists of scientists from many countries.

(d) It provides a basis for UNFCCC meetings.

9. Which of the following statements is **not** true with regard to global warming and climate change?

(a) The Arctic is melting fast.

(b) There are many extreme weather events now.

(c) Global warming will stop the moment we stop burning fossil fuels.

(d) There is an overwhelming agreement among scientists that climate change is happening.

10. Which of the following statements is true with regard to Clean Development Mechanism?

(a) A country with large emissions cannot implement a CDM project.

(b) Usually, CDM projects are implemented by developing countries in the industrialized countries.

(c) Very few CDM projects are found in Africa.

(d) A large thermal plant could be a CDM project.

Short-answer questions

1. Explain the causes and effects of acid rain.

2. What is ozone layer and why is it getting depleted?

3. Outline the provisions of the Vienna Convention and the Montreal Protocol

4. What have been the results of implementation of the Montreal Protocol?

5. What is global warming and how does it occur?

6. What are the possible effects of global warming?

7. Outline the provisions of the Kyoto Protocol.

Long-answer questions

Carry out a survey in your area and write an essay on the topic:

How do educated people view global warming and climate change? Why do we have so many sceptics? How can we convince them of the urgency of climate change?

Think critically: Deeper questions for reflection and discussion

An African diplomat once told the delegates of the rich countries, 'If you do not share your wealth with us, we will share our poverty with you.' Currently, the rich countries are responsible for most of the greenhouse gas emissions. How should they support the poorer countries to develop and use cleaner technologies?

SOMETHING DIFFERENT FOR A CHANGE

A poem from Our Earth Music

Global Warming, Can't You See?

Hope for the earth and
Hope for the human race.
Lets do something for change,
Its within our choice and range.

We must make it cool to be green.
To live, air and water must be clean.
Don't let our leaders convince us to fear

All but what will always be here.

Our earth, our atmosphere
Discrediting scientists. Refusing to hear
Anything against the status quo
Glaciers melting, what else is there to show?

Don't let terrorism and money sway you
Into thinking the earth doesn't need you.
Join with those working for life
A sustainable future will end the strife.

ACTIVITIES

Act: What you can do to mitigate the impact of global warming and climate change

Join 350.org, an international campaign that is building a movement to unite the world around solutions to the climate crisis—the solutions that science and justice demand. Their mission is to inspire the world to rise to the challenge of the climate crisis—to create a new sense of urgency and of possibility for our planet.

Their focus is on the number 350—as in parts per million CO_2. If we cannot get below that figure for CO_2 concentration, the damage we are already seeing from global warming will continue and accelerate. For more information, access the website www.350.org.

Organize together: Eco-club activities and projects

Observe September 16 as the International Day for the Preservation of the Ozone Layer. The Day commemorates the date in 1987 on which the Montreal Protocol was signed. You can devote this day to promote concrete activities in accordance with the objectives and goals of the Montreal Protocol and its amendments. Every year an appropriate theme is chosen for the Day. You can get more information on the year's theme and promotional material from the UNEP website.

LEARN MORE

Books

Gelbspan, Ross 2004, *Boiling Point: How politicians, Big Oil and Coal, Journalists and Activists Have Fueled the Climate Crisis and What We Can Do to Avert Disaster,* Basic Books, New York.

Lynas, Mark 2008, *Six Degrees: Our Future in a Hotter Planet,* National Geographic Society, Washington D.C.

McGuire, Bill 2008, *Seven Years to Save the Planet: The Questions and Answers,* Weidenfeld and Nicholson, London.

Romm, Joseph 2007, *Hell and High Water: Global Warming—the Solution and the politics—and What We Should Do,* William Morrow, New York.

Article

Price, Tom 2003, 'High Tide in Tuvalu', *Sierra,* July/August, pp. 35–37.

Websites

Arctic Sea, melting:
  http://nsidc.org/arcticseaicenews/
Carbon dioxide in the atmosphere:
  www.co2now.org
Carbon footprint calculator:
  www.cleanindia.org/carbon/ClimateChange.htm

www.nature.org/initiatives/climatechange/calculator/
Global warming, 2009 UNEP Science Compendium:
  www.unep.org/compendium2009
Intergovernmental Panel on Climate Change:
  www.ipcc.org
Kyoto Protocol: http://unfccc.int/kyoto_protocol/
Ozone depletion, Montreal Protocol:
  http://ozone.unep.org/
UN Framework Convention on Climate Change:
  www.unfccc.int
Yale Project on Climate Change Communication:
  http://environment.yale.edu/climate/

Films on Global Warming and Climate Change

A Global Warning?, a documentary by History Channel (2007)

Age of Stupid, a documentary by Franny Armstrong and Pete Postlethwaite (2009)

An Inconvenient Truth, a documentary by Al Gore

Carbon Nation, a documentary by Peter Byck (2010)

Everything's Cool: A Toxic Comedy About Global Warming, a documentary by Daniel B.Gold and Judith Gelfand (2007)

Six Degrees Could Change the World, a documentary by National Geographic (2008)

CHAPTER 20

Environmental Laws and Regulations

I am not against anyone at any time,
as I am often perceived to be.
I am just for the environment at all times.

M.C.Mehta
(1946–)
Environmental lawyer

THIS CHAPTER IS ABOUT...

Environmental laws and regulations, implementation of laws, ethics, values, environmental justice

THE KEYWORDS AND PHRASES ARE...

environmental ethics   environmental impact assessment   judicial activism
public interest litigation   national green tribunal

THE STORY OF THE GANGA: THE RIVER THAT CAUGHT FIRE

Someone dropped by chance a burning match into the river and a whole one-km stretch caught fire. In fact, the fire went seven metres high and could not be extinguished for three hours. That was the River Ganga near Haridwar in 1984, when the effluents from two factories were so toxic that a match could light a fire.

Environmental lawyer M.C.Mehta heard this story and he filed a petition in the Supreme Court of India in 1985 against the two polluting factories. The scope of the case was later broadened to include all the industries and all the municipal towns in the river basin—from the beginning to the end of the Ganga.

Every Friday for over two years, Justice Kuldip Singh heard the Ganga Pollution Case, which became a landmark event in Indian public interest litigation and judicial activism. Justice Singh issued directions every week in an attempt to clean up the mess that was the Ganga.

There were several hundred parties to the case:
• Hundreds of polluting industries and numerous small units like tanneries in Uttar Pradesh, Bihar, and West Bengal
• A number of small municipalities discharging untreated sewage into the river

- Half a dozen municipal corporations in the three states
- The Eastern Railway
- Giant thermal plants in Bokaro and Patratu

Dismayed at the persistent violation of environmental laws by the polluters and the continued inaction of the pollution control boards, the Court took an unusual result-oriented approach. It bypassed many formal court procedures and statutory requirements in favour of quick decisions.

With the help of Mehta, the Court identified the polluters. Each polluter was given three months to meet the effluent standards. The result of non-compliance would be closure of the unit. What is more, the order was issued without hearing the party concerned.

The respective Pollution Control Board had to serve the Court's notice on the polluter and, at the end of the period, report back to the Court on the status. Willing units could get extension of time, but it was closure for the obstinate.

What was the result? Hundreds of factories installed effluent treatment plants, the two thermal power plants ordered equipment to cut their pollution, Eastern Railway agreed to treat its wastewater, and even municipalities started moving.

Where the Pollution Control Boards had failed, the Court succeeded in building up pressure on industries and civic bodies. It also created environmental awareness among administrators, the subordinate judiciary, police, and municipal officials, all of whom were involved in implementing the Court's orders.

Ganga near Haridwar
(Image courtesy: Nichalp, http://commons.
wikimedia.org/wiki/File:Ganga-Haridwar.png)

Justice Kuldip Singh retired in 1997 and the Friday hearings on Ganga stopped. Meanwhile, the Government of India initiated a Ganga Action Plan (GAP) to clean the river. Rs 5 billion was spent on the Plan without much result.

Since then, many more plans and projects for a clean Ganga have been tried without success. In February 2009, the Government of India accorded the Ganga the status of a National River and constituted the National Ganga River Basin Authority (NGRBA). The NGRBA is a planning, financing, monitoring and coordinating body of the centre and the states. The objective of the NGRBA is to ensure effective abatement of pollution and conservation of the Ganga by adopting a river basin approach for comprehensive planning and management. In 2010, a consortium of IITs took up the preparation of a Ganga Management Plan.

And so the story goes on. Meanwhile, the river flows as dirty as ever.

What does the Ganga pollution case teach us?

When we try to clean up the pollution of rivers and other places, we really have a complex and tough problem on hand. A question arises from the Ganga case: why do the thousands who take a dip in the dirty river, keep quiet? Why are they not demanding a clean river and why are they not doing something about it? Apart from some stray individuals and one or two NGOs, there is no public pressure to clean up the river. This apathy is everywhere, in our towns and in our villages.

The most common response would be that we need laws and regulations to conserve the environment. We will review in this chapter the many environmental laws that we have. We will also discuss judicial activism and environmental ethics.

What are the Indian constitutional provisions regarding the environment?

The Constitution (Forty-Second Amendment) Act of 1976 explicitly incorporates environmental protection and improvement. Article 48A, which was added to the directive principles of state policy, declares: 'The state shall endeavour to protect and improve the environment and to safeguard the forests and wild life of the country.'

Article 51A(g) in a new chapter entitled 'Fundamental Duties', imposes a similar responsibility on every citizen 'to protect and improve the natural environment including forests, lakes, rivers and wild life, and to have compassion for living creatures.'

> **KEY IDEA**
> The Indian Constitution contains two important provisions concerning environmental protection.

In addition, Article 21 of the Constitution states: 'No person shall be deprived of his life or personal liberty except according to procedure established by law.' This Article protects the right to life as a fundamental right. The courts have interpreted this Article to mean that the enjoyment of life, including the right to live with human dignity, encompasses within its ambit the protection and preservation of environment.

Do we have an environmental policy? In 1980, the Union Government established the Department of Environment. It became the Ministry of Environment and Forests (MoEF) in 1985. This Ministry initiates and oversees the implementation of environmental policies, plans, laws, and regulations.

MoEF prepared the first National Environmental Action Plan in December 1993, setting India's environmental priorities. Later, the Ministry has come out with a National Environmental Policy.

What was the beginning of environmental legislation in India?

The UN Conference on the Human Environment held in Stockholm in June 1972 as the first international meeting to address environmental issues. The participating countries agreed to take appropriate steps for the preservation of the natural resources of the earth. In consonance with this decision, India began enacting environmental laws.

Initially the laws were not very different from the general body of law. For example, the Water Act of 1974 was very much like other laws and created another agency-administered licensing system to control effluent discharges into water.

The Bhopal tragedy changed the situation. In the 1990s, a spate of laws were passed covering new areas like vehicular emissions, noise, hazardous waste, transportation of toxic chemicals, and environmental impact assessment.

Further, the old licensing regime was supplemented by regulatory techniques. The new laws included provisions like public hearings, citizens' right to information, deadlines for technology changes (in motor vehicles, for example), workers' participation, and penalties on higher management of companies.

> **KEY IDEA**
> After the Bhopal tragedy, India enacted a number of environmental laws.

The powers of the enforcing agencies like the pollution control boards were also increased to levels much higher than before. For example, previously a board had to approach a magistrate to get a factory to close down. Now, it was given the power to order closure, leaving the polluter to challenge the order in court.

Let us now briefly review the main environmental laws of the country.

What powers does the Environment (Protection) Act of 1986 give to the central government?

This Act is an *enabling* law, that is, it provides powers to the executive to frame various rules and regulations. The Act authorizes the central government to protect and improve environmental quality, control and reduce pollution from all sources, and prohibit or restrict the setting and / or operation of any industrial facility on environmental grounds

The Act defines terms such as environment, environmental pollutant, and hazardous substance. According to the Act, the Central Government has the power to

- take measures to protect and improve environment;
- give directions (such as to close, prohibit, or regulate any industry, operation, or process); and
- make rules to regulate environmental pollution (air, water quality standards; prohibition or restriction in handling hazardous materials, siting of industry, etc.).

The Chapter on the prevention, control, and abatement of environmental pollution includes controlling discharge of environmental pollutants, enforcing compliance with procedural safeguards, power of entry and inspection, and power to take samples, setting up of environmental laboratories, appointing environmental analysts, and prescription of penalties for contravening the Act.

What are the Environment (Protection) Rules, 1986? These rules set the standards for emission or discharge of environmental pollutants. In addition, more stringent standards may be laid down for specific industries or locations.

There are rules regarding the prohibition and restriction on the location of industries and the carrying on of processes and operations in different areas. Factors to be taken into consideration include topographic and climatic features of an area, environmentally compatible land use, the net adverse impact likely to be caused by an industry, proximity to areas protected under various other laws, proximity to human settlements, etc.

What is meant by Environmental Impact Assessment?

In 1994, an Environmental Impact Assessment (EIA) was made mandatory for certain types of projects. The regulations require the project proponent to submit an EIA report, an environmental management plan, details of the public hearing and a project report to MoEF.

The projects that require an EIA cover 30 categories such as nuclear power, river valley projects, ports, harbours (except minor ports and harbours), all tourism projects between 200 and 500 m of the High Water Line and at locations with an elevation of more than 1,000 m with investment of more than Rs 50 million, thermal power plants, mining projects (major minerals with leases more than 5 hectares), highway projects, and thermal power plants.

The Ministry's Impact Assessment Agency evaluates the EIA reports. The assessment is to be completed within 90 days from receipt of the requisite documents and data from the Project Authorities and completion of public hearing and decision conveyed within thirty days thereafter. The clearance granted would be valid for a period of five years from the commencement of the construction or operation of the project.

In recent years, the EIA Rules have been repeatedly amended, relaxing many conditions and making it easier to get environmental clearance. NGOs have protected against such changes.

What are the provisions of the Air (Prevention and Control of Pollution) Act of 1981?

The objective of this Act is to provide for the prevention, control and abatement of air pollution. The Act defines air pollution as the presence in the atmosphere of any solid, liquid, or gaseous substance (including noise) in such concentration as may be injurious to human beings, other organisms, property, or the environment.

The provisions of the Act are to be implemented by the Central Pollution Control Board along with the state boards. The Act lists a number of functions for the Board including the setting of air quality standards, collecting data on air pollution, organising training and awareness programmes, establishing laboratories, etc. The Board can specify air pollution control areas and set standards for vehicle emissions.

The Act lays down penalties for violation of its provisions. This applies to companies and their owners and managers as well as to government departments. Citizens can file complaints with the Board.

What are the water-related environmental laws in India?

The early Acts concerned with water issues were the following:

- Easement Act of 1882 allowed private rights to use groundwater by viewing it as an attachment to the land. It also states that all surface water belongs to the state and is a state property.
- Indian Fisheries Act of 1897 established two sets of penal offences whereby the government can sue any person who uses dynamite or other explosive substance in any way (whether coastal or inland) with intent to catch or destroy any fish or poisons fish in order to kill.
- Merchant Shipping Act of 1970 deals with waste arising from ships along the coastal areas within a specified radius.

What are the objectives of the Water (Prevention and Control of Pollution) Act 1974?

The objectives of the Water Act are to prevent and control water pollution and the maintenance or restoration of the wholesomeness of water. The Act defines water pollution as the contamination of water, alteration of its physical, chemical or biological properties, or the discharge of any sewage or trade effluent or any other liquid, gaseous or solid substance into water which may render such water harmful to public health or to domestic, commercial, industrial, agricultural or other legitimate uses, or to the life and health of organisms.

The Act establishes an institutional structure for preventing and abating water pollution. It establishes standards for water quality and effluent. Polluting industries must seek permission to discharge waste into effluent bodies.

The implementation is similar to the Air (Prevention and Control of Pollution) Act with the Central Pollution Control Board being the main agency. In fact, the Central Pollution Control Board (CPCB) was constituted under this act.

What does the Forest Conservation Act of 1980 specify?

This Act along with the Forest (Conservation) Rules of 1981 provide for the protection of and the conservation of the forests. The Act specifies the requirements that should be met before declaring an area as a Protected Forest, Wildlife Sanctuary, or a National Park.

Under the Act, a state government may regulate or prohibit in any forest the clearing of land for cultivation, pasturing of cattle, or clearing the vegetation for any of the following purposes:

- protection against storms, winds, floods and avalanches, for the preservation of the soil on the slopes, the prevention of landslips or of the formation of ravines and torrents, or the protection of land against erosion
- maintenance of a water supply in springs, rivers, and tanks
- protection of roads, bridges, railways and other lines of communication
- preservation of public health.

The Act makes it mandatory for the owner of a forest to seek permission before converting it to any non-forest purposes such as the cultivation of tea, coffee, spices, rubber, palms, oil-bearing plants, horticultural crops, or medicinal plants.

What are the objectives of the Wildlife Protection Act of 1972?

The Wildlife Protection Act of 1972 defines wildlife to include any animal, bees, butterflies, crustaceans, fish, and moths; and aquatic or land vegetation, which form part of any habitat. The Act along with the Wildlife Protection Rules of 1973 provide for the protection of birds and animals and for all matters that are connected to it whether it be their habitat or the waterhole or the forest that sustain them.

What are the other Acts and Rules concerning the environment?

The following are the other important environment-related Acts and Rules:

- Hazardous waste (Management and Handling) Rules of 1989 control the generation, collection, treatment, import, storage, and handling of hazardous waste.
- Manufacture, Storage and Import of Hazardous Chemical Rules of 1989 set up an Authority to inspect, once a year, the industrial activity connected with hazardous chemicals and isolated storage facilities.
- Manufacture, Use, Import, Export, and Storage of Hazardous Micro-organisms, Genetically Engineered Organisms, or Cells Rules of 1989 were introduced with a view to protect the environment, nature, and health, in connection with the application of genetic engineering.
- Public Liability Insurance Act and Rules of 1991 and Amendment, 1992 were drawn up to provide for public liability insurance for the purpose of providing immediate relief to the persons affected by accident while handling any hazardous substance.
- National Environmental Tribunal Act of 1995 was created to award compensation for damages to persons, property, and the environment arising from any activity involving hazardous substances.
- Biomedical waste (Management and Handling) Rules of 1998 constitute a legal binding on the health care institutions to streamline the process of proper handling of hospital waste such as segregation, disposal, collection, and treatment.
- Coastal Regulation Zone Notification of 1991 regulates various activities, including construction, in the coastal zone. It gives some protection to the backwaters and estuaries.

How are the environmental laws being enforced?

We saw that there is no dearth of laws for protecting and conserving the environment. However, the implementation of these laws continues to be poor. The government agencies have vast powers to regulate industries and others who are potential polluters. They are, however, reluctant to use these powers to discipline the polluters.

The Parliament and the state assemblies are ready to pass environmental laws, but do not provide funds for their implementation. Nor do they demand that the governments enforce the laws strictly.

The poor performance of the government agencies in enforcing the laws has compelled the courts to play a pro-active role in the matter of environment. They have directly responded to the complaints of citizens or public interest litigation and assumed the roles of policy makers, educators, administrators, and, in general, friends of the environment. The environmental lawyer M.C.Mehta has played a remarkable role in this process (Box 20.1).

Many petitions filed in courts by individual citizens, groups, and voluntary organizations have led to major decisions given by the courts forcing the state governments to act against

---

BOX 20.1

The story of M.C.Mehta: The Green Avenger

He visited the Taj Mahal for the first time in early 1984 and was shocked to see that the monument's marble had turned yellow and was pitted as a result of pollutants from nearby industries. Being a lawyer, he filed an environmental case in the Supreme Court of India on the issue.

In 1993, after a decade of hearings, the Supreme Court ordered 212 small factories surrounding the Taj Mahal to close because they had not installed pollution control devices. Another 300 factories were put on notice to do the same.

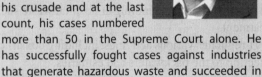

Mahesh Chandra Mehta did not stop with the Taj Case. In 1985, he filed a petition on the Ganga. As we saw, many positive actions to prevent the pollution of the river resulted from this case.

Mehta has continued his crusade and at the last count, his cases numbered more than 50 in the Supreme Court alone. He has successfully fought cases against industries that generate hazardous waste and succeeded in obtaining a court order to make lead-free gasoline available. He has also been working to ban intensive shrimp farming and other damaging activities along India's coast.

Through his work, Mehta has set the national agenda in the fields of water and air pollution, vehicular emission control, conservation of the coastal zone, and the translocation of heavy industry away from urban areas. Almost single-handedly, he has obtained more than 40 landmark judgements and numerous orders from the Supreme Court against polluters. In addition, responding to his petition, the Court has ordered the inclusion of environmental studies as a compulsory subject in all the schools, colleges, and universities of the country.

No other environmental lawyer in the world has perhaps done this much. He has inspired many lawyers in the lower courts to take up environmental cases. Mehta won the Goldman Environmental Prize in 1996 and the Ramon Magsaysay Award for Public Service in 1997.

Mehta has set up the M.C.Mehta Environmental Foundation for the protection of the environment, the rights of the people to clean and fresh water and air, the promotion of sustainable development, and the protection of the cultural heritage of India.

pollution and degradation of the environment. The Supreme Court, for example, has in numerous cases issued directions to close down or shift factories, change to less-polluting technologies, implement environmental norms, etc. Examples are the Ganga Pollution Case and the Shrimp Aquaculture Case (Box 20.2).

As a result of this 'judicial activism', hundreds of factories have installed effluent treatment plants and there is a much greater environmental awareness among the bureaucracy, police, and

---

BOX 20.2

The story of shrimp aquaculture: Mediating in prawn wars

Shrimp aquaculture production in India increased from 30,000 tons in 1990 to 102,000 tons in 1999, made possible by a rapid increase in the area under semi–intensive farms. The expansion was driven by the high profitability of shrimp farming and it attracted a wide range of investors ranging from individual farmers converting paddy fields to multi-national companies investing in large-scale semi-intensive and intensive shrimp farming.

Coastal areas are ideal for shrimp aquaculture since it needs both freshwater and seawater. The rapid expansion of shrimp aquaculture on the coast, particularly in Tamil Nadu and Andhra Pradesh, created many social and environmental problems:

- Polluted salty water from the prawn tanks was discharged into fields killing the soil and the crops. Wells became contaminated and the water undrinkable. Villagers were forced to walk many miles to fetch fresh water.

A prawn farm
(Image courtesy: Balaram Mahalder, http://commons.wikimedia.org/wiki/File:Freshwater_prawn_farm2.jpg)

- The salty water resulted in salinisation leading to the collapse of mud houses of the poor.
- The wastes from prawn farms containing pesticides, fertilizers, and antibiotics were often pumped back into the sea polluting the breeding zones for the fishes.
- The inlet and outlet pipes extending into the sea caused problems for fishing nets and boats.
- In many places, the farms prevented access for the fisherfolk to go to the sea
- Mangrove areas were converted into aquaculture farms. During the 1990s, shrimp aquaculture accounted for about 80 per cent of the conversion of mangrove land.

In 1994, S.Jagannathan, a Gandhian social worker from Tamil Nadu, filed a writ petition in the Supreme Court in public interest. The petition sought the enforcement of Coastal Zone Regulation Notification of 1991 and stoppage of intensive and semi-intensive type of prawn farming in the ecologically fragile coastal areas, prohibition from using the wastelands/wetlands for prawn farming and the constitution of a National Coastal Management Authority to safeguard marine life and coastal areas.

The Supreme Court bench, headed by Justice Kuldip Singh, issued many injunctions and directions. The shrimp aquaculture industry was prohibited in the coastal zone and existing farms were directed to be demolished. The workers, rendered unemployed, were to be compensated by the owners. Agricultural lands, salt-pan lands, mangroves, wetland, forestlands and land for village common purposes were not to be converted into shrimp ponds. The Court also directed the

Contd

Box 20.2 Contd

government to set up an Aquaculture Authority to regulate the industry.

Following the judgment, the government set up an Aquaculture Authority in 1997 to regulate new aquaculture farms and implement the Supreme Court directions with respect to closure of aquaculture farms that were violating coastal

regulations. However, a few months after its constitution and after the deadline for closure of aquaculture farms had expired, the government changed its charter. It longer had the responsibility for the closure of existing aquaculture farms that were violating coastal regulations.

The last word has not been said on this issue.

> **KEY IDEA**
> The implementation of environmental laws in India has been poor, forcing the people to turn to public interest litigation.

municipal officials, all of whom are involved in implementing the Court's orders. Judicial activism has certainly helped the cause of environment, but there is also the view that the courts should not be taking over the role of the executive.

Laws, regulations, and public interest litigation cannot save the environment if there is lack of environmental ethics among the citizens, government officials, companies, and industries.

What is the National Green Tribunal?

The Indian government established a National Green Tribunal in October 2010, headed by a former Judge of the Supreme Court. It is a tribunal exclusively dedicated to environmental issues. This Body, established by an Act of Parliament (National Green Tribunal Act of 2010) will have circuit benches across the country to try all matters related to and arising out of environmental issues.

The Tribunal shall also consist of members who are experts in the field of environmental and related sciences. It has been empowered to issue directions for the compensation and restitution of damage caused from actions of environmental negligence. In doing so, this is the first body of its kind that is required by its parent statute, to apply the 'polluter pays' principle and the principle of sustainable development.

The Ministry of Environment and Forests also intends to organise workshops in rural areas to educate people about issues of access and procedure related to the Tribunal.

What are environmental ethics?

Ethics are concerned with what is wrong and what is right, irrespective of the culture and society. For example, it is ethical to have reverence for all forms of life and any killing is unethical.

Morals reflect the predominant feelings of a culture about ethical issues. For example, in most cultures it is morally right to kill enemies in a war, though it is unethical.

Environmental ethics try to define the moral basis of environmental responsibility. There are three possible viewpoints:

Anthropocentric view Our environmental responsibility is to ensure that the earth remains hospitable and pleasant for human beings. This is the development ethic, the basis of the Idea of Progress (Chapter 1). In this view, nature has value only when humans utilize it.

Biocentric view   All forms of life—humans, animals, and plants—have an inherent right to exist and live without hindrance. This is the preservation ethic, which recognizes that nature has an intrinsic value apart from its use as a resource for humans.

Ecocentric view   Environment deserves care and consideration by itself and not out of the interests of humans, animals, and plants. This is the conservation ethic, which extends the preservation ethic to the entire earth and for all time.

It should be our aim to move from the current (widely held) anthropocentric view to an eco-centric view. That will change our relationship to nature and conserve the environment.

What is environmental justice?

Environmental justice has been defined as equal justice and equal protection for all under the environmental laws and regulations without discrimination based on race, caste, ethnicity, or socioeconomic status.

There are actually three categories of environmental equity issues.

Procedural Injustice   This refers to the uniform application of governing rules, regulations, and evaluation criteria. Examples of procedural injustice are:
- 'stacking' boards and committees with pro-business interests
- holding hearings in remote locations to minimize public participation
- using English-only material to communicate to non-English speaking communities.

Geographical Injustice   Some neighbourhoods, communities, and regions receive direct benefits, such as jobs and tax revenues, from industrial production while the costs, such as the burdens of waste disposal, are sent elsewhere. Communities hosting waste-disposal facilities receive fewer economic benefits than communities generating the waste.

Social Injustice   Environmental decisions often mirror the power arrangements of larger society. For example, toxic or waste dumps could be located in poor neighbourhoods, because the local people are unable to protect and resist the move.

> **KEY IDEA**
> Environment is basically an ethical issue and we need to move from an anthropocentric view to an eco-centric view. We also need to promote environmental justice.

Environmental justice is about social transformation directed towards meeting basic human needs and enhancing our quality of life—economic quality, health care, housing, human rights, environmental protection, and democracy. In linking environmental and social justice issues, the environmental justice movement seeks to challenge the abuse of power which results in poor people having to suffer the effects of environmental damage caused by the greed of others.

What lies ahead?

Judicial intervention alone cannot bring about systemic changes in such a large and complex country like India. It is one of many tools for promoting the environmental agenda. Public education, lobbying, and political action by organizing citizens may be far more effective in some cases.

In the long run, we need political commitment for conserving the environment shown in the form of substantial budgetary allocations for enforcing environmental laws. Courts can only supplement, and not replace, the administrative enforcement mechanism.

Ending on a hopeful note: Positive stories

In many cases of public interest litigation and citizen action on environmental issues, there is victory, but often a partial one. This was true of the Ganga Case, Shrimp Aquaculture Case, and also the Kodaikanal Mercury Case (Box 20.3).

BOX 20.3

The story of Kodaikanal Mercury Case: Send it back!

Normally, the waste would have slowly contaminated the soil and caused problems for years. In this case, however, the mercury was sent back to the US for recycling—thanks to a citizens' campaign and environmental litigation.

Hindustan Lever Ltd., a subsidiary of the Anglo-Dutch multinational Unilever, shut down a mercury thermometer factory in Watertown, New York and moved it to the hill station Kodaikanal, in Tamil Nadu in 1983. It imported mercury from the US and exported the finished thermometers back to the US. By 1997, the plant was making 125,000 thermometers every year.

(Image courtesy: Jurii, http://commons.wikimedia.org/wiki/File:Mercury-thermometer.jpg)

In 2001, the local people discovered tons of mercury waste from broken thermometers that had been dumped on a dirt lot near the factory. The community immediately purchased the mercury as evidence and informed the Tamil Nadu Pollution Control Board (TNPCB). The company initially denied it was their waste, but later admitted that it had been 'inadvertently sold'. The company had in fact sold the mercury to a scrap dealer over four years.

When liquid mercury is spilled, it forms droplets that can accumulate in the tiniest of spaces and then emit vapours into the air. Health problems caused by mercury depend on how much of it has entered the body. Hence, regardless of quantity, all mercury spills should be treated seriously.

In March 2003, the Tamil Nadu Pollution Control Board ordered the company to ship the mercury-laden waste back to the US for proper disposal. Under close supervision, some 300 tons of mercury-contaminated waste was packed into containers and taken to a mercury recycling plant in the US.

The story was not over yet. At a public hearing held in September 2002, the former workers of the factory said they had never been told about the poisonous nature of mercury and demanded that their health problems be addressed. 23 workers had died young and their symptoms had been those of mercury poisoning. Over 550 workers still living in Kodaikanal exhibit similar symptoms.

In 2006, the Ex-Mercury Employees Welfare Association filed a petition in the Chennai High Court seeking rehabilitation and healthcare treatment for all the ex-employees. The company has dismissed the workers' symptoms as having nothing to do with mercury exposure. The case is still on.

In September 2004, the Hazardous Waste Monitoring Committee appointed by the Supreme Court visited Kodaikanal. It ordered a cleanup of the site as well as medical aid for the affected people. The company admitted that over 360 kg of mercury remain spread over the factory site and started the remediation work in 2010.

Meanwhile, studies have shown that mercury levels in the Kodaikanal lakes are abnormally high. Will the factory's mercury convert into an even more dangerous form, methylmercury, as it happened in Minamata (Chapter 16, Box 16.3)? Will it get into the food chain? The citizens are worried.

REVIEW: A SUMMARY OF THE KEY POINTS

- India has many laws to protect the environment, but the implementation has been poor.
- Responding to public interest litigation by citizens and groups, the courts have been taking a pro-active role to enforce environmental laws in India.
- We have constitutional provisions to safeguard the environment
- The Bhopal tragedy gave the impetus for passing several environmental laws incorporating regulatory mechanisms.

- The Environment (Protection) Act of 1986 is an enabling law, providing powers to the executive to frame various rules and regulations.
- An Environmental Impact Assessment (EIA) is mandatory for certain types of projects.
- We have specific laws concerning air, water, forests, wild life, hazardous waste, etc., but the enforcement of all these laws is poor.
- Environmental ethics try to define the moral basis of environmental responsibility.

EXERCISES

Objective-type questions

For each question below, choose the best answer out of the given choices.

1. Which of the following statements is true with regard to the Constitution of India?
   (a) It contains one provision regarding environmental protection.
   (b) It contains no provision regarding environmental protection.
   (c) It contains two provisions regarding environmental protection.
   (d) According to it, right to life is not a fundamental right.

2. Which event gave an impetus for enacting many environmental laws in India?
   (a) Stockholm conference
   (b) Bhopal Tragedy
   (c) Arrival of the British
   (d) Independence

3. Which of the following statements is **not** true with regard to the Environment (Protection) Act?
   (a) It is an enabling law.
   (b) It sets the standards for emission or discharge of environmental pollutants.
   (c) It provides powers to the executive to frame various rules and regulations.
   (d) It authorizes the central government to protect and improve environmental quality.

4. An Environmental Impact Assessment is required for:
   (a) All projects
   (b) All tourism projects
   (c) All mining projects
   (d) Specified categories of projects

5. Which of the following views about the environment is currently dominant?
   (a) Eco-centric view
   (b) Anthropocentric view
   (c) Biocentric view
   (d) Ethical view

Short-answer questions

1. Outline the Indian constitutional provisions regarding the environment.
2. Describe the beginnings of environmental legislation in India.
3. Explain the requirement of an Environmental Impact Assessment for certain types of projects.
4. What are the main provisions of the following Acts?
   (a) Environment (Protection) Act
   (b) Air (Prevention and Control of Pollution) Act
   (c) Wildlife Protection Act
   (d) Water (Prevention and Control of Pollution) Act
   (e) Forest Conservation Act
5. Give two examples of public interest litigation and judicial activism in enforcing environmental laws in India.
6. Explain environmental ethics and the three different ways of viewing environmental responsibility

Long-answer questions

Write an essay on judicial activism in India. Give examples of cases in which the courts have assumed the roles of policy makers, educators, or administrators, and given directives that the government or the enforcement agency should have issued in the first instance.

Think critically: Deeper questions for reflection and discussion

Is judicial activism to be welcomed, given that the governments are not implementing the laws properly? How long can the courts continue to play the role of administrators? Will the fear of courts force the governments to enforce the laws strictly or will they let the court take on that task?

SOMETHING DIFFERENT FOR A CHANGE

A poem for reflection by the Chinese mystic philosopher Lao Tzu, who lived perhaps in the 6th Century BC:

The more laws and restrictions there are,
The poorer people become,
The sharper men's weapons,

The more trouble in the land.

The more ingenious and clever men are,
The more strange things happen,
The more rules and regulations,
The more thieves and robbers.

ACTIVITIES

Act: What you can do to promote awareness and proper implementation of environmental laws

Acquaint yourself with the basic environmental laws and take action when you come across any violation. File complaints with the appropriate authorities.

Learn by doing: Case study / Project

Get in touch with any individual or group of environmental lawyers in your area. Volunteer your services for a few weeks and help them with a case. Write a report on the case. What were the issues? Who are the parties to the case? Which of the laws are involved?

LEARN MORE

Book

Divan, Shyam and Armin Rosencranz 2001, *Environmental Law and Policy in India*, Second Edition, Oxford University Press, New Delhi.

Articles

Hiddleston, Sarah 2010, 'Poisoned Ground', *Frontline*, Vol. 27, No. 19, September 11–24, pp. 4–21. (Kodaikanal case)

Krishnakumar, Asha 2003, 'Mercury's Victims', *Frontline*, Vol. 20, No. 17, August 16–29, pp. 82–84. (Kodaikanal case)

Websites

Environmental law: www.elaw.org

M.C.Mehta Environmental Foundation: http://mcmef. org/index.html

M.C.Mehta: www.goldmanprize.org/

Module 8

Field Work

Chapter 21: Project Work

Project Work

The way to get started is to quit talking and begin doing.

Walt Disney
(1901–1966)
American film producer and animator

THIS CHAPTER IS ABOUT...

Carrying out a project or case study, writing and presenting a report

Why should you carry out a project work?

In this book, we have covered a wide variety of environmental problems facing India and the world. You may not have imagined that the state of the environment was so serious. You may not even believe that all that has been said in this book is true.

How does one verify and validate the various descriptions and ideas presented in the book? One way of doing this would be to embark on a project work. It can be either undertaken individually or as a group activity.

Project work gives you an opportunity to find out for yourself how things are in the real world. In doing the project, you will be involving yourself in a micro-level situation. You will then begin to appreciate the real nature and complexity of the environmental problems facing us today. You will also have the satisfaction of moving from being a part of the problem to becoming a part of the solution.

A group project also gives you to chance to work together with others who may not always agree with you. The lessons you will learn in working in a team will be of great value to you in your career and of course in your life itself.

How should you choose the project?

Choose a project that you can complete in the time that you have. It is far better to do a thorough job with a small project, instead of taking on a big one and leave it unfinished at the end.

Here are some criteria you can use while choosing a project. They are given in the form of a check list of questions you can ask yourself.

- *Attraction of topic*: Do I have a basic interest in the topic? Am I going along just because others have chosen the topic?
- *Usefulness*: Will I be able to make a modest and yet useful contribution to a given real life situation?
- *Specialist knowledge needed*: Does the project need any specialist information and if so, can I equip myself with it before I begin the work? Are there accessible experts whom I can consult?
- *Work by other groups*: Are there reports prepared by others who have been to the site earlier? Does the project sound interesting, judging from these reports?
- *Measurability*: Will I be able to measure the impact of my work?
- *Accessibility and facilities*: Is the project location easily accessible? If I am carrying out the project on a fulltime basis, is there any accommodation available at or near the project site?
- *Weekend projects*: If it is going to be a weekend project, will I be able to do some work each week, adding up to a meaningful whole?
- *Future work*: Given the short time frame, it may not possible for me to achieve all my objectives; is there scope to do things later on as follow up measures?

At the end of each chapter in this book, suggestions for project work were given. More ideas are listed below:

- Documenting environmental resources like river, forest, grassland, hill, mountain in a specific area
- Study of a polluted site in an urban, rural, industrial, agricultural area
- Study of simple ecosystems: ponds, river, hill slopes

Project ideas classified by discipline of student:

- Botany/zoology: Study of plants, insects, birds, etc. in a given area; tracing the origins of different plants, trees, vegetables, and fruits available in an area; study of any seed bank preserving indigenous species
- Science students: Testing water quality in an area, resource mapping of a village
- Design, fine arts, crafts, etc: Designing products with waste material, improving the design of solar energy products like lanterns and cookers
- Philosophy: Studies on environmental ethics
- Economics: Study of alternative economic models
- Architecture: Study buildings designed using ideas of ecological architecture
- Performing arts: Effective ways of communicating to people and mobilizing them for preserving our environment (street theatre performances, or designing a brochure on a specific topic).

Should you seek a project within an organization?　It is best to work as a volunteer / project trainee with an organization that has been working in the area or site. It could be a voluntary organization (NGO), a government department, or even a company that is funding and managing an environmental or social project.

How should you prepare yourself for the project work?

- Define objectives: Start with a list and revise it as you go along
- Formulate the questions: List the questions you expect to answer through the project

- *Conduct a literature survey*: Do a thorough study of the literature available on the topic (books, reports, news items, etc.).
- *Keep notes*: During the literature survey and throughout the project period, write down relevant information. A good practice is to use cards of about 10 cm x 15 cm size to write your notes. Each card should contain one main idea and should carry the name of the topic/ subtopic at the top right corner. This way it will be easy to shuffle and arrange the cards according to the topic. It will enormously simplify the writing process at the end. Remember to assign a card for each reference and write down the full bibliographic details right when you access the item the first time. Otherwise you will be desperately searching for the details while writing the report.
- *Meet concerned persons*: If you are going to interview a person, go prepared with a set of questions. Take a tape recorder along, but take the person's permission before recording the interview.
- *Obtain any permission needed* for entering the project site.
- *Letter from college/university*: Always carry a letter of introduction from your institution and your identity card.
- *Collect any equipment needed* for the project.

How should you conduct the field study?

- Plan each visit or trip meticulously.
- Keep a diary and make detailed notes on cards at the end of each day.
- Always be punctual and keep any deadlines you have agreed to.
- Keep your guides (on site and at your institution) informed of the progress and seek their advice
- At the end of the project, make sure that you return all borrowed material and leave the organization on a pleasant note.
- Take a certificate about your work from the organization. Your institution may ask for it and it will also be useful to you later on.
- Later, remember to give the organization a copy of your report

How should you write the report?

- Time frame: Allow yourself enough time to write a good report. Ultimately, what you have done comes out only through the report.
- The general format of the report could be the following, but follow any guidelines set by your institution or guide:
  - Executive summary
  - Contents
  - Acknowledgements
  - Preface
  - Introduction: The problem or ecosystem in brief; objectives of study
  - Background: literature survey
  - Observations and results
  - Conclusions and recommendations

       □ References

       □ Photographs

- Language and style: Read the slim volume *Elements of Style* by Strunk and White. It is a classic with very useful tips. Keep the language as simple as possible. If your language abilities are weak, get the draft corrected by a professional.
- Word processing: Do not depend too much on the software to correct the grammar and usage.
- Approval of the draft report: Get the draft approved by the organization, and your guides.
- Revision and final version: Check for typographical errors.
- Printing and submission: Follow any guidelines given on the size, number of copies, etc.

How should you prepare for a viva-voce examination, if there is one?

- Prepare a computer presentation.
- Each slide should have not more than 10 lines of text. Do not read out what everyone can see. The points on a slide are only to trigger your memory.
- Prepare ahead for possible questions.

In which other ways can you use the project work and the report?

- A good project report can be used in job interviews and in applications for admission to courses
- If you are looking for a career in environment, send an electronic copy of the report to organizations that have openings
- Write an article on your work for the appropriate journal, magazine, newspaper, or website

SOMETHING DIFFERENT FOR A CHANGE

Here is a part of the poem *Little Gidding*, one of the *Four Quartets* by the Anglo-American critic, dramatist, and poet, T.S.Eliot (1888–1965):

We shall not cease from exploration
and the end of all our exploring
shall be to arrive where we started
and know the place for the first time.

LEARN MORE

Book

Strunk, William and E.B. White 1972, *The Elements of Style,* Macmillan Publishing, New York.

Module 9

Conclusion

Chapter 22: Another World is Possible

Another World is Possible

Anyone who believes
exponential growth can go on forever
in a finite world is
either a madman or an economist.

Kenneth Boulding
(1910–1993)
American economist, systems scientist,
peace activist, and poet

If the world is saved,
it will be saved by people with changed minds,
people with a new vision.
It will not be saved by people
with old minds and new programs.
It will not be saved by people
with the old vision but a new program.

Daniel Quinn
(1935–)
American author and environmentalist

How can you move from despair to hope?

This (last) chapter is addressed directly to you, the reader. The book has been a catalogue of environmental destruction, sprinkled with signs of positive change. The state of the world can easily drive you to despair. But how can you move from a sense of despair to one of hope, from crisis to cure?

The first step is to realize that you have the power to change things. Mahatma Gandhi said:

The difference between what we do and what we are capable of doing would suffice to solve most of the world's problems.

There are three levels at which you can exercise the power you have:

• Power of One: You can take right actions as an individual.

- Power of a Group: You can join (or create) a group or community of like-minded people working for positive changes.
- Power of a Movement: You can join any one of the social and environmental movements that are determined to change the world.

Who is the real enemy?

Before you can act, you have to ask yourself: Who really is responsible for the environmental crisis? Who is the real enemy?

- Rich societies like that of the US that consume and pollute a lot?
- Governments and political parties that are only concerned about the next elections and hence do not take the necessary tough decisions?
- Companies that use natural resources and just throw away the waste?
- Corrupt officials who let the companies pollute?
- Municipalities that do not clear the garbage?
- Your neighbour, who throws the garbage on the street?

It is easy to blame others for the crisis, though some of them may well deserve a share of the blame. However, a little reflection shows that, at the very basic level, you are the cause and each one of us is the cause. As the cartoon character Pogo puts it, 'We have seen the enemy and it is us!'

The root causes of the crisis include:

- Your consumption and desire for more.
- The waste that you create and throw away mindlessly.
- Your NIMBY (Not In My BackYard) syndrome: The practice of objecting to something that would affect you or take place in your locality, even though it would benefit many others.
- The corruption that you support, directly or indirectly.

Your actions such as these lead to increasing production of goods and services, overexploitation of natural resources, more waste and pollution, and so on.

If you agree that you are part of the problem, one could ask you, 'Can you become a part of the solution?' Your response could well be, 'What can I do? I am just a powerless individual. How can I fight against the bureaucrats, politicians, or industrialists?'

What is the Power of One?

Many individuals all over the world have indeed tried to become part of the solution. They have acted to save the environment and brought about real changes. There are many such inspiring stories, some of which were given in the previous chapters (Box 22.1).

BOX 22.1

Inspirational heroes

- Jaime Lerner and the planning and building of Curitiba, an environment friendly city (Chapter 15, Box 15.6).

- Julia Butterfly Hill and her remarkable two-year struggle to save the redwood trees (Chapter 9, Box 9.8).

Contd

Box 22.1 Contd

- Laurie Baker and his ecological architecture (Chapter 15, Box 15.4)
- Lois Gibbs and her campaign for the cleanup of Love Canal and other toxic dumps (Chapter 16, Boxes 16.4 and 16.5).
- M.C.Mehta and public interest litigation (Chapter 20, Box 20.1)
- Rajendra Singh and water conservation (Chapter 7, Box 7.8).
- Rashida Bee and Champa Devi Shukla and their struggle for justice in Bhopal (Chapter 17, Box 17.4)
- Ray Anderson and his efforts to build a sustainable company (Chapter 18, Box 18.3)
- Romulus Whitaker and the conservation of snakes and crocodiles (Chapter 6, Box 6.7)
- S.R.Rao and the restoration of Surat after the plague (Chapter 15, Box 15.5).
- Sundarlal Bahuguna and his struggle to save the Himalayan ecosystem (Chapter 2, Box 2.1)
- Thimmakka and the trees she planted on a public road (Chapter 9, Box 9.7)
- Vellore Srinivasan and Zero Waste Management (Chapter 13, Box 13.5)
- Wangari Maathai and her Green Belt Movement (Chapter 9, Box 9.6)

Many more such environmental heroes can be found across the world. True tales of this kind have many uses:

- They can inspire us to act in our lives and in our context.
- By presenting environmental issues in the context of real places and events, they are more effective in spurring action than mere fear-inducing information.
- Through the stories, we understand the differences and commonalities of environmental problems and solutions around the world.
- The tales can be a great tool in education and creation of awareness among children and the youth.

Reading these extraordinary stories, we may be tempted to ask, 'What makes ordinary individuals take up seemingly impossible tasks in the face of heavy odds?' Clearly, given the depressing data, the driving force could not be just optimism, which arises from the head. It can only be hope that springs from the heart, as described by Vaclav Havel, writer and first President of the Czech Republic:

Hope is an orientation of the spirit, an orientation of the heart; it transcends the world that is immediately experienced, and is anchored somewhere beyond its horizons.

Havel (who led resistance groups against the Soviet Union), Nelson Mandela (who led the struggle against apartheid in South Africa), Martin Luther King, Jr., (who led the Civil Rights Movement in the US) and others like them were kept going, not by a sense of optimism, but undying hope. That hope did triumph at the end. In the same way, the environment may also be saved from a disaster.

What steps can you take?   You could become an inspiring hero, but until then you can still do your bit in healing this planet. You could take three steps:

- Be informed: Read books and magazines and scour websites to find out for yourself where the world stands.
- Examine yourself and your lifestyle by asking questions (Box 22.2)

- Take action at home and work place, in the neighbourhood, in your city, and so on. The previous chapters have given many suggestions for action.

BOX 22.2

Some questions to ask of yourself

- How much water and energy do I use every day?
- What do I buy? From where?
- What kind of food do I eat?
- What do I throw away? Where does the waste go?

- How do I travel?
- What types of medicines do I take?
- How do I build my house?
- How do I treat other living beings, plants?

What is the Power of a Group?

Every city has many NGOs that take up local environmental issues and conduct campaigns during weekends. There is strength in numbers and you may see better results when you work with such groups. The famous anthropologist Margaret Mead said:

Never doubt that a small group of thoughtful committed citizens can change the world. Indeed, it is the only thing that ever has.

You can also go beyond just working with local environmental groups and move into a community or create one. Often, such a community grows from the vision of an individual or a small and dedicated group. Some have ecology as a focus, while others are oriented towards religion and spirituality. Other communities concentrate on social work. In India, there are also Gandhian communities, inspired by the ideals of the Mahatma. Box 22.3 gives examples of communities that focus (among other things) on the environment. There are many more, large and small as well as old and new.

BOX 22.3

Examples of ecological communities

Gaviotas It was established in 1971 by Paulo Lugari on 25,000 acres of land on the impoverished eastern plains of Colombia. The Gaviotans are about 200 researchers, students, and workers and they produce 70 per cent of food and energy needed. The place is run by consensus and unwritten rules. The residents get good wages, free meals, medical care, schools, and housing. Over the years, Gaviotans have come up with an extraordinary number of inventions including efficient wind turbines, solar devices, self-cooling rooftops, cooling wind corridors, corkscrew manual well digger, and so on. Since Gaviotas does not patent its inventions, its ideas have spread in the region, from Central America to Chile.

Auroville Called also the City of Dawn, this is an international township in Tamil Nadu, near Puducherry, dedicated to human unity. It was founded in 1968 by the French visionary known as 'The Mother', a spiritual collaborator of the sage Sri Aurobindo. It is a remarkable story of ecological transformation achieved by a group of people (now about 2,000 in number) from 35 different countries

Contd

Box 22.3 Contd

The Matrimandir at Auroville
(Image courtesy: Sujit kumar, http://commons.wikimedia.org/wiki/
File:Matrimandir_Auroville.jpg)

including India. They have planted three million trees to convert barren land into lush greenery. They have also experimented with a range of environment friendly technologies covering water, energy, waste, building, and farming. Local biodiversity and medicinal knowledge is being recorded and revived.

Timbaktu Collective This community was established in 1990 on 32 acres of dry, degraded land in the drought prone Anantapur district of Andhra Pradesh. Slowly over the years not only Timbaktu but also the surrounding hills have greened themselves while insects, birds and animals have reappeared. A small community of volunteers, committed to developmental and ecological regeneration, has settled here. Timbaktu's vision is to stop the degradation of the land in the area and to find ways to reverse it. The aim is also to develop alternative lifestyles that are sustainable and provide more liberty and happiness, than those based upon exploitation.

Navadarshanam This small organization is located on 115 acres of land in Tamil Nadu, 50 km south of Bangalore. It investigates ecological and spiritual alternatives to the modern way of living and thinking. The areas of focus include eco-restoration of land, renewable energy, ecological architecture, healthier food and the science-spirituality connection. Navadarshanam organizes workshops and meetings on these aspects.

What is the Power of a Movement?

If the planet is to be saved from destruction, we need many Chipko-type people's movements. Paul Hawken, who has been studying such movements, believes that there are up to two million organizations in the world working toward ecological sustainability, social justice, and indigenous rights. 'It is a global humanitarian movement arising from the bottom up. It is in fact a coherent, organic, self-organized, worldwide movement involving tens of millions of people dedicated to positive change.'

Hawken puts it this way: 'If you look at the science that describes what is happening on earth today and aren't pessimistic, you don't have the correct data. If you meet the people in this unnamed movement and aren't optimistic, you haven't got a heart.'

Joanna Macy, American Buddhist scholar and peace activist, is sure that a 'Great Turning' is occurring in the world. 'This turning is a shift from the industrial growth society to a life-sustaining civilization. Future generations will look back at the epochal transition we are making to a life-sustaining society. It is happening now. To see this as the larger context of our lives clears our vision and summons our courage.'

David Korten, Macy's colleague and author of the book *The Great Turning*, believes that everything is going to change. He suggests that we should embrace the crisis as an opportunity and 'move from Empire to Earth Community, from Dominator story to Partnership story, and from Competition to Cooperation' (Box 22.4). Alex Steffen, author of *Worldchanging*, is clear that 'real solutions already exist for building the future we want. It is just a matter of grabbing hold and getting moving.'

Joining such movements and being part of a sustainable future is exhilarating, but not easy. It is akin to any creative work, about which the American dancer Martha Graham said:

[There is] no satisfaction whatever at any time. There is only a queer, divine dissatisfaction, **a blessed unrest** *that keeps us marching and makes us more alive than others.*

BOX 22.4

Change the story, change the future

Every society essentially plays out a story. One story has the theme, 'Man is an integral part of nature and is not separate from it.' This was the story of many indigenous peoples of the world. Today the dominant story tells us again and again in every way:

- Produce more and more products and services, be a strong economy and a powerful nation.
- Make more money, be happier.
- Consume more, enjoy more, that is your right.
- Compete or you will perish.

We can change the story to a new one that tells us:

- We are the stewards of the earth.
- Degrading the earth with the waste products of our luxurious living is a sin.
- The right path is to live as frugally and simply as possible.
- Reducing consumption is not a sacrifice; it is an elevating experience.
- Partnership and cooperation are the keys to survival.

What is stopping you from acting to save the planet?

Taking actions suggested in this book is necessary, but not sufficient. A profound change is possible only if all of us change our mindsets. Albert Einstein said, 'You cannot solve a problem with the same mindset which created it in the first place'.

We mistakenly see a difference between other beings and ourselves, between nature and ourselves. When we truly begin to see ourselves as an indivisible part of the universe, there will be a fundamental shift in our mindset.

Perhaps the first step in saving the planet is to fall in love with its beauty. The second step is to hear within us the sounds of the earth crying. The third step is to put this new understanding into action. Mahatma Gandhi captured it all in just a few words:

Be the change you wish to see in the world.

Begin changing yourself and you will then find that another world is possible!

SOMETHING DIFFERENT FOR A CHANGE

As an endpiece, here is a moving excerpt from a poem by the American poet, essayist and feminist Adrienne Rich (1929 -). It occurs towards the end of the poem 'Natural Resources' in her book *Dreams of a Common Language*.

> My heart is moved by all I cannot save:
> so much has been destroyed

> I have to cast my lot with those
> who age after age, perversely,
> with no extraordinary power,
> reconstitute the world.
> A passion to make, and make again
> where such un-making reigns.

LEARN MORE

Books

Hawken, Paul 2007, *Blessed Unrest: How the Largest Movement in the World Came into Being and Why No One Saw It Coming*, Viking, New York.

Korten, David C. 2006, *The Great Turning: From Empire to Earth Community*, Berret-Koehler Publishers, San Francisco.

Quinn, Daniel 1993, *Ishmael*, Bantam / Turner, New York.

Steffen, Alex 2008, *Worldchanging: A User's Guide for the 21st Century*, Abrams, New York.

Weisman, Alan 1999, *Gaviotas: A Village to Reinvent the World*, Chelsea Green, White River Junction, VT.

Websites

Auroville: www.auroville.org.in

Navadarshanam: www.navadarshanam.org

Paul Hawken: www.wiserearth.org

Worldchanging: www.worldchanging.com

Glossary

Abiotic components or conditions The non-living components or conditions of an ecosystem such as the natural resources and the atmospheric conditions.

Abyssal zone The cold and dark zone at the bottom of the ocean.

Acid rain Rain, mist or snow formed when atmospheric water droplets combine with a range of man-made chemical air pollutants.

Agent orange A compound herbicide used by the US army in the Vietnam War to kill all vegetation.

Agroforestry A system of land use that combines growing crops along with trees.

AIDS (Acquired Immune Deficiency Syndrome) A condition in which the body's immune system is weakened and therefore less able to fight certain infections and diseases. It is caused by the Human Immunodeficiency Virus.

Algal bloom A population explosion of some pigmented marine algae seen as an explosion of colour on the ocean—orange, red, or brown.

Aquaculture The artificial production of fish in ponds or underwater cages.

Aquatic life zone The non-terrestrial part of the biosphere including wetlands, lakes, rivers, estuaries, inter-tidal zone, coastal ocean, and open ocean.

Aquifer An underground layer of rock or sand that contains water.

Asbestos A fibrous silicate mineral used as construction material and insulation. It is very dangerous to health when the fibres are inhaled.

Background extinction The gradual disappearance of species due to changes in local environmental conditions.

Bathyal zone The dimly lit middle level zone in the ocean, roughly between 200 m and 1500 m in depth.

Benthos Bottom-dwelling organisms adapted to living on the floor of a water body.

Biodegradable waste Any waste item that breaks down into the raw materials of nature and becomes part of the environment in reasonable time.

Biodiversity (Biological diversity) The numbers, variety, and variability of living organisms and ecosystems. It covers diversity within species, between species, as well as the variation among ecosystems. It is concerned also with their complex ecological interrelationships.

Biodynamic farming A type of organic farming that exploits bio- and solar rhythms. It is based on the ideas of Rudolf Steiner.

Biofertilizer Living microorganisms, cultured and multiplied for use as fertilizer.

Biofuel Fuel oil from the seeds of certain trees; it can be mixed with diesel and used in engines.

Biogas Gas generated from human and animal waste.

Biogeochemical cycle A cycle (with biological, geological and chemical interactions) through which matter moves through ecosystems, powered directly or indirectly by solar energy. The water and carbon cycles are examples.

Bioinformatics A field of study that combines biology with computer science and thus uses the power of information technology to study and conserve biodiversity.

Biointensive farming A type of organic farming involving intensive garden cultivation using deep-dug beds.

Biological extinction The complete disappearance of a species. It is an irreversible loss with not a single member of the extinct species being found on earth.

Biological Oxygen Demand (BOD) Measure of the oxygen used by microorganisms to decompose organic waste.

Biological pest control The intentional introduction of predators, diseases, or parasites to control pests.

Biomagnification The increasing concentration of pollutants in organisms as we move up the food chain.

Biome A group similar or related ecosystems with a distinct climate and life forms adapted to the climate. A biome is more extensive and complex than an ecosystem. It is the next level of ecological organization above a community and an ecosystem.

Biomedical waste   Waste that originates mainly from hospitals and clinics and includes blood, diseased organs, poisonous medicines, etc.

Biopesticide   Pesticides derived from animals, plants, bacteria, and certain minerals.

Bioremediation   The use of biotechnology to clean up wastes and toxic pollutants.

Biosphere reserve   Area of land or water that is protected by law in order to support the conservation of the ecosystem.

Biosphere   The zone of the earth where life is found. It includes parts of the atmosphere, water bodies, and soil.

Biota   The living component of an ecosystem, also called the biotic community. The biotic community includes the plants, animals, and microorganisms.

Biotechnology   Technology that manipulates living organisms or cells to create a product or an effect.

Biotic components   The living components of an ecosystem.

Bottom trawling   The practice of fishing by scraping the sea floor with a net.

Bycatch   The species caught in the fishing nets along with the targeted ones.

Captive breeding   Reproduction of threatened animals in captivity.

Carbon cycle   Cyclic movement of carbon in various forms from the environment to organisms and back to the environment.

Carbon footprint   Total greenhouse gas emissions caused directly and indirectly by a person, organisation, event, product, or country.

Carnivores   Organisms that feed on other consumers.

Checkdam or johad   A small structure of earth and stones that blocks the path of any flow of water and helps recharge the groundwater.

Chlorofluorocarbon (CFC)   A type of chemical that is used as a refrigerant or aerosol propellants. When it breaks apart in the atmosphere and releases chlorine atoms, it causes ozone depletion.

Coastal zone   The area extending from the high tide mark on land to the edge of the continental shelf, where there is a sharp increase in the depth of water.

Common Effluent Treatment Plant (CETP)   A common plant where we collect the waste of several units from an industrial estate and make it safe by treatment.

Community (of populations)   The assemblage of all the interacting populations of different species existing in a geographical area. It is a complex interacting network of plants, animals, and microorganisms.

Composting   The process of converting organic waste into fertilizer.

Coniferous forest   A type of forest with an abundance of coniferous trees like spruce, fir, pine, and hemlock.

Consumer   An organism that feeds on producers or other organisms, also called heterotroph.

Continental shelf   The submerged part of the continent at the edge of the coastal zone, where there is a sharp increase in the depth of water. It marks the beginning of the open ocean.

Coral reefs   Colourful protective crust of limestone formed by colonies of tiny organisms called polyps.

Crude birth rate   The number of live births per 1000 people in a population in a given year.

Crude death rate   The number of deaths per 1000 people in a population in a given year.

Cyclone   Violent tropical storm in which strong winds move in a circle; occurs mainly in the Indian Ocean.

DDT (Dichloro-diphenol-trichloroethane)   An insecticide that protects crops and human beings from insects. Being harmful to organisms, it is now banned in many countries.

Decibel (db)   A logarithmic scale for measuring the intensity of sound.

Decomposer   An organism that gets its nourishment from dead organic material.

Desertification   Land degradation in arid and semiarid areas caused by human activities and climatic changes.

Detrivore   A consumer that feeds on detritus, which refers mainly to fallen leaves, parts of dead trees, and faecal wastes of animals.

Dioxin   A highly toxic chemical compound that occurs as contaminants in a number of industrial processes and products; also formed when we burn waste, plastics, coal or cigarettes.

Disaster management   Effective way of managing disasters including mitigation, preparedness, response, and recovery.

Disaster mitigation   Reducing the effects of potential disasters through suitable measures.

Displacement   The movement of people from their homes to new locations.

DNA   The molecule of an organism that contains information about its characteristics and behaviour.

Ecological architecture   Architecture that seeks to minimize the ecological footprint of the house, building, or complex that is being designed and constructed.

Ecological extinction   The state of a species when so few members are left that the species can no longer play its normal ecological role in the community.

Ecological footprint   A measure of the ecological impact of an entity, expressed as the extent of land needed to completely sustain the entity.

Ecological niche   All the physical, chemical, and biological factors that a species needs in order to live and reproduce.

Ecological pyramid   A graphical representation of the change that occurs as we move from one trophic level to the next in a food chain.

Ecological sanitation (EcoSan)   A sustainable closed-loop sanitation system that uses dry composting toilets.

Ecological succession   The orderly process of transition from one biotic community to another in a given area.

Ecologist   A scientist who works in the field of ecology.

Ecology   The science that studies the relationships between living things and their environment. It is often considered to be a discipline of biology.

Ecosystem   A defined area in which a living community (with its populations of species) with interactions taking place among the organisms and between the community and its non-living physical environment.

Ecosystem diversity   The variety of habitats found in an area, that is, the variety of forests, deserts, grasslands, aquatic ecosystems, etc., that occurs in the area.

Ecosystem service   The ecological service provided by an ecosystem such as the maintenance of the biogeochemical cycles, modification of climate, waste removal and detoxification, and control of pests and diseases.

Ecotone   The transitional zone between adjoining ecosystems.

Edge effect   The presence of rich and unique biological diversity found in an ecotone.

El Nino   An abnormal warming of the surface ocean waters in the eastern tropical Pacific in some years.

Electromagnetic radiation   A form of energy radiated as waves and caused by changing electric and magnetic fields.

Endangered species   The state of a species when the number of survivors is so small that it could soon become extinct over all or most of its habitat.

Endosulfan   A highly toxic pesticide used to protect many crops from pest attacks.

Energy flow   Flow of energy in a food chain from one organism to the next in a sequence.

Environment   The natural world in which people, animals, and plants live.

Environmental conservation   All the ways in which we protect nature and reverse the damage caused to the natural environment.

Environmental degradation   This term refers to the damage caused to the natural environment by human action and otherwise.

Environmental education   A subject concerned with all environmental issues. It has a wider coverage than environmental science or ecology. It includes the social aspects of the environment.

Environmental ethics   Moral principles that try to define our responsibility towards the environment.

Environmental health   Those aspects of human health that are determined by physical, chemical, biological, social, and psychosocial factors in the environment.

Environmental Impact Assessment (EIA)   The study of the likely short-term and long-term impact of a new project on the natural and social environment.

Environmental refugee   A person who has been displaced due to environmental degradation or a development project,

Environmental science The systematic and scientific study of our environment and our role in it.

Environmental stability The maintenance of natural processes in a state of balance. Forests contribute to environmental stability.

Environmental studies The branch of study concerned with environmental issues. It has a broader canvas than environmental science and includes the social aspects of the environment.

Environmentalist A person who helps in the conservation of the environment.

Estuary The wide part of a river where it flows into the sea.

Euphotic zone The upper part of the open ocean where there is enough light for the phytoplankton to carry out photosynthesis.

Eutrophication The excessive addition of chemical nutrients like nitrogen or phosphorus into the soil or a standing water body, which promotes the excessive growth of some species leading to the death of others.

E-waste Electronic waste that results from discarded devices like computers, televisions, telephones, and music systems.

Exclusive Economic Zone (EEZ) The area of the ocean up to a distance of 200 nautical miles from a country's shoreline over which the country has the exclusive right to exploit the resources.

Exponential growth The growth of a quantity with time in such a way that the curve is relatively flat in the beginning, but becomes steeper and steeper with time.

Ex situ conservation Conservation of biodiversity and wildlife in artificial settings outside the natural habitats of the species.

Extractive reserve Protected forests, in which local communities are allowed to harvest non-timber products in ways that do not harm the forest.

Fauna All the animals living in an area.

Flora All the plants of a particular area.

Fluorosis An ailment caused by the excess intake of fluoride.

Food chain A sequence of species, in which each is the food for the next in the chain.

Food web An interconnected set of food chains.

Forest certification A system for certifying forests that adopt sustainable management practices.

Forest Protection Committee A committee consisting of local people as well as forest and local officials that helps in protecting the forest and managing it in a sustainable manner.

Fossil fuel Remains of organisms that lived 200–500 million years ago that were converted by heat and pressure into coal, oil, and natural gas.

Fuel cell An electrochemical unit that burns hydrogen to produce electricity.

Genetic diversity The variety in the genetic makeup among individuals within a species.

Genetic engineering The manipulation of the genes in an organism to change its characteristics, for example, moving a favourable gene from one organism to another.

Genetically Modified food (GM food) Food derived from genetically modified organisms, which have had specific changes introduced into their DNA by genetic engineering.

Geothermal energy Energy from the hot liquid rock under the earth's crust tapped from the hot water that comes to the surface.

Global warming Warming of the earth's atmosphere due to an abnormal increase in the concentration of greenhouse gases.

Grassland Regions where the average annual precipitation is high enough for grass and a few trees to grow.

Green business Enterprise that has no negative impact on the global or local environment, community, society, or economy.

Green economy Economic activity related to reducing the use of fossil fuels, decreasing pollution and greenhouse gas emissions, increasing the efficiency of energy usage, recycling materials, and developing and adopting renewable sources of energy.

Green livelihood Productive and sustainable livelihoods based on natural resources.

Green revolution A way of agriculture that greatly increases crop yields, using new seed varieties, large quantities of chemical fertilizers, pesticides, and water.

Greenhouse gas A gas like carbon dioxide that surrounds the earth and prevents some of the Sun's heat from being reflected back out again.

Gross World Product The total value of all the products made and services offered in the world.

Groundwater Water contained underneath the earth's surface.

Habitat fragmentation The process by which continuous areas of species habitat are reduced in extent or divided into patchwork of isolated fragments due to human impact.

Habitat The area where a species is biologically adapted to live. It is marked by the physical and biological features of its environment such as the vegetation, climatic conditions, presence of water and moisture, and soil type.

Herbivore An organism that feeds directly on producers.

HIV Human Immunodeficiency Virus that causes AIDS.

Hubbert curve A curve proposed by the geophysicist M.King Hubbert that describes the pattern of oil availability in a field over time.

Human rights The rights and freedoms to which human beings in all countries are entitled.

Hurricane Violent storm with very strong winds experienced mainly in the western Atlantic Ocean.

Idea of progress The belief that humankind would move on an unceasing path of better material conditions and a better life through economic and industrial development, exploiting natural resources.

Indicator species Species that are very sensitive indicators of environmental problems. They give us early warning of problems that could potentially affect other species.

Indigenous knowledge The traditional and local knowledge held by the members of a given community.

In situ conservation Conservation that tries to protect species where they are, that is, in their natural habitat.

Intertidal zone The area of shoreline between the low and high tides. It is the transition between the land and the ocean.

Joint Forest Management Sustainable management of forests involving local communities in the planning and execution of the conservation programme.

Judicial activism The pro-active role of the judiciary in responding to the complaints of citizens or public interest litigation and assuming the roles of policy makers, educators, administrators, and, in general, friends of the environment.

Keystone species Species that play roles affecting many other organisms in an ecosystem. They determine the ability of a large number of other species to survive.

Landfill An area, usually located just outside the city, on which municipal waste is dumped.

Local extinction The state of a species when it is no longer found in the area it once inhabited. It is, however, present elsewhere in the world.

Mangrove A unique salt-tolerant tree with interlacing roots that grows in shallow marine sediments.

Marine Protected Area (MPA) Area set up by a country to protect a marine ecosystem, its natural processes, habitats, and species.

Marsh Wetland with few trees.

Mass extinction A global, catastrophic extinction of species, with more than 65% of all species becoming extinct over some millions of years. It is characterized by a rate of disappearance significantly higher than the background extinction.

Maximum sustainable yield (MSY) The yield of a species of fish that we could harvest annually leaving enough breeding stock for the population to renew itself. MSY is the amount we can catch every year indefinitely.

Mesosphere This layer occupies the space above the stratosphere up to about 80 km above the earth's surface.

Methyl Isocyanate (MIC) Highly poisonous chemical used in pesticide manufacture.

Monocropping   Planting only a single species over a piece of land.

Natural farming   No-tillage and organic farming, pioneered by Masanobu Fukuoka of Japan.

Naturalist   A person who studies animals, plants, birds, and other living things.

Nautical mile   The unit of distance used in the ocean. One nautical mile equals 1.85 km.

Nekton   The strong swimmers of the ocean including all the larger organisms like fishes, turtles and whales.

New economics   See green economics

NIMBY (Not In My BackYard) syndrome   Practice of objecting to something that would affect one or take place in one's locality, even though it would benefit many others.

Nonpoint source of water pollution   A large area over which water flows and picks up pollutants.

Non-renewable energy source   An energy source that is limited in supply and gets depleted by use.

Nutrient   Any food, element, or compound that is essential for an organism to live and grow.

Old-growth forest   Forests that have not been seriously disturbed by human activities or natural disasters for several hundred years or more.

Omnivore   An organism that eats producers as well as other consumers.

Open ocean   The area of the ocean beyond the coastal zone.

Opportunistic infection   Infection that attacks the body when its immune system has broken down, say, by the HIV.

Organic farming   A method of farming that does not use chemical fertilizers and chemical pesticides. It is a return to the traditional methods like crop rotation, use of animal and green manures, and some forms of biological control of pests.

Organism   Any living thing - an animal, a plant, or a microbe.

Ozone depleting potential (ODP)   The amount of ozone depletion caused by a substance.

Ozone layer   A layer of ozone that exists in the upper atmosphere, or stratosphere, between 10 and 50 km above the earth.

PCBs (Polychlorinated biphenyls)   Group of toxic chemical compounds that are very stable, have good insulation qualities, are fire resistant, and have low electrical conductivity.

Peak oil   The maximum rate of the production of oil in any area under consideration, recognising that it is a finite natural resource, subject to depletion.

Permaculture   A way of designing sustainable human settlements through an approach to land use, which weaves together microclimate, annual and perennial plants, animals, soils, water management, and human needs into intricately connected, productive communities.

Persistent Organic Pollutants (POPs)   A group of persistent, toxic chemicals that can accumulate in organisms and can contaminate sites far removed from their source. They cause reproductive, immunological, and neurological problems in marine organisms and possibly in humans.

Photochemical smog   A form of outdoor air pollution formed by the chemical reactions between sunlight, unburnt hydrocarbons, ozone, and other pollutants.

Photosynthesis   The process in which green plants take in carbon dioxide from the atmosphere, water from the soil and energy from the Sun to make food.

Photovoltaic (PV) cell   A device that converts solar energy directly into electricity.

Phytoplankton   Photosynthetic producers forming the basis of the ocean's food web.

Plankton   Free-floating microorganisms that cannot swim easily and are buffeted about by the waves and currents.

Point source of water pollution   Specific places like factories that discharge pollutants into water bodies.

Polychlorinated Biphenyls (PCBs)   Chemicals widely used in electrical equipment. They remain in the environment for long and are extremely toxic.

Polyp   Tiny organism that forms the coral.

Population The members of a species living and interacting within a specific geographical region. The term refers only to those members of a certain species that live within a given area.

Precipitation All the forms in which water comes down on earth, including rain, snow, and hailstorm.

Primary air pollutant Harmful chemical that is released directly from a source into the atmosphere.

Producer An organism such as a green plant that can produce food from simple inorganic substances through photosynthesis. Also called autotroph.

Protected area Area in which the biodiversity and wildlife are protected from human exploitation. National parks, sanctuaries, and biosphere reserves are examples.

Public Interest Litigation (PIL) Petitions filed in courts by individual citizens, groups, and voluntary organizations seeking justice in matters involving public interest.

Pyramid of biomass A graphical representation of the reduction in biomass of organisms as we move from one trophic level to the next.

Pyramid of energy A graphical representation of the reduction in usable energy of organisms as we move from one trophic level to the next.

Rainforest A type of forest found in the hot and humid regions near the Equator. These regions have abundant rainfall and little variation in temperature over the year.

Rainwater harvesting Harvesting rainwater where it falls, either by collecting and storing it, or by letting it recharge the groundwater.

Rangeland Land that is not suitable for crop production and is used for grazing by animals.

Recycle To convert waste back into a useful form

Reduce To reduce the amount of things we buy and consume.

Rehabilitation The provision of opportunities and facilities to displaced people to help them find livelihoods and shelter in the new area.

Renewable energy source An energy source that is replenished by natural processes and hence can be used indefinitely.

Renewable energy Type of energy (like solar energy) that is replaced by natural processes and can be used forever.

Resettlement The relocation of displaced persons in new areas.

Reuse To extend the life of an item or to find a new use for it.

Reverse Osmosis or RO method Purifying water by forcing it through a semi-permeable membrane.

Richter scale A measure of the severity of an earthquake. It is a measure of the amount of energy released, which is indicated by the vibrations in a seismograph.

Sacred grove A forest that is protected by the local community through social traditions and taboos that incorporate spiritual and ecological values.

Salinization of soil The building up of salt in the soil flowing the evaporation of excess water.

Sanitary landfill Land waste disposal site that is located to minimize water pollution from runoff and leaching. Waste is spread in thin layers, compacted and covered with a fresh layer of soil each day to minimize pest, aesthetic, disease, air pollution, and water pollution problems.

Savanna Tropical grasslands with widely scattered clumps of low trees. They are marked by low rainfall and prolonged dry periods.

Secondary air pollutant Harmful chemical that is produced from chemical reactions involving primary pollutants.

Second-growth forest A forest that results from secondary ecological succession that takes place when forests are cleared and then left undisturbed for long periods of time.

Seismograph An instrument that measures the amount of energy released in an earthquake by sensing the vibrations.

Sentinel species Species that are very sensitive indicators of environmental problems.

Seventh generation principle Being cautious while taking decisions in a community by considering the effects of each decision on the next seven generations.

Ship-breaking   The process of breaking up decommissioned ships for recycling the parts to the extent possible.

Sludge   The toxic material left behind after the treatment of sewage.

Smog   A form of outdoor pollution that is localized in urban areas, where it reduces visibility. The term was originally used to describe a combination of smoke, fog, and chemical pollutants that poisoned the air in industrialised cities.

Social environment   The environment that surrounds a person, any living organism, a citizen, a company, etc.

Social fencing   Voluntary agreement by people to prevent their livestock from grazing on the degraded lands.

Social forestry   The planting of trees, often with the involvement of local communities, in wasteland or common land.

Species diversity   The number of plant and animal species present in a community or an ecosystem.

Species extinction   The situation in which no members of the species are found to exist anywhere on earth.

Species   A set of organisms that resemble one another in appearance and behaviour. The organisms in a species are potentially capable of reproducing naturally among themselves.

Stratosphere   This layer is above the troposphere and extends to about 50 km above the earth's surface.

Sustainable development   Development that meets the needs of the present without compromising the ability of future generations to meet their own needs.

Sustainable forest management   The use of the world's forests in such a way that that they continue to provide resources now without depriving future generations of their needs.

Swamp   Wetland dominated by trees and shrubs.

Tailings   Waste products that come out of the initial processing of the uranium ore.

Temperate forest   A type of forest with seasonal variations in climate, freezing in winter and warm and humid in summer.

Thermosphere   This is the space above the mesosphere up to about 600 km above the earth's surface.

Threatened species   A species that is facing a high risk of global extinction.

Tidal energy   Energy from the large changes in tides.

Topsoil   Topmost layer of the soil, where most plant roots, microorganisms, and other animal life are located.

Toxic waste   Waste that contains poisons, which could kill certain organisms.

Trophic level   The specific feeding stage of an organism in the ecosystem.

Troposphere   The part of the atmosphere up to a distance of 17 km from the earth's surface.

Tsunami   An undersea high-energy wave set off by an (undersea) earthquake; when the wave hits the coast, giant waves result.

Tundra   The forests in the Arctic. They occur in the extreme northern latitudes, where the snow melts seasonally.

Typhoon   Violent storm with very strong winds experienced mainly in western Atlantic Ocean.

Urbanization   The process by which more and more people live and work in cities rather than in the rural areas.

UV method   Use of ultraviolet radiation to kill harmful organisms in water.

Vermicomposting   Composting organic waste more efficiently using earthworms.

Virtual water   Amount of water used in making the items that we eat, drink, or use.

Water cycle   A process that continually recycles and transports water among the atmosphere, land, and ocean.

Water footprint   Total volume of freshwater that is used to produce the goods and services consumed by an individual or community or produced by a business. It is an indicator that measures both direct and indirect water use.

Water harvesting   The process of catching the rain when and where it falls.

Watershed   A region from which water flows (or drains) into a stream, lake, reservoir, wetland, or other body of water.

Wave energy   The kinetic energy in the moving waves tapped by suitable methods.

Wetland   Land surface covered or saturated with water for a part or whole of the year.

Zooplankton   Primary consumers that feed on phytoplankton.

Zooxanthellae   The tiny single-celled algae that live inside the tissues of the polyps that form the corals. They produce food and oxygen through photosynthesis and give the colours to the corals.

Units of Measure

Some Common Prefixes

Prefix and Symbol	Meaning	Example		
Giga (G)	billion	1 gigaton	=	1,000,000,000 tons
Mega (M)	million	1 megawatt (MW)	=	1,000,000 watts
kilo	thousand	1 kilogram (kg)	=	1,000 grams
centi	hundredth	1 centimetre (cm)	=	0.01 metre
milli	thousandth	1 millilitre (ml)	=	0.001 litre
micro	millionth	1 micrometre	=	0.000001 metre
nano	billionth	1 nanometre	=	0.000000001 metre
pico	trillionth	1 picocurie	=	0.000000000001 curie

Numbers

1 million	=	1,000,000 (10 lakh or lac)
1 billion	=	1,000 million (100 crores)

Length

1 metre	=	39.37 inches
1 inch	=	2.54 cm
1 mile	=	1.6 km

Area

1 hectare (ha)	=	10,000 sq m
	=	2.471 acres
1 sq km	=	1,000,000 sq m
	=	100 hectares

Volume

1 litre	=	1000 cu. cm
1 US gallon	=	3.785 litres
1 Barrel (oil)	=	159 litres

Mass

1 metric ton (tonne)	=	1000 kg
1 pound	=	453.6 grams

Index